DOCUMENTS

OF

WESTERN CIVILIZATION

VOLUME I: TO 1715

Documents

of

Western Civilization

Volume I: To 1715

Janice Archer, Editor

West / Wadsworth

I⟨T⟩P® An International Thomson Publishing Company

Belmont, CA • Albany, NY • Bonn • Boston • Cincinnati • Detroit • Johannesburg • London
Madrid • Melbourne • Mexico City • New York • Paris • Singapore • Tokyo • Toronto • Washington

For more information, contact Wadsworth Publishing Company, 10 Davis Drive, Belmont, CA 94002, or
electronically at http://www.thomson.com/wadsworth.html

International Thomson Publishing Europe
Berkshire House 168-173
High Holborn
London, WC1V 7AA, England

International Thomson Editores
Campos Eliseos 385, Piso 7
Col. Polanco
11560 México D.F. México

Thomas Nelson Australia
102 Dodds Street
South Melbourne 3205
Victoria, Australia

International Thomson Publishing Asia
221 Henderson Road
#05-10 Henderson Building
Singapore 0315

Nelson Canada
1120 Birchmount Road
Scarborough, Ontario
Canada M1K 5G4

International Thomson Publishing Japan
Hirakawacho Kyowa Building, 3F
2-2-1 Hirakawacho
Chiyoda-ku, Tokyo 102, Japan

International Thomson Publishing GmbH
Königswinterer Strasse 418
53227 Bonn, Germany

International Thomson Publishing Southern Africa
Building 18, Constantia Park
240 Old Pretoria Road
Halfway House, 1685 South Africa

ISBN 0-314-20864-X

DOCUMENTS OF WESTERN CIVILIZATION

INTRODUCTION

In an introductory math class, students work out the answers to math problems. In a first sociology class, they may construct and carry out simple sociological surveys. Students learn, by doing, what it means to be a mathematician or a sociologist. In education courses all over the country, prospective teachers are being taught that students learn best not by hearing or by observing, but by doing. Yet on most college and university campuses, history is still taught mainly through lectures. Professors talk; students listen. There is a reason for this. Lecture is the quickest, most efficient means for transferring large amounts of information from the mind of the professor to the minds of the students—or at least to their notebooks. Unfortunately, it leaves beginning students with little idea of what historians do.

When I begin a history course, I challenge my students to hold me accountable by constantly asking me two questions: "How do you know that?" and "So what?" These questions go to the heart of what history is and what historians do. Historians consult the record of the past to attempt to determine what happened. From the results, we construct an interpretation of the past that will help us to understand how the experiences and acts of our predecessors have helped to make us what we are and how our acts and experiences will, in turn, help to shape the future.

In the middle of this century, an attempt was made to make history one of the social sciences—to invest it with the rigor of scientific method. In one sense this can never happen. Though science has opened new approaches for acquiring information about the past, such as radio-carbon dating and computer-based analysis of numerical data, we cannot prove that particular historical events happened in a certain way; we cannot reenact the Battle of Actium or the burning of Joan of Arc. Historical method is, rather, the method of the detective. We search for clues, we compare the stories of witnesses, we analyze the physical evidence, and we construct a narrative that best fits the results of our search. We even "try" our cases. We publish our results, along with the evidence, and wait for our colleagues, like opposing lawyers, to cross-examine us or bring out evidence pointing to a different conclusion.

Detecting history is fun! The purpose of this collection of documents is to allow students to participate in the fun. Using the documents provided, you can question your professor's description or explanation, or you can construct another narrative. Or you can find clues that support his or her position.

What are the raw materials of history? Where do we find our clues? Traditionally they have come from written sources, which make up most of the documents in this collection. You should ask several questions to help you evaluate the reliability of a written account. Was the writer an eyewitness to or a participant in the event? If not, where did he or she get the information? Who is the intended audience? What does the writer stand to gain by putting a particular "slant" on a description? Are the people being described friends or foes of the writer? A second series of questions one needs to ask of a written source concerns how it relates to other documents. Are the writer's statements supported or contradicted by other accounts?

For the earliest societies, many of the written sources available were recorded only after centuries of being passed orally from one generation to the next. They mix elements from the writer's society with the story of a previous event. Some may be wholly fantasy. We can guess at which parts are true only by comparing the story with other evidence.

Physical remains make up another category of historical evidence. Excavations expose skeletons, which can be analyzed to reveal the approximate age of death, illnesses suffered, and general health of the people who lived in a certain location. Jewelry and household objects buried with the bodies can indicate the level of technology of a society and can suggest their physical surroundings, but we can only guess at the uses to which the objects were put, unless they are accompanied by other evidence.

Sometimes physical and written evidence are mingled. The Code of Hammurabi was carved on a large stone, or stele. A drawing above the laws shows the sun god handing the laws to Hammurabi. The written preface to the Code proclaims that Hammurabi is promulgating these laws "to cause justice to prevail in the country, to destroy the wicked and the evil, and so that the strong may not oppress the weak." From the contradiction between the drawing and the inscription, we can deduce that there was some ambiguity in the people's understanding of the source of law. From the fact that it was inscribed on a monumental stone, we can guess that it was set up in a central place so that people might know the law and not be subject to arbitrary punishment at the whim of an official.

This collection of documents was put together following the plan of the Western Civilization textbook by Jackson Spielvogel, third edition, published by West Publishing Company. Its organization into units should, however, make it suitable for use with other texts or standing alone. I had several goals in mind when I suggested yet another collection of documents for Western Civilization. One goal was to integrate social history, the history of women, of working people, and of minorities into the more traditional political, intellectual, and religious history. A second goal was to avoid a mere collection of the most important documents. This book is not the "Greatest Hits of Western Civilization". To create a book of manageable size means finding a balance between the need for many documents, to provide context and continuity, and the need for length, so that an author's words are not misrepresented by being broken into pithy bits. I have chosen to limit the number of topics so that I could include, for each, at least one fairly lengthy segment, accompanied by shorter items that reflect the mileu in which it was created.

Unit 1: Mesopotamia

For the earliest civilizations of the land between the Tigris and the Euphrates Rivers, records are sparse. There are written records in a style called cuneiform because the characters are incised in clay with a wedge-shaped tool. Records of commercial transactions, inventories, and contracts predominate. There are myths and legends, written down centuries after the alleged events. Some of the details are supported by archaeological evidence. For instance, the Epic of Gilgamesh speaks of the ramparts of Uruk, made of burnt brick. Archaeologists have uncovered the ruins of walls five miles long, protected by 900 semicircular towers. They enclosed about two square miles of houses, palaces, workshops, and temples.

from *The Epic of Gilgamesh*

The *Epic of Gilgamesh* is the best-known Mesopotamian story. Gilgamesh was probably a real king of the city of Uruk about 2,700 B.C.E. Tradition says that during his reign the great walls of Uruk were built and the ziggurat, or temple, enlarged. The oldest written fragments of the Epic date from about 1,700 B.C.E. and the most complete version, from which this selection is taken, from about 1,000 years later.

Gilgamesh went abroad in the world, but he met with none who could withstand his arms till he came to Uruk. But the men of Uruk muttered in their houses, 'Gilgamesh sounds the tocsin for his amusement, his arrogance has no bounds by day or night. No son is left with his father, for Gilgamesh takes them all, even the children; yet the king should be a shepherd to his people. His lust leaves no virgin to her lover, neither the warrior's daughter nor the wife of the noble; yet this is the shepherd of the city, wise, comely, and resolute.'

The gods heard their lament, the gods of heaven cried to the Lord of Uruk, to Anu the god of Uruk: 'A goddess made him, strong as a savage bull, none can withstand his arms. No son is left with his father, for Gilgamesh takes them all; and is this the king, the shepherd of his people? His lust leaves no virgin to her lover, neither the warrior's daughter nor the wife of the noble.' When Anu had heard their lamentation the gods cried to Aruru, the goddess of creation, 'You made him O Aruru, now create his equal; let it be as like him as his own reflection, his second self, stormy heart for stormy heart. Let them contend together and leave Uruk in quiet.'

So the goddess conceived an image in her mind, and it was of the stuff of Anu of the firmament. She dipped her hands in water and pinched off clay, she let it fall in the wilderness, and noble Enkidu was created. There was virtue in him of the god of war, of Ninurta himself. His body was rough, he had long hair like a woman's; it waved like the hair of Nisaba, the goddess of corn. His body was covered with matted hair like Samuqan's, the god of cattle. He was innocent of mankind; he knew nothing of the cultivated land.

Enkidu ate grass in the hills with the gazelle and lurked with wild beasts at the water-holes; he had joy of the water with the herds of wild game. But there was a trapper who met him one day face to face at the drinking-hole, for the wild game had entered his territory. On three days he met him face to face, and the trapper was frozen with fear. He went back to his house with the game that he had caught, and he was dumb, benumbed with terror. His face was altered like that of one who has made a long journey. With awe in his heart he spoke to his father: 'Father, there is a man, unlike any other, who comes down from the hills. He is the strongest in the world, he is like an immortal from heaven. He ranges over the hills with wild beasts and eats grass; he rages through your land and comes down to the wells. I am afraid and dare not go near him. He fills in the pits which I dig and tears up my traps set for the game; he helps the beasts to escape and now they slip through my fingers.'

His father opened his mouth and said to the trapper, 'My son, in Uruk lives Gilgamesh; no one has ever prevailed against him, he is strong as a star from heaven. Go to Uruk, find Gilgamesh, extol the strength of this wild man. Ask him to give you a harlot, a wanton from the temple of love; return with her, and let her woman's power overpower this man. When next he comes down to drink at the wells she will be there, stripped naked; and when he sees her beckoning he will embrace her, and then the wild beasts will reject him.'

So the trapper set out on his journey to Uruk and addressed himself to Gilgamesh saying, 'A man unlike any other is roaming now in the pastures; he is as strong as a star from heaven and I am afraid to approach him. He helps the wild game to escape; he fills in my pits and pulls up my traps.' Gilgamesh said, 'Trapper, go back, take with you a harlot, a child of pleasure. At the drinking-hole she will strip, and when he sees her beckoning he will embrace her and the game of the wilderness will surely reject him.'

Now the trapper returned, taking the harlot with him. After a three days' journey they came to the drinking-hole, and there they sat down; the harlot and the trapper sat facing one another and waited for the game to come. For the first day and for the second day the two sat waiting, but on the third day the herds came; they came down to drink and Enkidu was with them. The small wild creatures of the plains were glad of the water, and Enkidu with them, who ate grass with the gazelle and was born in the hills; and she saw him, the savage man, come from far-off in the hills. The trapper spoke to her: 'There he is. Now, woman, make your breasts bare, have no shame, do not delay but welcome his love. Let him see you naked, let him possess your body. When he comes near, uncover yourself and lie with him; teach him, the savage man, your woman's art, for when he murmurs love to you the wild beasts that shared his life in the hills will reject him.'

She was not ashamed to take him, she made herself naked and welcomed his eagerness; as he lay on her murmuring love she taught him the woman's art. For six days and seven nights they lay together, for Enkidu had forgotten his home in the hills; but when he was satisfied he went back to the wild beasts. Then, when the gazelle saw him, they bolted away; when the wild creatures saw him they fled. Enkidu would have followed, but his body was bound as though with a cord, his knees gave way when he started to run, his swiftness was gone. And now the wild creatures had all fled away; Enkidu was grown weak, for wisdom was in him, and the thoughts of a man were in his heart. So he returned and sat down at the woman's feet, and listened intently to what she said. 'You are wise, Enkidu, and now you have become like a god. Why do you want to run wild with the beasts in the hills? Come with me. I will take you to strong-walled Uruk, to the blessed temple of Ishtar and of Anu, of love and of heaven; there Gilgamesh lives, who is very strong, and like a wild bull he lords it over men.'

When she had spoken Enkidu was pleased; he longed for a comrade, for one who would understand his heart. 'Come, woman, and take me to that holy temple, to the house of Anu and of Ishtar, and to the place where Gilgamesh lords it over the people. I will challenge him boldly, I will cry out aloud in Uruk, "I am the strongest here, I have come to change the old order, I am he who was born in the hills, I am he who is strongest of all."'

She said, 'Let us go, and let him see your face. I know very well where Gilgamesh is in Great Uruk. O Enkidu, there all the people are dressed in their gorgeous robes, every day is holiday, the young men and the girls are wonderful to see. How sweet they smell! All the great ones are roused from their beds. O Enkidu, you who love life, I will show you Gilgamesh, a man of many moods; you shall look at him well in his radiant manhood. His body is perfect in strength and maturity; he never rests by night or day. He is stronger than you, so leave your boasting. Shamash the glorious sun has given favours to Gilgamesh, and Anu of the heavens, and Enlil, and Ea the wise has given him deep understanding. I tell you, even before you have left the wilderness, Gilgamesh will know in his dreams that you are coming.'

Now Gilgamesh got up to tell his dream to his mother, Ninsun, one of the wise gods. 'Mother, last night I had a dream. I was full of joy, the young heroes were round me and I walked through the night under the stars of the firmament, and one, a meteor of the stuff of Anu, fell down from heaven. I tried to lift it but it proved too heavy. All the people of Uruk came round to see it, the common people jostled and the nobles thronged to kiss its feet; and to me its attraction was like the love of woman. They helped me, I braced my forehead and I raised it with thongs and brought it to you, and you yourself pronounced it my brother.'

Then Ninsun, who is well-beloved and wise, said to Gilgamesh, 'This star of heaven which descended like a meteor from the sky; which you tried to lift, but found too heavy, when you tried to move it would not budge, and so you brought it to my feet; I made it for you, a goad and spur, and you were drawn as though to a woman. This is the strong comrade, the one who brings help to his friend in his need. He is the strongest of wild creatures, the stuff of Anu; born in the grass-lands and the wild hills reared him; when you see him you will be glad; you love him as a woman and he will never forsake you. This is the meaning of the dream.'

Gilgamesh said, 'Mother, I dreamed a second dream. In the streets of strong-walled Uruk there lay an axe; the shape of it was strange and the people thronged round. I saw it and was glad. I bent down, deeply drawn towards it; I loved it like a woman and wore it at my side.' Ninsun answered, 'That axe, which you saw, which drew you so powerfully like the love of a woman, that is the comrade whom I give you, and he will come in his strength like one of the host of heaven. He is the brave companion who rescues his friend in necessity.' Gilgamesh said to his mother, 'A friend, a counsellor has come to me from Enlil, and now I shall befriend and counsel him.' So Gilgamesh told his dreams; and the harlot retold them to Enkidu.

And now she said to Enkidu, 'When I look at you you have become like a god. Why do you yearn to run wild again with the beasts in the hills? Get up from the ground, the bed of a shepherd.' He listened to her words with care. It was good advice that she gave. She divided her clothing in two and with the one half she clothed him and with the other herself; and holding his hand she led him like a child to the sheepfolds, into the shepherds' tents. There all the shepherds crowded round to see him, they put down bread in front of him, but Enkidu could only suck the milk of wild animals. He fumbled and gaped, at a loss what to do or how he should eat the bread and drink the strong wine. Then the woman said, 'Enkidu, eat bread, it is the staff of life; drink the wine, it is the custom of the land.' So he ate till he was full and drank strong wine, seven goblets. He became merry, his heart exulted and his face shone. He rubbed down the matted hair of his body and anointed himself with oil. Enkidu had become a man; but when he had put on man's clothing he appeared like a bridegroom. He took arms to hunt the lion so that the shepherds could rest at night. He caught wolves and lions and the herdsmen lay down in peace; for Enkidu was their watchman, that strong man who had no rival.

He was merry living with the shepherds, till one day lifting his eyes he saw a man approaching. He said to the harlot, 'Woman, fetch that man here. Why has he come? I wish to know his name.' She went and called the man saying, 'Sir, where are you going on this weary journey?' The man answered, saying to Enkidu, 'Gilgamesh has gone into the marriage-house and shut out the people. He does strange things in Uruk, the city of great streets. At the roll of the drum work begins for the men, and work for the women. Gilgamesh the king is about to celebrate marriage with the Queen of Love, and he still demands to be first with the bride, the king to be first and the husband to follow, for that was ordained by the gods from his birth, from the time the umbilical cord was cut. But now the drums roll for the choice of the bride and the city groans.' At these words Enkidu turned white in the face. 'I will go to the place where Gilgamesh lords it over the people, I will challenge him boldly, and I will cry aloud in Uruk, "I have come to change the old order, for I am the strongest here."'

Now Enkidu strode in front and the woman followed behind. He entered Uruk, that great market, and all the folk thronged round him where he stood in the street in strong-walled Uruk. The people jostled; speaking of him they said, 'He is the spit of Gilgamesh.' 'He is shorter.' 'He is bigger of bone.' 'This is the one who was reared on the milk of wild beasts. His is the greatest strength.' The men rejoiced; 'Now Gilgamesh has met his match. This great one, this hero whose beauty is like a god, he is a match even for Gilgamesh.'

In Uruk the bridal bed was made, fit for the goddess of love. The bride waited for the bridegroom, but in the night Gilgamesh got up and came to the house. Then Enkidu stepped out, he stood in the street and blocked the way. Mighty Gilgamesh came on and Enkidu met him at the gate. He put out his foot and prevented Gilgamesh from entering the house, so they grappled, holding each other like bulls. They broke the doorposts and the walls shook, they snorted like bulls locked together. They shattered the doorposts and the walls shook. Gilgamesh bent his knee with his foot planted on the ground and with a turn Enkidu was thrown. Then immediately his fury died. When Enkidu was thrown he said to Gilgamesh, 'There is not another like you in the world. Ninsun, who is as strong as a wild ox in the byre, she was the mother who bore you, and now you are raised above all men, and Enlil has given you the kingship, for your strength surpasses the strength of men.' So Enkidu and Gilgamesh embraced and their friendship was sealed.

The Code of Hammurabi, c. 1750 B.C.E.

Hammurabi was king of Babylon in the first half of the eighteenth century. He is best known for his code of law, which was inscribed, in cuneiform, on a block of stone nearly eight feet high, so that his subjects (at least those who could read) could know the laws and could seek legal redress when appropriate. While a sculpture at the top of the stone stele shows Hammurabi receiving the laws from the sun god, the prologue makes it clear that Hammurabi himself has collected and pronounced these laws "to promote the welfare of the people, cause justice to prevail in the land, destroy the wicked and the evil, that the strong might not oppress the weak." The laws describe a rather sophisticated society, with written contracts, crime victims compensated by the government, and a sometimes Draconian sense of justice.

21. If a man has broken into a house, he shall be killed before the breach and walled in it.

22. If a man has robbed and has been captured, that man shall be put to death.

23. If the robber has not been caught, the man who has been despoiled shall recount before the god what he has lost, and the city and governor in whose territory the robbery took place shall make good to him his loss.

25. If a fire broke out in a man's house and a man who has come to extinguish the fire has lifted up his eyes to the property of the householder and has taken the property of the householder, that man shall be thrown into the fire.

48. If a man has a debt upon him and a thunderstorm ravaged his field or carried away the produce, or the corn has not grown for lack of water, in that year he shall make no return of corn to his creditor; he shall alter his contract-tablet and he shall not pay interest for that year.

53. If a man has neglected to strengthen the dyke of his canal, and a breach has opened in his dyke, and the waters have ravaged the meadow, the man in whose dyke the breach has been opened shall make good the corn that he caused to be lost.

54. If he is not able to make good the corn, they shall sell him and his goods for money, and the farmers of the meadow whose corn the water carried away shall share it.

128. If a man has married a wife and has not drawn up a contract, that woman is no wife.

129. If the wife of a man has been caught lying with another man, they shall bind them and throw them into the waters. If the owner of the wife would save his wife then in turn the king could save his servant.

130. If a man has forced the wife of a man, who has had no intercourse with a male and is dwelling in her father's house, and has lain in her bosom, and he has been caught, that man shall be killed, the woman will go free.

131. If a wife has been accused by her husband and she has not been caught lying with another male, she shall swear by god and shall return to her house.

132. If a wife has the finger pointed at her on account of another male but has not been caught lying with another male, for the sake of her husband she shall throw herself into the holy river.[1]

---

1 This may refer to the practice of trial by ordeal. The woman throws herself into the river. Her tendency to sink or to float determines her guilt or innocence.

133. If a man has been taken captive and in his house there is maintenance, if his wife has gone out from her house and entered into the house of another, because that woman has not guarded her body and has entered the house of another, they shall prove it against that woman and throw her into the waters.

134. If a man has been taken captive and in his house there is no maintenance, and his wife has entered into the house of another; that woman has no blame.

135. If a man has been taken captive and in his house there is no maintenance, if his wife has entered the house of another and has borne children and afterwards her husband returns and regains his city, that woman shall return to her first husband; the children shall go after their father.

138. If a man has put away his bride who has not borne him children, he shall return her dowry and pay her the marriage portion which she brought from her father's house, and shall put her away.

139. If there was no dowry, he shall give her one *mina* of silver for a divorce.

140. If he is a poor man, he shall give her one third of a *mina* of silver.

141. If the wife of a man who is living in the house of her husband has made up her mind to leave the house to engage in business and has acted the fool, neglecting the house and humiliating the husband, it shall be proved against her; and if her husband has said "I put her away," he shall put her away and she shall go her way, and he shall not give her anything for her divorce.

142. If a woman hates her husband and has said "You shall not possess me," they shall inquire into her record and if she has been economical and has no vice and her husband has gone out and greatly belittled her, that woman has no blame; she will take her marriage portion and go off to her father's house.

143. If she has not been economical, a gadabout, has neglected her house and humiliated her husband, that woman they shall throw into the waters.

229. If a builder has built a house and not made his work strong and the house he built has fallen and so has caused the death of the owner of the house, that builder shall be put to death.

230. If he has caused the son of the owner of the house to die, they shall put to death the son of the builder.

231. If he has caused the slave of the owner of the house to die, he shall give slave for slave to the owner of the house.

232. If he has caused the loss of goods, he shall restore whatever losses he has caused, and because he did not make strong the house he built and it fell, he shall rebuild the house that fell at his own cost.

233. If a builder has built a house for a man and has not jointed his work, and the wall has fallen, that builder shall repair that wall at his own cost.

from *The Oldest Code of Laws in the World*. tr. C. H. W. Johns. Edinburgh. 1903.

Unit 2: Egypt

Because of elaborate preparations for the afterlife, at least for royalty, much of the evidence for the earliest Egyptian civilization comes from tombs. Baskets, pottery, and bone carvings from the fifth and fourth millenia B.C.E. attest to settled agriculture. About 3,000 B.C.E. writing developed in two forms, hieroglyph and hieratic. Writing and a literate bureaucracy were major instruments in the formation of a centralized state. Massive pyramids, temples, and tombs demonstrate a high level of knowledge in the third millenium.. Treatises on mathematics, astronomy, medicine, and magic date from around 2,500 B.C.E. Written records were undeciphered until the discovery of the Rosetta Stone during Napoleon's expedition to Egypt in 1798. The stone contains a decree of Ptolemy V Epiphenes in hieroglyphs, demotic, and Greek. A comparison of the three texts led to its decipherment in 1822.

Protest of an Egyptian Farmer, c. 2050 B.C.E.

In this text, a farmer is robbed by an official. He appeals to the Lord High Steward, who is so impressed with the farmer's eloquence that he informs the king, who orders the farmer detained through nine appeals. His family is secretly cared for while his words are recorded. At the end, the peasant is rewarded and the bureaucrat punished.

Once, there was a farmer named Khun-Anup, who lived in The Salt-Field District near Thebes. One day he said to Marye, his wife: "I am going down to the city for food. Go into the barn and see how much grain is left from last year's harvest." After determining that there were twenty-six measures of barley, the farmer took six with him to trade and left the rest to feed his family.

The farmer loaded the asses with salt, reeds, leopard skins, wolf hides, doves, and other goods from his district to trade. Then he set out for the city. He traveled south toward Herakleopolis through Per-fefi, north of Medenit. Tut-nakht, son of Isri—who was an official of The Chief Steward, Rensi, the son of Meru--was standing on the bank of the canal and saw the farmer coming.

As he watched the farmer approach, Tut-nakht said to himself: "I think I have a scheme I can use to steal this farmer's goods!"

At one point the public path along the embankment of the canal in front of Tut-nakht's house was no wider than a loincloth. One side of the path was flooded with water, and the other side was overgrown with barley from Tut-nakht's field. Tut-nakht told one of his slaves: "Get me some clothes from my house!" When the slave brought them, Tut-nakht laid the clothes down over the water.

Just then, the farmer came down the path. Tut-nakht shouted to him: "Be careful, you farmer! You are about to step on my garments."

The farmer answered: "I am being careful! I do not wish to offend you, but your garments are right in my way. I cannot climb the steep embankment along the canal on one side of them, nor do I want to trample the grain in your field on the other. Please give me permission to pass."

As he stood there talking, one of the asses bit off a stalk of barley. Then Tut-nakht said: "Now I am going to confiscate your ass for eating my grain. I will sentence it to the threshing floor for this offense."

But the farmer pleaded: "My intentions are good. Only one stalk has been damaged. If you do not let me pay for the damage done and buy back my donkey, I will appeal to Rensi, the son of Meru, who is The Chief Steward and Governor of this district. Is it likely that he will allow me to be robbed in his own district?"

Tut-nakht answered. "Why do the poor always want to speak to masters? You are speaking to me, not to The Chief Steward!" Then he took a stick and beat the farmer and confiscated his asses.

The farmer protested his painful sentence and the injustice done to him.

Tut-nakht tried to silence him in the name of Osiris, The God of Silence.

The farmer protested the attempt to silence him and swore by Osiris that he would not keep quiet until his property was returned.

For ten days, the farmer appealed to Tut-nakht without results. So, he went to Herakleopolis to appeal to Rensi, the son of Meru, who was The Chief Steward. As he was rushing off to board his barge, the official asked the farmer to file his protest with a lower court, which finally took his statement.

Eventually, Rensi and his council considered the case and decided that Tut-nakht was guilty only of harassing a farmer who no longer worked for him and should be sentenced only to return the farmer's goods. However, Rensi did not announce the verdict. So the farmer went to see about his appeal in person.

> "You are The Chief Steward, You are my lord!
> You are my last hope, You are my only judge.
> When you sail The Lake of Justice, Fairness fills your sail!
> You father the orphan, You husband the widow.
> You brother the divorced,
> You mother the motherless.
> I will extol your name throughout the land,
> I will proclaim you a just judge!
> . . .a ruler without greed, . . .a great man without fault.
> . . .a destroyer of lies, . . .a just judge, who hears the cry of the poor.
> Hear me when I speak, Give me justice.
> Relieve me of this burden of poverty, . . .the care which weighs me down!"

The farmer appealed to Rensi in the name of Neb-kau-Ra, Pharaoh of Upper and Lower Egypt.

So, Rensi went to the Pharaoh and said: "My lord, I am hearing the case of a truly eloquent farmer. His goods have been stolen by a man in my service and he has come to me for justice."

The Pharaoh said: "I am ordering you to keep this man waiting without giving him any reply. Just keep him talking. You must write down each of his speeches and send them to me.

Furthermore, without letting this farmer know, I want you to provide for his wife and children as well as for his own needs."

Each day, a friend of The Chief Steward delivered ten loaves of bread and two jars of beer to the farmer. Rensi also ordered the governor of The Field-of-Salt District to deliver three measures of grain to the farmer's wife every day.

The second time the farmer comes to see about his appeal, The Chief Steward asks him whether these goods were really worth going to prison over.

The farmer replies.

"The Distributor puts more grain in his own pile, The Giver of Full Measure shorts his people.
The Lawmaker approves of robbery,—who is left to punish the wrongdoer?—The Inspector condones corruption.

"One is publicly criminal, The other tolerates injustice.
Do not learn from such as these!

"Punishment lasts for a moment, Injustice goes on forever.
Good example is remembered forever, Follow this teaching--
Do unto others, As you would have others do unto you.

"Thank others for their work, Parry blows before they strike,
Give jobs to the most qualified." . . .
The third time, the farmer said:

"Do justice, And live!
Carry out sentences on convicts, And fulfill your duty beyond all others.
Does the hand-scale lie? Is the Stand-scale tilted?
Is Thoth, God of The Scales, looking the other way?
Do not be tempted by corruption. . . Do not return evil for good,
Do not substitute lesser for better goods.

Reprinted from *Old Testament Parallels: Stories and Laws from the Ancient Near East,* by Victor H. Matthews and Don C. Benjamin. © 1991 by Victor H. Matthews and Don C. Benjamin. Used by permission of Paulist Press, Mahwah, N.J.

"Declaration of Innocence" from the *Egyptian Book of the Dead*

The Book of the Dead is a collection of texts written on papyrus (or, occasionally, on linen, vellum, on the walls of tombs or on coffins), which were placed with the dead to help them to pass through the dangers of the Underworld. There are nearly two hundred spells, or chapters, in all. A wealthy person about to die could choose certain chapters to be written for him by a scribe. The less wealthy could buy ready-made texts with blank spaces to insert the name of the individual. The earliest existing papyri containing these spells date from the fifteenth century B.C.E.

THE FOLLOWING WORDS SHALL BE SAID BY THE STEWARD OF THE KEEPER OF THE SEAL, NU, WHOSE WORD IS TRUTH, WHEN HE COMES FORTH TO THE HALL OF MAATI,[2] SO THAT HE MAY BE SEPARATED FROM EVERY SIN WHICH HE HAS COMMITTED, AND MAY BEHOLD THE FACES OF THE GODS.

Homage to you, O Great God, Lord of Maati! I have come unto you, O my Lord, and I have brought myself here that I may behold your beauties. I know you, I know your name, I know the names of the Forty-two Gods who live with you in this Hall of Maati, who live by keeping ward over sinners, and who feed upon their blood on the day when the consciences of men are reckoned up in the presence of the god Un-Nefer. In truth your name is "Rehti-merti-nebti-Maati." In truth I have come unto you, I have brought Maati to you. I have done away sin for you. I have not committed sins against men. I have not opposed my family and kinsfolk. I have not committed perjury. I have not known worthless or profligate men. I have not done evil. I have not made it to be the first consideration daily that unnecessary work should be done for me. I have not brought forward my name for dignities. I have not attempted to direct servants. I have not defrauded the humble man of his property. I have not done what the gods abominate. I have not vilified a slave to his master. I have not inflicted pain. I have not caused anyone to go hungry. I have not made any man to weep. I have not committed murder. I have not given the order for murder to be committed. I have not caused calamities to befall men and women.

I have not plundered the offerings in the temples. I have not defrauded the gods of their cake-offerings. I have not carried off the *fenkhu* cakes offered to the Spirits. I have not had intercourse with men. I have not masturbated in the sanctuaries of the god of my city. I have not diminished from the bushel. I have not filched land from my neighbour's estate and added it to my own acre. I have not encroached upon the fields of others. I have not added to the weights of the scales. I have not depressed the pointer of the balance. I have not carried away the milk from the mouths of children.

I have not driven the cattle away from their pastures. I have not snared the geese in the goose-pens of the gods. I have not caught fish with bait made of the bodies of the same kind of fish. I have not stopped water when it should flow. I have not made a cutting in a canal of running water. I have not extinguished a fire when it should burn. I have not violated the times of offering the chosen meat offerings. I have not driven away the cattle on the estates of the gods. I have not turned back the god at his appearances. I am pure. I am pure. I am pure. I am pure. My pure offerings are the pure offerings of that great Benu which dwells in Hensu. For behold, I am the nose of Neb-nefu, who gives sustenance unto all mankind, on the day of the full moon in Anu, in the second month of the season Pert, on the last day of the month. I have seen the filling of the Utchat in Anu, therefore let not calamity befall me in this land, or in this Hall of Maati, because I know the names of the gods who are therein.

THE DECLARATION OF INNOCENCE BEFORE THE GODS OF THE TRIBUNAL

Ani says: Hail, you whose strides are long, who come forth from Annu, I have not done iniquity.

Hail, you who are embraced by flame, who come forth from Kheraba, I have not robbed with violence.

Hail, Fentiu, who come forth from Khemennu, I have not stolen.

---

2 Usually translated into English as justice or truth.

Hail, Devourer of the Shade, who come forth from Qernet, I have done no murder; I have done no harm.

Hail, Nehau, who come forth from Re-stau, I have not defrauded offerings.

Hail, god in the form of two lions, who come forth from heaven, I have not minished oblations.

Hail, you whose eyes are of fire, who come forth from Saut, I have not plundered the god.

Hail, you Flame, which comes and goes, I have spoken no lies.

Hail, Bone-crusher, who come forth from Suten-henen, I have not snatched away food.

Hail, Flame-shooter, who come forth from Het-Ptah-ka, I have not caused pain.

Hail, Qerer, who come forth from Amentet, I have not committed fornication.

Hail, you whose face is turned back, who come forth from your hiding place, I have not caused the shedding of tears.

Hail, Bast, who come forth from the secret place, I have not dealt deceitfully.

Hail, you whose legs are of fire, who come forth out of the darkness, I have not transgressed.

Hail, Devourer of Blood, who come forth from the block of slaughter. I have not acted guilefully.

Hail, Devourer of the inward parts, who come forth from Mabet, I have not laid waste the ploughed land.

Hail, Lord of Right and Truth, who come forth from the city of Right and Truth, I have not eavesdropped.

Hail you who stride backward, who come forth from the city of Bast, I have not set my lips in motion (against any man.)

Hail, Sertiu, who come forth from Annu, I have not been angry and wrathful except for a just cause.

Hail, you being of two-fold wickedness, who comes forth from Ati, I have not defiled the wife of any man.

Hail, you two-headed serpent, who come forth from the torture-chamber, I have not defiled the wife of any man.

Hail, you who regard what is brought to you, who come forth from Pa-Amsu, I have not polluted myself.

Hail, you Chief of the mighty, who come forth from Amentet, I have not caused terror.

Hail, you Destroyer, who come forth from Kesiu, I have not transgressed.

Hail, you who order speech, who come forth from Urit, I have not burned with rage.

Hail, you Babe, who come forth from Uab, I have not shut my ears against the words of Right and Truth.

Hail, Kenemti, who come forth from Kenemet, I have not created grief.

Hail, you who bring your offering, I have not acted insolently.

Hail you who order speech, who come forth from Unaset, I have stirred up strife.

Hail, Lord of faces, who come forth from Netchfet, I have not judged hastily.

Hail Sekheriu, who come forth from Utten, I have not eavesdropped.

Hail, Two-horned Lord who comes forth from Saïs, I have not been exceedingly talkative.

Hail, Nefer-Tmu, who come forth from Het-Pyah-ka, I have done neither harm nor ill.

Hail, Tmu in your hour, who come forth from Tattu, I have never cursed the king.

Hail you who work your will, who come forth from Tebu, I have never polluted the water.

Hail, Bearer of the Sistrum, who come forth from Nu, I have not spoken scornfully.

Hail, you who cause mankind to flourish, who come forth from Saïs, I have never cursed God.

Hail, Neheb-ka, who come forth from your hiding place, I have not defrauded the offerings of the gods.

Hail, you who set the head in order, who come forth from your shrine, I have not plundered the offerings to the blessed dead.

Hail, you who bring your arm, who come forth from the city of Maati, I have not stolen the infant's food; neither have I sinned against the god of my native town.

Hail, you White-toothed One, who come forth from Ta-she, I have not slaughtered with evil intent the cattle of the god.

Translated by E. A. Wallis Budge, *The Book of the Dead: The Papyrus of Ani*. New York: Dover. 1895.

CHAPTER 2: THE HEBREWS AND ASSYRIANS

Unit 3: The Hebrews

Nearly all of the evidence for the civilization of the ancient Hebrews comes from the Hebrew Bible. Excavators of the city of Mari, in Mesopotamia, found tablets containing names such as Abraham and Jacob and referring to a people called the Habiru, which lend some support to the biblical story of the migration from Ur.

The Hebrew Bible is known also as the TaNaKh, an acronym derived from the names of its three divisions: Torah, Nevi'im, and Ketuvim. The Torah, also called the Pentateuch, is made up of five books, traditionally attributed to Moses. It contains the history up to Moses' time and the Law. The Nevi'im are the Prophets and four historical works. The Ketuvim consist of religious poetry and wisdom literature. There is no reliable evidence indicating when or by whom these works were written. The Torah must have existed as a recognized sacred writing by 622 B.C.E. A narrative describing the reformation under King Josiah describes the discovery of a "book of the Torah" during the renovation of the Temple at that time. The histories were apparently based on other written records which have since disappeared. They make numerous references to "the annals of the kings of Israel."

from *The Torah*

Modern Jews and Muslims claim descent from Abraham. The first selection describes the migration that is the traditional beginning of these two peoples and of their claims to land in the Middle East.

The Hebrew faith is sometimes described as the earliest religion based on moral and ethical principles. In the second selection, Abraham calls god to account, insisting that he abide by the same moral principles he expects of his people. This is in contrast to the arbitrary gods of neighboring peoples, who act capriciously and are accountable to no one. The third selection is from the law said to have been given by God to Moses at Mt. Sinai. Some of its provisions have parallels in the Code of Hammurabi. There is a difference, though. Each law of Hammurabi carries a specific penalty for infraction—a penalty to be enacted by the authorities. The Mosaic laws are stated as moral imperatives. Transgressors will incur the anger of god.

GENESIS 11:27-12:9: THE CALL OF ABRAM

Now this is the line of Terah: Terah begot Abram, Nahor, and Haran; and Haran begot Lot. Haran died in the lifetime of his father Terah, in his native land, Ur of the Chaldeans. Abram and Nahor took to themselves wives, the name of Abram's wife being Sarai and that of Nahor's wife Milcah, the daughter of Haran, the father of Milcah and Iscah. Now Sarai was barren, she had no child.

Terah took his son Abram, his grandson Lot the son of Haran, they settled there. The days of Terah came to 205 years; and Terah died in Haran.

The Lord said to Abram, "Go forth from your native land and from your father's house to the land that I will show you.

> I will make of you a great nation,
> And I will bless you;
> I will make your name great,
> And you shall be a blessing:
> I will bless those who bless you,
> And curse him that curses you;
> All the families of the earth
> Shall bless themselves by you.

Abram went forth as the Lord had spoken to him, and Lot went with him. Abram was seventy-five years old when he left Haran. Abram took his wife Sarai and his brother's son Lot, and all the wealth that they had amassed, and the persons that they had acquired in Haran; and they set out for the land of Canaan. When they arrived in the land of Canaan, Abram passed through the land as far as the site of Shechem, at the *terebinth* of Moreh. The Canaanites were then in the land.

The Lord appeared to Abram and said, "I will give this land to your offspring." And he built an altar there to the Lord who had appeared to him. From there he moved on to the hill country east of Bethel and pitched his tent, with Bethel on the west and Ai on the east; and he built there an altar to the Lord and invoked the Lord by name. Then Abram journeyed by stages toward the Negeb.

GENESIS 18: 16-33: GOD IS HELD TO HIS OWN MORAL STANDARDS

The men set out from there and looked down toward Sodom, Abraham walking with them to see them off.[3] Now the Lord had said, "Shall I hide from Abraham what I am about to do, since Abraham is to become a great and populous nation and all the nations of the earth are to bless themselves by him? For I have singled him out, that he may instruct his children and his posterity to keep the way of the Lord by doing what is just and right, in order that the Lord may bring about for Abraham what He has promised him." Then the Lord said, "The outrage of Sodom and Gomorrah is so great, and their sin so grave! I will go down to see whether they have acted altogether according to the outcry that has come to Me; if not, I will know."

The men went on from there to Sodom, while Abraham remained standing before the Lord. Abraham came forward and said, "Will You sweep away the innocent along with the guilty? What if there should be fifty innocent within the city; will You then wipe out the place and not forgive it for the sake of the innocent fifty who are in it? Far be it from you to do such a thing, to bring death upon the innocent as well as the guilty, so that innocent and guilty fare alike. Far be it from You! Shall not the Judge of all the earth deal justly?" And the Lord answered, "If I find within the city of Sodom fifty innocent ones, I will forgive the whole place for their sake." Abraham spoke up, saying "Here I venture to speak to the Lord, I who am but dust and ashes: What if the fifty innocent should lack five? Will You destroy the whole city for want of the five?" And He answered, "I will not destroy if I find forty-five there." But he spoke to Him

---

3 Abram's name had recently been changed to Abraham when God confirmed the earlier covenant, promising him a son through whom he would have many descendents.

again, and said, "What if forty should be found there?" And He answered, "I will not do it, for the sake of the forty." And he said, "Let not the Lord be angry if I go on: What if thirty should be found there?" And He answered, "I will not do it if I find thirty there." And he said, "I venture again to speak to the Lord: What if twenty should be found there?" And He answered, "I will not destroy, for the sake of the twenty." And he said, "Let not the Lord be angry if I speak but this last time: What if ten should be found there?" And He answered, "I will not destroy, for the sake of the ten."

When the Lord had finished speaking to Abraham, He departed; and Abraham returned to his place.

EXODUS 22:20-23:13: SOCIAL RESPONSIBILITY

You shall not wrong a stranger or oppress him, for you were strangers in the land of Egypt.

You shall not mistreat any widow or orphan. If you do mistreat them, I will heed their outcry as soon as they cry our to Me, and My anger shall blaze forth and I will put you to the sword, and your own wives shall become widows and your children orphans.

If you lend money to My people, to the poor who is in your power, do not act toward him as a creditor: exact no interest from him. If you take your neighbor's garment in pledge, you must return it to him before the sun sets; it is his only clothing, the sole covering for his skin. In what else shall he sleep? Therefore, if he cries out to Me, I will pay heed, for I am compassionate.

You shall not offend God, nor put a curse upon a chieftain among your people.

You shall not put off the skimming of the first yield of your vats. You shall give Me the first-born among your sons. you shall do the same with your cattle and your flocks: seven days it shall remain with its mother; on the eighth day you shall give it to Me.

You shall be men holy to me; you must not eat flesh torn by beasts in the field; you shall cast it to the dogs.

You must not carry false rumors; you shall not join hands with the guilty to act as an unjust witness. Do not side with the mighty to do wrong, and do not give perverse testimony in a dispute by leaning toward the mighty; nor must you show deference to a poor man in his dispute.

When you encounter your enemy's ox or ass wandering, you must take it back to him. When you see the ass of your enemy prostrate under its burden and would refrain from raising it, you must nevertheless raise it with him.

You shall not subvert the rights of your needy in their disputes. Keep far from a false charge; do not bring death on the innocent and the righteous, for I will not acquit the wrongdoer. Do not take bribes, for bribes blind the clear-sighted and upset the pleas of the just.

You shall not oppress a stranger, for you know the feelings of the stranger, having yourselves been strangers in the land of Egypt.

Six years you shall sow your land and gather in its yield; but in the seventh you shall let it rest and lie fallow. Let the needy among your people eat of it, and what they leave let the wild beasts eat. You shall do the same with your vineyards and your olive groves.

Six days you shall do your work, but on the seventh day you shall cease from labor, in order that your ox and your ass may rest, and that your bondman and the stranger may be refreshed.

Be on guard concerning all that I have told you. Make no mention of the names of other gods; they shall not be heard on your lips.

from The Torah. The New JPS Translation. Jewish Publication Society. 1963. Used by permission.

from *The Histories*

The Hebrew people split into the Northern and the Southern Kingdom after the reign of King Solomon, which ended in 931 B.C.E. The Northern Kingdom, called Israel, was conquered by the Assyrians in 722. Many Hebrews were deported. They merged with neighboring peoples and lost their identity. The Southern Kingdom, known as Judah, was conquered in 586 by the Babylonians. Unlike their Northern kin, they maintained their identity during their captivity in Babylon, and were allowed to return to Jerusalem in 538.

II KINGS 24:8-25:12: THE BABYLONIAN CAPTIVITY

Jehoiachin was eighteen years old when he began to reign, and he reigned in Jerusalem three months. And his mother's name was Nehushta, the daughter of Elnathan of Jerusalem. And he did that which was evil in the sight of the Lord, according to all that his father had done.

At that time the servants of Nebuchadnezzar king of Babylon came up against Jerusalem, and the city was besieged. And Nebuchadnezzar king of Babylon came against the city, and his servants did besiege it. And Jehoiachin the king of Judah went out to the king of Babylon, he, and his mother, and his servants, and his princes, and his officers: and the king of Babylon took him in the eighth year of his reign. And he carried out thence all the treasures of the house of the Lord, and the treasures of the king's house, and cut in pieces all the vessels of gold which Solomon king of Israel had made in the temple of the Lord, as the Lord had said. And he carried away all Jerusalem, and all the princes, and all the mighty men of valour, even ten thousand captives, and all the craftsmen and smiths: none remained, save the poorest sort of the people of the land. And he carried away Jehoiachin to Babylon, and the king's mother, and the king's wives, and his officers, and the mighty of the land, those carried he into captivity from Jerusalem to Babylon. And all the men of might, even seven thousand, and craftsmen and smiths a thousand, all that were strong and apt for war, even them the king of Babylon brought captive to Babylon. And the king of Babylon made Mattaniah his father's brother king in his stead, and changed his name to Zedekiah.

Zedekiah was twenty and one years old when he began to reign, and he reigned eleven years in Jerusalem. And his mother's name was Hamutal, the daughter of Jeremiah of Libnah. And he did that which was evil in the sight of the Lord, according to all that Jehoiakim had done. For through the anger of the Lord it came to pass in Jerusalem and Judah, until he had cast them out from his presence, that Zedekiah rebelled against the king of Babylon.

And it came to pass in the ninth year of his reign, in the tenth month, in the tenth day of the month, that Nebuchadnezzar king of Babylon came, he, and all his host, against Jerusalem, and pitched against it; and they built forts against it round about. And the city was besieged unto the eleventh year of king Zedekiah. And on the ninth day of the fourth month the famine prevailed in the city, and there was no bread for the people of the land. And the city was broken up, and all the men of war fled by night by the way of the gate between two walls, which is by the king's garden: (now the Chaldees were against the city round about:) and the king went the way toward the plain. And the army of the Chaldees pursued after the king, and overtook him in the plains of Jericho: and all his army were scattered from him.

So they took the king, and brought him up to the king of Babylon to Riblah; and they gave judgment upon him. And they slew the sons of Zedekiah before his eyes, and put out the eyes of Zedekiah, and bound him with fetters of brass, and carried him to Babylon. And in the fifth month, on the seventh day of the month, which is the nineteenth year of king Nebuchadnezzar king of Babylon, came Nebuzaradan, captain of the guard, a servant of the king of Babylon, unto Jerusalem: And he burnt the house of the Lord, and the king's house, and all the houses of Jerusalem, and every great man's house burnt he with fire. And all the army of the Chaldees, that were left in the city, and the fugitives that fell away to the king of Babylon, with the remnant of the multitude, did Nebuzaradan the captain of the guard carry away. But the captain of the guard left of the poor of the land to be vinedressers and husbandmen.

from the King James version of the Bible, 1601

Psalm 37

Fret not thyself because of evildoers, neither be thou envious against the workers of iniquity.
For they shall soon be cut down like the grass, and wither as the green herb.
Trust in the Lord, and do good; so shalt thou dwell in the land, and verily thou shalt be fed.
Delight thyself also in the Lord; and he shall give thee the desires of thine heart.
Commit thy way unto the Lord; trust also in him; and he shall bring it to pass.
And he shall bring forth thy righteousness as the light, and thy judgment as the noonday.
Rest in the Lord, and wait patiently for him; fret not thyself because of him who prospereth in his
    way, because of the man who bringeth wicked devices to pass.
Cease from anger, and forsake wrath: fret not thyself in any wise to do evil.
For evildoers shall be cut off; but those that wait upon the Lord, they shall inherit the earth.
For yet a little while, and the wicked shall not be; yea, thou shalt diligently consider his place,
    and it shall not be.
But the meek shall inherit the earth; and shall delight themselves in the abundance of peace.
The wicked plotteth against the just, and gnasheth upon him with his teeth.
The Lord shall laugh at him; for he seeth that his day is coming.
The wicked have drawn out the sword, and have bent their bow, to cast down the poor and needy,
    and to slay such as be of upright conversation.
Their sword shall enter into their own heart, and their bows shall be broken.
A little that a righteous man hath is better than the riches of many wicked.
For the arms of the wicked shall be broken; but the Lord upholdeth the righteous.
The Lord knoweth the days of the upright; and their inheritance shall be for ever.
They shall not be ashamed in the evil time; and in the days of famine they shall be satisfied.
But the wicked shall perish, and the enemies of the Lord shall be as the fat of lambs; they shall
    consume; into smoke shall they consume away. . . .

from the King James version of the Bible, 1601

Unit 4: Assyria

The Hebrew Psalmist had confidence that his god would reward the righteous and punish evildoers. The Mesopotamian prayed to more gods than he could name. The desires of the gods were unknowable. Their judgments were unfathomable.

The Hebrews' most powerful neighbor from about 1360 to about 610 B.C.E. was Assyria, whose kings kept records, in chilling detail and hypnotic repetition, of the ferocious and bloody deeds by which they conquered their neighbors and then kept them in a terrified subjection.

Penitential Prayer to Every God, c. 650 B.C.E.

May the wrath of the heart of my god be pacified!
May the god who is unknown to me be pacified!
May the goddess who is unknown to me be pacified!
May the known and unknown god be pacified!
May the known and unknown goddess be pacified! . . .

The sin which I have committed I know not.
The misdeed which I have committed I know not.

A gracious name may my god announce!
A gracious name may my goddess announce!
A gracious name may my known and unknown god announce!
A gracious name may my known and unknown goddess announce!

Pure food have I not eaten.
Clear water have I not drunk.

An offence against my god I have unwittingly committed.
A transgression against my goddess I have unwittingly done.
O Lord, my sins are many, great are my iniquities!
My god, my sins are many, great are my iniquities! . . .

The sin, which I have committed, I know not.
The iniquity, which I have done, I know not.
The offence, which I have committed, I know not.
The transgression I have done, I know not.

The lord, in the anger of his heart, hath looked upon me.
The god, in the wrath of his heart, hath visited me.
The goddess hath become angry with me, and hath grievously stricken me.
The known or unknown god hath straitened me.
The known or unknown goddess hath brought affliction upon me.

I sought for help, but no one taketh my hand.
I wept, but no one came to my side.

I lamented, but no one hearkens to me.
I am afflicted, I am overcome, I cannot look up.

Unto my merciful god I turn, I make supplication.
I kiss the feet of my goddess and [crawl before her] . . .

How long, my god . . .
How long, my goddess, until thy face be turned toward me?
How long, known and unknown god, until the anger of thy heart be pacified?
How long, known and unknown goddess, until thy unfriendly heart be pacified?

Mankind is perverted and has no judgment.
Of all men who are alive, who knows anything?
They do not know whether they do good or evil.

O lord, do not cast aside thy servant!
He is cast into the mire; take his hand.

The sin which I have sinned, turn to mercy!
The iniquity which I have committed, let the wind carry away!
My many transgressions tear off like a garment!

My god, my sins are seven times seven; forgive my sins!
My goddess, my sins are seven times seven, forgive my sins!
Known and unknown god, my sins are seven times seven; forgive my sins!
Known or unknown goddess, my sins are seven times seven; forgive my sins!
Forgive my sins and I will humble myself before thee.

Translated by Robert F. Harper, *Assyrian and Babylonian Literature.* New York, 1901.

From the Annals of Assur-nasir-Pal, c. 870 B.C.E.

I am a king, I am a lord, I am glorious, I am great, I am mighty.
I have arisen, I am a chief, I am a prince.
I am a warrior, I am great and I am glorious,
Assur-nasir-habal, a mighty king of Assyria,
 proclaimer of the Moongod,
 worshipper of Anu, exalter of Yav,
suppliant of the gods am I, servant unyielding,
subduing the lands of his foes,
a king mighty in battle,
 destroyer of cities and forests,
 chief over opponents,
 king of the four regions,
 expeller of his foes,
 prostrating all his enemies,
 prince of a multitude of lands and of all kings, even of all,
a prince subduing those disobedient to him
who is ruling all the multitudes of men.

These aspirations have gone up to the face of the great gods;
on my destiny they have steadfastly determined;
at the wishes of my heart and the uplifting of my hand, Istar, exalted lady, has favored me in my intentions
and has applied her heart to the conduct of my battles and warfare.
In those days I Assur-nasir-pal,
> glorious prince,
> worshipper of the great gods, the wishes of whose heart Bel will cause him to attain, and
> who has conquered all kings who disobey him, and
who in difficult places has beaten down assemblages of rebels;
when Assur,
> mighty lord,
> proclaimer of my name,
> aggrandizer of my royalty over the kings of the four regions,
has bountifully added his invincible power to the forces of my government
putting me in possession of lands,
and mighty forests for exploration has he given and urgently impelled me—
by the might of Assur my lord, perplexed paths,
difficult mountains by the impetuosity of my hosts I crossed and an equal there was not.

In the beginning of my reign and in my first campaign when the Sun-god, guider of the lands threw over me his beneficent protection,
on the throne of my dominion I firmly seated myself.
A sceptre, the dread of man, I took into my hands.
My chariots and my armies I collected.
I passed rugged paths, difficult mountains,
ill-suited for the passage of chariots and armies
and I went to the land of Nairi:
Libie, their capital city,
The cities Zurra and Abuqua, Arura, Arubie, situated within the limits of the land
of Aruni and Etini, fortified cities, I took,
their fighting men in numbers I slew.
Their spoil, their wealth, their cattle I spoiled.
Their soldiers were discouraged.
They took possession of a difficult mountain, a mountain exceedingly difficult.
After them I did not proceed
for it was a mountain ascending up like lofty points of iron, and
the beautiful birds of heaven had not reached up into it.
Like nests of the young birds in the midst of the mountain
they placed their defences into which none of the kings my fathers had ever penetrated. . .

Along the feet of that mountain I crept and hid;
their nests, their tents I broke up;
two hundred of their warriors with weapons I destroyed;
their spoil in abundance like the young of sheep I carried off;
their corpses like rubbish on the mountains I heaped up;

their relics in tangled hollows of the mountains I consumed;
their cities I overthrew, demolished and burnt in fire.

From the land of Nummi to the land of Kirruri I came down.
The tribute of Kirruri . . . ,
horses, fish, oxen, horned sheep in numbers,
copper as their tribute I received.
An officer to guard boundaries over them I placed.
While in the land of Kirruri they detained me,
the fear of Assur my lord overwhelmed the lands of Gilzanai and Khubuskai;
horses, silver, gold, tin, copper, *kams* of copper as their tribute they brought me.

From the land of Kirruri I withdrew
and passed to a territory close to the town Khulun in Kurdistan.
Their cities I occupied.
Their soldiers in numbers I slew.
Their spoil, their riches I carried off.
Their soldiers were discouraged;
the summits rising over against the city of Nistun,
which were menacing like the storms of heaven, I captured,
into which none among the princes my sires had ever penetrated.
My soldiers like birds of prey rushed upon them.
260 of their warriors by the sword I smote down;
their heads cut off in heaps I arranged;
the rest of them like birds in a nest in the rocks of the mountains nestled;
their spoil, their riches from the midst of the mountains I brought down;
cities which were situated in the midst of vast forests I overthrew,
    destroyed,
    burned in fire,.
The rebellious soldiers fled from before my arms;
they came down;
my yoke they received;
impost tribute and a Viceroy I set over them.
Bubu, son of Bubua son of the Prefect of Nistun,
in the city of Arbela I flayed;
his skin I stretched in contempt upon the wall.

Translated by J. M. Rodwell, *Babylonian and Assyrian Literature*. New York, 1901.

CHAPTER 3: ANCIENT GREECE

Unit 5: Archaic Greece

Before about 1200 B.C.E. the Mycenaeans, those who occupied what is now Greece, had a written language known as Linear B. Clay tablets contain detailed records of royal possessions. After about 1200, writing disappeared and sources are limited to such artifacts as weapons, painted vases, and the remains of city walls and canals.

Around 800, writing was reintroduced. During the archaic period, about 800 to 550, Greece was still an oral culture. Composed works were in the form easiest to remember, that of poetry. The poetry of Homer and Sappho has been revered through the centuries not only for what it reveals about the people of its time, but for its timeless elegance and for the depth of feeling it portrays. Tyrtaeus of Sparta has not been as well known. The mood of his poetry fits with the descriptions of later authors, such as Plutarch and Aristotle, of a state dedicated to military strength.

from *The Iliad*, c. 800 B.C.E.

While it was written down about 800, probably but not certainly by the poet Homer, The Iliad tells the story of the Trojan War, fought about 400 years earlier. In this selection, Achilles, the greatest of the Greek warriors, rages against Agamemnon, leader of the Greek forces. The conflict is attributed to the gods, but it is obvious that the men are responsible for their own passions and for the choices they make.

Rage--Goddess, sing the rage of Peleus' son Achilles,
murderous, doomed, that cost the Achaeans countless losses,
hurling down to the House of Death so many sturdy souls,
great fighters' souls, but made their bodies carrion,
feasts for the dogs and birds,
and the will of Zeus was moving toward its end.
Begin, Muse, when the two first broke and clashed,
Agamemnon lord of men and brilliant Achilles.

What god drove them to fight with such a fury?
Apollo the son of Zeus and Leto. Incensed at the king
he swept a fatal plague through the army--men were dying
and all because Agamemnon spurned Apollo's priest.
Yes, Chryses approached the Achaeans' fast ships
to win his daughter back, bringing a priceless ransom
and bearing high in hand, wound on a golden staff,
the wreaths of the god, the distant deadly Archer.
He begged the whole Achaean army but most of all
the two supreme commanders, Atreus' two sons,

"Agamemnon, Menelaus--all Argives geared for war
May the gods who hold the halls of Olympus give you
Priam's city to plunder, then safe passage home.
Just set my daughter free, my dear one . . .here,
accept these gifts, this ransom. Honor the god
who strikes from worlds away--the son of Zeus, Apollo!"

And all ranks of Achaeans cried out their assent:
"Respect the priest, accept the shining ransom!"
But it brought no joy to the heart of Agamemnon.
The king dismissed the priest with a brutal order
ringing in his ears: "Never again, old man,
let me catch sight of you by the hollow ships!
Not loitering now, not slinking back tomorrow.
The staff and the wreaths of god will never save you then.
The girl--I won't give up the girl. Long before that,
old age will overtake her in my house, in Argos,
far from her fatherland, slaving back and forth
at the loom, forced to share my bed.

                              Now go,
don't tempt my wrath--and you may depart alive."

The old man was terrified. He obeyed the order,
turning, trailing away in silence down the shore
where the roaring battle lines of breakers crash and drag.
And moving off to a safe distance, over and over
the old priest prayed to the son of sleek-haired Leto,
lord Apollo, "Hear me, Apollo! God of the silver bow
who strides the walls of Chryse and Cilla sacrosanct—
lord in power of Tenedos--Smintheus, god of the plague!
If I ever roofed a shrine to please your heart,
ever burned the long rich bones of bulls and goats
on your holy altar, now, now bring my prayer to pass.
Pay the Danaans back--your arrows for my tears!"

His prayer went up and Phoebus Apollo heard him.
Down he strode from Olympus' peaks, storming at heart
with his bow and hooded quiver slung across his shoulders.
The arrows clanged at his back as the god quaked with rage,
the god himself on the march and down he came like night.
Over against the ships he dropped to a knee, let fly a shaft
and a terrifying clash rang out from the great silver bow.
First he went for the mules and circling dogs but then,
launching a piercing shaft at the men themselves,
he cut them down in droves—
and the corpse-fires burned on, night and day, no end in sight.

Nine days the arrows of god swept through the army.

On the tenth Achilles called all ranks to muster—
the impulse seized him, sent by white-armed Hera
grieving to see Achaean fighters drop and die.
Once they'd gathered, crowding the meeting grounds,
the swift runner Achilles rose and spoke among them:
"Son of Atreus, now we are beaten back, I fear,
the long campaign is lost. So home we sail . . .
 if we can escape our death--if war and plague
are joining forces now to crush the Argives.
But wait: let us question a holy man,
a prophet, even a man skilled with dreams—
dreams as well can come our way from Zeus—
come, someone to tell us why Apollo rages so,
whether he blames us for a vow we failed, or sacrifice.
If only the god would share the smoky savor of lambs
and full-grown goats, Apollo might be willing, still,
somehow, to save us from this plague."

                                    So he proposed
and down he sat again as Calchas rose among them,
Thestor's son, the clearest by far of all the seers
who scan the flight of birds. He knew all things that are,
all things that are past and all that are to come,
the seer who had led the Argive ships to Troy
with the second sight that god Apollo gave him.
For the armies' good the seer began to speak:
"Achilles, dear to Zeus . . .
you order me to explain Apollo's anger,
the distant deadly Archer? I will tell it all.
But strike a pact with me, swear you will defend me
with all your heart, with words and strength of hand.
For there is a man I will enrage--I see it now—
a powerful man who lords it over all the Argives,
one the Achaeans must obey . . .A mighty king,
raging against an inferior, is too strong.
Even if he can swallow down his wrath today,
still he will nurse the burning in his chest
until, sooner or later, he sends it bursting forth.
Consider it closely, Achilles. Will you save me?"

    And the matchless runner reassured him: "Courage!
Out with it now, Calchas. Reveal the will of god,
whatever you may know. And I swear by Apollo
dear to Zeus, the power you pray to, Calchas,
when you reveal god's will to the Argives--no one,
not while I am alive and see the light on earth, no one
will lay his heavy hands on you by the hollow ships.

None among all the armies. Not even if you mean
Agamemnon here who now claims to be, by far, the best of the Achaeans."
                                        The seer took heart
and this time he spoke out, bravely: "Beware—
he casts no blame for a vow we failed, a sacrifice.
The god's enraged because Agamemnon spurned his priest,
he refused to free his daughter, he refused the ransom.
That's why the Archer sends us pains and he will send us more
and never drive this shameful destruction from the Argives,
not till we give back the girl with sparkling eyes
to her loving father--no price, no ransom paid—
and carry a sacred hundred bulls to Chryse town.
Then we can calm the god, and only then appease him."

    So he declared and sat down. But among them rose
the fighting son of Atreus, lord of the far-flung kingdoms,
Agamemnon--furious, his dark heart filled to the brim,
blazing with anger now, his eyes like searing fire.
With a sudden, killing look he wheeled on Calchas first:
"Seer of misery! Never a word that works to my advantage!
Always misery warms your heart, your prophecies—
never a word of profit said or brought to pass.
Now, again, you divine god's will for the armies,
bruit it out, as fact, why the deadly Archer
multiplies our pains: because I, I refused
that glittering price for the young girl Chryseis.
Indeed, I prefer her by far, the girl herself,
I want her mine in my own house! I rank her higher
than Clytemnestra, my wedded wife--she's nothing less
in build or breeding, in mind or works of hand.
But I am willing to give her back, even so,
if that is best for all. What I really want
is to keep my people safe, not see them dying.
But fetch me another prize, and straight off too,
else I alone of the Argives go without my honor.
That would be a disgrace. You are all witness,
look--my prize is snatched away!"
                                        But the swift runner
Achilles answered him at once, "Just how, Agamemnon,
great field marshal . . .most grasping man alive,
how can the generous Argives give you prizes now?
I know of no troves of treasure, piled, lying idle,
anywhere. Whatever we dragged from towns we plundered,
all's been portioned out. But collect it, call it back
from the rank and file? That would be the disgrace.
So return the girl to the god, at least for now.

We Achaeans will pay you back, three, four times over,
 if Zeus will grant us the gift, somehow, someday,
to raze Troy's massive ramparts to the ground."

    But King Agamemnon countered, "Not so quickly,
brave as you are, godlike Achilles--trying to cheat *me*.
Oh no, you won't get past me, take me in that way!
What do you want? To cling to your own prize
while I sit calmly by--empty-handed here?
Is that why you order me to give her back?
No--if our generous Argives will give me a prize,
a match for my desires, equal to what I've lost,
well and good. But if they give me nothing
I will take a prize myself--your own, or Ajax'
or Odysseus' prize--I'll commandeer her myself
and let that man I go to visit choke with rage!
Enough. We'll deal with all this later, in due time.
 Now come, we haul a black ship down to the bright sea,
gather a decent number of oarsmen along her locks
and put aboard a sacrifice, and Chryseis herself,
in all her beauty . . .we embark her too.
Let one of the leading captains take command.
Ajax, Idomeneus, trusty Odysseus or you, Achilles,
you--the most violent man alive--so you can perform
the rites for us and calm the god yourself."
                                        A dark glance
and the headstrong runner answered him in kind: "Shameless—
armored in shamelessness--always shrewd with greed!
How could any Argive soldier obey your orders,
freely and gladly do your sailing for you
or fight your enemies, full force? Not I, no.
It wasn't Trojan spearmen who brought me here to fight.
The Trojans never did me damage, not in the least,
they never stole my cattle or my horses, never
in Phthia where the rich soil breeds strong men
did they lay waste my crops. How could they?
Look at the endless miles that lie between us . . .
shadowy mountain ranges, seas that surge and thunder.
No, you colossal, shameless--we all followed you,
to please you, to fight for you, to win your honor
back from the Trojans--Menelaus and you, you dog-face!
What do you care? Nothing. You don't look right or left.
And now you threaten to strip me of my prize in person—
the one I fought for long and hard, and sons of Achaea
handed her to me.

My honors never equal yours,
whenever we sack some wealthy Trojan stronghold—
my arms bear the brunt of the raw, savage fighting,
true, but when it comes to dividing up the plunder
the lion's share is yours, and back I go to my ships,
clutching some scrap, some pittance that I love,
when I have fought to exhaustion.

                                                No more now—
back I go to Phthia. Better that way by far,
to journey home in the beaked ships of war.
I have no mind to linger here disgraced,
brimming your cup and piling up your plunder."

     But the lord of men Agamemnon shot back,
"Desert, by all means--if the spirit drives you home!
I will never beg you to stay, not on my account.
Never--others will take my side and do me honor.
Zeus above all, whose wisdom rules the world.
You--I hate you most of all the warlords
loved by the gods. Always dear to your heart,
strife, yes, and battles, the bloody grind of war.
What if you are a great soldier? That's just a gift of god.
Go home with your ships and comrades, lord it over your Myrmidons!
You are nothing to me--you and your overweening anger!
But let this be my warning on your way:
since Apollo insists on taking my Chryseis,
I'll send her back in my own ships with my crew.
But I, I will be there in person at your tents
to take Briseis in all her beauty, your own prize—
so you can learn just how much greater I am than you
and the next man up may shrink from matching words with me,
from hoping to rival Agamemnon strength for strength!"

     He broke off and anguish gripped Achilles.
The heart in his rugged chest was pounding, torn . . .
Should he draw the long sharp sword slung at his hip,
thrust through the ranks and kill Agamemnon now?—
or check his rage and beat his fury down?
As his racing spirit veered back and forth,
just as he drew his huge blade from its sheath,
down from the vaulting heavens swept Athena,
the white-armed goddess Hera sped her down:
Hera loved both men and cared for both alike.
Rearing behind him Pallas seized his fiery hair—
only Achilles saw her, none of the other fighters—
struck with wonder he spun around, he knew her at once,

Pallas Athena! the terrible blazing of those eyes,
and his winged words went flying· "Why, why now?
Child of Zeus with the shield of thunder, why come now?
To witness the outrage Agamemnon just committed?
 I tell you this, and so help me it's the truth—
he'll soon pay for his arrogance with his life!"

    Her gray eyes clear, the goddess Athena answered,
"Down from the skies I come to check your rage
if only you will yield.
The white-armed goddess Hera sped me down:
she loves you both, she cares for you both alike.
Stop this fighting, now. Don't lay hand to sword.
Lash him with threats of the price that he will face.
And I tell you this--and I know it is the truth—
one day glittering gifts will lie before you,
three times over to pay for all his outrage.
Hold back now. Obey us both."
                So she urged
and the swift runner complied at once: "I must—
when the two of you hand down commands, Goddess,
a man submits though his heart breaks with fury.
Better for him by far. If a man obeys the gods
they're quick to hear his prayers."
                And with that
Achilles stayed his burly hand on the silver hilt
and slid the huge blade back in its sheath.
He would not fight the orders of Athena.
Soaring home to Olympus, she rejoined the gods
aloft in the halls of Zeus whose shield is thunder.

from *The Iliad* by Homer, translated by Robert Fagles. Translation © 1990 Robert Fagles. Used by permission of Viking Penguin, a division of Penguin Books USA Inc.

Sappho of Lesbos: Fragment 31, c. 600 B.C.E.

Sappho lived on the isle of Lesbos, in the Aegean sea. She probably had a school for girls, where she taught music, poetry, and perhaps weaving. She wrote love poems to both men and women.

He seems to me to be like the gods
--whatever man sits opposite you
and close by hears you talking sweetly

And laughing charmingly; which
makes the heart within my breast take flight;
for the instant I look upon you, I cannot
    anymore

speak one word.

But in silence my tongue is broken, a fine
fire at once runs under my skin,
with my eyes I see not one thing, my ears
    buzz,

Cold sweat covers me, trembling

seizes my whole body, I am more moist than
    grass;

I seem to be little short of dying . . .

from *The Woman and the Lyre: Women Writers in Classical Greece and Rome.* Jane McIntosh Snyder. Southern Illinois University Press. 1989. © 1989 by the Board of Trustees, Southern Illinois University.

Tyrtaeus of Sparta; c. 700 B.C.E.

I would not say anything for a man nor take
    account of him for any speed of his feet
    or wrestling skill he might have,
not if he had the size of a Cyclops and
    strength to go with it,
not if he could outrun Boreas, the North
    Wind of Thrace,
not if he were more handsome and
    gracefully formed than Tithonos, or had
    more riches than Midas had, or Kinyras
    too,
not if he were more of a king than Tantalid
    Pelops, or had the power of speech and
    persuasion Adrastos had,
not if he had all splendors except for a
    fighting spirit.

For no man ever proves himself a good man
    in war unless he can endure to face the
    blood and the slaughter,
go close against the enemy and fight with his
    hands.
Here is courage, mankind's finest
    possession,
here is the noblest prize that a young man
    can endeavor to win,
and it is a good thing his city and all the
    people share with him when a man
    plants his feet and stands in the
    foremost spears relentlessly, all thought
    of foul flight completely forgotten,
and has well trained his heart to be steadfast
    and to endure,
and with words encourages the man who is
    stationed beside him.
Here is a man who proves himself to be
    valiant in war.

With a sudden rush he turns to flight the
    rugged battalions of the enemy, and
    sustains the beating waves of assault.
And he who so falls among the champions
    and loses his sweet life, so blessing with
    honor his city, his father, and all his
    people,
with wounds in his chest, where the spear
    that he was facing has transfixed that
    massive guard of his shield, and gone
    through his breastplate as well,
why, such a man is lamented alike by the
    young and the elders,
and all his city goes into mourning and
    grieves for his loss.
His tomb is pointed to with pride, and so are
    his children, and his children's children,
    and afterward all the race that is his.
His shining glory is never forgotten,
his name is remembered, and he becomes an
    immortal, though he lies under the
    ground,
when one who was a brave man has been
    killed by the furious War God standing
    his ground and fighting hard for his
    children and land.

But if he escapes the doom of death, the
    destroyer of bodies, and wins his battle,
    and bright renown for the work of his
    spear,
all men give place to him alike, the youth
    and the elders, and much joy comes his
    way before he goes down to the dead.
Aging, he has reputation among his citizens.
No one tries to interfere with his honors or
    all he deserves;
all men withdraw before his presence, and
    yield their seats to him, the youth, and

the men his age, and even those older
than he.
Thus a man should endeavor to reach this
high place of courage with all his heart,

and, so trying, never be backward in
war.

Translated by Richard Lattimore, in *Greek Lyrics*.
©University of Chicago Press. 1960.

Unit 6: The Golden Age of Athens

For Athens in the fourth and fifth centuries B.C.E., there is such a richness of sources of every kind—literary, artistic, philosophical, political, economic, and even self-consciously historical—that it is impossible to justify choosing a handful as representative. For every page chosen, a hundred had to be rejected. This chapter is the longest in the book, because the ideas contained in these works form the bedrock of Western thinking for the subsequent two millenia and beyond.

The earliest Greek prose writing, in the middle of the sixth century, shows a spirit of critical inquiry that is still characteristic of Western thinking. Anaximander and Hecataeus both wrote descriptions of the earth based on their travels. Hecataeus distinguished between myth and history when he began his work: "Hecataeus the Milesian speaks thus: I write these things as they seem true to me; for the stories told by the Greeks are various and in my opinion absurd." By the fifth century, we have accounts that are recognizably and consciously historical.

Herodotus: Queen Artemisia of Halicarnassus at Salamis, c. 480 B.C.E.

Herodotus was known as the "father of history." His nine-book *History* is the earliest Greek book in prose to have survived intact. It goes far beyond the basic account of the conflict between Greece and Persia that came to a head in 480 B.C.E. On this framework Herodotus built a description of the known world, including the geography, customs, and beliefs of each civilization known to him from his travels. This selection depicts a woman commanding a Persian ship.

As far as the generality of them went, I cannot exactly say how each of the barbarians or the Greeks fought. But in respect to Artemisia the following thing happened, as a result of which she gained even greater renown with the King. For when the King's fortunes had been reduced to utter confusion, at that very moment the ship of Artemisia was pursued by an Attic ship. And she, not being able to make her escape, inasmuch as there were other friendly ships in front of her and she herself happened to be nearest to the enemy, she resolved to do this, which turned greatly to her advantage when she had done it: being pursued by the Attic vessel, she charged and rammed a friendly ship, of men of Calyndus, with the king of the Calyndians himself on board, Damasithymus. Whether there had been some quarrel between her and him while they were both still at the Hellespont, I cannot say, nor whether she did what she did deliberately or whether it was pure accident that the ship of the Calyndians happened to fall in her way. But when she rammed him and sank him, by her good luck she gained doubly by what she had done. For the trierarch of the Attic ship, when he saw her ramming a ship manned by barbarians, believed that Artemisia's ship was either Greek itself or must be deserting from the barbarians to the Greek side and helping them, and so he turned his line of pursuit to other vessels.

That is the way her stroke of luck befell her, that she escaped and did not meet destruction there. But there is the additional fact that, having done evil to Xerxes, as a result of that very evil she won particular renown with him. For it is said that, as the King watched, he noticed the vessel doing the ramming, and some one of his courtiers, standing by, said, "Master, do you see Artemisia, how well she fights? And lo, she has sunk a vessel of the enemy." He asked if the action was really that of Artemisia, and they said yes, for they could clearly read the ensign on her ship. The destroyed vessel they concluded was an enemy. As I said, everything happened to her good luck in this, and most of all that the ship of the Calyndians that was destroyed had not a single man escape alive to accuse her. So Xerxes, they say, in answer to what they had told him, observed, "My men have become women, and my women men." That is what they say Xerxes said.

Herodotus, VIII. 87-88, translated by David Grene, *The History of Herodotus*. ©University of Chicago Press, 1987.

~~~~~~~~~~~~~~~~

Thucydides on the Accuracy of his Histories

Thucydides was a participant in the Peloponnesian War, exiled from Athens in 424 B.C.E. after failing to prevent the capture of Amphipolis by the Spartans. Concerned with accuracy, he often describes the sources of his information, yet he admits, when reporting speeches, to recording not what the speaker actually said, but what Thucydides thinks should have been said in that situation.

I do not think that one will be far wrong in accepting the conclusions I have reached from the evidence which I have put forward. It is better evidence than that of the poets, who exaggerate the importance of their themes, or of the prose chroniclers, who are less interested in telling the truth than in catching the attention of their public, whose authorities cannot be checked, and whose subject matter, owing to the passage of time, is mostly lost in the unreliable streams of mythology. We may claim instead to have used only the plainest evidence and to have reached conclusions which are reasonably accurate, considering that we have been dealing with ancient history. As for the present war, even though people are apt to think that the war in which they are fighting is the greatest of all wars and, when it is over, to relapse again into their admiration of the past, nevertheless, if one looks at the facts themselves, one will see that this was the greatest war of all.

In this history I have made use of set speeches, some of which were delivered just before and others during the war. I have found it difficult to remember the precise words used in the speeches which I listened to myself and my various informants have experienced the same difficulty: so my method has been, while keeping as closely as possible to the general sense of the words that were actually used, to make the speakers say what, in my opinion, were called for by each situation.

Thucydides, I.21-22, tr. Rex Warner, *The Peloponnesian War*, Penguin Books Ltd. 1954. Reproduced by permission of Penguin Books Ltd.

~~~~~~~~~~~~~~

Pericles' Funeral Speech, 431-430 B.C.E.

This speech, given at a funeral for Athenian warriors killed in the early battles of the Peloponnesian War, was recorded by Thucydides. As noted above, the words are those of Thucydides, not necessarily those actually spoken by Pericles. In it, Pericles justifies the war, and the deaths, by comparing the culture and policies of Athens with those of its enemies, mainly Sparta.

Most of my predecessors in this office have commended him who added such a speech as this to our customary funeral rites, on the ground that it is fit and proper to have such an address made over the bodies of those who are brought home from the wars for burial. To me, however, it would seem sufficient, in the case of men who have proved themselves brave by their deeds, by deeds also to set forth their honors, as for instance by this public burial rite which you see provided here, without setting faith in the virtues of many men at hazard on the lips of one, according as he may speak well or ill. It is hard for a speaker to observe due moderation in a case where his hearer can scarcely be made to cherish a proper conception of the truth. For the hearer who is acquainted with the facts and well disposed toward the dead, will possibly deem the setting forth of praise all too sparing in the light of his own desires and knowledge; while he who is without knowledge in the case will suspect exaggeration here and there, because he is jealous on hearing of aught that surpasses his own powers. Men tolerate the praises of other men only so far as they think themselves capable, every one, of performing the deeds recited to them; but when such deeds are beyond them, they are jealous at once and incredulous. However, since our forefathers have sanctioned this practice, it is meet that I in my turn should observe the custom, and try to satisfy your wishes and beliefs, in every case, to the utmost of my powers.

I will speak first of our remoter ancestors, for it is not only right but proper as well that on an occasion like this such honorable mention of them be made. It was they who inhabited this Attic land of ours from time immemorial, generation after generation, and it was due to their valor that we received it from them the free land it is today. They are worthy of our praises, but still more than they our nearer fathers, who added to their inheritance the great empire we now possess, not without great toils, and bequeathed it to us of the present day. Most of its development has been due to those of us who are still in perhaps the most competent years of life, and we have equipped our city with all that can make her most sufficient unto herself in war and in peace. Of the military exploits by which our various possessions were won, or of the zeal with which either our fathers or we ourselves have driven off invaders, Hellenic or Barbarian, I will not speak; the tale would be long, and you know it well. I wish rather to prelude my praise of these dead warriors of ours with an exposition of the general principles by virtue of which we came to empire, and of the civic institutions and manners of life in consequence of which our empire became great. I conceive that such utterances are not unsuited to the occasion, and that it will profit all this throng of citizens and strangers to hear them.

We enjoy a form of government which is not in rivalry with the institutions of our neighbors, nay, we ourselves are rather an example to many than imitators of others. By name, since the administration is not in the hands of few but of many, it is called a democracy. And it is true that before the law and in private cases all citizens are on an equality. But in public life every man is advanced to honor according to his reputation for ability—not because of his party, but because of his excellence. And further, provided he is able to do the city good service, not even in poverty does he find any hindrance, since this cannot obscure men's good opinion of him. It is with a free spirit that we engage in public life, and in our scrutiny of one another's private life we are not filled with wrath at our neighbor if he consults his pleasure now and then, nor do we cast sour glances at him. These may do him no actual harm, but they offend his eye. Our private intercourse is thus free from all constraint, but in public matters we are kept back from transgression, and that too, for the most part, by a wholesome fear. This leads us to obey the regular magistrates and the laws, especially such as are enacted for the aid of the oppressed, and such as are unwritten and therefore involve their transgressor in a universal reprobation.

Furthermore, we above all men provide ourselves with spiritual refreshment after toil. Regular games and religious festivals fill our year, while the life we lead in private is refined. The daily enjoyment of all these blessings keeps dull care at bay. Because of the greatness of our city, the products of the whole earth stream in upon us, so that we enjoy the rich fruits of other men's labors with as intimate a relish as our own.

Moreover, even in our military training we surpass our rivals. We give all men the freedom of our city, and never banish strangers merely to keep them from learning or seeing what, if there is no concealment, may a foe might see to his advantage. We put our trust not so much in deceitful diplomacy as in our own courageous efficiency. And in the matter of education, they devote themselves to toilsome exercises, from their very youth up, in order to achieve manliness; while we live far less strenuous lives, and yet are no less able to cope with the dangers which confront us. This can be proved. The Lacadaemonians invade our land not by themselves, but with their whole confederacy, whereas we go alone into the land of our neighbors. And yet, though we are fighting on a foreign soil with men who are defending their homes, we usually have no difficulty in overpowering them. No foe has yet met our entire military force, because we not only support a navy, but on land too must send our own citizen soldiers on many undertakings. But they, when they happen to engage a small band of us, if they conquer a few of us, boast of having routed our whole force. If they are beaten, they protest that they were worsted by us all. If then we are determined to meet our perils with light hearts rather than after toilsome training, and with a valor based on character rather than on compulsion, the advantage is with us. We are not always anticipating the pain of future sufferings, and yet, as we face a crisis, we show ourselves no whit less daring than those who are forever enduring hardships.

And besides, our city deserves men's admiration for other things as well as for her exploits in war. For we cherish beauty in all simplicity, and wisdom without effeminacy. Our wealth supports timely action rather than noisy speech. As for poverty, the admission of it is no disgrace to a man; not to forge one's way out of it is the real disgrace.

The same citizens among us will be found devoted to their homes and to the state, and others who are immersed in business have no mean knowledge of politics. We are the only people to regard the man who takes no interest in politics not as careless, but as useless. In one and the same citizen body we either decide matters, or seek to form correct opinions about them, and we do not regard words as incompatible with deeds, but rather the refusal to learn by discussion before advancing to the necessary action. We are preeminent in this, that we combine in the same citizen body great courage to undertake, and ample discussion of our undertakings; whereas in other men it is ignorance that gives boldness, and discussion that produces hesitation. Surely they will rightly be judged the bravest souls who most clearly distinguish the pains and pleasures of life, and therefore do not avoid danger.

In our benevolence also we are the opposite of most men; it is not be receiving, but by conferring favors that we win our friends. And he is a more constant friend who confers the favor and then tries to keep alive in the recipient, by continued kindness, a sense of obligation for it; whereas he who owes a favor is not so keen a friend, because he knows that when he repays the benevolence it will not be counted him as a favor conferred, but as a debt paid. We are the only men who aid our fellows not from calculation of our own advantage, but rather with a fearless trust which springs from true liberality.

To sum up: I declare that our city in general is the school of Hellas, and that each individual man of us will, in my opinion, show himself able to exercise the most varied forms of activity with the greatest ease and grace. That this is no passing boast, but an actual truth, is shown by the power which our city has acquired in virtue of these traits of ours. She is the only city which surpasses her fame when put to the test; the only one which inspires neither resentment in her enemy for the disastrous consequences of attacking her, nor scorn in her subject because her empire is an unworthy one. Accompanied by great tokens and by no means without witness is this power which we display for the admiration of present and future generations. We need no Homer to sing our praises, nor any poet whose verses shall give fleeting delight, while his notion of the facts suffers at the hands of truth; nay, we have forced every sea and land to be pathways for our daring, and have everywhere established reminders of what our enmity or our friendship means, and they will abide forever. It was for such a city, then, that these dead warriors of ours so nobly gave their lives in battle; they deemed it their right not to be robbed of her, and every man who survives them should gladly toil in her behalf. . .

Translated by Bernadotte Perrin. *Plutarch's Cimon and Pericles*. New York: Charles Scribner's Sons, 1910.

Unit 7: Greek Drama

Greek drama grew out of religious ritual and mythical tale-telling, becoming more secular and more fictional in the fifth century B.C.E. The earliest tragedies were recognized at the Dionysian Festival in 534. Cleisthenes later introduced a competition. At first, three poets presented three plays each, plus a satyr play. The best play received a prize. Staging was simple, with first one, later two or three actors and a chorus of twelve or fifteen. The use of masks allowed a minute company of actors to play many characters. Greek tragedy took its pace, its rhythm, and its themes from epic poetry. Aeschylus, the first great tragedian, claimed that "We are all eating crumbs from the great table of Homer."

Comedy was first recognized at the Dionysian Festival in 487. While in tragedy, the chorus was usually the elders of the community, putting the action of the play in its social context, choruses in a comedy were often animals or humorous objects—Wasps, or Clouds or Caterpillars. Comedies were more directly political than tragedies. In later comedy, political satire was largely replaced by social satire.

Theatre was an essential part of the public life of Athens. One of the public duties of a wealthy citizen was to pay the costs of a theatrical production. Soon after an entrance fee was introduced around 450 B.C.E., Pericles established a fund to provide free admission to the poor.

Sophocles' *Oedipus Rex*, c. 420 B.C.E.

Aristotle, in his *Poetics*, refers to this play as the most nearly perfect of the Greek tragedies. It describes the gradual realization by Oedipus, king of Thebes, that he has gained the throne by murdering his father and marrying his mother. While these horrendous misdeeds were accidental and seem to indicate that man cannot escape the fate for which he is destined, Oedipus' handling of the investigation of the murder reveals a hubris, or arrogance, that Greek thought associated with the downfall of a hero. The play begins with the people of Thebes seeking the cause of a plague that is devastating the city.

OEDIPUS

My children, the newest to descend
from ancient Kadmos into my care:
why have you rushed here, to these seats,
your wool-strung boughs begging
for god's help? Our city is oppressed—
with incense smoke and cries of mourners
and prayers sung to the Healing God.
I thought it wrong to let messengers
Speak for you, my sons, I must hear
your words myself, so I have come out, I
Oedipus, the name that all men know.
(To the Priest) Speak to me, old man. Yours
is the natural voice for the rest.
What concerns drive you to me?
Fear? Reassurance? Be certain
I will give all the help I can.
I would be hard indeed if I didn't
pity those who approach me like this.

PRIEST

You rule my country, Oedipus, and you see
who comes to your altars, how mixed
we are in years: children too weak
to travel far, old men worn down by age,
priests like myself, the priest of Zeus,
a picked group of our best young men.
More of us wait with wool-strung boughs
in the markets, or at Athena's two temples,
or watch the embers at Ismenus' shrine
for the glow of prophecy.
                You can see for yourself
our city going under, too weak to lift
its head clear of each deadly surge.
Plague is killing our flowering farmland,
It's killing our grazing cattle. Our women
in labor give birth to nothing.
                A burning god
rakes his fire through our city;
he hates us with fever, he empties
the House of Kadmos—but he makes
black Hades rich, with our groans and tears.
We don't believe you are the gods' equal, King,

but I, and these children, ask help here,
at your hearth, because we put you first, of all men,
at handling trouble—or confronting gods.
You came to Thebes, you broke us free
of the tax we paid with our lives
to the rasping Singer. No one prompted you,
you were not taught by any of us.
We tell ourselves, you had a god's help
when you pulled us back to life.
Once more, Oedipus, we need your power.
We beg you, each in our own pain—
find our lost strength—by learning
what you can from a god's voice
or what some man can tell you.
                                    I know this:
advice from men proven right in the past
will meet a crisis with the surest force.
Act as our greatest man! Act
as you did when you first seized fame!
Our country believes your nerve saved us then.
Don't let us look back on your rule, saying,
once he raised us, but later let us fall.
Lift us to safety!—so that no misstep
ever again will bring Thebes down.

Good luck came with you, a bird from god's will,
the day you rescued us. Be that same man now.
If you are going to rule us, King, it's better
to rule the living that a lifeless waste.
A walled city is nothing, a ship is nothing,
when there's no one aboard to man it.

OEDIPUS

I do pity you, children. Don't think I'm unaware.
I know what need brings you: this sickness
harms you all. Yet, sick as you are,
not one of you suffers a sickness like mine.
Yours is a private grief, you feel
only what touches you. But my heart grieves
for you, for myself, and for our city.
You've come to wake me to all this.
There was truly no need. I haven't been asleep.
I have wept tears enough, for long enough;
my thoughts have raced down every twisting path.
The only cure all my thinking found
I've set in motion: I've sent Kreon,
my wife's brother, to Phoebus at Delphi,

              to hear what action or what word of mine
will save this town. Already, counting what day
this is, I'm anxious: what is Kreon doing?
He takes too long, more than he needs.
But when he comes, I'd be the criminal
not to do all the god shows me to do.

PRIEST   Your words have just been made good: your men
are now signaling me that Kreon's here.

OEDIPUS   O Lord Apollo,
may the luck he brings save us! Luck so bright
we can see it—just as we see him now.

(Kreon enters from *the countryside, wearing a laurel crown.)*

PRIEST   Only a man whose news is sweet comes home
wearing a crown of laurel speckled with berries.

OEDIPUS   We'll soon know, he's within earshot. Prince!
Brother kinsman, son of Menoikeos!
What kind of answer have you brought from god?

KREON   A good one. I call nothing unbearable
if luck can straighten it, and bless the outcome.

OEDIPUS   But what did the god say? There's nothing in your words
so far—to cheer me or to frighten me.

KREON   Will you hear it in front of these men?
If so, I'll speak. Otherwise we go inside.

OEDIPUS   Speak here, to all of us. I suffer more
for these men than for my own life.

KREON   Then I'll report what I heard from Apollo,
who did not hide his meaning.
He commands we drive out what corrupts us,
what makes our land sick. We now harbor
something incurable. He says: purge it.

OEDIPUS   Tell me the source of our trouble.
How do we cleanse ourselves?

KREON   By banishing a man—or by killing him. It's blood,
it's kin-murder that brings this storm on our city.

OEDIPUS   Did god name this man whose luck dooms him?

KREON	You know, King, that our city was ruled once by Laius, before you came to take the helm?
OEDIPUS	So I've heard. Though I never saw him.
KREON	Laius was murdered. Now, to avenge him, god wills you to strike down with your own hands those men whose hands struck Laius down.
OEDIPUS	Where do I find these men? How do I track vague footprints from a bygone crime?
KREON	The god said: look here, in our land. Nothing's caught that we don't chase— what we ignore goes free.
OEDIPUS	Was Laius killed at home? Or in the countryside? Or did they murder him on foreign ground?
KREON	He said when he left that his journey would take him into god's presence. But he never came home.
OEDIPUS	Did none of his troop see and report what happened? Is there no one to question whose answers might help?
KREON	All killed but a single terrified survivor, able to tell us but one fact.
OEDIPUS	What fact? One fact might point to many, if we had one small clue to raise our hopes.
KREON	They had the bad luck, he said, to meet bandits who struck them with a force many hands strong. It wasn't the violence of one man.
OEDIPUS	What bandit would risk such a huge crime unless somebody here hired him to do it?
KREON	That was our thought, but fresh trouble obsessed us. With Laius dead, who was to lead our revenge?
OEDIPUS	But here was your kingship murdered! What kind of trouble could have blockd your search?
KREON	The Sphinx's song. So wily, so baffling!—

she forced us to forget the dark past
to confront what lay at our feet.

OEDIPUS

I will go back, start fresh,
and clear up all this darkness.
Apollo was exactly right, and so were you,
to turn our minds back to the murdered man.
 And now it's time I joined your search
for vengeance, which our land and the god deserve.

I don't do it to placate any distant kin,
I will dispel this poison for my own sake.
 Laius' killer might one day come for me,
exacting vengeance with that same hand.
So to defend the dead man serves my interest.
Rise, children, quick, up from the altar,
raise those branches that appeal to god.
Someone go call the people of Kadmos here.
Tell them I'm ready to do anything.
If god is with us, we will survive.
If not, our ruin has already happened.

(Exit Oedipus, *into the palace.)*

PRIEST

Stand, children. The thing we came for
the king himself has promised to do.
Let god Apollo, who commands us to act,
lift this plague off our lives! Apollo our savior!

(The Theban *suppliants leave; the Chorus enters.)*

CHORUS

What will you say to Thebes,
Voice from Zeus? What sweet sounds
bring your will from golden Delphi
to our bright city? We're at the breaking point,
terror ranges through our minds.
Our wild cries reach for you,
Healing God from Delos—
in holy dread we ask: does your will
bring a new threat, or an old doom
come back as the years wheel by?
Say it, Great Voice,
you who answer us always,
speak as Hope's golden child.

Athena, your help is the first we ask,

immortal daughter of Zeus,
then Artemis your sister
who protects our land, sitting throned
in the heart of our marketplace.
And Apollo, whose shots
hit from far off! Our three
defenders from death: come now!
If once you fought off destruction
by blowing away the fires of our pain,
come to us now!

The blows I suffer are past count.
Plague kills my friends,
thought finds no spear
to keep a man safe.
Our rich earth shrivels what it grows,
our women in labor scream
but nothing's born. One life
after another flies,
you see them go, birds driving their strong wings
faster than flash-fire
to the shore of the sunset god.

Our city dies as its people die
those countless deaths, her children
rot in the streets, unmourned,
spreading more death.
Young wives and gray mothers
wash to our altars, their cries
carry from all sides, sobbing
for help, each lost in her pain.
A hymn shining to the Healer
is darkened by a grieving voice,
a flute in a courtyard.
Help us, Goddess,
golden child of Zeus,
send us the bright face
we need: Strength.

Force that raging killer, the god Ares,
to turn his back and run from our land.
He murders without armor now
but we, the victims of his fever,
shout in the hot blast of his charge.
Blow Ares to the great searoom
of Amphitrité, banish him

under a booming wind
to jagged harbors in the seas
roiling off Thrace. If night
doesn't finish the god's black work,
the day will finish it.
The lightning waits
in your fiery will,
Zeus, Father, Send its blast,
to kill the god killing us.

Apollo,
lord of the morning light, draw back
your curving bowstring
of twined gold—fire the sure arrows
that rake our attackers and keep them at bay.
Artemis, carry your radiance
into battle, on bright quick feet
down through the morning hills.
I call on the god whose hair
flows through its golden band,
whose name is our country's own,
Bakkhos! –the wine-flushed!—who comes
to the maenads' cries, who runs
in their midst: Bakkhos!—
come here on fire,
a pine-torch flaring,
to face with us the one god
all the gods hate: Ares!

(Oedipus has *entered while the Chorus was singing. Now he speaks.)*

OEDIPUS

I heard your prayer. Prayer may save you yet—
if you will trust me and do what I say:
work with me toward the one cure
this plague demands of us.
Help will come, the plague will lift.
I now outlaw the killer myself, by these words.
I act as a stranger, not familiar
either with this crime or accounts of it.
Unless I can mesh some clue I hold
with something known of the killer,
I will be tracking him alone, on a cold trail.
Since I came later to join your ranks,
when the crime itself was past history,
there are some things that you,
the sons of Kadmos, must tell me.

If any of you knows how Laius,
son of Labdacus, died, he must
instantly tell me all he knows.
He must not be frightened of naming
himself the guilty one: I swear
he'll suffer nothing worse than exile.
Or if you know of someone else,
a foreigner who struck the blow, speak up.
I will reward you now, I will thank you always.
But if you know the killer and don't speak,
out of fear, to shield kin or yourself,
listen to what that silence will cost you.
I order everyone in my land
where I hold power and sit as king:
don't let that man under your roof,
don't speak with him, no matter who he is.
Don't pray or sacrifice with him,
don't pour purifying water for him.
I say this to all my people:
drive him from your houses.
He is our sickness. He poisons us.
This the Pythian god has shown me.
Believe me, I am the ally in this
both of the god and the dead king.
I pray god that the unseen killer,
whoever he is, and whether he killed
alone or had help, be cursed with a life
as evil as he is, a life
of utter human deprivation.
I pray this, too: if he's found at my hearth,
inside my house, and I know that he's there,
may the curses I aimed at others punish me.
I charge you all—give my words force,
for my sake and the god's for our dead land
stripped barren of its harvests,
forsaken by its gods. Even if god
had not forced the issue,
this crime should not have gone uncleansed.
You should have looked to it!—the dead man
not only being noble, but your king.
But as my luck would have it,
I have his power, his bed—a wife
who shares our seed, and had she borne
the children of us both, she
might have linked us closer still. But Laius

had no luck fathering children, and fate
itself soon struck a blow at his head.
It's these concerns make me defend Laius
as I would my own father. There is nothing
I won't try, to trace his murder
back to the killer's hand.
I act in this for Labdacus and Polydorus,
for Kadmos and Agenor—for our whole line of kings.
I warn those who disobey me:
god make their fields harvest dust,
their women's bodies harvest death.

                                      O you gods,
kill them with something worse
than this plague killing us now.
For all the rest of us, who are
loyal sons of Kadmos:
may Justice fight with us,
the gods be always at our side.

CHORUS	King, your curse forces me to speak.
	None of us is the killer.
	And none of us can point to him.
	Apollo ordered us to search,
	now *hè* must find the killer.
OEDIPUS	So he must. But what man could force
	a god against his will?
LEADER	Let me suggest a second course of action.
OEDIPUS	Don't stop at two if you have more.
LEADER	Tiresias is the man whose power of seeing
	shows him most nearly what Apollo sees.
	King, he might make brilliantly clear
	what you most want to learn.
OEDIPUS	I've acted already not to lose this chance.
	At Kreon's urging I've sent for him—twice now.
	The fact that he still hasn't come I find strange.
LEADER	There were some old rumors—too faint to help us now.
OEDIPUS	I'll study every word. What did those rumors say?
LEADER	That Laius was killed by some travelers.

OEDIPUS That's something even I have heard. But the man
who actually did it—no one sees.

LEADER If fear means anything to him
he won't linger in Thebes
once he has heard that curse of yours.

OEDIPUS If murder didn't frighten him, my words won't.

LEADER There is the man who will convict him:
god's prophet, led here at last.
God gave to him what he gave no one else.
The truth is living in his mind.

(Enter Tiresias, *led by a boy.)*

OEDIPUS Tiresias, you are master of the hidden world.
You can read earth and sky, you know
what omens to expound, what to keep secret.
Though your eyes can't see it,
you are aware of the plague
attacking us. To fight it, we can find
no savior or defense but you, my Lord.
For we now have Apollo's answer—
you will have heard it from others:
to end this plague we must root out Laius' killers.
Find them, then kill them or banish them.
Help us do it. Don't begrudge us
what you divine from birdcries, show us
any escape prophecy has shown you.
Rescue Thebes! Rescue yourself, and me!
Take charge of our defilement, and stop
this poison from the murdered man
which sickens and destroys us.
We're in your hands. To help another
is the best use a man can make of his powers.

TIRESIAS The most terrible knowledge is the kind
it would pay no wise man to use.
I knew this, but I forgot it.
I should never have come.

OEDIPUS What's this? You've come—but with no desire to help?

TIRESIAS Let me go home. Take my advice now. Your life
will be easier to bear—so will mine.

OEDIPUS	Strange words. And hardly kind—to hold back god's crucial guidance from your own people.
TIRESIAS	I see that you've spoken out today when silence was called for. I'm silent now to spare me your mistake.
OEDIPUS	For god's sake do not turn your back if you understand any of this! We kneel and beg.
TIRESIAS	You beg out of ignorance. I'll never speak. If I made my griefs plain, you would see your own.
OEDIPUS	Then you know and won't help us? You intend to betray us all and destroy Thebes?
TIRESIAS	I'll cause no grief to you or me. Why ask futile questions? You'll learn nothing.
OEDIPUS	So the traitor won't answer. You would enrage a rock. Still won't speak? Are you without feelings—or beyond their reach?
TIRESIAS	You blame this rage on me, do you? Rage? You haven't seen her yet, the kind that's married to your life. *You* find fault with *me*?
OEDIPUS	Who wouldn't be enraged at the words you're using to insult Thebes?
TIRESIAS	Truth will come. My silence can't hide it.
OEDIPUS	Must it come? Good reason to speak it now.
TIRESIAS	I prefer not to speak. Rage at that, if you like, with the most savage fury your heart knows.
OEDIPUS	I'm angry enough now to speak my mind. I think you helped plot the murder. No, you can't have struck the blow itself. Had you eyes, though, I would have said you alone were the killer.
TIRESIAS	That's your truth? Hear mine: I say honor the curse your own mouth spoke. From today, don't you speak to me,

or to your people here. You are the plague.
You ruin your own land.

OEDIPUS
So the appalling charge has been at last
flushed out, into the open.
Now where will you run?

TIRESIAS
Where you can't reach. To truth, where I'm strong.

OEDIPUS
Who put this truth in your mouth? Not your prophet's trade.

TIRESIAS
You did. By forcing me to speak.

OEDIPUS
Speak what? Repeat it so I understand.

TIRESIAS
I made no sense the first time?
Are you provoking me to use the word?

OEDIPUS
You made no sense at any time. Try once more.

TIRESIAS
I say: you are the killer you would find.

OEDIPUS
The second time is even more outrageous. You'll wish you'd never
spoken.

TIRESIAS
Shall I feed your fury with more words?

OEDIPUS
Say anything. It's all the same worthless noise.

TIRESIAS
I say that you are living unaware
in the most hideous intimacy
with your nearest and most loving kin.
You have arrived at evil—which you cannot see.

OEDIPUS
You think you can savage Me? Forever? Unscathed?

TIRESIAS
Forever. Truth lasts.

OEDIPUS
Truth lasts for some, but your "truth" won't—
you have blind eyes, blind ears, and a blind brain.

TIRESIAS
And you're a wretched fool, lashing me with taunts
every man here will soon aim at you.

OEDIPUS
You survive in the care of black
unbroken night! You can't hurt me
or any man who sees the sunlight.

TIRESIAS   It isn't I who will cause your fall.
             Apollo is enough. You're his concern.

OEDIPUS   Did you invent these lies? Or did Kreon?

TIRESIAS   Kreon is not your disease. You are.

OEDIPUS   Wealth, and a king's power,
             the skill that wins every time—
             how much envious malice they provoke!
             To rob me of power—power I didn't want,
             but which this city thrust into my hands—
             my oldest friend here, loyal Kreon, worked
             quietly against me—aching to steal my throne.
             He hired for the purpose this fortuneteller—
             conniving bogus beggar-priest!—
             who sees the main chance clearly
             but is a blind groper in his art.

             Tell us now, where did you ever
             prove your claim to a seer's power?
             Why—when the Sphinx who barked black songs
             was hounding us—why wasn't it *your* answer
             that freed the city? Her riddle wasn't the sort
             just anyone who happened by could solve:
             prophetic skill was needed then,
             the kind you didn't have, skill learned
             from birds or from a god. Yet it was Oedipus,
             who knew nothing, that silenced her,
             because my wit seized the answer,
             needing no help from birds.
             Now it is I, this same man, for whom you plot
             disgrace and exile, thinking you will
             maneuver close to Kreon's throne.
             But your scheme to rid Thebes of this plague
             will destroy only you—and the man who planned it.
             You look now so near death—otherwise I'd make you
             the first victim of your own plot.

LEADER   He spoke in anger, Oedipus—
             but so did you, if you'll hear what we think.
             We don't need angry words, we need insight—
             how best to manage what the god commands.

TIRESIAS   You may be king, but my right to
             answer makes me your equal.

In this respect, I am as much
my own master as you are.
You do not own my life.
Apollo does. Nor am I Kreon's man.
Hear me out.
Since you have thrown my blindness at me
I will tell you what your eyes don't see:
the evil you are mired in.
                            You don't see
where you live or who shares your house.
Do you know your parents?
You are their enemy
in this life and down there with the dead.
And soon their double curse—
your father's and your mother's lash—
will whip you out of Thebes
on terrorstruck feet.
Your eyes will then see darkness
which now see life.
                            Your shriek
will try to hide itself in every cave.
What mountain outcrop on Cithairon
won't roar your screaming back at you,
when what your marriage means strikes home,
shows you the house that took you in: you sailed
your lucky wind to a most foul harbor.
Evils you can't guess
will level you to what you are,
to what your children are.
Go on, throw muck at Kreon, and at
the warning spoken through my mouth.
But there will never be a man
ground into wretchedness as you shall be.

OEDIPUS

Shall I wait for him to attack me more?
May you be damned. Go. Leave my doors
now! Turn your back and go.

TIRESIAS

I'm here only because you sent for me.

OEDIPUS

Had I known the madness you would speak
I wouldn't have hurried to get you here.

TIRESIAS

I may seem crazed to you, but your natural
parents thought I had an able mind.

OEDIPUS	My parents? Wait. Who is my father?
TIRESIAS	Today, you will be born. Into ruin.
OEDIPUS	You always have a murky riddle in your mouth.
TIRESIAS	Don't you excel us all at finding answers?
OEDIPUS	Sneer at my mind. But you must face the power it won.
TIRESIAS	That very luck is what destroyed you.
OEDIPUS	If I save Thebes, I won't care what happens to me.
TIRESIAS	I will leave you to that. Boy, guide me out.
OEDIPUS	Yes, let him take you home. Here you are painfully underfoot. Gone, you'll take away a great source of grief.

TIRESIAS

I'll go. But first I must finish
what you brought me to do—
your face won't frighten me.
The man you have been looking for,
the one your curses threaten, the man
you had outlawed in Laius' death:
I say that man is here—

        You think him a foreigner,
but he will prove himself a Theban native,
though he'll find no joy in that news.
A blind man who has eyes now,
a beggar who's now rich, he'll jab
his stick, feeling the road to foreign lands.

(Oedipus enters *the palace.)*

He will soon be shown father and brother to
his own children, son and husband
to the mother who bore him—she took
his father's seed and his seed,
and he took his own father's life.

You go inside. Think through what I have said.
If I have lied, say of me then
I am a prophet with no mind.

(Exit Tiresias.)

Translated by Robert Bagg. *Oedipus the King.* University of Massachusetts Press. ©1982 by Robert Bagg

Aristophanes' *Lysistrata*, 411 B.C.E.

Lysistrata is a comedy, written after twenty years of war between the Delian League, led by Athens, and the Peloponnesian League, with Sparta at its head. Lysistrata brings together a group of women who vow to end the war by refusing to have sex until the men agree to stop fighting. While the play portrays the women as strong and wise, one must keep in mind that it was written by a man at a time when most Greek women were kept secluded in their homes and denied any role in politics. The idea that women might do such a thing was preposterous—that is what provides the comedy. In this scene, the women have seized the Acropolis, where the Treasury is located, and they describe, in housewifely images, how they propose to settle the disputes causing the war.

COMMISSIONER   *You* will save us?

LYSISTRATA   Who else?

COMMISSIONER   But this is unscrupulous!

LYSISTRATA   We'll save you. You can't deter us.

COMMISSIONER   Scurrilous!

LYSISTRATA   You seem disturbed.
This makes it difficult. But, still--we'll save you.

COMMISSIONER   Doubtless illegal!

LYSISTRATA   We deem it a duty. For friendship's sake.

COMMISSIONER   Well, forsake this friend:
I DO NOT WANT TO BE SAVED, DAMMIT!

LYSISTRATA   All the more reason.
It's not only Sparta; now we'll have to save you from *you.*

COMMISSIONER   Might I ask where you women conceived this concern about War and Peace?

LYSISTRATA   We shall explain.

COMMISSIONER   Hurry up, and you won't get hurt.

Making a fist

LYSISTRATA   Then listen. And do try to keep your hands to yourself.

COMMISSIONER   I can't. Righteous anger forbids restraint, and decrees . . .

*Moving
threateningly
toward her*

KLEONIKE   Multiple fractures?

*Brandishing a
chamber pot*

COMMISSIONER   Keep those croaks for yourself, you old crow!

(to Lysistrata): All right, lady, I'm ready. Speak.

LYSISTRATA   I shall proceed:

When the War began, like the prudent, dutiful wives that we are, we tolerated you men, and endured your actions in silence (Small wonder--you wouldn't let us say boo.)

                  You were not precisely the answer to a matron's prayer--we knew you too well, and found out more. Too many times, as we sat in the house, we'd hear that you'd done it again--manhandled another affair of state with your usual staggering incompetence. Then masking our worry with a nervous laugh,

                we'd ask you, brightly, "How was the Assembly today, dear? Anything in the minutes about Peace?"

                And my husband would give his stock reply. "What's that to you? Shut up!" And I did.

KLEONIKE   I never shut up!

COMMISSIONER   I trust you were shut up. Soundly.

LYSISTRATA   Regardless, I shut up.

And then we'd learn that you'd passed another decree, fouler than the first, and we'd ask again: "Darling, how did you manage anything so idiotic?" And my husband, with his customary glare, would tell me to spin my thread, or else get a clout on the head.

And of course he'd quote from Homer:

                Y^e menne must husband ye warre.

COMMISSIONER   Apt and irrefutably right.

LYSISTRATA   Right, you miserable misfit?

To keep us from giving advice while you fumbled the City away in the Senate? Right, indeed!

But this time was really too much: Wherever we went, we'd hear you engaged in the same conversation:

"What Athens needs is a Man."

            "But there isn't a Man in the country."

                  "You can say that again."

There was obviously no time to lose. We women met in immediate convention and passed a unanimous resolution: To work in concert for safety and Peace in Greece. We have valuable advice to impart, and if you can possibly deign to emulate our silence, and take your turn as audience, we'll

	rectify you--we'll straighten you out and set you right.
COMMISSIONER	*You'll* set *us* right? You go too far. I cannot permit such a statement to. . .
LYSISTRATA	Shush.
COMMISSIONER	I categorically decline to shush for some confounded woman, who wears--as a constant reminder of congenital inferiority, and injunction to public silence--a veil! Death before such dishonor!
LYSISTRATA	If that's the only obstacle. . . I feel you need a new panache, so take the veil, my dear Commissioner, and drape it thus—

and SHUSH!

As she winds the veil around the startled Commissioner's head, Kleonike and Myrrhine, with a carding- comb and wool-basket, rush forward and assist in transforming him into a woman.

KLEONIKE	Accept, I pray, this humble comb.
MYRRHINE	Receive this basket of fleece as well.
LYSISTRATA	Hike up your skirts, and card your wool, and gnaw your beans—and stay at home! While we rewrite Homer: Y^e WOMEN must WIVE ye warre!

Enter a Chorus of Women, as the Commissioner struggles to remove his new outfit.

CHORUS OF WOMEN	Women, weaker vessels, arise! Put down your pitchers. It's our turn, now. Let's supply our friends with some moral support.

The Chorus of Women dances to the same tune as the Men, but with much more confidence.

Singly	Oh, yes! I'll dance to bless their success. Fatigue won't weaken my will. Or my knees. I'm ready to join in any jeopardy, with girls as good as these!
Tutte	A tally of their talents convinces my they're giants of excellence. To commence: there's Beauty, Duty, Prudence, Science, Self-Reliance, Compliance, Defiance, and Love of Athens in balanced alliance with Common Sense!
KORYPHAIOS OF WOMEN	Autochthonous daughters of Attika, sprung from the soil that bore your mothers, the spiniest, spikiest nettles known to man, prove your mettle and attack! Now is no time to dilute your anger. You're running ahead of the

wind!

LYSISTRATA We'll wait for the wind from heaven. The gentle breath of Love and his Kyprian mother will imbue our bodies with desire, and raise a storm to tense and tauten these blasted men until they crack. And soon we'll be on every tongue in Greece--the *Pacifiers*.

COMMISSIONER That's quite a mouthful. How will you win it?

LYSISTRATA First, we intend to withdraw that crazy Army of Occupation from the downtown shopping section.

KLEONIKE Aphrodite be praised!

LYSISTRATA The pottery shop and the grocery stall are overstocked with soldiers, clanking around like those maniac Korybants, armed to the teeth for a battle.

COMMISSIONER A Hero is Always Prepared!

LYSISTRATA I suppose he is. But it does look silly to shop for sardines from behind a shield.

KLEONIKE I'll second that. I saw a cavalry captain buy vegetable soup on horseback. He carried the whole mess home in his helmet.

And then that fellow from Thrace, shaking his buckler and spear--a menace straight from the stage. The saleslady was stiff with fright. He was hogging her ripe figs--free.

COMMISSIONER I admit, for the moment, that Hellas' affairs are in one hell of a snarl. But how can you set them straight?

LYSISTRATA Simplicity itself.

COMMISSIONER Pray demonstrate

LYSISTRATA It's rather like yarn. When a hank's in a tangle, we lift it--so--and work out the snarls by winding it up on spindles, now this way, now that way.

That's how we'll wind up the War, if allowed: We'll work out the snarls by sending Special Commissions-- back and forth, now this way, now that way—to ravel these tense international kinks.

COMMISSIONER I lost your thread, but I know there's a hitch. Spruce up the world's disasters with spindles--typically woolly female logic.

LYSISTRATA If you had a scrap of logic, you'd adopt our wool as a master plan for Athens.

COMMISSIONER What course of action does the wool advise?

LYSISTRATA   Consider the City as fleece, recently shorn. The first step is Cleansing: Scrub it in a public bath, and remove all corruption, offal, and sheepdip.

Next, to the couch for Scutching and Plucking: Cudgel the leeches and similar vermin loose with a club, then pick the prickles and cockleburs out.

As for the clots--those lumps that clump and cluster in knots and snarls to snag important posts--you comb these out, twist off their heads, and discard.

Next, to raise the City's nap, you card the citizens together in a single basket of common weal and general welfare. Fold in our loyal Resident Aliens, all Foreigners of proven and tested friendship, and Disenfranchised Debtors. Combine these closely with the rest.

Lastly, cull the colonies settled by our own people: these are nothing but flocks of wool from the City's fleece, scattered throughout the world. So gather home these far-flung flocks, amalgamate them with the others.

Then, drawing this blend of stable fibers into one fine staple, you spin a mighty bobbin of yarn--and weave, without bias or seam, a cloak to clothe the City of Athens!

from *Four Comedies by Aristophanes*. Translated by Douglass Parker. University of Michigan Press. 1977. © 1961, 1962, 1969.

Unit 8: Classical Greek Philosophy

The first century of Greek philosophy is known to us only through fragments and quotations in later work, though whole schools of thought have been reconstructed from these bits and pieces. They are known collectively as preSocratic, and include the Pythagoreans and the Sophists.

From the time that Socrates began his street-corner conversations, three men dominated Greek philosophy—Socrates, Plato, and Aristotle. For none of them do we possess straight-forward accounts of their teachings.

Socrates did not teach for money, nor did he found a school. He refused to put his ideas in writing, insisting that true knowledge comes from within and can be found only by self-searching. We know of Socrates only through the descriptions of his students and friends. The greatest of these, Plato, wrote almost entirely in the form of dialogues, of which the chief protagonist was Socrates. This was a stylistic device, not a mere parroting of Socrates' ideas, so that it is impossible to separate the thought of Socrates' from that of his pupil and reporter.

Aristotle did write, including many works in dialogue form for the general public. These survive only in fragments. What we read as the corpus of Aristotle's thinking consists of lectures and notes from the courses he offered at his school. They were grouped together by an editor into the books we now know as the *Phy-*

sics, *Metaphysics*, and so on. This may help to explain why Aristotle's works are choppy, confusing, and inelegant compared to the polished style of Plato.

Plato: *The Republic*

Plato was disillusioned with democracy after seeing the defeat of Athens by Sparta in the Peloponnesian War and the condemnation of his teacher, Socrates, by his fellow-Athenians. In The Republic he describes an ideal government, headed by people chosen for their innate intelligence and goodness. He prescribes a course of education which will fit them for a role often described as that of "philosopher-king." The Allegory of the Cave demonstrates Plato's belief that truth cannot be discovered by experience. Indeed, he insists, our senses often mislead us. The story of the bed is another attempt to explain his theory of where reality resides.

ALLEGORY OF THE CAVE

And now, I said, let me show you by a parable to what extent our nature may be enlightened or unenlightened. Imagine human beings living in an underground den, with a mouth open to the light, which reaches all along the cave. They have been here since childhood, with their legs and necks chained so that they cannot move, and can see only what is in front of them, because the chains prevent them from turning their heads. Above and behind them, at a distance, is a fire blazing; between the fire and the prisoners there is a raised walkway; and you can see a low wall built against the walkway, like the screen that puppeteers set in front of themselves, above which they show the puppets.

I see.

And do you see, I said, men passing along the wall carrying all sorts of containers, and statues and figures of animals made of wood and stone and various materials, which appear above the wall?

This is a strange image, and they are strange prisoners.

Like ourselves, I replied; and they see only their own shadows, or the shadows of one another, which the fire throws on the wall of the cave opposite the opening.

True, he said. How could they see anything but the shadows if they were never allowed to move their heads?

And of the objects which are being carried, they likewise would see only the shadows.

Yes, he said.

And if they were able to talk to one another, would they not suppose that their words named the things in front of them?

Very true.

And suppose that, in addition, the prison had an echo which came from the other side. Would they not believe, when one of the people passing behind them spoke, that the sound came from the shadow in front of them?

No question, he replied.

To them, I said, the truth would be literally nothing but the shadows of the images.

That is certain.

And now consider what will happen if the prisoners are released and discover their error. At first, when one of them is liberated and suddenly compelled to stand up, turn around, and walk and look toward the light, he will suffer sharp pains; the glare will make it impossible for him to see the objects whose shadows he had previously watched. Then imagine someone saying to him that what he had seen before was an illusion, but that now, as he is approaching reality and his head is turned toward more real objects, his vision is clearer. What will be his reply? Imagine further that his instructor is pointing to the objects as they pass and asking him to name them. Will he not be perplexed? Will he not believe that the shadows to which he was accustomed are more real than the objects now being shown to him?

Far more real.

And suppose that he is compelled to look straight at the light, will he not suffer pain—a pain that will make him turn away and take refuge in the shadows that he can see? And will he not imagine these shadows to be more real than the objects now being shown to him?

And suppose once more that he is reluctantly dragged up a steep and rugged slope and held tightly and forced into the presence of the sun itself, will he not be pained and irritated? When he approaches the light, his eyes will be dazzled, and he will not be able to see anything at all of what he is now told are realities.

No, he won't see them immediately.

He would need, then, to grow accustomed to the sight of that upper world. First he would see shadows best, next the reflections of men and other objects in the water, then the objects themselves. Then he would gaze upon the light of the moon and the stars and the night sky; and he would see the sky and the stars by night better than the sun or the light of the sun by day.

Certainly.

Last of all he would be able to see the sun, and not mere reflections of it in the water, but the sun in its proper place, and not in another, and contemplate it as it is.

Certainly.

He would then begin to assert that it is the sun that produces the seasons and the years, and is the guardian of all that is in the visible world and, in a sense, the cause of the shadows that he and his companions were accustomed to seeing.

Clearly, he said, he would first see the sun, then reason about it.

And when he remembered his old habitation, and what passed for wisdom among his fellow-prisoners in the den, do you not suppose that he would be happy with his change, and pity his former companions?

Certainly, he would.

Suppose that they had been in the habit of conferring honours on those among them who were quickest to recognise the shadows as they passed, and to name the one that came before, and the one after, and the ones that came together, and thus could predict which ones would come next? Do you think that he would care for such honours and glories, or envy the possessors of them? Would he not say with Homer,

Better to be the poor servant of a poor master,

and to endure anything, rather than think as they do and live as he had been accustomed to live?

Yes, I think that he would rather endure anything than to live in this miserable fashion, with these false notions.

Imagine once more, I said, such a person coming suddenly out of the sun and being placed again in his old situation. Would his eyes not be filled with darkness?

To be sure, he said.

And if there were a contest, and he had to compete with the prisoners who had never moved out of the den, while his sight was still weak and before his eyes had become steady (which might be quite some time), would he not seem ridiculous to them? They would say of him that he had gone up and had come down with his eyes ruined, and that it was better not even to think of going up. And if anyone tried to release another prisoner and lead him up into the light, if they could catch the offender they would kill him.

No question, he said.

This entire allegory, I said, you may now add to the previous argument, my dear Glaucon. The prisonhouse is the world of sight, the light of the fire is the sun, and you will not misunderstand me if you think of the journey upwards as the ascent of the soul into the intellectual world according to my poor belief--a belief I have expressed as you asked, whether rightly or wrongly, God knows. Whether true or false, my opinion is that in the world of knowledge the idea of good appears last of all, and is seen only with an effort. When seen, it is understood to be the universal author of all things beautiful and right, parent of light and of the lord of light in this visible world, and the immediate source of reason and truth in the intellectual. He who would act rationally either in public or private life must have his eye fixed on this power.

BEDS AND THEIR MAKERS

Socrates: Well, then, shall we begin the enquiry in our usual manner: Whenever a number of individuals have a common name, we assume them to have also a corresponding idea or form. Do you understand me?

Glaucon: I do.

Let us take any common instance; there are beds and tables in the world—plenty of them, are there not?

Yes.

But there are only two ideas or forms of them—one the idea of a bed, the other of a table.

True. And the maker of either of them makes a bed or he makes a table for our use, in accordance with the idea—that is our way of speaking in this and similar instances—but no artificer makes the ideas themselves: How could he?

Impossible.

And there is another artist—I should like to know what you would say of him.

Who is he?

One who is the maker of all the works of all other workmen.

What an extraordinary man!

Wait a little, and there will be more reason for your saying so. For this is he who is able to make not only vessels of every kind, but plants and animals, himself and all other things—the earth and heaven, and the things which are in heaven or under the earth; he makes the gods also.

He must be a wizard and no mistake.

Oh! You are incredulous, are you? Do you mean that there is no such maker or creator, or that in one sense there might be a maker of all these things but in another not? Do you see that there is a way in which you could make them all yourself?

What way?

An easy way enough; or rather, there are many ways in which the feat might be quickly and easily accomplished, none quicker than that of turning a mirror round and round—you would soon enough make the sun and the heavens, and the earth and yourself, and other animals and plants, and all the other things of which we were just now speaking, in the mirror.

Yes, he said; but they would be appearances only.

Very good, I said, you are coming to the point now. And the painter too is, as I conceive, just such another—a creator of appearances, is he not?

Of course.

But then I suppose you will say that what he creates is untrue. And yet there is a sense in which the painter also creates a bed?

Yes, he said, but not a real bed.

And what of the maker of the bed? Were you not saying that he too makes, not the idea which, according to our view, is the essence of the bed, but only a particular bed?

Yes, I did.

Then if he does not make that which exists he cannot make true existence, but only some semblance of existence; and if any one were to say that the work of the maker of the bed, or of any other workman, has real existence, he could hardly be supposed to be speaking the truth.

At any rate, he replied, philosophers would say that he was not speaking the truth.

trans. B. Jowett. *The Republic*. New York. Modern Library. n.d.

Aristotle's *Politics*

Aristotle was born in 384 B.C.E. and died in 322, a year after the death of his student, Alexander the Great. His father was court physician to the former king of Macedon, which may help to explain his preoccupation with nature. A student of Plato, he rejected his teacher's insistence that understanding comes through reason alone, and not through experience. Aristotle's *Politics* is based on his examination of the constitutions of 158 states. After comparing and analyzing them, he concluded that "different peoples create for themselves different ways of life and different constitutions." Nevertheless, his concern for determining the ideal constitution and his insistence that the purpose of the state is to attain the highest good show that he shared Plato's conviction that philosophy is a search for the highest good.

BOOK I, CHAPTERS 1 AND 2

Every state is a community of some kind, and every community is established with a view to some good; for mankind always act in order to obtain that which they think good. But, if all communities aim at some good, the state or political community, which is the highest of all, and which embraces all the rest, aims at good in a greater degree than any other, and at the highest good.

Some people think that the qualifications of a statesman, king, householder, and master are the same, and that they differ, not in kind, but only in the number of their subjects. For example, the ruler over a few is called a master; over more, the manager of a household; over a still larger number, a statesman or king, as if there were no difference between a great household and a small state. The distinction which is made between the king and the statesman is as follows; When the government is personal, the ruler is a king; when, according to the rules of the political science, the citizens rule and are ruled in turn, then he is called a statesman.

But all this is a mistake; for governments differ in kind, as will be evident to any one who considers the matter according to the method which has hitherto guided us. As in other departments of science, so in politics, the compound should always be resolved into the simple elements or least parts of the whole. We must therefore look at the elements of which the state is composed, in order that we may see in what the different kinds of rule differ from one another, and whether any scientific result can be attained about each one of them.

He who thus considers things in their first growth and origin, whether a state or anything else, will obtain the clearest view of them. In the first place there must be a union of those who cannot exist without each other; namely, of male and female, that the race may continue (and this is a union which is formed, not of deliberate purpose, but because, in common with other animals and with plants, mankind have a natural desire to leave behind them an image of themselves), and of natural ruler and subject, that both may be preserved. For that which can plan ahead by the exercise of mind is by nature intended to be lord and master, and that which can with its body carry out the plan is a subject, and by nature a slave; hence master and slave have the same interest. Now nature has distinguished between the female and the slave. For she is not niggardly, like the smith who fashions the Delphian knife for many uses; she makes each thing for a single use, and every instrument is best made when intended for one and not for many uses. But among barbarians no distinction is made between women and slaves, because there is no natural ruler among them; they are a community of slaves, male and female. Wherefore the poets say

'It is meet that barbarous peoples should be governed by the Greeks'

--the assumption being that barbarian and slave are by nature one and the same. . .

Out of these two relationships between man and woman, master and slave, the first thing to arise is the family, and Hesiod is right when he says

'First house, and wife, and ox to draw the plough,'

for oxen serve the poor in lieu of household slaves. The family is the association established by nature for the supply of men's everyday wants, and the members of it are called by Charondas 'companions of the cupboard,' and by Epimenides the Cretan, 'companions of the manger.' But when several families are united, and the association aims at something more than the supply of daily needs, the first society to be formed is the village.

And the most natural form of the village appears to be that of a colony from the family, composed of the children and grandchildren, who are said to be 'suckled with the same milk.' And this is the reason why each Greek *polis* was originally governed by a king; because the Greeks were under royal rule before they came together, as the peoples of the barbarian world still are. Families are always ruled by the eldest; therefore villages retained the kingly form of government because they were made up of kinship groups. As Homer says:

'Each of them ruleth

Over his children and wives,'

for they lived in scattered groups, as indeed men generally did in ancient times. Wherefore men say that the Gods have a king, because they themselves either are or were in ancient times under the rule of a king. For they imagine, not only the forms of the Gods, but their ways of life to be like their own.

When several villages are united in a single complete community, large enough to be nearly or quite self sufficient, the *polis* comes into existence, originating in the bare needs of life, and continuing in existence for the sake of a good life. And therefore, if the earlier forms of society are natural, so is the *polis*, for it is the end or consummation of them, and the nature of a thing is its end. For what each thing is when fully developed, we call its nature, whether we are speaking of a man, a horse, or a family. Besides, the final cause and end of a thing is the best, and to be self-sufficient is both the end and the best.

Hence it is evident that the *polis* is a natural being, and that man is by nature an animal intended to live in a *polis*. And he who by nature and not by mere accident is without a *polis*, is either a poor example of a man or a being higher than man. He is like the man whom Homer denounces:

'Clanless and lawless and hearthless is he.'

The man who is isolated by nature becomes a lover of war. He is like an isolated piece in a game of checkers.

Now it is evident that man is more a political animal than bees or any other gregarious animal. Nature, as we often say, makes nothing in vain, and man is the only animal whom she has endowed with the gift of language. And whereas mere making of sounds is but an indication of pleasure or pain, and is therefore found in other animals (for their nature attains to the perception of pleasure and pain and the intimation of them to one another, and no further), the power of language is intended to set forth what is advantageous and what is not, and likewise what is just and what is unjust. And it is a characteristic of man that he alone has a sense of good and evil, of just and unjust, and of other similar qualities. It is the association of beings who have this sense that makes a family and a *polis*.

Further, the *polis* is by nature clearly prior to the family and to the individual, since the whole is necessarily prior to the part. For example, if the whole body be destroyed, there will be no foot or hand, except in an equivocal sense, as we might speak of a stone hand; for when the body is destroyed the hand will be no better than a stone hand. But things are defined by their function and capacity. When they can no longer serve their function, we ought not to say that they are the same, but merely that they have the same name.

The proof that the *polis* is a natural being and prior to the individual is that the isolated individual is not self-sufficient. Therefore he is like a part in relation to the whole. The man who is unable to live in a political community--or who does not need it because he is self-sufficient-- must be either a beast or a god. A social instinct is implanted in all men by nature, and yet he who first founded the *polis* was the greatest of benefactors. For man, when perfected, is the best of animals, but, when separated from law and justice, he is the worst. Injustice is more danger- ous when it is armed injustice, and man is equipped at birth with arms, meant to be used with intelligence and virtue, but which may be used for opposite ends. That is why a man without virtue is the most unholy and the most savage of animals, and the most full of lust and gluttony. But justice bonds men in the *polis*; for justice, which is the determination of what is just, is the principle of order in the political association.

BOOK VII, CHAPTERS 8 AND 9

In a state, as in other natural compounds, the conditions of the whole are not necessarily organic parts of it. Just so, not all the elements which are necessary conditions of a state are parts of it. The members of an association must have something in common, identical for all—yet their shares in it may be equal or unequal; for example, food, or land, or any other thing. But where there are two things—one the means to an end and the other the end served by the means—they have nothing in common except that the one receives that which the other produces. Such, for example is the relation of a builder and his tools to the product of his work. The house and the builder have nothing in common. The builder's skill exists to create the product—the house. Just so, a state requires property, but property is not a part of the state. This is true even if the property includes living beings (i.e., slaves). For a state is not merely a community of living beings, but a community of equals, aiming at the best life possible. The highest good is happiness, which is the realization and perfect practice of virtue. Some can attain this; others have little or none of it. The various qualities of men are clearly the reason why there are various kinds of states and many forms of government; for different men seek after happiness in different ways and by different means, and so make for themselves different modes of life and forms of government.

It remains for us to see what are the indispensable elements of a state, for what we call the parts of a state will be found among its indispensable elements. Let us then enumerate the functions of a state, and we shall easily elicit what we want: First, there must be food; secondly, arts, for life requires many tools. Thirdly, there must be arms, for the members of a community have need of them, and in their own hands, too, in order to maintain authority both against disobedient subjects and against external assailants. Fourthly, there must be a certain amount of revenue, both for internal needs, and for the purposes of war. Fifthly, or rather first, there must be a care of religion, which is commonly called worship. Sixthly, and most necessary of all, there must be a system for deciding what is in the public interest and what is just in men's dealings with one another.

These are the services which every state may be said to need. For a state is not a mere casual group of persons, but a union which is self-sufficient for the purposes of life. If any of these things is lacking, we maintain that it is impossible for the community to be self-sufficient. A state then should be created with the purpose of fulfilling these functions. There must be farmers to produce food, artisans, a military force, a wealthy class, priests, and judges to decide what is necessary and expedient.

Having determined these points, we have next to consider whether all ought to share in every sort of occupation. Shall every man be simultaneously farmer, artisan, councillor, and judge, or shall each occupation be assigned to different persons? or, thirdly, shall some services be assigned to certain individuals and others shared by all? The same arrangement, does not occur in every constitution. Hence arise the differences of constitutions, for in democracies all men share in all functions, while in oligarchies the opposite practice prevails. Now, we are here speaking of the best form of government, i.e. that under which the state will be most happy (and happiness, as has been already said, cannot exist without virtue). It clearly follows that in the state which is best governed—one that possesses men who are absolutely just, not merely just in relation to their particular constitution—the citizens must not lead the lives of mechanics or shopkeepers, for such a life is ignoble and not conducive to virtue. And they must not be farmers, since leisure is necessary both for the development of virtue and for the performance of political duties.

Again, there is in a state a class of warriors, and another of councillors, who advise about matters of public interest and give decisions in matters of justice. These are, in a special sense, parts of a state. Now should these two classes be kept separate, or should both functions be assigned to the same persons? Here again it is easy to see that both functions will in one sense belong to the same persons, in another sense to different persons. To different persons, in that these employments are suited to different primes of life; one requires wisdom, the other strength. On the other hand, those who are able to use or to resist force will not be willing to remain always in subjection. From this point of view the two functions should go to the same set of persons, for those who carry arms can always determine the fate of the constitution. It remains therefore that—in the ideal constitution—both functions will be entrusted to the same persons. But they will not exercise them at the same time, but rather in the order prescribed by nature, who has given to young men strength and to older men wisdom. Such a distribution of duties will be expedient and also just, and has the advantage of giving to each that which he deserves.

Besides, the ruling class should be the owners of property, for they are citizens, and the citizens of a state should be comfortably well-off. Mechanics or any other class that is not a producer of goodness has no share in the state. This follows from our first principle, for happiness cannot exist without virtue, and a city cannot be called happy with regard to only a portion of its citizens, but with regard to all. Clearly, property should belong to them, since the farmers ought to be slaves or barbarian serfs.

Of the six classes we enumerated there remain only the priests. The manner in which that office should be regulated is obvious. No farmer or mechanic should be appointed to it, for the gods should receive honour only from the citizens. Citizens are divided into two classes, the warriors and the councillors. The duties of the priesthood should be assigned to the old men of these two classes, so that the worship of the gods will be duly performed; at the same time, this will provide a rest in their service for those who have given up the active life because of age.

We have shown both the necessary conditions and the parts of a state. Farmers, craftsmen, and labourers of all kinds are necessary to the existence of states, but the parts of the state are the warriors and councillors. These are distinguished from each other, the distinction being in some cases permanent, in others not.

Adapted from the translation of Benjamin Jowett. *The Works of Aristotle*, vol. X. Oxford: Clarendon Press. 1921.

CHAPTER 4: THE HELLENISTIC WORLD

Unit 9: Alexander the Great

Alexander died in 323 B.C.E. Many of those who accompanied him in his conquest of most of the Western world wrote about it. Callisthenes, the nephew of Aristotle, wrote the official version—up until his arrest and execution for treason. Other accounts were written by Chares, the royal chamberlain, Aristobulus, an engineer, Nearchus, the commander of Alexander's fleet on its voyage from India to the Persian Gulf, and Ptolemy, who became ruler of Egypt after Alexander's death. In these accounts are mixed exaggerated heroics, sensationalist muck-raking, and unabashed legend. For instance, Callisthenes recounted how once the sea retreated from Alexander's path and bowed in homage before him. No contemporary account has survived.

The earliest extant account of Alexander's conquests was written 300 years after his death. It makes up the seventeenth book of the *Universal History* of Diodorus, a Sicilian Greek. Arrian, who wrote nearly 500 years after the events, relied on a number of the contemporary accounts. He says that there are "so many of them and more mutually conflicting, than of any other historical character." He says that he relied mainly on the accounts of Ptolemy and Aristobulus. When they disagreed, he chose the more probable and interesting.

from *The Campaigns of Alexander*, by Arrian, c. 150 C. E.

In this speech to soldiers who threatened to mutiny and return home, Alexander reminds them of what they owe to his father, Philip of Macedon.

He found you vagabonds and destitute, most of you clad in hides, feeding a few sheep up the mountain sides for the protection of which you had to fight with small success against Illyrians, Tribalians, and the border Thracians. Instead of the hides he gave you cloaks to wear, and from the mountains he led you down into the plains, and made you capable of fighting the neighboring barbarians so that you were no longer forced to save yourselves by trusting more to your inaccessible strongholds than to your valor. Colonists of cities, too, he made you, and he adorned them with useful laws and customs; and from being slaves and subjects he made you rulers over the very barbarians by whom you yourselves, as well as your property, had previously been liable to be carried off or ravaged.

Then again he added the bulk of Thrace to Macedonia, and by seizing the best situated places on the coast, he made the land prosper by commerce, and made the workings of the mines safe business. He made you rulers over the Thessalians—of whom you had once been mortally afraid; and by humbling the folk of the Phocians, he made the road into Hellas[4] broad for you and easy—not narrow and difficult as before. The Athenians and Thebans, always waiting to assail Macedonia, he humbled to such a degree . . . that instead of paying tribute to Athens and being

---

4 Greece

vassals to Thebes, those states must perforce get security for themselves by our aid. He penetrated into Peloponnesus, and after regulating its affairs, was publicly declared commander in chief for all the rest of Hellas in the expedition against the Persian, adding this glory not more to himself than to the commonwealth of the Macedonians.

These then were the advantages which you gained from my father Philip!

From *Readings in Ancient History*, edited by William Stearns Davis, Boston: Allyn and Bacon, 1912.

This story of the defeat of Darius, the Persian king, at Issus, demonstrates attributes that may account for the loyalty of Alexander's men and the respect of his enemies. On the other hand, it may be just a good story.

The moment the Persian left went to pieces under Alexander's attack and Darius, in his war-chariot, saw that it was cut off, he incontinently fled--indeed, he led the race for safety. Keeping to his chariot as long as there was smooth ground to travel on, he was forced to abandon it when ravines and other obstructions barred his way; then, dropping his shield and stripping off his mantle—and even leaving his bow in the war-chariot—he leapt upon a horse and rode for his life. Darkness soon closed in; and that alone saved him from falling into the hands of Alexander, who, while daylight held, relentlessly pressed the pursuit; but when there was no longer light enough to see what he was coming to, he turned back—but not without taking possession of Darius' chariot together with his shield, mantle, and bow. In point of fact his pursuit would have been more rapid had he not turned back at the moment when his line of heavy infantry broke, in the first stage of the battle; he had than waited until he saw that both the Greek mercenaries and the Persian cavalry had been forced back from the river bank.

Among the Persian dead were Arsames, Rheomithres, and Atizyes—all three of whom had served as cavalry officers at the battle on the Granicus; also Sabaces, governor of Egypt, and Bubaces, another person of distinguished rank; of the common soldiers, something like 100,000 were killed, including over 10,000 of the cavalry. Ptolemy, son of Lagus, who was serving with Alexander at this time, says in his account of the battle that the Macedonians in their pursuit of Darius actually crossed a ravine on the bodies of the Persian dead. Darius' headquarters were stormed and captured; his mother was taken, together with his wife (who was also his sister) and his infant son; in addition to these, two of his daughters fell into Alexander's hands with a few noble Persian ladies who were in attendance upon them. The Persian officers had sent their gear and womenfolk to Damascus, and Darius, too, had sent thither most of his treasure and the various paraphernalia which the luxurious life of a great king seems to require, even on campaign; so that a mere 3,000 talents were found at his headquarters. In point of fact, however, the treasure at Damascus, too, was seized not long afterwards by Parmenio, who was ordered there for the purpose. Such, then, was the result of the battle of Issus, fought in the month of November, during the archonship of Nicocrates at Athens.

Alexander had been hurt by a sword-thrust in the thigh, but this did not prevent him from visiting the wounded on the day after the battle, when he also gave a splendid military funeral to the dead in the presence of the whole army paraded in full war equipment. At the ceremony he spoke in praise of every man who be his own observation or from reliable report he knew had distinguished himself in the fighting, and marked his approval in each case by a suitable reward. He appointed Balacrus, son of Nicanor, a member of the Royal Guard, as governor of Cilicia, promoting Menes, son of Dionysisus, to fill the place thus left vacant, and Polysperchon, son of

Simmias, was promoted to command the battalion of Ptolemy, son of Seleucus, who had been killed. The people of Soli still owed fifty talents of the fine imposed upon them, but he canceled the debt and returned their hostages.

His sympathy was extended, moreover, even to Darius' mother, wife, and children. According to some accounts, on the night when he returned from the pursuit he heard upon entering Darius' tent, which had been set aside as his own special portion of the spoils of war, the confused sound of women's voices raised in lamentation somewhere close at hand. He asked who the women were and why they should be in a tent so close to him. 'Sire,' he was told, 'they are Darius' mother and wife and children. They know that you have his bow and his royal mantle and that his shield has been brought back, and they are mourning for his death.' Alexander at once sent Leonnatus, one of his Companions, to tell them that Darius was alive--his mantle and weapons he had left, as he fled for safety, in his war chariot, and these, and nothing else, had fallen into Alexander's hands. Leonnatus entered their tent, gave the message about Darius, and added that Alexander wished them to retain all the marks, ceremonies, and titles of royalty, as he had not fought Darius with any personal bitterness, but had made legitimate war for the sovereignty of Asia. This is the account given by Ptolemy and Aristobulus; there is also another story to the effect that Alexander on the following day entered the tent accompanied only by Hephaestion, and that Darius' mother, in doubt, owing to the similarity of their dress, which of the two was the King, prostrated herself before Hephaestion, because he was taller than his companion. Hephaestion stepped back, and one of the Queen's attendants rectified her mistake by pointing to Alexander; the Queen withdrew in profound embarrassment, but Alexander merely remarked that her error was of no account, for Hephaestion, too was an Alexander—a 'protector of men.' I record this anecdote not as necessarily true, though it is credible enough. If such were indeed the facts, I cannot but admire Alexander both for treating these women with such compassion and for showing such respect and confidence towards his friend; if the story is apocryphal, it was at least inspired by Alexander's character; thus he would have acted, thus he would have spoken--and on that account I admire him no less. . . .

There is a story about Darius that shortly after the battle of Issus the eunuch who had charge of his wife succeeded in making his way to him. Darius' first question was whether his mother, wife, and children were still alive, and hearing that they not only were, but were also addressed by the title of princess and treated with as much ceremony as when he was on the throne, he proceeded to inquire if his wife still preserved her chastity.

'She does,' replied the eunuch.

'And has Alexander offered her no violence--no insult?'

'My lord,' exclaimed the eunuch with an oath, 'your wife is as you left her, and Alexander is the best of men and the least ready to yield to temptation.'

Darius raised his hands to heaven in prayer. 'My lord Zeus,' he cried, ' to whom it is given to order the affairs of kings in this world, keep safe for me now the empire over the Medes and Persians, even as once you gave it me; but, if it is no longer your will that I be King of Asia, then entrust my throne, I pray, to no man but Alexander.' Thus even enemies are not indifferent to honourable deeds.

from Arrian, *The Campaigns of Alexander.* Translated by Aubrey de Sélincourt. © The Estate of Aubrey de Sélincourt 1958. New York: Penguin. 1971. pp.120-23, 235-36. Printed by permission of Penguin Books Ltd.

Unit 10: Hellenistic Life

While philosophy, art, and drama flourished in Athens in the fourth and fifth centuries, it was in Hellenistic times that science, especially in its practical applications, came to the fore. The Ptolemaic kings established a major research center in Alexandria, in Egypt, and libraries in Alexandria, Pergamum, Antioch, Rhodes, and Smyrna, Astronomy and mathematics, medicine and mechanics flourished in Alexandria. Aristarchus suggested that the planets revolve around the sun and that the stars were at enormous distances from the earth. Hipparchus of Nicaea calculated the length of a mean lunar month to within one second of modern findings. Euclid's geometry was the standard until the nineteenth century.

Archimedes as Described by Plutarch

Archimedes is known for his discovery of the principle of specific gravity. He calculated the value of π and invented integral calculus. His practical inventions include the pulley and the endless screw, which was used to drain water from the holds of ships and for irrigation. Archimedes died in 211, killed by a Roman soldier .

The first that turned their thoughts to mechanics, a branch of knowledge which came afterwards to be so much admired, were Eudoxus and Archytas, who thus gave a variety and an agreeable turn to geometry, and confirmed certain problems by sensible experiments and the use of instruments, which could not be demonstrated in the way of theorem. That problem, for example, of two mean proportional lines, which cannot be found out geometrically, and yet are so necessary for the solution of other questions, they solved mechanically, by the assistance of certain instruments called mesolabes, taken from conic sections. But when Plato inveighed against them, with great indignation, as corrupting and debasing the excellence of geometry, by making her descend from incorporeal and intellectual to corporeal and sensible things, and obliging her to make use of matter, which requires much manual labour, and is the object of servile trades; then mechanics were separated from geometry, and being a long time despised by the philosopher, were considered as a branch of the military art.

Archimedes one day asserted to king Hiero, whose kinsman and friend he was, this proposition, that with a given power he could move any given weight whatever; nay, it is said, from the confidence he had in his demonstration, he ventured to affirm, that if there was another earth besides this we inhabit, by going into that, he would move this wherever he pleased. Hiero, full of wonder, begged of him to evince the truth of his proposition by moving some great weight with a small power. In compliance with which, Archimedes caused one of the king's galleys to be drawn on shore with many hands and much labour; and having well manned her, and put on board her usual loading, he placed himself at a distance, and without any pains, only moving with his hand the end of a machine, which consisted of a variety of ropes and pulleys, he drew her to him in as smooth and gentle a manner as if she had been under sail. The king, quite astonished when he saw the force of his art, prevailed with Archimedes to make for him all manner of engines and machines which could be used either for attack or defence in a siege. These, however, he never made use of, the greatest part of his reign being blessed with tranquillity; but they were extremely serviceable to the Syracusans on the present occasion,[5] who with such a number of machines, had the inventor to direct them.

When the Romans attacked them both by sea and land, they were struck dumb with terror, imagining they could not possibly resist such numerous forces and so furious an assault. But Archimedes soon began to play his engines, and they shot against the land forces all sorts of missive weapons and stones of an enormous size, with so incredible a noise and rapidity that nothing could stand before them; they overturned and crushed whatever came in their way, and spread terrible disorder throughout the ranks. On the side towards the sea were erected vast machines, putting forth on a sudden, over the walls, huge beams with the necessary tackle, which striking with a prodigious force on the enemy's galleys, sunk them at once; while other ships hoisted up at the prows by iron grapples or hooks, like the beaks of cranes, and set on end on the stern, were plunged to the bottom of the sea; and others again by ropes and grapples, were drawn towards the shore, and after being whirled about, and dashed against the rocks that projected below the walls, were broken to pieces, and the crews perished. Very often a ship lifted high above the sea, suspended and twirling in the air, presented a most dreadful spectacle. There it swung till the men were thrown out by the violence of the motion, and then it split against the walls, or sunk, on the engine's letting go its hold. As for the machine which Marcellus brought forward upon eight galleys, and which was called sambuca, on account of its likeness to the musical instrument of that name, while it was at a considerable distance from the walls, Archimedes discharged a stone of ten talents weight, and after that a second and a third, all which striking upon it with an amazing noise and force, shattered and totally disjointed it.

Marcellus, in this distress, drew off his galleys as fast as possible, and sent orders to the land forces to retreat likewise. He then called a council of war, at which it was resolved to come close to the walls, if it was possible, next morning before day. For Archimedes's engines, they thought, being very strong and intended to act at a considerable distance, would then discharge themselves over their heads; and if they were pointed at them when they were so near, they would have no effect. But for this Archimedes had long been prepared, having by him engines fitted to all distances, with suitable weapons and shorter beams. Besides, he had caused holes to be made in the walls, in which he placed *scorpions*, that did not carry far, but could be very fast discharged; and by these the enemy was galled, without knowing whence the weapon came.

When, therefore, the Romans were got close to the walls, undiscovered as they thought, they were welcomed with a shower of darts, and huge pieces of rocks, which fell as it were perpendicularly upon their heads; for the engines played from every quarter of the walls. This obliged them to retire; and when they were at some distance, other shafts were shot at them, in their retreat, from the larger machines, which made terrible havoc among them, as well as greatly damaged their shipping, without any possibility of their annoying the Syracusans in their turn. For Archimedes had placed most of his engines under cover of the walls; so that the Romans, being infinitely distressed by an invisible enemy, seemed to fight against the gods.

Marcellus, however, got off, and laughed at his own artillery-men and engineers. "Why do not we leave off contending," said he, "with this mathematical Briaraeus, who, sitting on the shore, and acting as it were but in jest, has shamefully baffled our naval assault; and, in striking us with such a multitude of bolts at once, exceeds even the hundred-handed giants in the fable?"

---

5 The occasion was a war in which the Romans, led by Marcellus, besieged the city of Syracuse

And, in truth, all the rest of the Syracusans were no more than the body in the batteries of Archimedes, while he himself was the informing soul. All other weapons lay idle and unemployed; his were the only offensive and defensive arms of the city. At last the Romans were so terrified, that if they saw but a rope or a stick put over the walls, they cried out that Archimedes was levelling some machine at them, and turned their backs and fled. Marcellus seeing this, gave up all thoughts of proceeding by assault, and leaving the matter to time, turned the siege into a blockade.

Yet Archimedes had such a depth of understanding, such a dignity of sentiment, and so copious a fund of mathematical knowledge, that, though in the invention of these machines he gained the reputation of man endowed with divine rather than human knowledge, yet he did not vouchsafe to leave any account of them in writing. For he considered all attention to mechanics, and every art that ministers to common uses, as mean and sordid, and placed his whole delight in those intellectual speculations, which, without any relation to the necessities of life, have an intrinsic excellence arising from truth and demonstration only. Indeed, if mechanical knowledge is valuable for the curious frame and amazing power of those machines which it produces, the other infinitely excels on account of its invincible force and conviction. And certainly it is, that abstruse and profound questions in geometry are nowhere solved by a more simple process and upon clearer principles, than in the writings of Archimedes. Some ascribe this to the acuteness of his genius, and others to his indefatigable industry, by which he made things that cost a great deal of pains appear unlaboured and easy. In fact, it is almost impossible for a man of himself to find out the demonstration of his propositions, but as soon as he had learned it from him, he will think he could have done it without assistance; such a ready and easy way does he lead us to what he wants to prove. We are not, therefore, to reject as incredible, what is related of him, that being perpetually charmed by a domestic siren, that is, his geometry, he neglected his meat and drink, and took no care of his person; that he was often carried by force to the baths, and when there he would make mathematical figures in the ashes, and with his finger draw lines upon his body, when it was anointed, so much was he transported with intellectual delight, such an enthusiast in science. And though he was the author of many curious and excellent discoveries, yet he is said to have desired his friends only to place on his tombstone a cylinder containing a sphere, and to set down the proportion which containing solid bears to the contained.[6] Such was Archimedes, who exerted all his skill to defend himself and the town against the Romans.

From Plutarch's Life of Marcellus. Langhorne translation. London: Frederick Warne, 1884.

Marriage Contract

In this contract, Ptolemy is still referred to as a satrap of Alexander IV, indicating that the contract was made early in the Hellenistic period. It concerns the marriage of two Greeks, immigrants in Egypt. The bride is given in marriage by her parents, and her father even has the privilege of helping to choose where the couple will live. The wife does have rights, however, which are reinforced with economic sanctions.

In the reign of Alexander son of Alexander, in the seventh year, in the satrapship of Ptolemy in the fourteenth yeaar, in the month of Daisios. Marriage contract of Herakleides and Demetria. Herakleides (the Temnitan) takes as his lawful wife Demetria the Koan, both being

---

6 It was Archimedes who discovered the proportion between these two solids.

freeborn, from her father Leptines, Koan, and her mother Philotis, bringing clothing and ornaments to the value of 1000 drachmas, and Herakleides shall supply to Demetria all that is proper for a freeborn wife, and we shall live together wherever it seems best to Leptines and Herakleides consulting in common. If Demetria is discovered doing any evil to the shame of her husband Herakleides, she shall be deprived of all that she brought, but Herakleides shall prove whatever he alleges against Demetria before three men whom they both accept. It shall not be lawful for Herakleides to bring home another wife in insult of Demetria nor to have children by another woman nor to do evil against Demetria on any pretext. If Herakleides is discovered doing any of these things and Demetria proves it before three men whom they both accept, Herakleides shall give back to Demetria the dowry of 1000 drachmas which she brought and shall moreover forfeit 1000 drachmas of the silver coinage of Alexander. Demetria and those aiding Demetria to exact payment shall have the right of execution, as derived from a legally decided action, upon the person of Herakleides and upon all the property of Herakleides both on land and on water. This contract shall be valid in every respect, wherever Herakleides may produce it against Demetria, or Demetria and those aiding Demetria to exact payment may produce it against Herakleides, as if the agreement had been made in the place. Herakleides and Demetria shall have the right to keep the contracts severally in their own custody and to produce them against each other. Witnesses: Kleon, Gelan; Antikrates, Temnitan; Lysis, Temnitan; Dionysios, Temnitan; Aristomachos, Cryrenaean; Aristodikos, Koan.

From *Greek Historical Documents: The Hellenistic Period*, edited by Roger S. Bagnall and Peter Derow. © Society of Biblical Literature, 1981. Reprinted by permission.

Flooding of a Field

In this suit, a farmer complains that neighbors have ruined his crop by flooding his land, probably by accidentally discharging water from a holding basin. The *Code of Hammurabi* also addresses issues such as this, indicating the importance of irrigation to these ancient societies.

To King Ptolemy greeting from Idomeneus, one of the farmers from the gift-estate of Chrysermos, from the village of Kaminoi. I am wronged by Petobastis son of Taos and Horos son of Kelesis, from the same village. For after I leased two *arouras* from the gift estate of Chrysermos and sowed the land with *arakos*, the aforementioned Petobastis and Horos flooded my sown field, so that my *arakos* became lost and I cannot even pay the expenses I have accrued on the land. I beg of you therefore, O king, if it seems right to you, to order Diophanes and, if I show that they have flooded my sown field, to compel them to take over my sown land and pay the rent on it, and to give me an equal amount from the land which they cultivate in place of that which they have flooded. If this is done, by fleeing to you, O king, I shall be able to pay the rent to Chrysermos, and I shall have experienced kindness at your hands. Farewell.

(Strategos' note) To Hephaistion. If possible reconcile them; if not, send them to _____ after the 10th of Choiach, so that they may be judged before the proper court. Year 4, Daisios 27, Hathyr 29.

(Docket) Year 4, Daisios 27, Hathry 29. Idomeneus, farmer of the gift-estate of Chrysermos, against Petobastis and Horos about flooding of land.

From *Greek Historical Documents: The Hellenistic Period*, edited by Roger S. Bagnall and Peter Derow. © Society of Biblical Literature, 1981. Reprinted by permission.

Letter From a Man in Jail, c. 250 B.C.E.

This letter is from a man who is apparently being held in jail pending trial. His proposed solution is an interesting one.

To Zenon greeting from Kalippos. Have you fallen asleep, regardless of me in prison? Think of your flocks and herds. Know that if the goats of Demetrios remain here, they will perish; for the road down which he drives them to the pastures is enough to kill them. Think too about the hay already cut in Senaru, that it not be lost; for not small is the profit you will gain from it; I reckon there will be as many as 3000 sheaves. I pray and beseech you, be not unmindful of me in prison. Much loss have I suffered since I was led to jail from the allotment which I leased, trusting in your support. No little loss have you suffered since I was led to jail; and the sheep which I have acquired since I came to you have been carried off by the shepherds since I was led to jail. And if it seems good to you, I will leave my wife in prison to be answerable for me, until you inquire into the matters about which they accuse. Farewell.

CHAPTER 5: THE ROMAN REPUBLIC

Unit 11: Founding of Rome and Evolution of the Republic

At the end of the first century B.C.E., Caesar Augustus commissioned Titus Livius (Livy) to write a history of Rome. He wrote 142 books describing Rome from the founding of the city (753 B.C.E.) to 9 B.C.E. Only forty-five books have survived, plus synopses of the others. The histories of Livy and his contemporaries, Diodorus Siculus and Dionysius of Halicarnassus, are the earliest surviving works on this period. Tacitus and Plutarch, writing in the first century C.E. are the other two important historians for this period. They relied on earlier works, now lost, such as those of Quintus Fabius Pictor, and on literary works. They could also draw on family traditions, which were carefully handed down at funerals, where a son or close relative entoned the exploits of dead ancestors over the body.

For the chronology of early Rome, the best evidence is the *Fasti Capitolini*, a list of magistrates kept in the Temple of Jupiter beginning in the sixth century B.C.E. Most of them were destroyed when Rome was sacked by the Gauls in 390 B.C.E. Another list on "linen rolls" was found in the first century B.C.E., but Cicero and Livy agreed that the lists had been falsified, probably by families seeking to exalt themselves by ties to ancient heroes.

Archaeological findings tend to confirm the bare outlines of the literary histories. There were wattle-and-daub houses on several of the hills of Rome in the eighth century. Between 700 and 625, isolated villages began to merge. Between 625 and 575, the forum area was cleared of houses to make room for administrative buildings, indicating a central authority for the city. Houses of brick or wood were located on regularly patterned streets.

Livy: Romulus and Remus, c. 24 B.C.E.

Livy wrote his history of Rome more than seven hundred years after the events reported here. Livy reports the story as it has come down to him, and he admits, in his introduction, that there is no evidence for its accuracy: "Events before Rome was born or thought of have come to us in old tales with more of the charm of poetry than of a sound historical record, and such traditions I propose neither to affirm nor refute."

Proca ruled next.[7] He begat Numitor and Amulius; to Numitor, the elder, he bequeathed the ancient realm of the Silvian family. Yet violence proved more potent than a father's wishes or respect for seniority. Amulius drove out his brother and ruled in his stead. Adding crime to crime, he destroyed Numitor's male issue; and Rhea Silvia, his brother's daughter, he appointed a Vestal under pretence of honouring her, and by consigning her to perpetual virginity, deprived her of the hope of children.

---

7 In Alba Longa.

But the Fates were resolved, as I suppose, upon the founding of this great city, and the beginning of the mightiest of empires, next after that of Heaven. The Vestal was ravished, and having given birth to twin sons, named Mars as the father of her doubtful offspring, whether actually so believing, or because it seemed less wrong if a god were the author of her fault. But neither gods nor men protected the mother herself or her babes from the king's cruelty. The priestess he ordered to be manacled and cast into prison, the children to be committed to the river. It happened by singular good fortune that the Tiber having spread beyond its banks into stagnant pools afforded nowhere any access to the regular channel of the river, and the men who brought the twins were led to hope that being infants they might be drowned, no matter how sluggish the stream. So they thought to carry out the king's command by exposing the babes at the nearest point of the overflow, where the Ruminal fig-tree—formerly called the fig-tree of Romulus—now stands.

In those days this was a wild and uninhabited region. The story persists that when the floating basket in which the children had been exposed was left high and dry by the receding water, a she-wolf, coming down out of the surrounding hills to slake her thirst, turned her steps towards the cry of the infants, and with her teats gave them suck so gently, that the keeper of the royal flock found her licking them with her tongue. Tradition assigns to this man the name of Faustulus, and adds that he carried the twins to his hut and gave them to his wife Larentia to rear. Some think that Larentia, having been free with her favours, had got the name of "she-wolf" among the shepherds, and that this gave rise to this marvellous story. . . .Some think that the origin of this fable was the fact that Larentia was a common whore and was called Wolf by the shepherds. . . .

The Alban state having been turned over to Numitor as I described,[8] Romulus and Remus were seized with the desire to found a city in the region where they had been exposed and brought up. And in fact the population of Albans and Latins was too large; besides, there were the shepherds. All together, their numbers might easily lead men to Hope that Alba would be small, and Lavinium small, compared with the city which they should build. These considerations were interrupted by the curse of their grandfather and Amulius—a greed for kingly power—and by the shameful quarrel which grew out of it, upon an occasion innocent enough. Since the brothers were twins, and respect for their age could not determine between them, it was agreed that the gods who had those places in their protection should choose by augury who should give the new city its name, and govern it once it was built. Romulus took the Palatine for his augural observation post, Remus the Aventine. Remus is said to have been the first to receive an augury, from the flight of six vultures. The omen had been already reported when twice that number appeared to Romulus. Thereupon each was saluted king by his own followers, one side basing its claim on priority, the other on the number of birds. They then engaged in a battle of words and angry taunts leading to bloodshed. Remus was killed in the fight. The commoner story is that Remus leaped over the new walls in mockery of his brother, whereupon Romulus in great anger slew him, and in a menacing way added the words "So perish whoever else shall leap over my walls!

Thus Romulus acquired sole power, and the city thus founded was called by his name.

---

8 Romulus and Remus had helped their grandfather, Numitor, stage a rebellion against his brother, Amulius, in which Amulius was killed and Numitor restored to the throne.

Translated by B. O. Foster, in *Livy*. London: William Heinemann, 1919.

Polybius: The Roman Constitution

Polybius was a Greek historian taken as a hostage to Rome in 167 B.C.E. He became an admirer of Rome and sought an explanation for its success in bringing under its administration much of the western world. Here he describes the Roman constitution, with its three branches—Consuls, Senate, and people—as the best that can be found, because each branch can serve as a check against excesses of the others.

As for the Roman constitution, it had three elements, each of them possessing sovereign powers: and their respective share of power in the whole state had been regulated with such a scrupulous regard to equality and equilibrium, that no one could say for certain, not even a native, whether the constitution as a whole were an aristocracy or democracy or despotism. And no wonder: for if we confine our observation to the power of the Consuls we should be inclined to regard it as despotic; if on that of the Senate, as aristocratic; and if finally one looks at the power possessed by the people it would seem a clear case of a democracy. What the exact powers of these several parts were and still, with slight modifications, are, I will now state.

The consuls, before leading out the legions, remain in Rome and are the supreme masters of the administration. All other magistrates, except the Tribunes, are under them and take their orders. They introduce foreign ambassadors to the Senate; bring matters requiring deliberation before it; and see to the execution of the decrees. If, again, there are any matters of state which require the authorization of the people, it is their business to see to them, to summon the popular meetings, to bring the proposals before them, and to carry out the decrees of the majority. In the preparations for war also, and in a word in the entire administration of a campaign, they have all but absolute power. It is competent to them to impose on the allies such levies as they think good, to appoint the military tribunes, to make up the roll for soldiers and select those that are suitable. Besides they have absolute power of inflicting punishment on all who are under their command while on active service; and they have authority to expend as much of the public money as they choose, being accompanied by a *quaestor* who is entirely at their orders. A survey of these powers would in fact justify our describing the constitution as despotic, a clear case of royal government. Nor will it affect the truth of my description if any of the institutions I have described are changed in our time or in that of our posterity; and the same remarks apply to what follows.

The Senate has first of all control of the treasury, and regulates the receipts and disbursements alike. For the *Quaestors* cannot issue any public money for the various departments of the state without a decree of the Senate, except for the service of the Consuls. The Senate controls also what is by far the largest and most important expenditure, that, namely, which is made by the censors every *lustrum* for the repair or construction of public buildings; this money cannot be obtained by the censors except by the grant of the Senate. Similarly all crimes committed in Italy requiring a public investigation, such as treason, conspiracy, poisoning, or willful murder, are in the hands of the Senate. Besides, if any individual or state among the Italian allies requires a controversy to be settled, a penalty to be assessed, help or protection to be afforded, all this is the province of the Senate. Or again, outside Italy, if it is necessary to send an embassy to reconcile warring communities or to remind them of their duty, or sometimes to impose requisitions upon them, or to receive their submission, or finally to proclaim war against them, this too is the business of the Senate. In like manner, the reception to be given to foreign ambassadors in Rome and the answers to be returned to them, are decided by the Senate. With such business the people have nothing to do. Consequently, if one were staying at Rome when the Consuls were not in town, one would imagine the constitution to be a complete aristocracy; and this has been the idea entertained by many Greeks, and by many kings as well, from the fact that nearly all the business they had with Rome was settled by the Senate.

After this one would naturally be inclined to ask what part is left for the people in the constitution, when the Senate has these various functions, especially the control of the receipts and expenditure of the exchequer; and when the Consuls, again, have absolute power over the details of military preparation and an absolute authority in the field? There is, however, a part left the people, and it is a most important one. For the people is the sole fountain of honor and of punishment; and it is by these two things and these alone that dynasties and constitutions and, in a word, human society are held together; for where the distinction between them is not sharply drawn both in theory and practice, there no undertaking can be properly administered, as indeed we might expect when good and bad are held in exactly the same honor. The people then are the only court to decide matters of life and death; and even in cases where the penalty is money, if the sum to be assessed is sufficiently serious, and especially when the accused have held the higher magistracies. And in regard to this arrangement there is one point deserving especial commendation and record. Men who are on trial for their lives at Rome, while sentence is in process of being voted, if even only one of the tribes whose votes are needed to ratify the sentence has not voted, have the privilege at Rome of openly departing and condemning themselves to a voluntary exile. Such men are safe at Naples, or Praeneste or at Tibur, and at other towns with which this arrangement has been duly ratified on oath.

Again, it is the people who bestow offices on the deserving, which are the most honorable rewards of virtue. It has also the absolute power of passing or repealing laws; and, most important of all, it is the people who deliberate on the question of peace or war. And when provisional terms are made for alliance, suspension of hostilities, or treaties, it is the people who ratify them or the reverse.

These considerations, again, would lead one to say that the chief power in the state was the people's, and that the constitution was a democracy.

Such, then, is the distribution of power between the several parts of the state. I must now show how each of these several parts can, when they choose, oppose or support each other.

The Consul, then, when he has started on an expedition with the powers I have described, is to all appearance absolute in the administration of the business in hand; still he has need of the support both of people and Senate, and, without them, is quite unable to bring the matter to a successful conclusion. For it is plain that he must have supplies sent to his legions from time to time; but without a decree of the Senate they can be supplied neither with grain, nor clothes, nor pay, so that all the plans of a commander must be futile if the Senate is resolved either to shrink from danger or hamper his plans. And, again, whether a Consul shall bring any undertaking to a conclusion or no depends entirely upon the Senate; for it has absolute authority at the end of a year to send another Consul to supersede him, or to continue the existing one in his command. Again, even to the successes of the generals the Senate has the power to add distinction and glory, and on the other hand to obscure their merits and lower their credit. For these high achievements are brought in tangible form before the eyes of the citizens by what are called "triumphs." But these triumphs the commanders cannot celebrate at all, unless the Senate concurs and grants the necessary money. As for the people, the Consuls are pre-eminently obliged to court their favor, however distant from home may be the field of their operations; for it is the people, as I have said before, that ratifies or refuses to ratify terms of peace and treaties; but most of all because when laying down their office they have to give an account of their administration before it. Therefore in no case is it safe for the Consuls to neglect either the Senate or the good will of the people.

As for the Senate, which possesses the immense power I have described, in the first place it is obliged in public affairs to take the multitude into account, and respect the wishes of the people; and it cannot put into execution the penalty for offences against the republic which are punishable with death, unless the people first ratify its decrees. Similarly, even in matters which directly affect the Senators, for instance in the case of a law diminishing the Senate's traditional authority, or depriving Senators of certain dignities and offices, or even actually cutting down their property, even in such cases the people have the sole power of passing or rejecting the law. But most important of all is the fact that, if the Tribunes interpose their veto, the Senate not only are unable to pass a decree, but cannot even hold a meeting at all, whether formal or informal. Now, the Tribunes are always bound to carry out the decree of the people, and above all things to have regard to their wishes; therefore, for all these reasons, the Senate stands in awe of the multitude and cannot neglect the feelings of the people.

In like manner the people on its part is far from being independent of the Senate, and is bound to take its wishes into account both collectively and individually. For contracts too numerous to count are given out by the censors in all parts of Italy for the repairs or construction of public buildings; there is also the collection of revenue from many rivers, harbors, gardens, mines, and land; everything, in a word, that comes under the control of the Roman government. And in all these the people at large are engaged; so that there is scarcely a man, so to speak, who is not interested either as a contractor or as being employed in the works. For some purchase the contracts from the censors for themselves; and others go partners with them; while others again go security for these contractors, or actually pledge their property to the treasury for them. Now over all these transactions the Senate has absolute control. It can grant an extension of time; and in case of unforeseen accident can relieve the contractors from a portion of their obligation, or release them from it altogether if they are absolutely unable to fulfill it. And there are many details in which the Senate can inflict great hardships, or, on the other hand, grant great indulgences to the contractors; for in every case the appeal is to it. But the most important point of all is that the judges are taken from its members in the majority of trials, whether public or private, in which the charges are heavy. Consequently, all citizens are much at its mercy; and being alarmed at the uncertainty as to when they may need its aid, are cautious about resisting or actively opposing its will. And for a similar reason men do not rashly resist the wishes of the Consuls, because one and all may become subject to their absolute authority on a campaign.

The result of this power of the several estates for mutual help or harm is a union sufficiently firm for all emergencies, and a constitution than which it is impossible to find a better. For whenever any danger from without compels them to unite and work together, the strength which is developed by the State is so extraordinary that everything required is unfailingly carried out by the eager rivalry shown by all classes to devote their whole minds to the need of the hour, and to secure that any determination come to should not fail for want of promptitude; while each individual works, privately and publicly alike, for the accomplishment of the business in hand. Accordingly, the peculiar constitution of the State makes it irresistible, and certain of obtaining whatever it determines to attempt. Nay, even when these external alarms are past, and the people are enjoying their good fortune and the fruits of their victories, and, as usually happens, growing corrupted by flattery and idleness, show a tendency to violence and arrogance--it is in these circumstances more than ever that the constitution is seen to possess within itself the power of correcting abuses. For when any one of the three classes becomes puffed up, and manifests an inclination to be contentious and unduly encroaching, the mutual interdependence of all the three and the possibility of the pretensions of one being checked and thwarted by the others, must plainly check this tendency; and so the proper equilibrium is maintained by the impulsiveness of the one part being checked by its fear of the other. . . .

Translated by Evelyn S. Shuckburgh in The Histories of Polybius. London. 1889.

The Twelve Tables, c. 450 B.C.E.

> The Twelve Tables, or tablets, contained the first written Roman law. It is essentially a codification of existing customs, and was written at the insistence of the plebeians during their struggle to attain equality (at least equality before the law) with the patricians during the Struggle of the Orders. The law was never formally repealed and remained the foundation of Roman law until the *Corpus Juris Civilis* of Justinian 1,000 years later.

TABLE I: PRELIMINARIES TO AND RULES FOR A TRIAL

If plaintiff summons defendant to court, he shall go. If he does not go, plaintiff shall call witness thereto. Then only shall he take defendant by force.

If defendant shirks or takes to his heels, plaintiff shall lay hands on him

If disease or age is an impediment, he (who summons defendant to court) shall grant him a team; he shall not spread with cushions the covered carriage if he does not so desire.

For a landowner, a landowner shall be surety; but for a proletarian person, let any one who is willing be his protector.

There shall be the same right of bond and conveyance with the Roman people for a person restored to allegiance as for a loyal person.

When parties make a settlement of the case, the judge shall announce it. If they do not reach a settlement, they shall state the outline of their case in the meeting place or Forum before noon.

They shall plead it out together in person. After noon, the judge shall adjudge the case to the party present. If both be present, sunset shall be the time limit (of proceedings.)

TABLE IV: *PATRIA POTESTAS*: RIGHTS OF THE HEAD OF FAMILY

Quickly kill . . .a dreadfully deformed child.

If a father thrice surrender a son for sale, the son shall be free from the father.

A child born ten months after the father's death will not be admitted into a legal inheritance.

TABLE VI: ACQUISITION AND POSSESSION

Usucapio[9] of movable things requires one year's possession for its completion; but *usucapio* of an estate and buildings two years.

Any woman who does not wish to be subjected in this manner to the hand of her husband should be absent three nights in succession every year, and so interrupt the *usucapio* of each year.[10]

TABLE VIII: TORTS OR DELICTS

If any person has sung or composed against another person a song such as was causing slander or insult to another, he shall be clubbed to death.

If a person has maimed another's limb, let there be retaliation in kind unless he makes agreement for settlement with him. . .

If theft has been done by night, if the owner kill the thief, the thief shall be held lawfully killed.

It is forbidden that a thief be killed by day . . . unless he defend himself with a weapon; even though he has come with a weapon, unless he use his weapon and fight back, you shall not kill him. And even if he resists, first call out.

In the case of all other thieves caught in the act, if they are freemen, they should be flogged and adjudged to the person against whom the theft has been committed, provided that the malefactors have committed it by day and have not defended themselves with a weapon; slaves caught in the act of theft should be flogged and thrown from the Rock; boys under the age of puberty should, at the praetor's discretion, be flogged, and the damage done by them should be repaired.

TABLE XI: SUPPLEMENTARY LAWS

Intermarriage shall not take place between plebeians and patricians.

from *Roman Civilization* by Naphtali Lewis and Meyer Reinhold. ©Columbia University Press. 1951. Reprinted with permission of the publisher.

Unit 12: The Roman Family

Letter From Pliny to His Wife, c. 110 B.C.E.

Pliny was governor of Bithynia under the emperor Trajan. This letter indicates the passion and emotional attachment that were possible in a Roman marriage.

---

9 ownership acquired through long-term possession.

10 Ordinarily, a woman, when she married, moved from the guardianship of her father to the guardianship of her husband. This law represents a form of marriage without *manus*. The husband does not gain legal control of his wife. She remains in the guardianship of her father. Because her father would probably die before her husband, she might by this means hope to gain control of her own life at an earlier age.

I am seized by unbelievable longing for you. The reason is above all my love, but secondarily the fact that we are not used to being apart. This is why I spend the greater part of the night haunted by your image; this is why from time to time my feet lead me (the right expression!) of their own accord to your room at the times I was accustomed to frequent you; this is why, in short, I retreat, morbid and disconsolate, like an excluded lover from an unwelcoming doorway. The only time free of these torments is time spent in the forum and in friends' law cases. Just imagine what my life is like—I, for whom you are the respite from toil, the solace of my wretchedness and anxieties. Farewell.

Pliny, *Epistles*, 7.5. From Suzanne Dixon, *The Roman Family*. © 1992. The Johns Hopkins University Press.

Protest Speech of Hortensia, 42 B.C.E.

The Second Triumvirate (Octavian, Marc Antony, and Lepidus) made an edict that fourteen hundred of the richest women in Rome should submit valuations of their personal property in anticipation of a war tax to be imposed on them. Hortensia protested their action in a speech in the Forum. Contemporary written versions of the speech have disappeared. This selection is from a paraphrase by Appian, written in the late first or early second century C.E. It demonstrates that Roman women could own substantial property and could participate in public life to the extent of protesting political actions they deemed wrong.

As was appropriate for women such as ourselves in need of something from you, we dispatched ourselves to your womenfolk. But we were rudely treated by Fulvia[11] and have thus been forced to come to the Forum. You have already taken away from us our fathers, sons, husbands, and brothers, whom you accused of having done wrong to you; if you should also take away our possessions, you will reduce us to straits unworthy of our birth, manners, and female nature. If you claim that you have been wronged at our hands, as you say you have by our husbands, then proscribe us as you do them. But if we women have neither voted any of you an enemy, nor torn down your houses, nor destroyed your army, nor led one of you against another, nor prevented you from obtaining public office or honor--then why should we have a share in the penalty even though we had no share in the guilt?

Why should we pay taxes when we have no share at all in public office, in honors, in military commands, or in government—all of which you fight over to our detriment? "Because," do you say, "this is war?" And when have there not been wars? When have women ever been taxed--whose very nature exempts them among all peoples?

Still our mothers once did go beyond what is natural and did pay taxes, when you were in danger of losing the entire empire and the City itself during the Carthaginian troubles. But they contributed the tax of their own free will—and not from their land or estates or dowry or houses, without which life is unlivable for freeborn women; rather, they contributed only from their jewelry, and these items were not appraised by informers and accusers through force or violence. The women themselves gave whatever amount they wished.

What, then, is your fear now on behalf of the empire or our fatherland? Let there be war with the Celts or the Parthians, and we will come to the rescue no less readily than our mothers did. But may we never contribute towards civil war nor lend aid for you to fight with each other.

---

11 wife of Marc Antony.

We did not help Caesar or Pompey, nor did Marius or Cinna or even Sulla—that tyrant of the fatherland—impose taxes on us. And you—you claim to be re-establishing legal government!

Appian, *Bellium Civile* 4:32-33, in *Appian's Roman History*, edited and translated by Horace White, 4 vols. London: Heinemann, 1912-13.

Unit 13: Demise of the Roman Republic

Sources for the last two centuries of the Republic are more plentiful and more varied than for its inception. Polybius wrote histories in the second century, Livy, Sallust, and Julius Caesar in the first. For the second century, we have the plays of Plautus and Terence; for the first century, the poetry of Ovid, Horace, and Catullus and the philosophy of Lucretius. Varro, a scholar and satirist, wrote 74 works in 600 books. Much of his work has been lost, but it was available to historians during the early Empire.

Tacitus in the first century C.E. and Appian in the second wrote histories of the Republic. Though they did not themselves witness the events they describe, they relied on earlier works which have since disappeared. Plutarch's *Parallel Lives*, in which he compares Roman heroes with their Greek counterparts, is an important biographical source.

The crucial years in the destruction of the Republic, from 82 to 44 B.C.E., are documented in more detail than any other period of Roman history, due to the abundance of speeches and letters by a man who was deeply involved, holding the highest state offices and considered the greatest orator of ancient times—Cicero.

Plutarch: from *The Life of Tiberius Gracchus*

The Roman constitution was not a written document, but a collection of traditions and laws developed over centuries. They are described above by Polybius. The tribune was the plebians' representative in the Senate. His veto (meaning "I object") could invalidate the actions of consuls, other magistrates, and the plebian assembly itself. A tribune was inviolable. To kill a tribune was to defy the Constitution and to call down the wrath of the gods. He could not be ousted from office. Because of his extensive power, a tribune could serve only one term. Tiberius Gracchus, in his passion for land reform, which would help to relieve poverty, defied two Constitutional prohibitions—he ousted a fellow tribune and he ran for office for a second term. His murder, encouraged if not committed by Senators, defied another. These events are often considered the beginning of the downfall of the Roman Republic.

. . . When the Romans in their wars made any acquisitions of lands from their neighbours, they used formerly to sell part, to add part to the public demesnes, and to distribute the rest among the necessitous citizens; only reserving a small rent to be paid into the treasury. But when the rich began to carry it with a high hand over the poor, and to exclude them entirely, if they did not pay exorbitant rents, a law was made that no man should be possessed of more than 500 acres of land. This statute for awhile restrained the avarice of the rich, and helped the poor, who, by virtue of it, remained upon their lands at the old rents. But afterwards their wealthy neighbours took their farms from them, and held them in other names; though, in time, they scrupled not to claim them in their own. The poor thus expelled, neither gave in their names readily to the levies, nor attended to the education of their children. The consequence was a want of freemen all over Italy, for it was filled with slaves and barbarians, who, after the poor Roman citizens were dispossessed, cultivated the ground for the rich. Caius Laelius, the friend of Scipio, attempted to correct this disorder; but finding a formidable opposition from persons in power, and fearing the matter could not be decided without the sword, he gave it up. This gained him the name of Laelius the wise. But Tiberius was no sooner appointed tribune of the people, that he embarked in the same enterprise. . . .

. . .His brother Caius writes that, as Tiberius was passing through Tuscany on his way to Numantia, and found the country almost depopulated, there being scarce any husbandmen or shepherds, except slaves from foreign and barbarous nations, he then first formed the project which plunged them into so many misfortunes. It is certain, however, that the people inflamed his spirit of enterprise and ambition, by putting up writings on the porticoes, walls and monuments, in which they begged of him to restore their share of the public lands to the poor.

Yet he did not frame the law without consulting some of the Romans that were most distinguished for their virtue and authority. Among these were Crassus the chief pontiff, Mutius Scaevola the lawyer, who at that time was also consul, and Appius Claudius, father-in-law to Tiberius. There never was a milder law made against so much injustice and oppression. For they who deserved to have been punished for their infringement on the rights of the community, and fined for holding the lands contrary to law, were to have a consideration for giving up their groundless claims, and restoring the estates to such of the citizens as were to be relieved. But though the reformation was conducted with so much tenderness, the people were satisfied; they were willing to overlook what was passed, on condition that they might guard against future usurpations.

On the other hand, persons of great property opposed the law out of avarice, and the lawgiver out of a spirit of resentment and malignity; endeavouring to prejudice the people against the design, as if Tiberius intended by the Agrarian law to throw all into disorder and subvert the constitution. But their attempts were vain. For, in this just and glorious cause, Tiberius exerted an eloquence which might have adorned a worse subject, and which nothing could resist. How great was he, when the people were gathered about the rostrum, and he pleaded for the poor in such language as this:

The wild beasts of Italy have their caves to retire to; but the brave men who spill their blood in her cause have nothing left but air and light. Without houses, without any settled habitations, they wander from place to place with their wives and children; and their generals do but mock them, when, at the head of their armies, they exhort their men to fight for their sepulchres and domestic gods; for, among such numbers, perhaps there is not a Roman who has an altar that belonged to his ancestors, or a sepulchre in which their ashes rest. The private soldiers fight and die to advance the wealth and luxury of the great; and they are called masters of the world, while they have not a foot of ground in their possession.

Such speeches as this, delivered by a man of such spirit, and flowing from a heart really interested in the cause, filled the people with an enthusiastic fury; and none of his adversaries durst pretend to answer him. Forbearing, therefore, the war of words, they addressed themselves to Marcus Octavius, one of the tribunes, a grave and modest young man, and an intimate acquaintance of Tiberius. Out of reverence for his friend, he declined the task at first; but upon a number of applications from men of the first rank, he was prevailed upon to oppose Tiberius, and prevent the passing of the law; for the tribune's power chiefly lies in the negative voice, and if one of them stands out, the rest can effect nothing.

Incensed by this behaviour, Tiberius dropped his moderate bill, and proposed another more agreeable to the commonalty, and more severe against the usurpers. For by this they were commanded immediately to quit the lands which they held contrary to former laws. On this subject there were daily disputes between him and Octavius on the *rostra*; yet not one abusive or disparaging word is said to have escaped either of them in all the heat of speaking. Indeed an ingenuous disposition and liberal education will prevent or restrain the sallies of passion, not only during the free enjoyment of the bottle, but in the ardour of contention about points of a superior nature.

Tiberius, observing that Octavius was liable to suffer by the bill, as having more land than the laws could warrant, desired him to give up his opposition, and offered, at the same time, to indemnify him out of his own fortune, though that was not great. As this proposal was not accepted, Tiberius forbade all other magistrates to exercise their functions, till the Agrarian law was passed. He likewise put his own seal upon the doors of the temple of Saturn, that the *quaestors* might neither bring anything into the treasury, nor take anything out. And he threatened to fine such of the praetors as should attempt to disobey his command. This struck such a terror that all departments of government were at a stand. Persons of great property put themselves in mourning, and appeared in public with all the circumstances that they thought might excite compassion. Not satisfied with this, they conspired the death of Tiberius, and suborned assassins to destroy him; for which reason he appeared with a tuck, such as is used by robbers, which the Romans call a *dolon*.[12]

When the day appointed came, and Tiberius was summoning the people to give their suffrages, a party of the people of property carried off the balloting vessels, which occasioned great confusion. Tiberius, however, seemed strong enough to carry his point by force, and his partisans were preparing to have recourse to it, when Manlius and Fulvius, men of conular dignity, fell at Tiberius's feet, bathed his hands with tears, and conjured him not to put his purpose into execution. He now perceived how dreadful the consequences of his attempt might be, and his reverence for those two great men had its effect upon him; he therefore asked what they would have him do. They said, they were not capable of advising him in so important an affair, and earnestly entreated him to refer it to the senate. The senate assembled to deliberate upon it, but the influence of the people of fortune on that body was such that the debates ended in nothing.

Tiberius then adopted a measure that was neither just nor moderate. He resolved to remove Octavius from the tribuneship, because there was no other means to get his law passed. He addressed him indeed in public first, in a mild and friendly manner, and taking him by the hand, conjured him to gratify the people, who asked nothing that was unjust, and would only receive a small recompense for the great labours and dangers they had experienced. But Octavius absolutely refused to comply. Tiberius then declared, "That as it was not possible for two magistrates of equal authority, when they differed in such capital points, to go through the remainder of their office without coming to hostilities, he saw no other remedy but the deposing of them." He therefore desired Octavius to take the sense of the people first with respect to him; assuring him

---

12 A staff with a concealed dagger

that he would immediately return to a private station, if the suffrages of his fellow-citizens should order it so. As Octavius rejected this proposal too, Tiberius told him plainly that he would put the question to the people concerning him, if upon farther consideration he did not alter his mind.

Upon this he dismissed the assembly. Next day he convoked it again; and when he had mounted the *rostra*, he made another trial to bring Octavius to compliance. But finding him inflexible, he proposed a decree for depriving him of the tribuneship, and immediately put it to the vote. When, of the five and thirty tribes, seventeen had given their voices for it, and there wanted only one more to make Octavius a private man, Tiberius ordered them to stop, and once more applied to his colleague. He embraced him with great tenderness in the sight of the people, and with the most pressing instances besought him neither to bring such a mark of infamy upon himself, nor expose him to the disreputation of being promoter of such severe and violent measures. It was not without emotion that Octavius is said to have listened to these entreaties. His eyes were filled with tears, and he stood a long time silent. But when he looked towards the persons of property, who were assembled in a body, shame and fear of losing himself in their opinion brought him back to his resolution to run all risks, and, with a noble firmness, he bade Tiberius do his pleasure. The bill, therefore, was passed; and Tiberius ordered one of his freedmen to pull down Octavius from the tribunal. For he employed his own freedmen as lictors. This ignominious manner of expulsion made the case of Octavius more pitiable. The people, notwithstanding, fell upon him; but by the assistance of those of the landed interest, who came to his defence, and kept off the mob, he escaped with his life. However, a faithful servant of his, who stood before him to ward off the danger, had his eyes torn out. This violence was much against the will of Tiberius, who no sooner saw the tumult rising, than he hastened down to appease it.

The Agrarian law then was confirmed, and three commissioners appointed to take a survey of the lands, and see them properly distributed. Tiberius was one of the three; his father-in-law, Appius Claudius, another; and his brother, Caius Gracchus, the third. The latter was then making the campaign under Scipio at Numantia. Tiberius having carried these point without opposition, next filled up the vacant tribune's seat; into which he did not put a man of any note, but Mutius, one of his own clients. These proceedings exasperated the patricians extremely, and as they dreaded the increase of his power, they took every opportunity to insult him in the senate. When he desired, for instance, what was nothing more than customary, a tent at the public charge, for his use in dividing the lands, they refused him one, though such things had been often granted on much less important occasions. And, at the motion of Publius Nasica, he had only nine *oboli* a day allowed for his expenses. Nasica, indeed was become his avowed enemy, for he had a great estate in the public lands, and was of course unwilling to be stripped of it. . . .

> (The land reform, though passed by the Senate, was not carried out. In continuing to agitate for the se and other reforms, Tiberius got himself elected to the tribuneship for a second year. In a riot allegedly started by Nasica, Tiberius was killed. The Senate refused to release his body to his brother Gaius for a proper burial; it was thrown into the river.)

The senate, now desirous to reconcile the people to these acts of theirs, no longer opposed the Agrarian law; and they permitted them to elect another commissioner, in the place of Tiberius, for dividing the lands.

From Plutarch's *Lives*, translated by Langhorne. London: Frederick Warne, 1884.

Plutarch: Julius Caesar

The Roman Republic used a lunar calendar, with 355 days. In order to keep it from becoming too far out of step with the solar year, an extra month was inserted every two years, between February 23 and 24. The intercalation was the duty of the priests. They sometimes manipulated it for their own political gain. Caesar instituted a solar calendar of 365 days, with an added day every fourth year. This was still out of step with the solar year by 11 minutes and 14 seconds, but the Julian calendar was used until 1582 C.E., when it was adjusted by Pope Gregory XIII.

According to tradition, when the Romans expelled King Tarquin and formed a Republic in 509 B.C.E., they swore that the title Rex, or King, would never again be used in Rome. Julius Caesar had already subverted the republic by being named dictator for life, but it may have been his flirting with the possibility of being named king that pushed his detractors to assassinate him. His disrespect for the office of tribune also played a part.

He completed, however, the regulations of the calendar, and corrected the erroneous computation of time, agreeably to a plan which he had ingeniously contrived, and which proved of the greatest utility. For it was not only in ancient times that the Roman months so ill agreed with the revolution of the year, that the festivals and days of sacrifice, by little and little, fell back into seasons quite opposite to those of their institution; but even in the time of Caesar, when the solar year was made use of, the generality lived in perfect ignorance of the matter; and the priests, who were the only persons that knew any thing about it, used to add, all at once, and when nobody expected it, an intercalary month, called Mercidonius, of which Numa was the inventor. That remedy, however, proved much too weak, and was far from operating extensively enough to correct the great miscomputations of time; as we have observed in that prince's life.

Caesar having proposed the question to the most able philosophers and mathematicians, published, upon principles already verified, a new and more exact regulation, which the Romans still go by, and by that means are nearer the truth than other nations with respect to the difference between the sun's revolution and that of the twelve months. Yet this useful invention furnished matter of ridicule to the envious, and to those who could but ill brook his power. For Cicero, (if I mistake not), when some one happened to say,—"Lyra will rise tomorrow," answered,—"Undoubtedly; there is an edict for it:" as if the calendar was forced upon them, as well as other things.

But the principal thing that excited the public hatred, and at last caused his death, was his passion for the title of king. It was the first thing that gave offence to the multitude, and it afforded his inveterate enemies a very plausible plea. Those who wanted to procure him that honour, gave it out among the people, that it appeared, from the Sibylline books,—"The Romans could never conquer the Parthians, except they went to war under the conduct of a king." And one day, when Caesar returned from Alba to Rome, some of his retainers ventured to salute him by that title. Observing that the people were troubled at this strange compliment, he put on an air of resentment, and said,—"He was not called king, but Caesar." Upon this, a deep silence ensued, and he passed on in no good humour.

Another time the senate having decreed him some extravagant honours, the consuls and praetors, attended by the whole body of patricians, went to inform him of what they had done. When they came, he did not rise to receive them, but kept his seat, as if they had been persons in a private station; and his answer to their address was,—"That there was more need to retrench his honours, than to enlarge them." This haughtiness gave pain not only to the senate, but the people, who thought the contempt of that body reflected dishonour upon the whole commonwealth; for all who could decently withdraw, went off greatly dejected.

Perceiving the false step he had taken, he retired immediately to his own house; and laying his neck bare, told his friends,—"He was ready for the first hand that would strike." He then bethought himself of alleging his distemper as an excuse, and asserted, that those who are under its influence, are apt to find their faculties fail them when they speak standing; a trembling and giddiness coming upon them, which bereaves them of their senses. This, however, was not really the case; for it is said he was desirous to rise to the senate; but Cornelius Balbus, one of his friends, or rather flatterers, held him, and had servility enough to say,—"Will you not remember that you are Caesar, and suffer them to pay their court to you as their superior." These discontents were greatly increased by the indignity with which he treated the tribunes of the people. In the Lupercalia, which, according to most writers, is an ancient pastoral feast, and which answers in many respects to the Lycaea among the Arcadians, young men of noble families, and indeed many of the magistrates, run about the streets naked, and, by way of diversion, strike all they meet with leather thongs with the hair upon them. Numbers of women of the first quality put themselves in their way, and present their hands for stripes (as scholars do to a master), being persuaded that the pregnant gain an easy delivery by it, and that the barren are enabled to conceive. Caesar wore a triumphal robe that day, and seated himself in a golden chair upon the *rostra*, to see the ceremony.

Antony ran among the rest, in compliance with the rules of the festival, for he was consul. When he came into the forum, and the crowd had made way for him, he approached Caesar, and offered him a diadem wreathed with laurel. Upon this some plaudits were heard, but very feeble, because they proceeded only from persons placed there on purpose. Caesar refused it, and then the plaudits were loud and general. Antony presented it once more, and few applauded his officiousness; but when Caesar rejected it again, the applause again was general. Caesar, undeceived by his second trial, rose up, and ordered the diadem to be consecrated in the Capitol.

A few days after, his statues were seen adorned with royal diadems; and Flavius and Marullus, two of the tribunes, went and tore them off. They also found out the persons who first saluted Caesar king, and committed them to prison. The people followed with cheerful acclamations, and called them Brutuses, because Brutus was the man who expelled the kings, and put the government in the hands of the senate and people. Caesar, highly incensed at their behaviour, deposed the tribunes; and by way of reprimand to them, as well as insult to the people, called them several times Brutes and Cumoeans.

From Plutarch's Lives, translated by John Langhorne and William Langhorne. London, 1819.

Cicero: The Third Philippic, 44/43 B.C.E.

After the death of Julius Caesar, Cicero wrote fourteen Philippics,[13] in which he tried to rouse the senate to oppose Marc Antony's bid to claim for himself the dictatorial power that Cacsar had exercised.. In this speech, he compares Marc Antony to King Tarquin, who had been overthrown to create the Republic.

---

13 so called because they imitated the speeches of Demosthenes against Philip of Macedon.

Soon after Antony, Octavian, and Lepidus formed the Second Triumvirate, Cicero was captured and executed. His head and hands were displayed on the *rostra*, the speakers' platform in the Forum.

We have been assembled at length, O conscript fathers,[14] altogether later than the necessities of the republic required; but still we are assembled; a measure which I, indeed, have been every day demanding; inasmuch as I saw that a nefarious war against our altars and our hearths, against our lives and our fortunes, was, I will not say being prepared, but being actually waged by a profligate and desperate man. People are waiting for the first of January. But Antonius is not waiting for that day, who is now attempting with an army to invade the province of Decimus Brutus, a most illustrious and excellent man. And when he has procured reinforcements and the equipments there, he threatens that he will come to this city. What is the use then of waiting, or of even a delay for the very shortest time? For although the first of January is at hand, still a short time is a long one for people who are not prepared. For a day, or I should rather say an hour, often brings great disasters, if no precautions are taken. And it is not usual to wait for a fixed day for holding a council, as it is for celebrating a festival. But if the first of January had fallen on the day when Antonius first fled from the city, or if people had not waited for it, we should by this time have no war at all. For we should easily have crushed the audacity of that frantic man by the authority of the senate and the unanimity of the Roman people. And now, indeed, I feel confident that the consuls elect will do so, as soon as they enter on their magistracy. For they are men of the highest courage, of the most consummate wisdom, and they will act in perfect harmony with each other. But my exhortations to rapid and instant action are prompted by a desire not merely for victory, but for speedy victory.

For how long are we to trust to the prudence of an individual to repel so important, so cruel, and so nefarious a war? Why is not the public authority thrown into the scale as quickly as possible?

Caius Caesar,[15] a young man, or I should rather say, almost a boy, endued with an incredible and godlike degree of wisdom and valour, at the time when the frenzy of Antonius was at its height, and when his cruel and mischievous return from Brundusium was an object of apprehension to all, while we neither desired him to do so, nor thought of such a measure, nor ventured even to wish it, (because it did not seem practicable,) collected a most trustworthy army from the invincible body of veteran soldiers, and has spent his own patrimony in doing so. Although I have not used the expression which I ought,—for he has not spent it,—he has invested it in the safety of the republic.

And although it is not possible to requite him with all the thanks to which he is entitled, still we ought to feel all the gratitude towards him which our minds are capable of conceiving. For who is so ignorant of public affairs, so entirely indifferent to all thoughts of the republic, as not to see that, if Marcus Antonius could have come with those forces which he made sure that he should have, from Brundusium to Rome, as he threatened, there would have been no description of cruelty which he would not have practised? A man who in the house of his entertainer at

---

14 the formal title by which Roman Senators were addressed.

15 Octavian, Caesar's great-nephew, had been adopted by Caesar and so bore his name. Cicero backed Octavian against Marc Antony, hoping that, once Antony was out of the way, Rome could return to a republican model of government. Octavian was only eighteen at this time. Cicero wrongly thought he would be unable to take the sort of control held by Caesar and sought by Antony.

Brundusium ordered so many most gallant men and virtuous citizens to be murdered, and whose wife's face was notoriously besprinkled with the blood of men dying at his and her feet. Who is there of us, or what good man is there at all, whom a man stained with this barbarity would ever have spared; especially as he was coming hither much more angry with all virtuous men than he had been with those whom he had massacred there? And from this calamity Caesar has delivered the republic by his own individual prudence, (and, indeed, there were no other means by which it could have been done). And if he had not been born in this republic we should, owing to the wickedness of Antonius, now have no republic at all.

For this is what I believe, this is my deliberate opinion, that if that one young man had not checked the violence and inhuman projects of that frantic man, the republic would have been utterly destroyed. And to him we must, O conscript fathers, (for this is the first time, met in such a condition, that, owing to his good service, we are at liberty to say freely what we think and feel,) we must, I say, this day give authority, so that he may be able to defend the republic, not because that defence has been voluntarily undertaken by him but also because it has been entrusted to him by us.

Nor (since now after a long interval we are allowed to speak concerning the republic) is it possible for us to be silent about the Martial legion. For what single man has ever been braver, what single man has ever been more devoted to the republic than the whole of the Martial legion? Which, as soon as it had decided that Marcus Antonius was an enemy of the Roman people, refused to be a companion of his insanity; deserted him though consul; which, in truth, it would not have done if it had considered him as consul, who, as it saw, was aiming at nothing and preparing nothing but the slaughter of the citizens, and the destruction of the state. And that legion has encamped at Alba. What city could it have selected either more suitable for enabling it to act, or more faithful, or full of more gallant men, or of citizens more devoted to the republic?

The fourth legion, imitating the virtue of this legion, under the leadership of Lucius Egnatuleius, the *quaestor*, a most virtuous and intrepid citizen, has also acknowledged the authority and joined the army of Caius Caesar.

We, therefore, O conscript fathers, must take care that those things which this most illustrious young man, this most excellent of all men has of his own accord done, and still is doing, be sanctioned by our authority; and the admirable unanimity of the veterans, those most brave men, and of the Martial and of the fourth legion, in their zeal for the reestablishment of the republic, be encouraged by our praise and commendation. And let us pledge ourselves this day that their advantage, and honours, and rewards shall be cared for by us as soon as the consuls elect have entered on their magistracy.

And the things which I have said about Caesar and about his army are, indeed, already well known to you. For by the admirable valour of Caesar, and by the firmness of the veteran soldiers, and by the admirable discernment of those legions which have followed our authority, and the liberty of the Roman people, and the valour of Caear, Antonius has been repelled from his attempts upon our lives. But these things, as I have said, happened before; but this recent edict of Decimus Brutus, which has just been issued, can certainly not be passed over in silence. For he promises to preserve the province of Gaul in obedience to the senate and people of Rome. O citizen, born for the republic; mindful of the name he bears; imitator of his ancestors! Nor, indeed, was the acquisition of liberty so much an object of desire to our ancestors when Tarquinius was expelled, as, now that Antonius is driven away, the preservation of it is to us. Those men had learnt to obey kings ever since the foundation of the city, but we from the time when the kings were driven out have forgotten how to be slaves. And that Tarquinius, whom our ancestors expelled, was not either considered or called cruel or impious, but only The Proud. That vice which we have often borne in private individuals, our ancestors could not endure even in a king.

Lucius Brutus could not endure a proud king. Shall Decimus Brutus submit to the kingly power of a man who is wicked and impious? What atrocity did Tarquinius ever commit equal to the innumerable acts of the sort which Antonius has done and is still doing? Again, the kings were used to consult the senate; nor, as is the case when Antonius holds a senate, were armed barbarians ever introduced into the council of the king. The kings paid due regard to the auspices, which this man, though consul and augur, has neglected, not only by passing laws in opposition to the auspices, but also by making his colleague (whom he himself had appointed irregularly, and had falsified the auspices in order to do so) join in passing them. Again, what king was ever so preposterously impudent as to have all the profits, and kindnesses, and privileges of his kingdom on sale? But what immunity is there, what rights of citizenship, what rewards that this man has not sold to individuals, and to cities, and to entire provinces? We have never heard of anything base or sordid being imputed to Tarquinius. But at the house of this man gold was constantly being weighed out in the spinning room, and money was being paid, and in one single house every soul who had any interest in the business was selling the whole empire of the Roman people. We have never heard of any executions of Roman citizens by the orders of Tarquinius; but this man both at Suessa murdered the man whom he had thrown into prison, and at Brundusium massacred about three hundred most gallant men and most virtuous citizens. Lastly, Tarquinius was conducting a war in defence of the Roman people at the very time when he was expelled. Antonius was leading an army against the Roman people at the time when, being abandoned by the legions, he cowered at the name of Caesar and at his army, and neglecting the regular sacrifices, he offered up before daylight vows which he could never mean to perform; and at this very moment he is endeavouring to invade a province of the Roman people. The Roman people, therefore, has already received and is still looking for greater services at the hand of Decimus Brutus than our ancestors received from Lucius Brutus,[16] the founder of this race and name which we ought to be so anxious to preserve.

But, while all slavery is miserable, to be slave to a man who is profligate, unchaste, effeminate, never, not even while in fear, sober, is surely intolerable. He, then, who keeps this man out of Gaul, especially by his own private authority, judges, and judges most truly, that he is not consul at all. We must take care, therefore, O conscript fathers, to sanction the private decision of Decimus Brutus by public authority. Nor, indeed, ought you to have thought Marcus Antonius consul at any time since the Lupercalia.[17] For on the day when he, in the sight of the Roman people, harangued the mob, naked, perfumed, and drunk, and laboured moreover to put a crown on the head of his colleague, on that day he abdicated not only the consulship, but also his own freedom. At all events he himself must at once have become a slave, if Caesar had been willing to accept from him that ensign of royalty. Can I then think him a consul, can I think him a Roman citizen, can I think him a freeman, can I even think him a man, who on that shameful and

---

16 Lucius Brutus led the rebellion in which Tarquinius was overthrown.
17 A fertility festival that took place in February.

wicked day showed what he was willing to endure while Caesar lived, and what he was anxious to obtain himself after he was dead? . . .

Translated by C. D. Yonge. London: G. Bell & Sons, 1872.

CHAPTER 6: THE ROAMN EMPIRE

Unit 13: Creation of an Empire

The period of the Civil Wars and the conversion of the Republic to an Empire was also the period when Rome produced its greatest writing—the poetry of Horace, Virgil, Ovid, and Juvenal, the novels of Petronius, the biographies of Plutarch, the histories of Livy and Tacitus, the letters of Pliny the Younger, the plays, philosophy, and speeches of Seneca.

Physical evidence from this era is abundant. The reign of Augustus was an age of architectural and artistic fervor. Paintings, mosaics, and sculpture depict Romans at work and play. Many of the great building projects of the early Empire—roads, baths, theatres, and aqueducts—can still be seen, and some are still in use. The eruption of Mt. Vesuvius in 79 C.E. left two towns, Pompeii and Herculaneum, almost perfectly preserved beneath a bed of ash. Excavations have revealed houses, gardens, furnishings, jewelry, and even the remains of food prepared but uneaten when the disaster struck.

The Deeds of Augustus

Octavian, or Augustus, was a masterful manipulator of public opinion. In this account he tells plainly the many steps he took to gather control of the Roman state into his own hands, but insists throughout that he was only acting as a concerned citizen of the Republic.

In my twentieth year, acting upon my own judgment and at my own expense, I raised an army by means of which I restored to liberty the commonwealth which had been oppressed by the tyranny of a faction. On account of this the senate by laudatory decrees admitted me to its order, in the consulship of Gaius Pansa and Aulus Hirtius, and at the same time gave me consular rank in the expression of opinion, and gave me the imperium. It also voted that I as *propraetor*, together with the consuls, should see to it that the commonwealth suffered no harm. In the same year, moreover, when both consuls had perished in war, the people made me consul, and triumvir for organizing the commonwealth.

Those who killed my father I drove into exile by lawful judgments, avenging their crime, and afterwards, when they waged war against the commonwealth, I twice defeated them in battle. . .

The dictatorship which was offered to me by the people and the senate, both when I was absent and when I was present, in the consulship of Marcus Marcellus and Lucius Arruntius, I did not accept. At a time of the greatest dearth of grain I did not refuse the charge of the food supply, which I so administered that in a few days, at my own expense, I freed the whole people from the anxiety and danger in which they then were. The annual and perpetual consulship offered to me at that time I did not accept.

During the consulship of Marcus Vinucius and Quintus Lucretius, and afterwards in that of Publius and Cnaeus Lentulus, and a third time in that of Paulius Fabius Maximus and Quintus Tubero, by the consent of the senate and the Roman people I was voted the sole charge of the laws and of morals, with the fullest power; but I accepted the proffer of no office which was contrary to the customs of the country. The measures of which the senate at that time wished me to take charge, I accomplished in virtue of my possession of the tribunitial power. In this office I five times associated with myself a colleague, with the consent of the senate. . .

To each man of the roman plebs I paid three hundred *sesterces* in accordance with the last will of my father; and in my own name, when consul for the fifth time, I gave four hundred *sesterces* from the spoils of the wars; again, moreover, in my tenth consulship I gave from my own estate four hundred *sesterces* to each man by way of *congiarum*; and in my eleventh consulship I twelve times made distributions of food, buying grain at my own expense; and in the twelfth year of my tribunitial power I three times gave four hundred *sesterces* to each man. These my donations have never been made to less than two hundred and fifty thousand men. In my twelfth consulship and the eighteenth year of my tribunitial power I gave to three hundred and twenty thousand of the city plebs sixty *denarii* apiece. In the colonies of my soldiers, when consul for the fifth time, I gave to each man a thousand *sesterces* from the spoils; about a hundred and twenty thousand men in the colonies received that triumphal donation. When consul for the thirteenth time I gave sixty *denarii* to the plebs who were at that time receiving public grain; these men were a little more than two hundred thousand in number. . . .

Four times I have aided the public treasury from my own means, to such extent that I have furnished to those in charge of the treasury one hundred and fifty million *sesterces*. And in the consulship of Marcus Lepidus and Lucius Arrantius I paid into the military treasury which was established by my advice that from it gratuities might be given to soldiers who had served a term of twenty or more years, one hundred and seventy million *sesterces* from my own estate.

The Capitol and the Pompeian theatre have been restored by me at enormous expense for each work, without any inscription of my name. Aqueducts which were crumbling in many places by reason of age I have restored, and I have doubled the water which bears the name Marcian by turning a new spring into its course. The Forum Julium and the basilica which was between the temple of Castor and the temple of Saturn, works begun and almost completed by my father, I have finished; and when that same basilica was consumed by fire, I began its reconstruction on an enlarged site, inscribing it with the names of my sons; and if I do not live to complete it, I have given orders that it be completed by my heirs. In accordance with a decree of the senate, while consul for the sixth time, I have restored eighty-two temples of the gods, passing over none which was at that time in need of repair. In my seventh consulship I constructed the Flaminian way from the city to Ariminum, and all the bridges except the Mulvian and Minucian. . . .

Three times in my own name, and five times in that of my sons or grandsons, I have given gladiatorial exhibitions; in these exhibitions about ten thousand men have fought. Twice in my own name, and three times in that of my grandson, I have offered the people the spectacle of athletes gathered from all quarters. I have celebrated games four times in my own name, and twenty-three times in the turns of other magistrates. In behalf of the college of *quindecemvirs*, I, as master of the college, with my colleague Agrippa, celebrated the Secular Games in the consulship of Gaius Furnius and Gaius Silanus. When consul for the thirteenth time, I first celebrated the Martial games, which since that time the consuls have given in successive years. Twenty-six times in my own name, or in that of my sons and grandsons, I have given hunts of African wild beasts in the circus, the forum, the amphitheatres, and about thirty-five hundred beasts have been killed. . .

In my sixth and seventh consulships, when I had put an end to the civil wars, after having obtained complete control of affairs by universal consent, I transferred the commonwealth from my own dominion to the authority of the senate and Roman people. In return for this favor on my part I received by decree of the senate the title Augustus, the door-posts of my house were publicly decked with laurels, a civic crown was fixed above my door, and in the Julian Curia was placed a golden shield, which, by its inscription, bore witness that it was given to me by the senate and Roman people on account of my valor, clemency, justice and piety. After that time I excelled all others in dignity, but of power I held no more than those also held who were my colleagues in any magistracy.

from *Translations and Reprints from the Original Sources of European History.* Vol. 5 # 1. Philadelphia: University of Pennsylvania Press. 1897.

Tacitus: from *The Annals of Imperial Rome*

Looking back after one hundred years, Tacitus gives quite a different, one might even say a cynical, description of Augustus' accomplishments.

. . .When the last army of the Republic had fallen with Brutus and Cassius on the field; when Sextus Pompeius had been crushed in Sicily; and when the deposition of Lepidus, followed by the death of Antonius, had left Augustus sole leader of the Julian party, he laid aside the title of Triumvir, assumed the Consulship, and professed himself content with the Tribunitian Power for the protection of the plebs. But when he had won the soldiery by bounties, the populace by cheap corn, and all classes alike by the sweets of peace, he rose higher and higher by degrees, and drew into his own hands all the functions of the Senate, the magistrates and the laws. And there was no one to oppose; for the most ardent patriots had fallen of the field, or in the proscriptions; and the rest of the nobles, advanced in wealth and place in proportion to their servility, and drawing profit out of the new order of affairs, preferred the security of the present to the hazards of the past.

Nor did the provinces resent the change; for the rule of the Senate and the People had become odious to them from the contests between great leaders, and the greed of magistrates, against whom the laws, upset by force, by favour, and, in fine, by bribery, were powerless to protect them. . . .

All wars had now ceased except that against the Germans; and even that was being continued rather to wipe out the disgrace of the loss of Quintilius Varus and his legions, than from a desire to extend the empire, or for any profitable end. Tranquillity reigned at home; the magistrates were called by their old names; the younger generation had been born since Actium,[18] the elder, for the most part, during the course of the Civil Wars: how many were there left who had beheld the Republic?

---

[18]   The battle in which Octavian defeated Marc Antony.

Thus a revolution had been accomplished. The old order had passed away; everything had suffered change. The days of equality were gone: men looked to the Prince for his commands, having no anxiety for the present, so long as Augustus was of the age, and had the strength, to keep himself, his house and the public peace secure. But when he advanced in years, when his health and strength failed, and his approaching end gave birth to new hopes, some few discoursed idly on the blessings of liberty; many dreaded war; some longed for it. . . .

Translated by G. G. Ramsey. London: John Murray, 1904.

from Petronius' *Trimalchio's Dinner*

Petronius was at the court of Nero until he committed suicide in 66 C.E. His satire
describes the conspicuous consumption that some felt was ruining Roman society.

Presently we took our places, and Alexandrian slaves poured water cooled with snow over our hands, while others approached our feet and with great skill began paring our corns; nor were they silent even over this rather disagreeable task, but kept singing all the time. I wanted to find out whether the whole household sang; and so I asked for something to drink; whereupon a slave served me, singing the while, like the others, a shrill ditty; and in fact, every slave who was asked for anything did exactly the same, so that you would have imagined yourself in the green-room of a comic opera troupe rather than in the dining-room of a private gentleman.

A very choice lot of hors d'oeuvres was then brought in; for we had already taken our places, all except Trimalchio himself for whom the seat of honor was reserved. Among the objects placed before us was a young ass made of Corinthian bronze and fitted with a sort of pack-saddle, which contained on one side pale green olives and on the other side dark ones. Two dishes flanked this; and on the margin of them Trimalchio's name was engraved and the weight of the silver. Then there were little bridge-like structures of iron which held dormice seasoned with honey and poppy-seed; and smoking sausages were arranged over a silver grill which had underneath it dark Syrian plums to represent black coals, and scarlet pomegranate seeds to represent red hot ones.

In the midst of all this magnificence Trimalchio was brought in to the sound of music and propped up on a pile of well-stuffed cushions. The very sight of him almost made us laugh in spite of ourselves; for his shaven pate was thrust out of a scarlet robe, and around his neck he had tucked a long fringed napkin with a broad purple stripe running down the middle of it. On the little finger of his left hand he wore a huge gilt rung, and on the last joint of the next finger a ring that appeared to be of solid gold, but having little iron stars upon it. Moreover, lest we should fail to take in all his magnificence, he had bared his right arm, which was adorned with a golden bracelet and an ivory circle fastened by a glittering clasp. . . .

A troupe immediately came in clattering their shields and spears. Trimalchio sat up on his couch, and while the Homeric actors in a pompous fashion began a dialogue in Greek verse, he read a book aloud in Latin, with a singsong tone of voice. Presently, when the rest had become silent, he said:

"Do you know what play they're acting? Diomede and Ganymede were two brothers. Their sister was Helen. Agamemnon carried her off and put a deer in her place for Diana, and so now Homer explains how the Trojans and the Parentines are waging war. Agamemnon, you must know, came off victor and gave his daughter Iphigenia to be the wife of Achilles. Thereupon Ajax went mad, and presently now will show us how it all ends."

As Trimalchio said this, the Homeric actors set up a shout, and while the slaves bustled about, a boiled calf was brought on in an enormous dish and with a helmet placed upon it. The actor who took the part of Ajax followed with a drawn sword, fell upon it as though he were mad, and hacking this way and that he cut up the calf and offered the bits to us on the point of his sword, to our great surprise.

We had no time to admire these elegant proceedings, for all of a sudden the ceiling of the room began to rumble and the whole dining-room shook. In consternation I jumped up, fearing lest some acrobat should come down through the roof; and all the other guests in surprise looked upward as though they expected some miracle from heaven. But, lo and behold, the panels of the ceiling slid apart, and suddenly a great hoop as though shaken off from a hogshead was let down, having gold crowns with jars of perfume hanging about its entire circumference. These things we were invited to accept as keepsakes, and presently a tray was set before us full of cakes with an image of Priapus as a centre piece made of confectionery and holding in its generous bosom apples of every sort and grapes, in the usual fashion, as being the god of gardens. We eagerly snatched at this magnificent display, and suddenly renewed our mirth at discovering a novel trick; for all the cakes and all the apples, when pressed the least bit, squirted saffron water into our faces.

Thinking that there was something of a religious turn to a course that was so suggestive of divine worship, we all rose up together and pronounced the formula, "Success to Augustus, Father of his Country!" But some of us, even after this solemn act, snatched up the apples and filled our napkins with them to carry away, a thing which I did myself, for I thought that I could not heap up enough presents in Giton's lap.

While this was going on, three slaves dressed in white tunics entered, two of whom placed images of the household gods upon the table, and the other one carrying around a bowl of wine called out "God bless us all!" Trimalchio told us that one image was the image of the God of Business, the second the image of the God of Luck, and the third was a very striking bust of Trimalchio also, and as everybody else kissed it, I was ashamed not to do the same. . . .

Soon after, for the first time, our mirth was checked: for when a young slave who was by no means bad looking had come in among the new servants, Trimalchio pounced upon him and began to kiss him for a long time. Whereupon Fortunata[19] in order to prove her equal right in the household, began to abuse Trimalchio, styling him the scum of the earth and a disgraceful person. At last she called him a dog. Taking offence at this, Trimalchio threw a cup in her face, and she, as though she had lost an eye, shrieked and placed her trembling hands before her face. Scintilla also was very much disturbed and hid the cowering woman in her robe. A slave at once in an officious manner placed a cold jug against her cheek, leaning upon which Fortunata began to moan and cry.

On his side Trimalchio exclaimed: "How now? The jade doesn't remember that I took her off the stage and made an honest woman of her; she puffs herself up like a frog and fouls her own nest . . .

---

[19] Trimalchio's wife.

(After an extended quarrel, Trimalchio excuses himself): "I kissed this excellent young slave, not because of his good looks but because of his intelligence. He can say his multiplication table, he can read a book at sight, and he's saved up some money for himself out of his daily food allowance and bought a little stool and two ladles with his own money. So doesn't he deserve to have me keep my eye on him? . . . But come, let's think of something more cheerful. I hope you're all comfortable, my friends. I used to be myself the same sort of person that you all are, but, by my own merits, I became what I am. It's brain that makes men, and everything else is all rot. One man'll tell you one rule of life, and another'll tell you another. But I say, "Buy cheap and sell dear," and so you see I'm just bursting with wealth. (Well, grunter, are you still crying? Pretty soon I'll give you something to cry for!) Well, as I was going on to say, my clever management brought me my present good fortune. When I came from Asia, I was about the height of this candle stick here and, in fact, I used to measure myself against it every day. And so as to get a beard on my mug I used to smear my lips with lamp oil. I was a great favorite with my master for fourteen years, and I was on pretty good terms with my master's wife. You understand what I mean. I'm not saying anything about it, because I'm not one of the boastful kind; but, as the gods would have it, I was really master in the house myself and I took his fancy greatly. Well, there's no need of a long story. He made me his residuary legatee, and I came into a fortune fit for a senator. But nobody ever gets enough. I became crazy to go into business; and, not to bore you, I had five ships built, loaded them with wine (and wine at that time was worth its weight in gold) and sent them to Rome. You'd imagine that it had been actually planned that way, for every blessed ship was wrecked, and that's a fact not a fable. On one single day the sea swallowed down thirty million *sesterces*. Do you think I gave up? Not much! This loss just whetted my appetite as though it had been a mere nothing. I had other ships built, bigger and better, and they were luckier too, so that everybody said I was a plucky fellow. I loaded them with wine once more, with bacon, beans, ointment and slaves, and at that crisis Fortunata did a very nice thing, for she sold all her jewelry and even all her clothes, and put a hundred gold pieces in my hand. And this was really the germ of my good fortune. What the gods wish happens quickly. In a single round trip I piled up ten million *sesterces*, and immediately bought in all the lands that had belonged to my former owner. I built me a house and bought all the cattle that were offered for sale, and whatever I touched grew rich as a honey comb. After I began to have more money than my whole native land contains, then, says I, enough. I retired from business and began to lend money to freedmen."

Translated by Harry Thurston Peck. New York, 1898.

Unit 14: The Rise of Christianity

The story of Jesus' life, death, and teachings is contained in the four Gospels, written by his followers forty to sixty years after his death. During the second century, they were being read in many churches, as were the letters of Paul the Apostle to various churches. The Gospels, the letters of Paul, the Acts of the Apostles, the Apocalypse, or Revelation, and some other letters of church leaders were eventually recognized as the canon of sacred writings, known as the New Testament, or New Covenant. Christians also claim the Hebrew Bible as a sacred text, which they call the Old Testament.

In the early centuries of Christianity, a number of other gospels, letters, and apocalypses claimed to contain Christian teachings, but were rejected by church leaders. Decisions on orthodoxy, or "right belief", were made primarily in ecumenical councils, the first of which was held in Nicea in 325 C.E.

The writings of numerous theologians, such as Origen, Jerome, Tertullian, and Augustine, reveal struggles within the early church as well as its struggles with the pagan world.

Before the conversion of the Emperor Constantine, Christianity is known mainly through the writings of its members, but there is occasional mention of the sect from outside sources, such as the letters between Pliny and the Emperor Trajan.

Matthew 5:17-48

Jesus and his first disciples were Jews. It is the law of the ancient Hebrews to which Jesus refers in the following selection.

Do not suppose that I have come to abolish the law and the prophets; I did not come to abolish, but to complete. Truly I tell you: so long as heaven and earth endure, not a letter, not a dot, will disappear from the law until all that must happen has happened. Anyone therefore who sets aside even the least of the law's demands, and teaches others to do the same, will have the lowest place in the kingdom of Heaven, whereas anyone who keeps the law, and teaches others to do so, will rank high in the kingdom of Heaven. I tell you, unless you show yourselves far better than the scribes and Pharisees, you can never enter the kingdom of Heaven.

You have heard that our forefathers were told, "Do not commit murder; anyone who commits murder must be brought to justice." But what I tell you is this: Anyone who nurses anger against his brother must be brought to justice. Whoever calls his brother "good for nothing" deserves the sentence of the court; whoever calls him "fool" deserves hell-fire. So if you are presenting your gift at the altar and suddenly remember that your brother has a grievance against you, leave your gift where it is before the altar. First go and make your peace with your brother; then come back and offer your gift. If someone sues you, come to terms with him promptly while you are both on your way to court; otherwise he may hand you over to the judge, and the judge to the officer, and you will be thrown into jail. Truly I tell you: once you are there you will not be let out until you have paid the last penny.

You have heard that they were told, "Do not commit adultery." But what I tell you is this: If a man looks at a woman with a lustful eye, he has already committed adultery with her in his heart. If your right eye causes your downfall, tear it out and fling it away; it is better for you to lose one part of your body than for the whole of it to be thrown into hell. If your right hand causes your downfall, cut it off and fling it away; it is better for you to lose one part of your body than for the whole of it to go to hell.

They were told, "A man who divorces his wife must give her a certificate of dismissal." But what I tell you is this: If a man divorces his wife for any cause other than unchastity he involves her in adultery; and whoever marries her commits adultery.

Again, you have heard that our forefathers were told, "Do not break your oath," and "Oaths sworn to the Lord must be kept." But what I tell you is this: You are not to swear at all—not by heaven, for it is God's throne, nor by the earth, for it is his footstool, nor by Jerusalem, for it is the city of the great King, nor by your own head, because you cannot turn one hair of it white or black. Plain "Yes" or "No" is all you need to say; anything beyond that comes from the evil one.

You have heard that they were told, "An eye for an eye, a tooth for a tooth." But what I tell you is this: Do not resist those who wrong you. If anyone slaps you on the right cheek, turn and offer him the other also. If anyone wants to sue you and takes your shirt, let him have your cloak as well. If someone in authority presses you into service for one mile, go with him two. Give to anyone who asks; and do not turn your back on anyone who wants to borrow.

You have heard that they were told, "Love your neighbour and hate your enemy." But what I tell you is this: Love your enemies and pray for your persecutors; only so can you be children of your heavenly Father, who causes the sun to rise on good and bad alike, and sends the rain on the innocent and the wicked. If you love only those who love you, what reward can you expect? Even the tax collectors do as much as that. If you greet only your brothers, what is there extraordinary about that? Even the heathen do as much. There must be no limit to your goodness, as your heavenly Father's goodness knows no bounds.

from Luke 22, 23, 24

As soon as it was day, the elders of the people, chief priests, and scribes assembled, and he was brought before their Council. "Tell us," they said, "are you the Messiah?" "If I tell you," he replied, "you will not believe me; and if I ask questions, you will not answer. But from now on, the Son of Man will be seated at the right hand of Almighty God." "You are the Son of God, then?" they all said, and he replied, "It is you who say I am." At that they said, "What further evidence do we need? We have heard this ourselves from his own lips."

With that the whole assembly rose and brought him before Pilate. They opened the case against him by saying, "We found this man subverting our nation, opposing the payment of taxes to Caesar, and claiming to be Messiah, a king." Pilate asked him, "Are you the king of the Jews?" He replied, "The words are yours." Pilate then said to the chief priests and the crowd, "I find no case for this man to answer." But they insisted: "His teaching is causing unrest among the people all over Judaea. It started from Galilee and now has spread here." . . .

There were two others with him, criminals who were being led out to execution; and when they reached the place called The Skull, they crucified him there, and the criminals with him, one on his right and the other on his left. Jesus said, "Father, forgive them; they do not know what they are doing." . . .

But very early on the first day of the week they came to the tomb bringing the spices they had prepared. They found that the stone had been rolled away from the tomb, but when they went inside, they did not find the body of the Lord Jesus. While they stood utterly at a loss, suddenly two men in dazzling garments were at their side. They were terrified, and stood with eyes cast down, but the men said, "Why search among the dead for one who is alive? Remember how he told you, while he was still in Galilee, that the Son of Man must be given into the power of sinful men and be crucified, and must rise again on the third day." They recalled his words and, returning from the tomb, they reported everything to the eleven and all the others.

Letters of Trajan and Pliny, c. 111 C.E.

Pliny was governor of Bithynia, a province in Asia Minor, under the Emperor Trajan. The Romans had traditionally allowed conquered peoples to continue to worship their own gods, as long as they also made offerings to the Roman gods, including the emperors. This Christians refused to do, for which their religion was outlawed. Death was the prescribed penalty. Pliny wrote to Trajan asking how vigorously he should pursue the outlaws.

LETTER 97: PLINY TO TRAJAN

It is a rule, Sir, which I inviolably observe, to refer myself to you in all my doubts; for who is more capable of removing my scruples, or informing my ignorance? Having never been present at any trials concerning those who profess Christianity, I am unacquainted not only with the nature of their crimes, or the measure of their punishment, but how far it is proper to enter into an examination concerning them. Whether therefore any difference is usually made with respect to the ages of the guilty, or no distinction is to be observed between the young and the adult; whether repentance entitles them to a pardon; or if a man has been once a Christian, it avails nothing to desist from his error; whether the very profession of Christianity, unattended with any criminal act, or only the crimes themselves inherent in the profession are punishable; in all these points I am greatly doubtful. In the mean while the method I have observed towards those who have been brought before me as Christians, is this: I interrogated them whether they were Christians; if they confessed I repeated the question twice again, adding threats at the same time; when, if they still persevered, I ordered them to be immediately punished; for I was per-suaded, whatever the nature of their opinions might be, a contumacious and inflexible obstinacy certainly deserved correction.

There were others also brought before me possessed with the same infatuation, but being citizens of Rome, I directed them to be carried thither. But this crime spreading (as is usually the case) while it was actually under prosecution, several instances of the same nature occurred. An information was presented to me without any name subscribed, containing a charge against several persons, who upon examination denied they were Christians, or had ever been so. They repeated after me an invocation to the gods, and offered religious rites with wine and frankin-cense before your statue; (which for the purpose I had ordered to be brought together with those of the gods) and even reviled the name of Christ: whereas there is no forcing, it is said, those who are really Christians, into a compliance with any of these articles; I thought proper therefore to discharge them. Some among those who were accused by a witness in person, at first confessed themselves Christians, but immediately after denied it; while the rest own'd indeed that they had been of that number formerly, but had now (some above three, others more, and a few above twenty years ago) forsaken that error. They all worshipped your statue and the images of the gods, throwing out imprecations at the same time against the name of Christ. They affirmed, the whole of their guilt, or their error, was, that they met on a certain stated day before it was light, and addressed themselves in a form of prayer to Christ, as to some God, binding themselves by a solemn oath, not for the purposes of any wicked design, but never to commit any fraud, theft, or adultery, never to falsify their word, nor deny a trust when they should be called upon to deliver it up; after which, it was their custom to separate, and then reassemble, to eat in common a harmless meal. From this custom, however, they desisted after the publication of my edict, by which, according to your orders, I forbade the meeting of any assemblies. After receiving this account, I judged it so much the more necessary to endeavor to extort the real truth, by putting two female slaves to the torture, who were said to administer in their religious function: but I could discover nothing more than an absurd and excessive superstition.

I thought proper therefore to adjourn all farther proceedings in this affair, in order to consult with you. For it appears to be a matter highly deserving your consideration; more especially as great numbers must be involved in the danger of these prosecutions, this enquiry having already extended, and being still likely to extend, to persons of all ranks and ages, and even of both sexes. For this contagious superstition is not confined to the cities only, but has spread its infection among the country villages. Nevertheless, it still seems possible to remedy this evil and restrain its progress. The temples, at least, which were once almost deserted, begin now to be frequented; and the sacred solemnities, after a long intermission, are again revived; while there is a general demand for the victims, which for some time past have met with but few purchasers. From whence it is easy to imagine, what numbers might be reclaimed from this error, if a pardon were granted to those who shall repent.

LETTER 98: TRAJAN TO PLINY

The method you have pursued, my dear Pliny, in the proceedings against those Christians which were brought before you, is extremely proper; as it is not possible to lay down any fixed plan by which to act in all cases of this nature. But I would not have you officiously enter into any enquiries concerning them. If indeed they should be brought before you, and the crime is proved, they must be punished; with the restriction however that where the party denies himself to be a Christian, and shall make it evident that he is not, by invoking our Gods, let him (notwithstanding any former suspicion) be pardoned upon his repentance. Information without the accuser's name subscribed, ought not to be received in prosecutions of any sort, as it is introducing a very dangerous precedent, and by no means agreeable to the equity of my government.

from *The Letters of Pliny the Consul*, translated by William Melmoth. London: R. and J. Dodsley. 1757.

Edict of Milan, 313 C.E.

In 312, after a visionary experience that directed him to inscribe the Chi Rho emblem of Christ on the shields of his soldiers, Constantine won the Battle of the Milvian Bridge. He converted to Christianity, though he was not baptized until he was on his deathbed. In 313, the Edict of Milan allowed Christians and those of other faiths to worship freely, and returned confiscated properties to the churches.

When I, Constantine Augustus, as well as I, Licinius Augustus, had fortunately met near Mediolanum [Milan] and were considering everything that pertained to the public welfare and security, we thought that, among other things which we saw would be for the good of many, those regulations pertaining to the reverence of the Divinity ought certainly to be made first, so that we might grant to the Christians and to all others full authority to observe that religion which each preferred; whence any Divinity whatsoever in the seat of the heavens may be propitious and kindly disposed to us and all who are placed under our rule. And thus by this wholesome counsil and most upright provision we thought to arrange that no one whatsoever should be denied the opportunity to give his heart to the observance of the Christian religion, or of that religion which he should think best for himself, so that the supreme Deity, to whose worship we freely yield our hearts, may show in all things His usual favor and benevolence. Therefore, your Worship should know that it has pleased us to remove all conditions whatsoever, which were in the rescripts formerly given to you officially, concerning the Christians, and now any one of these who wishes to observe the Christian religion may do so freely and openly, without any disturbance or molestation. We thought it fit to commend these things most fully to your care that you may know that we have given to those Christians free and unrestricted opportunity of religious worship. When you see that this has been granted to them by us, your Worship will know that we have also conceded to other religions the right of open and free observance of their worship for the sake of the peace of our times, that each one may have the free opportunity to worship as he pleases; this regulation is made that we may not seem to detract aught from any dignity or any religion.

Moreover, in the case of the Christians especially, we esteemed it best to order that if it happens that anyone heretofore has bought from our treasury or from anyone whatsoever, those places where they were previously accustomed to assemble, concerning which a certain decree had been made and a letter sent to you officially, the same shall be restored to the Christians without payment or any claim of recompense and without any kind of fraud or deception. Those moreover, who have obtained the same by gift, are likewise to return them at once to the Christians. Besides, both those who have purchased and those who have secured them by gift, are to appeal to the vicar if they seek any recompense from our bounty, that they may be cared for through our clemency. All this property ought to be delivered at once to the community of the Christians through your intercession, and without delay. And since these Christians are known to have possessed not only those places in which they were accustomed to assemble, but also other property, namely the churches, belonging to them as a corporation and not as individuals, all these things which we have included under the above law, you will order to be restored, without any hesitation or controversy at all, to these Christians, that is to say to the corporations and their conventicles:--providing, of course, that the above arrangements be followed so that those who return the same without payment, as we have said, may hope for an indemnity from our bounty.

In all these circumstances you ought to tender your most efficacious intervention to the community of the Christians, that our command may be carried into effect as quickly as possible, whereby, moreover, through our clemency, public order may be secured. Let this be done so that, as we have said above, Divine favor towards us, which, under the most important circumstances we have already experienced, may, for all time, preserve and prosper our successes together with the good of the state. Moreover, in order that the statement of this decree of our good will come to the notice of all, this rescript, published by your decree, shall be announced everywhere and brought to the knowledge of all, so that the decree of this, our benevolence, cannot be concealed.

From *Translations and Reprints from the Original Sources of European History*. Vol. 4. University of Pennsylvania Press, 1898

Nicene Creed

The Council of Nicea was convoked by the Emperor Constantine in 325 C.E. to settle controversies over the nature of Christ and of the Trinity. The chief issue was the teaching of Arius, who held that, while Christ was truly God, "there was a time when he was not;" that is, he was not eternal and did not participate in the creation of the world. The chief issue at the Council of Constantinople in 381 was the nature of the Holy Spirit and his place in the Trinity. These texts are taken from the proceedings of the Council of Chalcedon, 451, where they were quoted. The proceedings of the earlier councils have disappeared.

CREED AS FRAMED AT THE COUNCIL OF NICEA

We believe in one God, the Father, Almighty, Maker of all things visible and invisible. And in one Lord Jesus Christ, the Son of God, begotten of the Father, God of God, Light of Light, very God of very God, begotten, not made, being of one essence with the Father; by whom all things were made, both in heaven and on earth; who for us men, and for our salvation, came down and was incarnate and was made man; he suffered, and the third day he rose again, ascended into heaven; and he shall come to judge the living and the dead. And in the Holy Ghost. But those who say: "There was a time when he was not," and "He was not before he was made"; and "He was made out of nothing," or "He is of another substance or essence," or "The Son of God is created," or "changeable," or "alterable"--they are condemned by the holy catholic and apostolic church.

CREED AS REVISED BY THE COUNCIL OF CONSTANTINOPLE

We believe in one God, the Father Almighty, Maker of heaven and earth and of all things visible and invisible. And in one Lord Jesus Christ, the only-begotten Son of God, begotten of the Father before all worlds, Light of Light, very God of very God, begotten, not made, being of one substance with the Father; by whom all things were made; who for us men and for our salvation came down from heaven, and was incarnate by the Holy Ghost of the Virgin Mary, and was made man; he was crucified for us under Pontius Pilate, and suffered, and was buried, and the third day he rose again, according to the Scriptures, and ascended into heaven, and sitteth on the right hand of the Father; and he shall come again, with glory, to judge the quick and the dead; whose kingdom shall have no end. And in the Holy Ghost, the Lord and Giver of life, who proceedeth from the Father, who with the Father and the Son together is worshipped and glorified, who spake by the prophets. In one holy catholic and apostolic church. We acknowledge one baptism for the remission of sins; we look for the resurrection of the dead, and the life of the world to come. Amen.

from *Translations and Reprints from the Original Sources of European History*. Vol. 4. University of Pennsylvania Press. 1897.

Unit 15: Fall of the Empire

Suggested causes for the Destruction of the Western Roman Empire range from the Christian focus on the afterlife to the use of lead in cooking vessels and water pipes. Certainly the causes were many and varied. One contributing factor was the migration of germanic tribes into the Empire. The traditions and lifestyle of the germanic tribes were also major factors in the creation of the medieval culture that followed the dissolution of the Empire.

Early written descriptions of the germanic peoples, before they were established within the Empire and converted to Christianity, were written by Romans, as the Germans had no written language. Tacitus wrote in 98 C.E., when the Germans had only begun to settle along the Rhine, making occasional raids against Romans, when the Empire was strong enough feel impregnable. Tacitus portrays the germanic peoples as "noble savages," in contrast to what he sees as the decadence of the Romans. Ammianus Marcellinus, who wrote in the fourth century, describes a more fearsome and dangerous people.

There is a Gothic translation of the Bible made in the fourth century by Ulfilas, a Greek who was raised among the Goths. Though it provides no direct evidence about the Goths, linguistic analysis provides some clues to their lifestyles.

The principal germanic sources are Gregory of Tours, Bede, and Paul the Deacon, all of who wrote much later—in the sixth, seventh and eighth centuries. All were clerics and interpreted the germanic migrations as a part of God's plan for the world.

Physical evidence for the lifestyles of the germanic peoples has been found in archaeological sites such as the Sutton Hoo burial in England and the grave of Childeric, the father of Clovis, in Tournai.

From Tacitus: *Germania*, 98 C.E.

There is no evidence that Tacitus knew about the germanic peoples from his own experience. He probably drew on the writings of Julius Caesar and of Pliny the Elder (the latter is now lost) and perhaps on the stories of soldiers and merchants of his own time.

IV. I myself subscribe to the opinion of those who hold that the German tribes have never been contaminated by intermarriage with other nations, but have remained peculiar and unmixed and wholly unlike other people. Hence the bodily type is the same among them all, notwithstanding the extent of their population. They all have fierce blue eyes, reddish hair and large bodies fit only for sudden exertion; they do not submit patiently to work and effort and cannot endure thirst and heat at all, though cold and hunger they are accustomed to because of their climate.

V. In general the country, though varying here and there in appearance, is covered over with wild forests or filthy swamps, being more humid on the side of Gaul but bleaker toward Noricum and Pannonia. It is suitable enough for grain but does not permit the cultivation of fruit trees; and though rich in flocks and herds these are for the most part small, the cattle not even possessing their natural beauty nor spreading horns. The people take pride in possessing a large number of animals, these being their sole and most cherished wealth. Whether it was in mercy or wrath that the gods denied them silver and gold, I know not. Yet I would not affirm that no vein of German soil produces silver or gold; for who has examined? They do not care for their possession and use as much as might be expected. There are to be seen among them vessels of silver that have been presented as gifts to their ambassadors and chiefs, but they are held in no more esteem than vessels of earthenware; however those nearest to us prize gold and silver because of its use in trade, and they recognize certain of our coins as valuable and choose those. The people of the interior practice barter and exchange of commodities in accordance with the simple and ancient custom. They like the old and well known coins, those with milled edges bearing the stamp of a two-horse chariot. They are more anxious also for silver coins than for gold, not because of any special liking, but because a number of silver coins is more convenient in purchasing cheap and common articles. . .

VII. They choose their kings on account of their ancestry, their generals for their valor. The kings do not have free and unlimited power and the generals lead by example rather than command, winning great admiration if they are energetic and fight in plain sight in front of the line. But no one is allowed to put a culprit to death or to imprison him, or even to beat him with stripes except the priests, and then not by way of a punishment or at the command of the general but as though ordered by the god who they believe aids them in their fighting. Certain figures and images taken from their sacred groves they carry into battle, but their greatest incitement to courage is that a division of horse or foot is not made up by chance or by accidental association but is formed of families and clans; and their dear ones are close at hand so that the wailings of the women and the crying of the children can be heard during the battle. These are for each warrior the most sacred witnesses of his bravery, these his dearest applauders. They carry their wounds to their mothers and their wives, nor do the latter fear to count their number and examine them while they bring them food and urge them to deeds of valor.

VIII. It is related how on certain occasions their forces already turned to flight and retreating have been rallied by the women who implored them by their prayers and bared their breasts to their weapons, signifying thus the captivity close awaiting them, which is feared far more intensely on account of their women than for themselves; to such an extent indeed that those states are more firmly bound in treaty among whose hostages maidens of noble family are also required. Further, they believe that the sex has a certain sanctity and prophetic gift, and they neither despise their counsels nor disregard their answers. We ourselves in the reign of the divine Vespasian saw Valaeda, who was considered for a long time by many as a sort of divinity; and formerly also Albruna and many others were venerated, though not out of servility nor as though they were deified mortals. . .

XI. Concerning minor matters the chiefs deliberate, but in important affairs all the people are consulted, although the subjects referred to the common people for judgment are discussed beforehand by the chiefs. Unless some sudden and unexpected event calls them together they assemble on fixed days either at the new moon or the full moon, for they think these the most auspicious times to begin their undertakings. They do not reckon time by the number of days, as we do, but by the number of nights. So run their appointments, their contracts; the night introduces the day, so to speak. A disadvantage arises from their regard for liberty in that they do not come together at once as if commanded to attend, but two or three days are wasted by their delay in assembling. When the crowd is sufficient they take their places fully armed. Silence is proclaimed by the priests, who have on these occasions the right to keep order. Then the king or a chief addresses them, each being heard according to his age, noble blood, reputation in warfare and eloquence, though more because he has the power to persuade than the right to command. If an opinion is displeasing they reject it by shouting; if they agree to it they clash with their spears. The most complimentary form of assent is that which is expressed by means of their weapons. . .

XV. In the intervals of peace they spend little time in hunting but much in idleness, given over to sleep and eating; all the bravest and most warlike doing nothing, while the hearth and home and the care of the fields is given over to the women, the old men and the various infirm members of the family. The masters lie buried in sloth by that strange contradiction of nature that causes the same men to love indolence and hate peace. It is customary for the several tribesmen to present voluntary offerings of cattle and grain to the chiefs which, though accepted as gifts of honor, also supply their wants. They are particularly delighted in the gifts of neighboring tribes, not only those sent by individuals, but those presented by states as such,--choice horses, massive arms, embossed plates and armlets. We have now taught them to accept money also.

XVI. It is well known that none of the German tribes live in cities, nor even permit their dwellings to be closely joined to each other. They live separated and in various places, as a spring or a meadow or a grove strikes their fancy. They lay out their villages not as with us in connected or closely-joined houses, but each one surrounds his dwelling with an open space, either as a protection against conflagration or because of their ignorance of the art of building. They do not even make use of rough stones or tiles. They use for all purposes undressed timber, giving no beauty or comfort. Some parts they plaster carefully with earth of such purity and brilliancy as to form a substitute for painting and designs in color. They are accustomed also to dig out subterranean caves which they cover over with great heaps of manure as a refuge against the cold and a place for storing grain, for retreats of this sort render the extreme cold of their winters bearable and, whenever an enemy has come upon them, though he lays waste the open country he is either ignorant of what is hidden underground or else it escapes him for the very reason that it has to be searched for.

XVII. . . .Almost alone among barbarian peoples they are content with one wife each, excepting those few who because of their high position rather than out of lust enter into more than one marriage engagement.

XVIII. The wife does not bring a dowry to the husband, but the husband to the wife. The parents and relatives are present at the ceremony and examine and accept the presents,--gifts not suited to female luxury nor such as a young bride would deck herself with, but oxen, a horse and bridle and a shield together with a spear and sword. In consideration of these offerings the wife is accepted, and she in her turn brings her husband a gift of weapons. This they consider as the strongest bond, these as their mystic rites, their gods of marriage. Lest the woman should think herself excluded from aspiring to share in heroic deeds and in the dangers of war, she is admonished by the very initiatory ceremonies of matrimony that she is becoming the partner of her husband's labors and dangers, destined to suffer and to dare with him alike in peace and in war. The yoke of oxen, the caparisoned horse, the gift of arms, give this warning. So must she live, so must she die. What things she receives she must hand down to her children worthy and untarnished and such that future daughters-in-law may receive them and pass them on to her grandchildren.

From *Translations and Reprints from the Original Sources of European History*, vol. 6. University of Pennsylvania Press, 1905.

Ammianus Marcellinus: The Germanic Invasions, 370 C.E.

Ammianus respected the work of Tacitus, but felt that no one since Tacitus had written a history of the same quality. He set out to record the history of the Empire from where Tacitus left off to his own time.

In the third consulate of the Emperor Valentinian a large band of Saxons came over the ocean and made an attack on the Roman boundary wall, laying waste the country with fire and sword. The first shock of this invasion was borne by Count Nannenus, the commander in that region, a careful and experienced veteran. But he had to do with a people who knew not the fear of death, and after he had lost a number of soldiers and had been himself wounded he had to admit himself unequal to carrying on the continuous strife. The Emperor having been informed of his necessity, Severus, the magister peditum, was allowed to come to his assistance. When he arrived with a force sufficient for the occasion and had drawn his troops up for battle the barbarians were so terrified that they did not dare risk an engagement, but awed by the splendor of the eagles and the battle standards, they sued for peace. Since this seemed to be for the best interests of the state, a treaty was agreed upon after a long discussion, whereby the Saxons were to furnish a large contingent of their warlike youth to serve under our standards while the remainder were allowed to depart, though without any plunder, and return whence they had come. And when their minds were now relieved of all anxiety and they were preparing to set out for home, a force of infantry was sent forward and quietly placed in ambush in a certain deep valley from which they were to make an attack on the barbarians as the latter passed by and so destroy them, as it was supposed, without difficulty. But it turned out very differently from what was hoped. For at the noise of their approach certain of the Romans in their excitement sprang forth too quickly, and no sooner were they seen than the barbarians with fearful whoops and yells made for them and overthrew them before they could form to resist the attack. Still our men drew quickly together in a circle and held their ground with the courage of despair. Many however were killed, and they would certainly have fallen to the last man had not the tumult been heard by a squadron of our heavy cuirassiers similarly placed at a fork of the road to attack the passing barbarians from the other side. These hastened to the rescue. Then the battle raged fiercely. The Romans with renewed courage rushed in on all sides, surrounded the enemy and cut them down with the sword. None of them ever saw again their native home. Not even a single one was allowed to survive the slaughter of his comrades. An upright judge might accuse us of baseness and perfidy in this affair, yet when one thinks the matter over one must admit that it was a just fate for a band of robbers to be thus destroyed when the opportunity was given us.

Though this affair had been so happily carried out, Valentinian continued to feel much anxiety and solicitude, turning over many projects in his mind and planning with what stratagems he might break the pride of the Alemanni and their king Macrian, whose restlessness was bringing endless disturbance to the Roman state. For the remarkable thing about this people is that, however great their losses through various causes from the very beginning on, yet they increase so fast that one would think that they had remained undisturbed for many ages. Finally after considering various plans it seemed best to the Emperor to weaken them by stirring up against them the Burgundians, a warlike people whose flourishing condition was due to the immense number of their young men, and who were therefore to be feared by all their neighbors.

From *Translation and Reprints from the Original Sources of European History*. vol. VI. University of Pennsylvania Press, 1895.

Law of the Salian Franks

The early Germans had no written records, but as they moved into the Roman Empire, they began to adopt some of the features of Roman government, including written law. The Law of the Salian Franks was promulgated by Clovis, the first of the germanic kings to convert to Roman Christianity. It was the most influential of the germanic law codes.

TITLE 2. CONCERNING THEFTS OF PIGS, ETC.

1. If any one steal a suckling pig, and it be proved against him, he shall be sentenced to 120 *denarii*, which make three *solidi*.

2. If any one steal a pig that can live without its mother, and it be proved on him, he shall be sentenced to 40 *denarii*—that is, 1 *solidi*.

14. If any one steal 25 sheep where there were no more in that flock, and it be proved on him, he shall be sentenced to 2500 *denarii*—that is, 62 *solidi*.

TITLE III. CONCERNING THEFTS OF CATTLE

1. If any one steal that bull which rules the herd and never has been yoked, he shall be sentenced to 1800 *denarii*, which make 45 *solidi*.

5. But if that bull is used for the cows of three villages in common, he who stole him shall be sentenced to three times 45 *solidi*.

6. If any one steal a bull belonging to the king, he shall be sentenced to 3600 *denarii*, which make 90 *solidi*.

TITLE IV. CONCERNING DAMAGE DONE AMONG CROPS OR IN ANY ENCLOSURE

1. If any one finds cattle, or a horse, or flocks of any kind in his crops, he shall not at all mutilate them.

2. If he do this and confess it, he shall restore the worth of the animal in place of it, and shall himself keep the mutilated one.

3. But if he has not confessed it, and it has been proved on him, he shall be sentenced, besides the value of the animal and the fines for delay, to 600 *denarii*, which make 15 *solidi*.

TITLE XIII. CONCERNING RAPE COMMITTED BY FREEMEN

1. If three men carry off a free born girl, they shall be compelled to pay 30 *solidi*.

2. If there are more than three, each one shall pay 5 *solidi*.

3. Those who shall have been present with boats shall be sentenced to three *solidi*.

4. But those who commit rape shall be compelled to pay 2500 *denarii*, which make 63 *solidi*.

5. But if they have carried off that girl from behind lock and key, or from the spinning room, they shall be sentenced to the above price and penalty.

6. But if the girl who is carried off is under the king's protection, then the *frith* shall be 2500 *denarii*, which make 63 *solidi*.

7. But if a bondsman of the king, or a leet, should carry off a free woman he shall be sentenced to death.

8. But if a free woman has followed a slave of her own will, she shall lose her freedom.

9. If a freeborn man shall have taken an alien bondswoman, he shall suffer similarly.

10. If anybody takes an alien spouse and joins her to himself in matrimony, he shall be sentenced to 2500 *denarii*, which make 63 *solidi*.

TITLE XIV. CONCERNING ASSAULT AND ROBBERY

1. If any one has assaulted and plundered a free man, and it be proved on him, he shall be sentenced to 2500 *denarii*, which make 63 *solidi*.

2. If a Roman has plundered a Salian Frank, the above law shall be observed.

3. But if a Frank has plundered a Roman, he shall be sentenced to 35 *solidi*.

4. If any man should wish to migrate, and has permission from the king, and shall have shown this in the public Thing: whoever, contrary to the decree of the king, shall presume to oppose him, shall be sentenced to 8000 *denarii*, which make 200 *solidi*.

TITLE XV. CONCERNING ARSON

1. If any one shall set fire to a house in which men were sleeping, as many freemen as were in it can make complaint before the Thing; and if any one shall have been burned in it, the arsonist shall be sentenced to 2500 *denarii*, which make 63 *solidi*.

TITLE XVII. CONCERNING WOUNDS

1. If any one has attempted to kill another person, and the blow has missed, he on whom it was proved shall be sentenced to 2500 *denarii*, which make 63 *solidi*.

2. If any person has attempted to strike another with a poisoned arrow, and the arrow has glanced aside, and it shall be proved on him: he shall be sentenced to 2500 *denarii*, which make 63 *solidi*.

3. If any person strike another on the head so that the brain appears, and the three bones which lie above the brain shall project, he shall be sentenced to 1200 *denarii*, which make 30 *solidi*.

4. But if it shall have been between the ribs or in the stomach, so that the wound appears and reaches to the entrails, he shall be sentenced to 1200 *denarii*—which make 30 *solidi*—besides five *solidi* for the physician's pay.

5. If any one shall have struck a man so that blood falls to the floor, and it be proved on him, he shall be sentenced to 600 *denarii*, which makes 15 *solidi*.

6. But if a freeman strike a freeman with his fist so that blood does not flow, he shall be sentenced for each blow—up to 3 blows—to 120 *denarii*, which make 3 *solidi*.

TITLE XVIII. CONCERNING HIM WHO, BEFORE THE KING, ACCUSES AN INNOCENT MAN

If any one, before the king, accuse an innocent man who is absent, he shall be sentenced to 2500 *denarii*, which make 63 *solidi*.

TITLE XXIV. CONCERNING THE KILLING OF LITTLE CHILDREN AND WOMEN

1. If any one has slain a boy under 10 years—up to the end of the tenth—and it has been proved on him, he shall be sentenced to 24000 *denarii*, which make 600 *solidi*.

3. If any one has hit a free woman who is pregnant, and she dies, he shall be sentenced to 28000 *denarii*, which make 700 *solidi*.

6. If any one has killed a free woman after she has begun bearing children, he shall be sentenced to 24000 *denarii*, which make 600 *solidi*.

7. After she can have no more children, he who kills her shall be sentenced to 8000 *denarii*, which make 200 *solidi*.

TITLE XXX. CONCERNING INSULTS

3. If any one, man or woman, has called a woman harlot, and has not been able to prove it, he shall be sentenced to 1800 *denarii*, which make 45 *solidi*.

4. If any person shall have called another "fox," he shall be sentenced to 3 *solidi*.

5. If any man shall have called another "hare," he shall be sentenced to 3 *solidi*.

6. If any man shall have brought it up against another that he has thrown away his shield, and shall not have been able to prove it, he shall be sentenced to 120 *denarii*, which make 3 *solidi*.

7. If any man shall have called another "spy" or "perjurer," and has not been able to prove it, he shall be sentenced to 600 *denarii*, which make 15 *solidi*.

TITLE XXXIV. CONCERNING THE STEALING OF FENCES

1. If any man shall have cut 3 staves by which a fence is bound or held together, or have stolen or cut the heads of 3 stakes, he shall be sentenced to 600 *denarii*, which make 15 *solidi*.

2. If any one shall have drawn a harrow through another's harvest after it has sprouted, or shall have gone through it with a wagon where there was no road, he shall be sentenced to 120 *denarii*, which make 3 *solidi*.

3. If any one shall have gone, where there is no way or path, through another's harvest which has already become thick, he shall be sentenced to 600 *denarii*, which make 15 *solidi*.

TITLE XLV. CONCERNING MIGRATORS.

1. If any one wishes to migrate to another village and if one or more who live in that village do not wish to receive him—if there is only one who objects, he shall not have permission to move there.

2. But if he shall have presumed to settle in that village in spite of his rejection by one or two men, then some one shall give him warning. And if he is unwilling to go away, he who gives him warning shall give him warning, with witnesses, as follows:

"I warn you that you may remain here tonight as the Salic law demands, and I warn you that within 10 nights you must leave this village."

After another 10 nights he shall come to him again and warn him again to go away within 10 nights. If he still refuses to go, another 10 nights shall be added to the command, so that the number of 30 nights shall be filled. If he will not go away even then, then he shall summon him to the Thing, and present his witnesses as to each of the commands to leave. If he who has been warned will not then move away, and no valid reason detains him, and all the above warnings which we have mentioned have been given according to law: then he who gave him warning shall take the matter into his own hands and request the comes to go to that place and expel him. And because he would not listen to the law, that man shall relinquish all that he has earned there, and besides, shall be sentenced to 1200 *denarii*, which make 30 *solidi*.

3. But if anyone has moved there, and within 12 months no one has given him warning, he shall remain as secure as the other neighbours.

Adapted from *Select Historical Documents of the Middle Ages*, edited by Ernest F. Henderson. London, 1912.

CHAPTER 7: CHRISTIANITY AND ISLAM

Unit 16: The Church Triumphant

During the fifth century, the Roman Empire in the West disintegrated. Invading tribes set up their own small kingdoms, each with its own laws and customs. Each tribe fought others for control over the newly conquered lands. One bureaucratic network remained in place, that of the Christian Church. With the West in chaos, the Church became a prime force in the shaping of a new society— that of medieval Europe. It was also during the fifth century that the bishop of Rome began to assert his supremacy over the Church. Pope Gelasius I suggested a division of power between religious and secular rulers.

Sources for this period include church records and the writings of theologians, plus the histories of Gregory of Tours , Bede, and Paul the Deacon.

Leo the Great and Attila—Two Versions

The story of Pope Leo's encounter with Attila is presented here in two versions. The first was written by Prosper in 455, three years after the event. In it, Leo is a good citizen of Rome, using his office for moral suasion. In the second, Leo faces a more ferocious Attila, who is quelled only by the miraculous intervention of Leo's apostolic predecessors.

PROSPER, 455

Now Attila, having once more collected his forces which had been scattered in Gaul, took his way through Pannonia into Italy. . . . To the emperor and the senate and Roman people none of all the proposed plans to oppose the enemy seemed so practicable as to send legates to the most savage king and beg for peace. Our most blessed Pope Leo—trusting in the help of God, who never fails the righteous in their trials—undertook the task, accompanied by Avienus, a man of consular rank, and the prefect Trygetius. And the outcome was what his faith had foreseen; for when the king had received the embassy, he was so impressed by the presence of the high priest that he ordered his army to give up warfare and, after he had promised peace, he departed beyond the Danube.

FROM A LATER LIFE OF LEO THE GREAT

Attila, the leader of the Huns, who was called the scourge of God, came into Italy, inflamed with fury, after he had laid waste with most savage frenzy Thrace and Illyricum, Macedonia and Moesia, Achaia and Greece, Pannonia and Germany. He was utterly cruel in inflicting torture, greedy in plundering, insolent in abuse. . . . He destroyed Aquileia from the foundations and razed to the ground those regal cities, Pavia and Milan; he laid waste many other towns, and was rushing down upon Rome.

Then Leo had compassion on the calamity of Italy and Rome, and with one of the consuls and a large part of the Roman senate he went to meet Attila. The old man of harmless simplicity, venerable in his gray hair and his majestic garb, ready of his own will to give himself entirely for the defense of his flock, went forth to meet the tyrant who was destroying all things. He met Attila, it is said, in the neighborhood of the river Mincio, and he spoke to the grim monarch, saying: "The senate and the people of Rome, once conquerors of the world, now indeed vanquished, come before you as suppliants. We pray for mercy and deliverance. O Attila, king of kings, you could nave no greater glory than to see suppliant at your feet this people before whom once all peoples and kings lay suppliant. You have subdued, O Attila, the whole circle of the lands which it was granted to the Romans, victors over all peoples, to conquer. Now we pray that you, who have conquered others, should conquer yourself. The people have felt your scourge; now as suppliants they wish to feel your mercy."

As Leo said these things Attila stood looking upon his venerable garb and aspect, silent, as if thinking deeply. And lo, suddenly there were seen the apostles Peter and Paul, clad like bishops, standing by Leo, the one on the right hand, the other on the left. They held swords stretched out over his head, and threatened Attila with death if he did not obey the pope's command. Wherefore Attila was appeased by Leo's intercession,—he who had raged as one mad. He straightway promised a lasting peace and withdrew beyond the Danube.

From *Readings in European History*, edited by J. H. Robinson. Boston: Ginn, 1906.

Two Views of Papal Power

There were bishops in the early church, and it was bishops, meeting in ecumenical councils, who settled important questions of faith. Bishops of lesser localities looked to the bishops of cities such as Jerusalem, Alexandria, Constantinople, and Rome for advice. By the fifth century, if not before, the bishop of Rome was claiming authority over all other bishops, citing the "doctrine of the keys." This doctrine was based on the tradition that Peter was the first bishop of Rome, added to the gospel story in which Jesus says to Peter, "You are Peter (*petra*, or rock) and upon this rock I will build my church. Whatever you bind on earth will be bound in heaven, and whatever you loose on earth will be loosed in heaven."

SAINT JEROME (DIED 420)

The church at Rome is not to be considered as one thing and the rest of the churches throughout the world as another. Those of Gaul and Britain, Africa, Persia, and India, as well as the various barbarous nations, adore one Christ and observe a single rule of truth. If you are looking for authority, the world is surely greater than the city of Rome. Wherever there is a bishop, whether at Rome or Eugubium, at Constantinople, Rhegium, or Alexandria, his rank and priesthood are the same. Neither the power that riches bring nor the humility of poverty makes a bishop higher or lower in rank. All are successors of the apostles. . . . Why urge the custom of a single city?

From *Readings in European History*, edited by J. H. Robinson. Boston: Ginn, 1906.

POPE LEO I, 446

Although the priests enjoy a common dignity, they are not all on the same footing, since even among the blessed apostles, who were alike in honor, there was a certain distinction in authority. All were alike chosen, but it was given to one that he should be preeminent among the others. Upon this model the distinction among the bishops is based, and it is salutarily provided that all should not claim the right to do all things, but in each province there should be one who should have the first word among his brethren. Again, in the greater cities others are appointed to greater responsibilities. Through these the oversight of the whole Church is concentrated in one see, that of Peter, and from this head there should never be any dissent.

From *Readings in European History*, edited by J. H. Robinson. Boston: Ginn, 1906.

EMPEROR VALENTINIAN, 445

Since, then, the primacy of the Apostolic See is established by the merit of St. Peter (who is the chief among the bishops), by the majesty of the city of Rome, and finally by the authority of a holy council, no one, without inexcusable presumption, may attempt anything against the authority of that see. Peace will be secured among the churches if every one recognize his ruler.

[He refers to independent actions of certain church officials in Gaul.]

Lest even a slight commotion should arise in the churches, or the religious order be disturbed, we herewith permanently decree that not only the bishops of Gaul, but those of the other provinces, shall attempt nothing counter to ancient custom without the authority of the venerable father[20] of the Eternal City. Whatever shall be sanctioned by the authority of the Apostolic See shall be law to them and to every one else; so that if one of the bishops be summoned to the judgment of the Roman bishop and shall neglect to appear, he shall be forced by the moderator of his province to present himself. In all respects let the privileges be maintained which our deified predecessors have conferred upon the Roman church.

From *Readings in European History*, edited by J. H. Robinson. Boston: Ginn, 1906.

$\Longrightarrow$ Gregory of Tours: The Conversion of Clovis

Many of the Germanic tribes that invaded the West had converted to Christianity, but most were Arians, adherents of a creed that had been declared heretical at the Council of Nicea in 325. Because of Clovis' conversion to Western Christianity, the Roman church supported the Franks in their bid to become the leaders of the West. The story of Clovis' conversion is markedly similar to that of the conversion of Constantine.

CHAPTER 30

The queen (Clothilde) ceased not to warn Clovis that he should acknowledge the true God and forsake idols. But in no way could he be brought to believe these things. Finally war broke out with the Alemanni. Then by necessity he was compelled to acknowledge what before he had denied with his will. The two armies met and there was a fearful slaughter, and the army of Clovis was on the point of being annihilated. When the king perceived that, he raised his eyes to heaven, his heart was smitten and he was moved to tears, and he said: "Jesus Christ, whom Clothilde declares to be the Son of the living God, who says that You will help those in need and give victory to those who hope in You, humbly I flee to You for Your mighty aid, that You will give me victory over these my enemies, and I will in this way experience Your power, which the people called by Your name claim that they have proved to be in You. Then will I believe on

---

[20] Papa (in English, pope).

You and be baptized in Your name. For I have called upon my gods but, as I have seen, they are far from my help. Therefore, I believe that they have no power who do not hasten to aid those obedient to them. I now call upon You and I desire to believe on You. Only save me from the hand of my adversaries." As he thus spoke, the Alemanni turned their backs and began to take flight. But when they saw that their king was dead, they submitted to Clovis and said: "Let not, we pray you, a nation perish; now we are yours." Thereupon he put an end to the war, exhorted the people, and returned home in peace. He told the queen how by calling upon the name of Christ he had obtained victory. This happened in the fifteenth year of his reign (496).

CHAPTER 31

Thereupon the queen commanded that the holy Remigius, bishop of Rheims, be brought secretly to teach the king the word of salvation. The priest was brought to him secretly and began to lay before him that he should believe in the true God, the creator of heaven and earth, and forsake idols, who could neither help him nor others. But he replied: "Gladly do I listen to you, most holy Father, but one thing remains, for the people who follow me do not permit me to forsake their gods. But I will go and speak to them according to your words." When he met his men, and before he began to speak, all the people cried out together, for the divine power had anticipated him: "We reject the mortal gods, pious king, and we are ready to follow the immortal God whom Remigius preaches." These things were reported to the bishop, who rejoiced greatly and commanded the font to be prepared. . . . The king first asked to be baptized by the pontiff. He went, a new Constantine, into the font to be washed clean from the old leprosy, and to purify himself in fresh water from the stains which he had long had. But as he stepped into the baptismal water, the saint of God began in moving tone: "Bend softly your head, Sicamber, reverence what you have burned, and burn what you have reverenced." . . .

Therefore the king confessed Almighty God in Trinity, and was baptized in the name of the Father and of the Son and of the Holy Ghost, and was anointed with the holy chrism[21] with the sign of the cross. Of his army more than three thousand were baptized.

Adapted from the translation of Joseph Cullen Ayer in *A Source Book for Ancient Church History*. New York: Scribner's, 1913.

Rule of St. Benedict, c. 530 C.E.

The custom of some Christians of living in isolation from the world, dedicating their lives to prayer, meditation, and, often, fasting, probably derived from pre-Christian groups such as the Essenes. Many such Christians lived in caves in the Egyptian desert. Benedict of Nursia thought this practice extreme, and proposed a rule for monks who would live in communities, eating together, combining prayer and study with a healthy and moderate lifestyle.

---

[21] Anointing a political leader with oil dates back to the anointing of Saul as the first king of the Hebrews. A later legend claims that, no oil being available for the anointing of Clovis, a dove, symbol of the Holy Spirit, descended from the heavens carrying a vial. Medieval French kings claimed that the oil that anointed them was from this vial, which never ran dry.

CHAPTER 22: THE SLEEPING ARRANGEMENTS OF THE MONKS

The monks are to sleep in separate beds. They receive bedding as provided by the abbot, suitable to monastic life.

If possible, all are to sleep in one place, but should the size of the community preclude this, they will sleep in groups of ten or twenty under the watchful care of seniors. A lamp must be kept burning in the room until morning.

They sleep clothed, and girded with belts or cords; but they should remove their knives, lest they accidentally cut themselves in their sleep. Thus the monks will always be ready to arise without delay when the signal is given; each will hasten to arrive at the Work of God before the others, yet with all dignity and decorum. The younger brothers should not have their beds next to each other, but interspersed among those of the seniors. On arising for the Work of God, they will quietly encourage each other, for the sleepy like to make excuses.

CHAPTER 33: MONKS AND PRIVATE OWNERSHIP

Above all, this evil practice must be uprooted and removed from the monastery. We mean that without an order from the abbot, no one may presume to give, receive or retain anything as his own, nothing at all—not a book, writing tablets or stylus—in short, not a single item, especially since monks may not have the free disposal even of their own bodies and wills. For their needs, they are to look to the father of the monastery, and are not allowed anything which the abbot has not given or permitted. All things should be the common possession of all, as it is written, so that no one presumes to call anything his own (Acts 4:32).

But if anyone is caught indulging in this most evil practice, he should be warned a first and a second time. If he does not amend, let him be subjected to punishment.

CHAPTER 39: THE PROPER AMOUNT OF FOOD

For the daily meals, whether at noon or in midafternoon, it is enough, we believe, to provide all tables with two kinds of cooked food because of individual weaknesses. In this way, the person who may not be able to eat one kind of food may partake of the other. Two kinds of cooked food, therefore, should suffice for all the brothers, and if fruit or fresh vegetables are available, a third dish may also be added. A generous pound of bread is enough for a day whether for only one meal or for both dinner and supper. In the latter case the cellarer will set aside one third of this pound and give it to the brothers at supper.

Should it happen that the work is heavier than usual, the abbot may decide—and he will have the authority—to grant something additional, provided that it is appropriate, and that above all overindulgence is avoided, lest a monk experience indigestion. For nothing is so inconsistent with the life of any Christian as overindulgence. Our Lord says: Take care that your hearts are not weighed down with overindulgence. (Luke 21:34).

Young boys should not receive the same amount as their elders, but less, since in all matters frugality is the rule. Let everyone, except the sick who are very weak, abstain entirely from eating the meat of four-footed animals.

CHAPTER 48: THE DAILY MANUAL LABOUR

Idleness is the enemy of the soul. Therefore, the brothers should have specified periods for manual labor as well as for prayerful reading.

We believe that the times for both may be arranged as follows: From Easter to the first of October, they will spend their mornings after Prime till about the fourth hour at whatever work needs to be done. From the fourth hour until the time of Sext, they will devote themselves to reading. But after Sext and their meal, they may rest on their beds in complete silence; should a brother wish to read privately, let him do so, but without disturbing the others. They should say None a little early, about midway through the eighth hour, and then until Vespers they are to return to whatever work is necessary. They must not become distressed if local conditions or their poverty should force them to do the harvesting themselves. Then they live by the labor of their hands, as our fathers and the apostles did, then they are really monks. Yet, all things are to be done with moderation on account of the fainthearted.

From the first of October to the beginning of Lent, the brothers ought to devote themselves to reading until the end of the second hour. At this time Terce is said and they are to work at their assigned tasks until None. At the first signal for the hour of None, all put aside their work to be ready for the second signal. Then after their meal they will devote themselves to their reading or to the psalms.

During the days of Lent, they should be free in the morning to read until the third hour, after which they will work at their assigned tasks until the end of the tenth hour. During this time of Lent each one is to receive a book from the library, and is to read the whole of it straight through. These books are to be distributed at the beginning of Lent.

Above all, one or two seniors must surely be deputed to make the rounds of the monastery while the brothers are reading. Their duty is to see that no brother is so apathetic as to waste time or engage in idle talk to the neglect of his reading, and so not only harm himself but also distract others. If such a monk is found—God forbid—he should be reproved a first and a second time. If he does not amend, he must be subjected to the punishment of the rule as a warning to others. Further, brothers ought not to associate with one another at inappropriate times.

On Sunday all are to be engaged in reading except those who have been assigned various duties. If anyone is so remiss and indolent that he is unwilling or unable to study or to read, he is to be given some work in order that he may not be idle.

Brothers who are sick or weak should be given a type of work or craft that will keep them busy without overwhelming them or driving them away. The abbot must take their infirmities into account.

CHAPTER 55: THE CLOTHING AND FOOTWEAR OF THE BROTHERS

The clothing distributed to the brothers should vary according to local conditions and climate, because more is needed in cold regions and less in warmer. This is left to the abbot's discretion. We believe that for each monk a cowl and tunic will suffice in temperate regions; in winter a woolen cowl is necessary, in summer a thinner or worn one; also a scapular for work and footwear—both sandals and shoes.

Monks must not complain about the color or coarseness of all these articles, but use what is available in the vicinity at a reasonable cost. However, the abbot ought to be concerned about the measurements of these garments that they not be too short but fitted to the wearers.

Whenever new clothing is received, the old should be returned at once and stored in a wardrobe for the poor. To provide for laundering and night wear, every monk will need two cowls and two tunics, but anything more must be taken away as superfluous. When new articles are received, the worn ones—sandals or anything old—must be returned.

Brothers going on a journey should get underclothing from the wardrobe. On their return they are to wash it and give it back. Their cowls and tunics, too, ought to be somewhat better than those they ordinarily wear. Let them get these from the wardrobe before departing, and on returning put them back.

For bedding the monks will need a mat, a woolen blanket and a light covering as well as a pillow.

The beds are to be inspected frequently by the abbot, lest private possessions be found there. A monk discovered with anything not given him by the abbot must be subjected to very severe punishment. In order that this vice of private ownership may be completely uprooted, the abbot is to provide all things necessary: that is, cowl, tunic, sandals, shoes, belt, knife, stylus, needle, handkerchief and writing tablets. In this way every excuse of lacking some necessity will be taken away.

The abbot, however, must always bear in mind what is said in the Acts of the Apostles: Distribution was made to each one as he had need (Acts 4:35). In this way the abbot will take into account the weaknesses of the needy, not the evil will of the envious; yet in all his judgments he must bear in mind God's retribution.

From *The Rule of St. Benedict*, edited by Timothy Fry. Collegeville, Minn.: The Liturgical Press, 1981.

Unit 17: Islam

The Qu'ran is the Holy Book of the Islamic faith. It is a collection of sayings that Muhammed claimed were revealed to him by God while he was meditating in a cave. While Muhammed lived, he governed his people personally, with a status similar to that of a wise man or judge. After his death, his teachings were gathered quite quickly into an authorized version, containing the principles by which Muslims were to live. Within one hundred years after Muhammed's death, Muslims had conquered vast territories reaching to the borders of the Byzantine Empire in the East and penetrating into the heart of Europe in the West. The personal governing style of Muhammed gave way to kingdoms and the teachings of the Qu'ran were supplemented by two other collections. The *Hadith* are stories from Muhammed's life and his teachings not contained in the Qu'ran, but handed down orally for several generations. The *Shari'a* is a collection of case law in which the principles found in the Qu'ran are applied to the changing life-styles of a people whose culture and mores often clashed with the other cultures with which they came into close contact.

The Qu'ran: Sura 22, Pilgrimage

The first part of this passage deals with heaven and hell, the second with pilgrimage to the Kaaba, an obligation of every Muslim and one of the Five Pillars of Islam.

15. If any one thinks that God cannot support him in this life, as well as in the hereafter, let him turn totally to God and sever (his idolization towards anyone else.) He will then find out that this plan eliminates his worries.

16. We thus reveal these clear revelations, then God guides whomever He wills.

17. Those who believe, those who are Jewish, the converts, the Christians, the Magi, and the idol worshipers; God will judge them all on the day of resurrection. God is witnessing all things.

18. Do you not realize that to God prostrate those in the heavens, and those in the earth, and the sun, and the moon, and the stars, and the mountains, and the trees, and the animals, and many people? Other people are committed to doom. Whomever God commits to humiliation, you will find none to honor him. God does what He wills.

19. Of the two opposing sides, with regard to their Lord, those who disbelieve have deserved garments of fire, and lava being poured on their heads.

20. Even their insides melt therefrom, and their skins.

21. They will be confined in iron cells.

22. Whenever they try to flee from the agony thereof, they will be returned therein: "Taste the retribution of burning."

23. As for those who believe and work righteousness, God will admit them into gardens with flowing streams. They are adorned therein with bracelets of gold, and their clothes are silk.

24. They have been guided to the right message; they have been guided in the path of God most praised.

25. Those who disbelieve and repel others from the path of God, and from the Sacred Mosque that we appointed for all the people to retreat therein or just visit, and those who introduce any wickedness therein, we will commit them to painful retribution.

26. We pointed out for Abraham the location of the shrine: "You shall never idolize anything besides Me, and purify My shrine for those who encircle it, retreat in it, and those who bow and prostrate therein.

27. "And announce that the people shall observe the *hajj* pilgrimage. They will come to you walking and riding; they will come from the farthest valleys.

28. "They will reap many benefits, commemorate God's name during the specified days, and show their appreciation for the livestock He provides for them. Eat therefrom, and feed the poor and the needy.

29. "They shall carry out the religious duties, fulfill their vows, and encircle the grand shrine."

30. Indeed, for those who respect the sacred duties decreed by God, it will be better for them at their Lord. All livestock are permitted for you as food, except what is already stated. You shall avoid the abomination of idol worship, and avoid false regulations.

31. You shall devote your worship to God alone; do not set up any idols besides Him. Anyone who idolizes anything besides God is like one who falls from the sky, and gets snatched away by the vultures, or gets blown away by the wind into a bottomless pit.

32. Indeed, those who honor the offerings decreed by God, demonstrate the righteousness of their hearts.

33. After reaping benefits from the livestock for awhile, they offer it as charity at the grand shrine.

34. We decreed certain rituals for each congregation, whereby they show their appreciation of God's provision of livestock. However, your God is the same God; you shall submit to Him. Give good news to the reverent;

35. whose hearts cringe upon remembering God, remain steadfast in the face of adversity, observe the salat prayers, and give to charity from our provisions to them.

36. The livestock offerings are part of the religious duties decreed by God, for your own good. Thus, you shall mention God's name as you sacrifice them. Once they fall on their sides, you shall eat therefrom, and feed the poor and needy. That is what we created them for, that you may be appreciative.

37. None of their meat or blood reaches God; what reaches Him is your righteousness. That is what He created them for; that you may magnify God for guiding you; give good news to the good doers.

Translated by Rashad Khalifa, in Qur'an: The Final Scripture. Tucson, Arizona: Islamic Productions, 1981.
Reprinted by permission.

Hadith

ON PRAYING FOR THE DEAD

It is related from Abu Qalaba that he saw in a dream a cemetery, and it was as if the graves were split open and the dead came out of them. They sat on the edges of the graves and each one had before him a light. He saw among them one of his neighbors with no light in front of him and he asked him about it, saying, "Why do I not see any light in front of you?" The dead person said, "These others have children and friends to pray for them and give alms for them and their light is produced by that. I have only one son and he is no good. He does not pray for me and does not give alms on my behalf, therefore I have no light. And I am ashamed in front of my neighbors." When Abu Qalaba woke up he called the man's son and told him what he had seen. So the son said, "I will mend my ways and will no more do what I have been doing. And he was obedient and prayed for his father and gave him alms on his behalf. And sometime later when Abu Qalaba saw the graveyard in his dream he saw the same man with a light brighter than the sun and greater than the light of his companions. And the man said, "O Abu Qalaba, may God reward you well for me. Because of what you said I am saved from shame in front of my neighbors."

Translated by Jane Idleman Smith and Yvonne Yazbeck Haddad in *The Islamic Understanding of Death and Resurrection*. Albany: State University of New York Press. 1981.

CHAPTER 8: THE EARLY MIDDLE AGES

Unit 18: The Carolingians

The inheritance laws of the Salian Franks required that property be divided among all the sons of the deceased. Following this rule, it was the custom, when a king died, to divide the kingdom among his sons. By the eighth century, the Merovingian kings had become weak, ceding many of their duties to their chief administrative officers, the "mayors of the palace." One of these mayors of the palace was Charles Martel, leader of the army that stopped the European conquest of the Muslims at the Battle of Poitiers in 732. It was probably the popularity and strength of Charles that allowed his son Pippin to actually take the crown and establish a new dynasty, which would be named for his son, Charles. Pippin's son, Charles the Great, once again brought much of the West under the rule of one man.

Charlemagne created a school in his palace at Aachen where he brought some of the finest scholars in Europe. Because he fostered learning, there are many written sources for the reigns of the early Carolingians, including theological works, administrative documents, letters and two contemporary biographies.

from Einhard's *Life of Charlemagne*, c. 830

Einhard was a close friend and adviser to Charlemagne. He modeled his biography on Suetonius' *Lives of the Emperors*

The Franks in olden times were wont to choose their kings from the family of the Merovingians. This royal line is considered to have come to an end in the person of Childeric III, who was deposed from the throne by command of Stephen, the Roman pontiff; his long hair was cut off[22] and he was thrust into a monastery.

Although the line of the Merovingians actually ended with Childeric, it had nevertheless for some time previously been so utterly wanting in power that it had displayed no mark of royalty except the empty kingly title.

All the resources and power of the kingdom had passed into the control of the prefects of the palace, who were called the "mayors of the palace," and who employed the supreme authority. Nothing was left to the king. He had to content himself with his royal title, his flowing locks, and long beard. Seated in a chair of state, he was wont to display an appearance of power by receiving foreign ambassadors on their arrival, and, on their departure, giving them, as if on his own authority, those answers which he had been taught or commanded to give.

---

[22]   The long hair of the Merovingians was a sign of their nobility. They were known as "the long-haired kings."

Thus, except for his empty title, and an uncertain allowance for his subsistence, which the prefect of the palace used to furnish at his pleasure, there was nothing that the king could call his own, unless it were the income from a single farm, and that a very small one, where he made his home, and where such servants as were needful to wait on him constituted his scanty household. When he went anywhere he traveled in a wagon drawn by a yoke of oxen, with a rustic oxherd for charioteer. In this manner he proceeded to the palace, and to the public assemblies of the people held every year for the dispatch of the business of the kingdom, and he returned home again in the same sort of state. The administration of the kingdom, and every matter which had to be undertaken and carried through, both at home and abroad, was managed by the mayor of the palace.

In the year of the Incarnation of our Lord, 750, Pippin sent ambassadors to Pope Zacharias to ask his opinion in the matter of the kings of the Franks, who, though of the royal line, and called kings, enjoyed in truth no power in the realm except that official documents were issued in their name. Otherwise they were destitute of power, and did only what the mayor of the palace told them.

Only upon the day when the people, according to ancient usage, were wont to bring gifts to their sovereign on the March Field, did the king, surrounded by the army, sit in his chair, the mayor of the palace standing before him, and proclaim such laws as had been established by the Franks. The next day he returned home, and stayed there during the remainder of the year.

Pope Zacharias, therefore, in virtue of apostolic authority, told the ambassadors that he judged it better and more advantageous that he should be king and be called king who had the power rather than he who was falsely called king.

The said pontiff accordingly enjoined the king and the people of the Franks that Pippin, who already exercised the regal power, should be called king and raised to the throne.

And this was done by St. Boniface, the archbishop, who anointed him king in the city of Soissons. And so it came about that Pippin was called king, while Childeric, falsely called king, was shaven and sent to the monastery.

From *Readings in European History*, J. H. Robinson. Boston: Ginn, 1906.

Charlemagne: Letter to Abbot Baugulf, c. 790

In another part of his biography, Einhard describes Charlemagne's love of learning. At a time when a knowledge of reading and writing was limited mainly to the clergy, Charlemagne invited the leading scholars of the day to his court, founded a school there, and admonished bishops to found a school in each diocese. During what is often called the Carolingian renaissance, scriptoria were established in monasteries for copying manuscripts, both religious and secular. The monks developed a new, more legible writing style known as Carolingian minuscule. In this letter he explains some of the reasons for his concern for education.

Charles, by the grace of God, King of the Franks and Lombards and Patrician of the Romans, to Abbot Baugulf, and to all the congregation, also to the faithful committed to you, we have directed a loving greeting by our messengers in the name of omnipotent God:

Be it known, therefore, to your Devotion pleasing to God, that we, together with our faithful, have considered it to be expedient that the bishoprics and monasteries entrusted by the favor of Christ to our government, in addition to the rule of monastic life and the intercourse of holy religion, ought to be zealous also in the culture of letters, teaching those who by the gift of God are able to learn, according to the capacity of each individual; so that just as the observance of the monastic rule imparts order and grace to moral conduct, so also zeal in teaching and learning may do the same for the use of words, so that those who desire to please God by living rightly should not neglect to please him also by speaking correctly. For it is written, "Either from thy words thou shalt be justified, or from thy words thou shalt be condemned."

Although it is better to do the right than to know it, nevertheless knowledge should precede action. Therefore, each one ought to study what he would accomplish, so that the mind may the better know what ought to be done, if the tongue utters the praises of omnipotent God without the hindrances of errors. For if errors should be shunned by all men, so much the more ought they to be avoided, as far as possible, by those who are chosen for the very purpose that they may be the servants of truth.

Yet, in recent years, when letters have been written to us from various monasteries to inform us that the brethren who dwelt there were offering up in our behalf holy and pious prayers, we noted in most of these letters correct thoughts but uncouth expressions; for what pious devotion dictated faithfully to the mind, the tongue, uneducated on account of the neglect of study, was not able to express without error. We, therefore, began to fear lest perchance, as the skill in writing was wanting, so also the wisdom for understanding the Holy Scriptures might be much less than it rightly ought to be. And we all know well that, although errors of speech are dangerous, far more dangerous are errors of the understanding.

Therefore, we exhort you not only not to neglect the study of letters, but also with most humble mind, pleasing to God, to pursue it earnestly in order that you may be able more easily and more correctly to penetrate the mysteries of the divine Scriptures. Since, moreover, figures of speech, tropes, and the like are found in the sacred pages, it cannot be doubted that in reading these one will understand the spiritual sense more quickly if previously he shall have been fully instructed in the mastery of letters. Such men truly are to be chosen for this work as have both the will and the ability to learn and a desire to instruct others. And may this be done with a zeal as great as the earnestness with which we command it.

From *Readings in European History*. J. H. Robinson. Boston: Ginn, 1906

Capitulary of Herstal. 779

This selection illustrates Charlemagne's dependence on counts, church officials, and his *missi dominici* to rule a territory so large that his personal supervision could be only slight and sporadic.

In the eleventh auspicious year of the reign of our lord and most glorious king, Charles, in the month of March, there was made a capitulary whereby, there being gathered together in one synod and council the bishops and abbots and illustrious counts, together with our most pious lord, decisions were agreed to concerning certain appropriate matters in accordance with God's will.

1   Concerning the metropolitans, that suffragan bishops should be placed under them in accordance with the canons, and that such things as they see needing correction in their ministry they should correct and improve with willing hearts.

2   Concerning bishops: where at present they are not consecrated they are to be consecrated without delay.

3   Concerning the monasteries that have been based on a rule, that they should live in accordance with that rule; and that convents should preserve their holy order, and each abbess reside in her convent without intermission.

4   That bishops should have authority over the priests and clerks within their dioceses, in accordance with the canons.

5   That bishops should have authority to impose correction on incestuous people, and should have the power of reproving widows within their dioceses.

6   That no one should be allowed to receive another's clerk, or to ordain him to any rank.

7   Concerning tithes, that each man should give his tithe, and that these should be disposed of according to the bishop's orders.

8   Concerning murderers and other guilty men who ought in law to die, if they take refuge in a church they are not to be let off, and no food is to be given to them there.

9   That robbers who are caught within an immunity area should be presented by the justices of that area at the count's court; and anyone who fails to comply with this is to lose his benefice and his office. Likewise a vassal of ours, if he does not carry this out, shall lose his benefice and his office; anyone who has no benefice must pay the fine.

10   Concerning a man who commits perjury, that he cannot redeem it except by losing his hand. But if an accuser wishes to press the charge of perjury they are both to go to the ordeal of the cross; and if the swearer wins, the accuser is to pay the equivalent of his *wergeld*.[23] This procedure is to be observed in minor cases; in major cases, or in cases involving free status, they are to act in accordance with the law.

11   Concerning the judgement of, and punishment inflicted upon robbers, the synod have ruled that the testimony given by the bishops is probably equivalent to that of the count, provided there is no malice or ill will, and there is no intervention in the case except in the interests of seeing justice done. And if he (the judge) should maim a man through hatred or ill intent and not for the sake of justice, he is to lose his office and is to be subject to the laws under which he acted unjustly and to the penalty which he sought to inflict.

12   The heads of procedure which our father of happy memory decided upon for his hearings and for his synods: these we wish to preserve.

13   Concerning the properties of the churches from which the census now comes, the tithes and ninths should be paid along with that census; likewise tithes and ninths are to be given for those properties from which they have not so far come--from fifty casati one shilling, from

---

[23]   Literally "man price," the *wergeld* was the fine imposed for a crime under Salic law. See Chapter 6 "The Laws of the Salian Franks."

thirty *casati* half a shilling, and from twenty a *tremissis*. And concerning precarial holdings, where they are now they are to be renewed, and where they are not they are to be recorded. And a distinction should be made between the precarial holdings established by our authority and those which they establish of their own volition from the property of the church itself.

14 Concerning the raising of an armed following, let no one dare to do it.

15 Concerning those who give tribute in candles, and those who are free by deed or charter, the long standing arrangements are to be observed.

16 Concerning oaths entered into by a swearing together in a fraternity, that no one should dare to perform them. Moreover, concerning alms-giving, and fire and shipwreck, even though men enter into fraternities they are not to dare to swear to them.

17 Concerning travellers who are going to the palace or anywhere else, that no one should dare to assault them with an armed band. And let no one presume to take away another's crop when the fields are enclosed, unless he is going to the host[24] or is acting as one of our *missi*; anyone who dares to do otherwise shall make amends for it.

18 Concerning the tolls that have before now been forbidden, let no one exact them except where they have existed from of old.

19 Concerning the sale of slaves, that it should take place in the presence of a bishop or count, or in the presence of an archdeacon or *centenarius*, or in that of a *vicedominus* or a count's justice, or before well-known witnesses; and let no one sell a slave beyond the march. Anyone who does so must pay the fine as many times over as the slaves he sold; and if he does not have the means to pay he must hand himself over in service to the count as a pledge, until such time as he can pay off the fine.

20 Concerning coats of mail, that no one should dare to sell them outside our kingdom.

21 If a count does not administer justice in his district he is to arrange for our missus to be provided for from his household until justice has been administered there; and if a vassal of ours does not administer justice, then the count and our missus are to stay at his house and live at his expense until he does so.

22 If anyone is unwilling to accept a payment instead of vengeance he is to be sent to us, and we will send him where he is likely to do least harm. Likewise, if anyone is unwilling to pay a sum instead of vengeance or to give legal satisfaction for it, it is our wish that he be sent to a place where he can do no further harm.

23 Concerning robbers, our instructions are that the following rules should be observed: for the first offence they are not to die but to lose an eye; for the second offence the robber's nose is to be cut off; for the third offence, if he does not mend his ways, he must die.

---

[24] Reporting for military service.

Donation of Constantine, 8th century

As the authority of the Roman Emperors declined in Western Europe, the church under the bishop at Rome tended to extend its authority in secular as well as religious matters, especially in the Italian peninsula. The church supported the Carolingians and, in return, asked first Pepin and later his grandson Charlemagne for military aid in subduing the Lombards and others who threatened to establish hegemony in Italy. To support the church's claim, a document surfaced that purported to be written by the Emperor Constantine in the fourth century, granting to the bishop of Rome and to his successors supremacy over all of the Christian church and over "all the provinces, districts and cities of Italy of the western regions." The document was later proven to be a forgery. (see Chapter 13, Lorenzo Valla)

In the name of the holy and indivisible Trinity, the Father, namely, and the Son and the Holy Spirit. The emperor Caesar Flavius Constantine in Christ Jesus, the Lord God our Saviour, one of that same holy Trinity,—faithful, merciful, supreme, beneficent, Alamannic, Gothic, Sarmatic, Germanic, Britannic, Hunic, pious, fortunate, victor and triumpher, always august: to the most holy and blessed father of fathers Sylvester, bishop of the city of Rome and pope, and to all his successors the pontiffs who are about to sit upon the chair of St. Peter until the end of time—also to all the most reverend and of God beloved catholic bishops, subjected by this our imperial decree throughout the whole world to this same holy Roman church, who have been established now and in all previous times—grace, peace, charity, rejoicing, long-suffering, mercy, be with you all from God the Father almighty and from Jesus Christ his Son and from the Holy Ghost. . .

(There follows an account of Constantine's suffering from leprosy, the intervention of Saints Peter and Paul, and his conversion to Christianity through the guidance of Pope Sylvester.)

And, when, the blessed Sylvester preaching them, I perceived these things, and learned that by the kindness of St. Peter himself I had been entirely restored to health: I—together with all our satraps and the whole senate and the nobles and all the Roman people, who are subject to the glory of our rule—considered it advisable that, as on earth he (Peter) is seen to have been constituted vicar of the Son of God, so the pontiffs, who are the representatives of that same chief of the apostles, should obtain from us and our empire the power of a supremacy greater than the earthly clemency of our imperial serenity is seen to have had conceded to it,—we choosing that same prince of the apostles, or his vicars, to be our constant intercessors with God. And, to the extent of our earthly imperial power, we decree that his holy Roman church shall be honoured with veneration; and that, more than our empire and earthly throne, the most sacred seat of St. Peter shall be gloriously exalted; we giving to it the imperial power, and dignity of glory, and vigour and honour.

And we ordain and decree that he shall have the supremacy as well over the four chief seats Antioch, Alexandria, Constantinople and Jerusalem, as also over all the churches of God in the whole world. And he who for the time being shall be pontiff of that holy Roman church shall be more exalted than, and chief over, all the priests of the whole world; and, according to his judgment, everything which is to be provided for the service of God or the stability of the faith of the Christians is to be administered. It is indeed just, that there the holy law should have the seat of its rule where the founder of holy laws, our Saviour, told St. Peter to take the chair of the apostleship; where also, sustaining the cross, he blissfully took the cup of death and appeared as imitator of his Lord and Master; and that there the people should bend their necks at the confession of Christ's name, where their teacher, St. Paul the apostle, extending his neck for Christ, was crowned with martyrdom. There, until the end, let them seek a teacher, where the holy body of the teacher lies; and, there, prone and humiliated, let them perform the service of the heavenly king, God our Saviour Jesus Christ, where the proud were accustomed to serve under the rule of an earthly king. . . .

In imitation of our own power, in order that for that cause the supreme pontificate may not deteriorate, but may rather be adorned with power and glory even more than is the dignity of an earthly rule: behold we—giving over to the oft-mentioned most blessed pontiff, our father Sylvester the universal pope, as well our palace, as has been said, as also the city of Rome and all the provinces, districts and cities of Italy or of the western regions; and relinquishing them, by our inviolable gift, to the power and sway of himself or the pontiffs his successors—do decree, by this our godlike charter and imperial constitution, that it shall be so arranged; and do concede that they (the palaces, provinces, etc.) shall lawfully remain with the holy Roman church.

Wherefore we have perceived it to be fitting that our empire and the power of our kingdom should be transferred and changed to the regions of the East; and that, in the province of Byzantium, in a most fitting place, a city should be built in our name; and that our empire should there be established. For, where the supremacy of priests and the head of the Christian religion has been established by a heavenly Ruler, it is not just that there an earthly ruler should have jurisdiction. . .

Given at Rome on the third day before the *Kalends* of April, our master the august Flavius Constantine, for the fourth time, and Galligano, most illustrious men, being consuls.

Translated by *Ernest F. Henderson in Select Historical Documents of the Middle Ages*. London: George Bell & Sons. 1910.

Unit 19: Invasions and the Creation of Feudalism

Feudalism is the general term for a variety of arrangements and institutions by which people of the Middle Ages sought to protect themselves from invaders and to keep order in a society without strong governmental institutions. A free man bound himself to a lord and promised to serve his lord faithfully in return for the lord's protection. The vassal was usually granted a fief, for which he performed military service.

The Capitulary of Mersen, 847

In the early years, mutual rights and obligations were not spelled out in detail.

We will moreover that each free man in our kingdom shall choose a lord, from us or our faithful, such a one as he wishes.

We command moreover that no man shall leave his lord without just cause, nor should any one receive him, except in such a way as was customary in the time of our predecessors.

And we wish you to know that we want to grant right to our faithful subjects and we do not wish to do anything to them against reason. Similarly we admonish you and the rest of our faithful subjects that you grant right to your men and do not act against reason toward them.

And we will that the man of each one of us (Lothair, Louis and Charles) in whosesoever kingdom he is, shall go with his lord against the enemy, or in his other needs unless there shall have been (as may there not be) such an invasion of the kingdom as is called a *landwer*, so that the whole people of that kingdom shall go together to repel it.

from *Translation and Reprints from the Original Sources of European History*. vol. IV. University of Pennsylvania. 1895.

Causes for Which a Vassal Might Leave his Lord, 816

Here are detailed the "just causes" referred to in the previous selection.

If any one shall wish to leave his lord, and is able to prove against him one of these crimes, that is, in the first place, if the lord has wished to reduce him unjustly into servitude; in the second place, if he has taken counsel against his life; in the third place, if the lord has committed adultery with the wife of his vassal; in the fourth place, if he has wilfully attacked him with a drawn sword; in the fifth place, if the lord has been able to bring defence to his vassal after he has commended his hands to him, and has not done so; it is allowed to the vassal to leave him. If the lord has perpetrated anything against the vassal in these five points it is allowed the vassal to leave him.

from *Translation and Reprints from the Original Sources of European History*. vol. IV. University of Pennsylvania. 1895.

A Summons to Military Service, c. 1072

This selection describes the organization of a medieval kingdom. The king deals directly with his vassals, who are responsible for summoning their own vassals when an army is needed.

William, king of the English, to Aethelwig, abbot of Evesham, greeting. I command you to summon all those who are under your charge and jurisdiction to have armed before me by the week after Whitsunday, at Clarendon, all the knights which are due to me. And do you also come to me on that day and bring with you armed those five knights which you owe to me from your abbey. Witness Eudo, the steward, at Winchester.

from *Translation and Reprints from the Original Sources of European History*. vol. IV. University of Pennsylvania. 1895.

Ceremony of Homage, 1127

The vassal became the "man" (Latin *homo*) of his lord. In return, he received a fief, a grant of land or some other privilege by which he could secure the wealth needed to outfit himself for battle. In theory the relationship was strictly personal, between the two men, and ended at the death of either of them. In practice, it tended to become hereditary. Upon the death of a lord, his vassals would become the vassals of his son, but a ceremony and declaration of homage to the new lord was needed to create a new personal allegiance.

Through the whole remaining part of the day those who had been previously enfeoffed by the most pious Count Charles did homage to the new count, taking up now again their fiefs and offices and whatever they had before rightfully and legitimately obtained. On Thursday, the seventh of April, homages were again made to the count, being completed in the following order of faith and security.

First they did their homage thus. The count asked the vassal if he were willing to become completely his man, and the other replied, "I am willing"; and with hands clasped, placed between the hands of the count, they were bound together by a kiss. Secondly, he who had done homage gave his fealty to the representative of the count in these words, "I promise on my faith that I will in future be faithful to Count William, and will observe my homage to him completely against all persons, in good faith and without deceit." And, thirdly, he took his oath to this upon the relics of the saints. Afterward the count, with a little rod which he held in his hand, gave investitures to all who by this agreement had given their security and accompanying oath.

From *Readings in European History*, edited by J. H. Robinson. Boston: Ginn, 1906.

Grant of a Fief, 1200

This selection alludes to the practice, common in later feudalism, of a man having more than one lord. If two of his lords went to war against each other, he faced a seemingly insoluble conflict—to fight for one meant to betray his obligation to the other. This led to the practice of naming a "liege lord," to whom he owed primary allegiance.

I, Thiebault, count palatine of Troyes, make known to those present and to come that I have given in fee to Jocelyn d'Avalon and his heirs the manor which is called Gillencourt, which is of the castellanerie of La Ferté sur Aube; and whatever the same Jocelyn shall be able to acquire in the same manor I have granted to him and his heirs in augmentation of that fief. I have granted, moreover, to him that in no free manor of mine will I retain men who are of this gift. The same Jocelyn, moreover, on account of this has become my liege man, saving, however, his allegiance to Gerard d'Arcy, and to the lord duke of Burgundy, and to Peter, count of Auxerre. Done at Chouaude, by my own witness, in the year of the Incarnation of our Lord 1200 in the month of January. Given by the hand of Walter, my chancellor; note of Milo.

from *Translation and Reprints from the Original Sources of European History*. vol. IV. University of Pennsylvania. 1895.

Fees for License to Marry, 1140-1282

If the widow of a vassal wanted to remarry, her new husband would, at least in theory, hold her land as a fief from the dead man's lord, and would become his vassal. The lord might thus insist on choosing as her new husband a man who would be loyal to him. A widow might be allowed to purchase the right to marry a man of her own choosing, or to remain single.

Ralph son of William owes 100 marks as a fine, to be allowed to marry Margery who was wife of Nicholas Corbet who held of the king in *capite*, and that the same Margery may be allowed to marry him.

Walter de Cancy renders account of 15 pounds to be allowed to marry a wife as he shall choose.

Wiverona wife of Iverac of Ipswich renders account 4 pounds and 1 mark of silver that she may not have to take any husband except the one she wishes.

Emma de Normanville and Roheisa and Margaret and Juliana, her sisters, render account of 10 marks for license to marry where they wish.

Roheisa de Doura renders account of 450 pounds to have half of all the lands which belonged to Richard de Lucy, her grandfather, and which the brother of the same Roheisa had afterward as well in England as in Normandy, and for license to marry where she wishes so long as she does not marry herself to any of the enemies of the king.

Alice, countess of Warwick, renders account of 1000 pounds and 10 palfreys to be allowed to remain a widow as long as she pleases, and not to be forced to marry by the king. And if perchance she should wish to marry, she shall not marry except with the assent and on the grant of the king, where the king shall be satisfied; and to have the custody of her sons whom she has by the earl of Warwick her late husband.

Hawisa, who was wife of William Fitz Robert renders account of 130 marks and 4 palfreys that she may have peace from Peter of Borough to whom the king has given permission to marry her; and that she may not be compelled to marry.

Geoffrey de Mandeville owes 20,000 marks to have as his wife Isabella, countess of Gloucester, with all the lands and tenements and fiefs which fall to her.

From *Translations and Reprints from the Original Sources of European History* , vol. 4. University of Pennsylvania Press, 1895.

Rules for Military Service, 1270

After feudalism was well established, the mutual obligations of lord and vassal tended to be spelled out in detail.

The baron and all vassals of the king are bound to appear before him when he shall summon them, and to serve him at their own expense for forty days and forty nights, with as many knights as each one owes; and he is able to exact from them these services when he wishes and when he has need of them. And if the king wishes to keep them more than forty days at their own expense, they are not bound to remain if they do not wish it. And if the king wishes to keep them at his expense for the defence of the realm, they are bound to remain. And if the king wishes to lead them outside of the kingdom, they need not go unless they wish to, for they have already served their forty days and forty nights.

from *Translation and Reprints from the Original Sources of European History*. vol. IV. University of Pennsylvania. 1895.

Freeing of a Serf, 1278

The feudal relationship was between two free men, lord and vassal. Their function was to fight, to protect society from dangers from within and without. The economic underpinning of feudalism was the fief, usually a grant of land consisting of one or more manors, whose land was worked by serfs. Serfs were unfree. They could not leave the land or refrain from their assigned labors without the permission of the lord of the manor. They were not, however, slaves. They could not be sold or dispossessed from the land. The labor or rent required of them was regulated by tradition. By the thirteenth century, with cities growing and the economy diversifying, the manumission of serfs was not uncommon.

To all the faithful of Christ to whom the present writing shall come, Richard, by the divine permission, Abbot of Peterborough and of the Convent of the same place, eternal greeting in the Lord:

Let all know that we have manumitted and liberated from all yoke of servitude William, the son of Richard of Wythington, whom previously we have held as our born bondsman, with his whole progeny and all his chattels, so that neither we nor our successors shall be able to require or exact any right or claim in the said William, his progeny, or his chattels, But the same William, with his whole progeny and all his chattels, shall remain free and quit and without disturbance, exaction, or any claim on the part of us or our successors by reason of any servitude forever.

We will, moreover, and concede that he and his heirs shall hold the messuages, land, rents and meadows in Wythington which his ancestors held from us and our predecessors, by giving and performing the fine which is called *merchet* for giving his daughter in marriage, and tallage from year to year according to our will,—that he shall have and hold these for the future from us and from our successors freely, quietly, peacefully, and hereditarily, by paying to us and our successors yearly 40s. sterling, at the four terms of the year, namely: at St. John the Baptist's day 10s., at Michaelmas 10s., at Christmas 10s., and at Easter 10s., for all service, exaction, custom, and secular demand; saving to us, nevertheless, attendance at our court of Castres every three weeks, wardship, and relief, and outside service of our lord the king, when they shall happen.

And if it shall happen that the said William or his heirs shall die at any time without an heir, the said messuage, land, rents, and meadows with their appurtenances shall return fully and completely to us and our successors. Nor will it be allowed to the said William or his heirs to give, sell, alienate, mortgage or encumber in any way, the said messuage, land, rents, and meadows, or any part of them, by which the said messuage, land, rents and meadows should not return to us and our successors in the form declared above. And if this should occur later, their deed shall be declared null, and what is thus alienated shall come to us and our successors.

Given at Borough, for the love of Lord Robert of good memory, once abbot, our predecessor and maternal uncle of the said William, and at the instance of the good man, Brother Hugh of Mutton, relative of the said abbot Robert, A.D. 1278, on the eve of Pentecost.

from *Translation and Reprints from the Original Sources of European History*. vol. 3. University of Pennsylvania. 1895.

CHAPTER 9: THE HIGH MIDDLE AGES

Unit 20: Popular Piety

The model for society in the early Middle Ages was that of The Three Orders. According to this model, society was divided into three classes, or orders: those who pray, those who fight, and those who work; that is, the clergy, the nobility, and everyone else. These functions were ordained by God. The clergy prayed for the spiritual well-being of all, as the nobility were responsible for their physical safety. In the High Middle Ages, relative peace, the beginnings of state building with paid armies, and the growth of an urban economy made it more difficult to divide the functions of society so neatly. One of the effects was a growing enthusiasm of lay people for pious activities on their own behalf.

Private confession of sins to a priest created a need for guidance for the priests who heard the confessions. Manuals were created, telling them how to go about questioning the penitent and what penances they should impose.

With safer roads, pilgrimages became popular. They served a number of purposes. Some pilgrimages were imposed as penances for particularly serious sins. Some were made in hopes of being healed by the saint whose relics reposed at the pilgrimage site. Some people no doubt went for the adventure and comradeship.

The intellectual concern of lay people for their own spirituality took two forms. The uneducated looked for manifestations of God around them, as in the story of the Devout Bees. Lay persons who were learning to read and write began to read the Bible and the works of theologians for themselves, and some interpreted these writings in ways that were unacceptable to the Church. The Roman inquisitorial process was adapted to hunt out and silence those who taught or encouraged unorthodox beliefs.

A Manual for Inquisitors at Carcasonne, 1248-1249

According to Roman law, action could be started in criminal matters in three ways. The first was accusation by another citizen. The second was denunciation by a public official. The third was inquisition, in which officials went into a locality and asked upstanding citizens if they knew of any crimes that had been committed. It was this third method that was used by the Church in the High Middle Ages (1000-1300) in its effort to stamp out heresy, or unorthodox beliefs. At the beginning of the thirteenth century there was no body of law that explicitly defined heresy or set out how it should be dealt with. Individuals appointed as inquisitors wrote down and then collected into manuals the methods they developed out of their experience in dealing with heretics. One of the earliest is the manual below, which includes forms for the various actions the inquisitors may take. In other criminal trials, Roman law gave the accused the right to be defended, to face his or her accuser, and to know the exact charges against him. These rights were denied a person accused of heresy.

LETTER OF COMMISSION

To the pious and discreet men, beloved in Christ, Friars William Raymond and Peter Durand of the Order of Preachers, Pons, a friar of the same order in the province of Provence, a servant of little use and unworthy, sends greetings and the spirit of charity.

With full confidence in your discretion and devotion, in virtue of the authority of the Lord Pope which is entrusted to us in this region, we have decided to send you, for remission of your sins, to make inquisition of heretics and their believers, *fautors*,[25] receivers, and defenders, and also of persons who are defamed, in the province of Narbonne, with the exception of the arch-deaconries of Villelongue and Villemur of the diocese of Toulouse and in the dioceses of Albi, Rodez, Mende, and Le Puy; by that same authority directing you to proceed vigorously and prudently in this business, pursuant to the mandate and decree of the Apostolic See. If both of you are unable to be present to carry out this commission, one of you nevertheless may accomplish it.

Given at Narbonne, 21 October 1244

THE PROCEDURE OF THE INQUISITION

This is the procedure. Within the limits of inquisition entrusted to and defined for us by the prior of the province under the authority stated above, we choose a place which seems to be well suited to the purpose, from which or in which we make inquisition of other localities. Calling the clergy and people together there, we deliver a general sermon, in which we read aloud the letters of both the Lord Pope and the prior of the province concerning the form and the authorization of the Inquisition, and we make what explanation is necessary; thereafter, we issue a general summons, either orally to those present or by letter to those who are absent, in the following form:

METHOD OF CITATION

The inquisitors of heretical depravity (send) greetings in the Lord to so and so, parish priest. We enjoin and strictly instruct you, in virtue of the authority we wield, to summon in our name and by our authority all the parishioners of such and such place, men from the age of fourteen, women from the age of twelve, or younger if perchance they shall have been guilty of an offense, to appear before us on such a day at such a place to answer for acts which they may have committed against the faith and to abjure heresy. And if no previous inquisition has been made in that place, we will grant indulgence from imprisonment to all from that place who have not been cited by name or who have not yet earned the indulgence, if, within a specified time, they come voluntarily as penitents to tell the exact and full truth about themselves and about others.

This we call the period of grace or of indulgence.

---

25 Protector.

METHOD OF ABJURATION AND THE FORM OF THE OATH

We require each and every person who presents himself for confession to abjure all heresy and to take oath that he will tell the full and exact truth about himself and about others, living and dead, in the matter of the fact or crime of heresy or Waldensianism;[26] that he will preserve and defend the Catholic faith; that he will neither harbor nor defend heretics of any sect whatever nor befriend them nor believe in them, but rather that he will in good faith pursue and seize them and their agents or, at least, will disclose them to the Church or to princes and their *baillis*[27] who are eager and able to seize them; and that he will not obstruct the Inquisition, but rather will set himself against those who impede it.

FORMULA FOR THE INTERROGATORY

Thereafter, the person is diligently questioned about whether he saw a heretic or Waldensian, where and when, how often and with whom, and about others who were present; whether he listened to their preaching or exhortation and whether he gave them lodging or arranged shelter for them; whether he conducted them from place to place or otherwise consorted with them or arranged for them to be guided or escorted; whether he ate or drank with them or ate bread blessed by them; whether he gave or sent anything to them; whether he acted as their financial agent or messenger or assistant; whether he held any deposit or anything else of theirs; whether he received the Peace from their book, mouth, shoulder, or elbow; whether he adored a heretic or bowed his head or genuflected and said "Bless us" before heretics or whether he was present at their baptisms or confessions; whether he was present at a Waldensian Lord's Supper, confessed his sins to them, accepted penance or learned anything from them; whether he was otherwise on familiar terms with or associated with heretics or Waldenses in any way; whether he made an agreement, heeded requests, or received gifts in return for not telling the truth about himself or others; whether he advised or persuaded anyone or caused anyone to be persuaded to do any of the foregoing; whether he knows any other man or woman to have done any of the foregoing; whether he believed in the heretics of Waldenses or their errors.

Finally, after that which he has confessed about himself or testified about other persons on all of these matters--and sometimes on others about which he was questioned, but not without good reason--has been written down, in the presence of one or both of us, with at least two other persons qualified for careful discharge of this task associated with us, he verifies everything which he caused to be recorded.[28] In this way we authenticate the records of the Inquisition as to confessions and depositions, whether they are prepared by the notary or by another scribe.

And when a region is widely infected we make general inquisition of all persons in the manner just described, entering the names of all of them in the record, even of those who insist that they know nothing about others and have themselves committed no crime, so that if they have lied or if subsequently they commit an offense, as is often found true of a number of persons, it is on record that they have abjured and have been interrogated in detail.

---

26 The Waldensians were a group who preached the virtue of poverty. The church's main complaint against them was that they preached on streetcorners without the permission of the local bishop.

27 Royal officials.

28 The proceedings were written down and read back to the accused, which theoretically assured that she or he could dispute any inaccuracies. However, they were written in Latin, while the defendant usually spoke the local vernacular language and could read neither Latin nor the vernacular.

Moreover, when we summon anyone individually we write in this form:

> In our name and by our authority, you (the priest) are to issue a summary citation to so and so, once and for all, to appear on such a day at such a place to answer for his faith (or for such and such an offense or to receive sentence of imprisonment, or more simply, penance for acts committed or to defend a deceased parent or to hear sentence in his own case or in the case of a deceased person whose heir he is).[29]

In individual as well as multiple summons, after describing the authority by which we issue them, which is on record for the region, we list in order of rank and locality the names of persons; we state the reasons for the summons; we assign safe places and the limit of delay without contempt. To no one do we deny a legitimate defense, nor do we deviate from established legal procedure, except that we do not make public the names of witnesses, because of the decree of the Apostolic See, wisely made by Lord Gregory (IX) and afterward renewed by our most blessed pope, Innocent (IV), as a prerogative and absolute necessity of the faith, on which point we have letters of confirmation from several cardinals. In this matter, we proceed according to the holy counsel of prelates, with all necessary prudence and are, as well in the case of those against whom inquisition is made as in the case of those who are witnesses.

We use this form in imposing penances and issuing condemnation: We require those who wish to return to ecclesiastical unity for that reason to abjure heresy again, and we solemnly bind them by official affidavits to observance and defense of the faith, to the pursuit of heretics, and to active assistance in inquisitions, as stated above, and to acceptance and fulfillment of penance imposed at our discretion. Thereafter, having granted the boon of absolution according to the usage of the Church, we impose on the penitent the penance of imprisonment with this formula:

METHOD AND FORM OF RECONCILING AND PUNISHING THOSE WHO RETURN TO ECCLESIASTICAL UNITY

> In the name of our Lord Jesus Christ. We inquisitors of heretical depravity, etc. Through the inquisition which by apostolic mandate we make of heretics and persons who are defamed, we find that you (so and so) as you have confessed in legal proceedings before us, have adored numerous heretics, harbored them, visited them, and believed in their errors. Having on that account been taken into custody, you nevertheless declare that you desire to return to ecclesiastical unity and to recant sincerely and unfeignedly, as recorded above; you subjugate yourself of your own will to the penalty for heretics if you act to the contrary; you recognize that you are absolved from the excommunication by which you were bound for previous acts, under the condition and reservation that if you are found to have suppressed the truth, either about yourself or about others, or if you do not carry out and fulfill the penance and commands which we lay upon you, the aforesaid absolution has no effect thereafter and you will be adjudged to be entirely noncompliant. With the cooperation and assistance of such and such

---

29 The property of a convicted heretic was often confiscated as part of his punishment. If the convicted heretic was deceased, his property would be seized from his heirs. A conviction also impugned the family honor, another reason for requiring the heirs to appear.

prelates and men learned in law, by their counsel and that of others, in accordance with apostolic command, and by virtue of the oath you have taken , we direct you to do penance for the acts stated above, by which you have shamefully offended God and the Church, and to betake yourself without delay to the decent and humane prison prepared for you in (such and such) a city, there to make your salutary and permanent abode. If, indeed, you refuse to carry out our command, either by delaying to enter or, perchance, by leaving after you have done so or by doing anything else in contradiction to what you abjured or swore or promised, whatever the time you came before us, thus revealing your fictitious confession (and your deceit) in festing repentance we hold you guilty thenceforward as impenitent and bound by worse sins; and, pursuant to the authority we wield, we bind by the chains of excommunication as *fautors*, receivers, and defenders, of heretics all who knowingly either harbor or defend you or in any way lend counsel and aid to your refusal to comply; and we decree that the reconciliation and mercy granted to you can have no further effect, at the same time, in full justice, relinquishing you as a heretic to the secular arm from that moment on.[30]

LETTERS CONCERNING THE PERFORMANCE OF PENANCES

In respect of the penances which we give to those who are not to be imprisoned, we issue letters in the following form:

To all faithful Christians who shall inspect the present letter, (so and so), inquisitors, etc. Since (so and so) the bearer sinned by the crime of heretical morbidity, as revealed by his own confession made in proceedings before us, and of his own will returns humbly to the bosom of Holy Church, at the same time abjuring heretical morbidity, and now has been absolved from the chains of excommunication according to the usages of the Church, we decree for him that in detestation of his error he shall wear two crosses, one on the breast and one on the shoulders, yellow in color, two palms in height, two in breadth, each arm three fingers in width. The clothing on which he wears the crosses shall never be yellow in color. As long as he lives he shall attend mass and vespers on Sundays and feast days, as well as a general sermon if one is delivered in the village where he shall follow processions for (so many) years, bearing large branches in his hand, walking between the clergy and the people, in each procession in which he appears displaying himself in such aspect that he reveals to the people that he is doing penance there because of acts he committed against the faith. He shall visit over (so many) years such and such sanctuaries, and in each of these pilgrimages just stated he is required to present our letter, which we wish him to have and carry to the prelate of the church he is visiting, and to bring back to us a letter from him attesting that the pilgrimage was accomplished in proper form. Therefore, dearly beloved, we request that you in no way molest or allow others to molest (so and so), who is carrying our letter and wearing crosses and fulfilling the things we have enjoined for him by reason of the acts stated above which he committed against the faith, when you find him deporting himself in all respects as a Catholic. If, however, you see him behaving otherwise or attempting to do so, you should hold him to be a perjurer and excommunicate and bound by even

---

30 The church did not allow its officials to shed blood, even in order to stamp out heresy. People convicted of the most serious offenses against the Church were turned over to secular officials for execution.

worse sins. And from that time on we decree that the reconciliation and mercy granted to him can have no further effect, and not only do we, pursuant to the authority we wield, bind him by the chain of excommunication as a heretic, but we do the same, as *fautors*, receivers, or defenders of heretics, for all who knowingly harbor or defend him or in any other way lend him aid, counsel, or favor.

FORM OF SENTENCE FOR RELEASE TO THE SECULAR ARM[31]

We condemn by sentences, such as the following, heretics and their believers, having first stated and exposed their crimes and errors and other matters, as is customary in procedures of this kind:

We, the inquisitors aforesaid, having heard and carefully weighed the crimes and defaults of (so and so), named above, and especially those circumstances which ought most significantly to influence us in the work of extirpating heretical morbidity and planting the faith, either by punishment or forgiveness, with the reverend fathers (so and so) associated and acting with us, by definitive sentence adjudge (so and so), named above, to be a heretic, because he believed in the errors of heretics and is proved still to believe them and because, when examined or when convicted and confessing, he flatly refused to be recalled and to give full obedience to the mandates of the Church. We relinquish him now to secular judgment and, by the authority which we wield, we not only condemn him as a heretic but also we bind with chain of excommunication as fautors, receivers, and defenders of heretics all persons who knowingly henceforth either harbor or defend him or lend him counsel, aid, or favor.

FORM OF SENTENCE FOR THOSE WHO DIED AS HERETICS

Likewise, we condemn deceased heretics and believers, having set forth their errors, crimes, and other matters in this way:

We, inquisitors, etc., having seen and carefully reviewed and considered the sins and defaults of (so and so), named above, and the defense offered in his behalf, and the circumstances which must be taken into account and evaluated in respect of the persons and the words of the witnesses, and other matters, with (so and so) associated and acting with us, adjudge (so and so) by definitive verdict to have died as a heretic and, condemning him and his memory with equal severity, we decree that his bones be exhumed from the cemetery, if they can be distinguished from others, and burned in detestation of so heinous an offense.

We issue and impose the condemnations and sentences here described solemnly and deliberately before a convocation of clergy and people, there requiring those on whom we impose the penances described here to abjure and to take an oath, as noted above; and an official record of the condemnations and of the penances of imprisonment is made, attested by our seals and the witness of others who are present.

The substance of letters in respect of the other penances which are imposed is entered in the records.

---

31 See footnote 13.

We do not proceed to the condemnation of anyone without clear and evident proof[32] or without his own confession, nor, God permitting, will we do so. And all the major condemnations and penances which we have issued and do issue, we pronounce with not only the general but also the specific signed counsel of prelates.

We do various other things, indeed, in procedure and in other matters which cannot easily be reduced to writing, holding in all things to the letter of the law or to specific apostolic ordinances. We cause the goods of heretics, the condemned and the imprisoned as well, to be confiscated, and we insist that this be done, as we are duty bound to do. It is in this way that heretics and believers are particularly confounded. And if justice is well done in respect of the condemned and those who relapse, if their property is surely confiscated, and if prisoners are adequately provided with necessities, the Lord will gloriously and wonderfully be made manifest in the fruit of the Inquisition.

from Walter L. Wakefield, *Heresy, Crusade and Inquisition in Southern France.* Berkeley: University of California Press. 1974

Excerpts from Penitential Manuals

In the early church, there was controversy over whether sins committed after baptism could be forgiven. A ritual of public confession and reconciliation gradually developed. By the twelfth century, the sacrament of penance had been formalized and became the norm. Forgiveness required "contrition of the heart, confession with the mouth, and satisfaction by works." Confession was made in private to a priest. Manuals were written to aid priests in prescribing appropriate acts of satisfaction.

FROM BOOK 19, "THE CORRECTOR AND PHYSICIAN" OF BURCHARD OF WORMS, C. 1010

This book is called "the Corrector" and "the Physician," since it contains ample corrections for bodies and medicines for souls and teaches every priest, even the uneducated, how he shall be able to bring help to each person, ordained or unordained; poor or rich; boy, youth, or mature man; decrepit, healthy, or infirm; of every age; and of both sexes.

Chapter 1: In the week preceding the beginning of Lent the priests of the parishes shall assemble the people to themselves and reconcile the contentious by canonical authority and settle all quarrels and then first give the penance to those who confess; so that before the beginning of the fast comes about, all shall have confessed and received their penance, that they may be able freely to say: "And forgive us our debts as we also forgive our debtors."

Chapter 11: If one is able to fast and to fulfill what is written in the penitential, it is good, and let him render thanks to God. But to him who is not able we, through God's mercy, give the following advice, that it be not necessary either for him or for anyone else either to despair or to perish.

Chapter 12: For one day on which he is to fast on bread and water he shall sing fifty psalms, kneeling, if possible, in a church; but if he cannot he shall do this in a convenient place and shall feed one poor man; and on that day, he shall eat what he chooses except wine, meat, and fat.

---

32 Without a confession, most manuals required the testimony of at least two witnesses.

Chapter 15: He who does not know the psalms shall redeem one day on which he is to do penance on bread and water, if he is rich, with three *denarii*, and if he is poor, with one denarius; and on that day he shall take what he chooses except wine, meat, and fat.

Chapter 19: For one month in which he is to fast on bread and water, he shall sing 1200 psalms, kneeling. But if he cannot do this, he shall sing 1680 psalms, sitting or standing, without kneeling; if possible, in a church; but if not, in one place. And, if he wishes, and if he cannot refrain, he shall dine at sext every day except Wednesday and Friday, when he shall fast until nones. And he shall abstain the whole month from meat and fat and wine. But he shall take other food after he has sung the before-mentioned psalms. By this plan the whole year is to be redeemed.

FROM REGINO'S ECCLESIASTICAL DISCIPLINE, C. 906

453: He who is not able to do penance as we have said above in the first year shall expend in alms twenty-six *solidi*, in the second year, twenty, in the third, eighteen; this comes to sixty-four *solidi*. Powerful men shall do for their sins as Zacchaeus did. For he said to the Lord: "Lord, the half of all my goods I give to the poor, and if I have wrongfully taken anything I restore it fourfold." And he shall set free some of his slaves and redeem captives, and from the heart forgive those who sin against him. And he who commits forbidden things shall abstain even from things permissible and afflict the body with fasts, vigils, and frequent prayers. For the flesh when gladsome drew us into guilt; afflicted, it leads us back to pardon.

FROM THE PENITENTIAL OF THEODORE, XIV:1 (DIED 690)

xiv:1: There are three legitimate fasts in a year for the people; the forty days before Easter, when we pay the tithes of the year, and the forty days before the Lord's nativity and the forty days and nights after Pentecost.

FROM THE PENITENTIAL OF BARTHOLOMEW ISCANUS, BISHOP OF EXETER, C. 1175

If anyone pays respect to soothsayers, augurs, enchanters, or makes use of philters, let him be anathema. Whoever by any magic turns aside a judgment of God, shall do penance for two years. He who is a magician for the sake of love and does not bring it to success shall do penance for two years. If he does, five years. If adultery results, ten years. . . He who strives to take away another's supply of milk or honey or of other things by any incantation, or tries by magic to gain it for himself, shall do penance for three years. . . A woman who by a magical trick prevents the consummation of a legal marriage shall do penance for five years. Those who make vows beside trees or water, those who keep the New Year with pagan rites, and those who make magical knots or charms and hide them in the grass or in a tree or at a cross roads to free their animals from pestilence must each do penance for two years. He who places his child upon a roof or in an oven in order to restore his health, or who for this purpose uses charms or characters or things fashioned for sorcery or any trick, and not godly prayers or the liberal art of medicine, shall do penance for forty days . . . He who believes that the masculine or feminine shape of any animal can be transformed into that of a wolf shall do penance for ten days.

FROM THE PENITENTIAL OF THORLAC THORHALLSON, C. 1180

For homosexuality and bestiality, a nine-year or a ten-year penance; the three thorough fasts yearly; the first before the feast of John the Baptist, the second before the feast of Michael, the third before the feast of Advent; however, fasts are to be kept on alternate days and on two nights of each week. He commanded that one hundred genuflexions be made each day of the fasts of Advent when nine lections are not held; and as many paternosters are to be said. Every Friday in Lent the "discipline" is to be used, at least five blows of the rod or strap so as to wound. Downy clothing, except cushions, and also linen clothing, are to be put aside during the lenten period and the fast of Advent; but on Friday or on a day of vigils he shall make some genuflexions, and for three years he shall not receive the Lord's body.

For violation of a woman . . . he shall perform the above-mentioned penance;[33] he shall also sing the paternoster fifty times on the festival days or make one hundred genuflexions on work days, repeating this penance as many times as he offended.

For theft, he shall be punished by the restitution of what was stolen if it can be made, and he shall perform a minor penance; but for a serious theft, a major penance, if he cannot make restitution, and if the theft was committed rather from malice than on account of need. He shall be punished for the theft with fasts and flagellations and prayers and genuflexions, and he shall perform other penance until what he stole is restored.

A rich man shall always be more severely punished than a poor man for the same sin; the hale, than the sick; the learned, than the unlearned; a man of superior, than a man of inferior rank; a fortunate man, than an unfortunate; and an adult, than one of minor age.

from *Medieval Handbooks of Penance*, edited by John T. McNeill and Helena M. Gamer. New York: © 1990 by Columbia University Press. Reprinted with permission of the publisher.

Pilgrim's Guide to Compostela

Pilgrimages to holy places, to visit relics of Christ and the saints, were common in Christianity as early as the second century. By the eleventh century, the three most important pilgrimage sites were Jerusalem, where Jesus walked, preached, and died, Rome, where Saints Peter and Paul were buried, and Compostela in northwestern Spain, said to contain the relics of St. James. The importance to Christians of Jerusalem and Rome is obvious. Compostela became a major pilgrimage site because of the political events of the time. Much of Spain was controlled by Muslims. Alphonso II, king of Asturias and Galicia was trying to consolidate his power at the time the supposed tomb of James was discovered. Europe was, in the words of Raoul Glaber, "covering itself with a white robe of churches." Alphonso built roads and did what he could to make them safe for travelers, while churches were built about every twenty miles along the major pilgrimage routes, creating convenient stopovers for the weary traveler. The Pilgrim's Guide provided travelers with warnings and suggestions for a safe and pleasant trip.

CHAPTER 1: OF THE ROUTES OF ST. JAMES

There are four roads which, leading to Santiago, converge to form a single road at Puente la Reina, in Spanish territory. One crosses Saint-Gilles, Montpellier, Toulouse, and the pass of Somport; another goes through Notre-Dame of Le Puy, Sainte-Foy of Conques and Saint-Pierre of Moissac; another traverses Sainte-Marie-Madeleine of Vézelay, Saint Léonard in the Limousin

---

33 Six to nine years according to circumstances.

as well as the city of Périgueux; still another cuts through Saint-Martin of Tours, Saint-Hilaire of Poitiers, Saint-Jean-d'Angély, Saint Eutrope of Saintes and the city of Bordeaux.

The road that traverses Sainte-Foy, the one that proceeds through Saint-Léonard, and the one that does so through Saint-Martin meet at Ostabat and, having gained the pass of Cize, join at Puente la Reina the road that comes from the Somport; thence a single road leads as far as Santiago.

Chapter 6: The Bitter and Sweet Waters Found Along This Road

These are the rivers one finds from the mountain passes of Cize and Somport as far as St. James: from the Somport descends a salubrious river called the Aragón which waters Spain; from the pass of Cize, to be sure, a healthy river issues called by many the Runa. This stream crosses Pamplona. At Puente la Reina both the Arga and the Runa flow by.

In a place called Lorca, towards the east, runs a river called Rio Salado. Beware from drinking its waters or from watering your horse in its stream, for this river is deadly. While we were proceeding towards Santiago, we found two Navarrese seated on its banks and sharpening their knives: they make a habit of skinning the mounts of the pilgrims that drink from that water and die. To our questions they answered with a lie saying that the water was indeed healthy and drinkable. Accordingly, we watered our horses in the stream, and had no sooner done so, than two of them died; these the men skinned them on the spot.

At Estella flows the Ega; its water is sweet, healthy and excellent. By the town called Los Arcos flows, on the other hand, a deadly stream; and beyond Los Arcos, next to the first hospice, that is to say between Los Arcos and the same hospice, flows a stream deadly for the horses no less than for the men that drink from it. By the town called Torres, to be sure in Navarrese territory, there is a river that is fatal to horses and men that drink from it. Thence and as far as a town called Cuevas runs an equally deadly stream. By Logroño, in contrast, there is a large river called Ebro which is healthy and abounds in fish.

The water of all rivers one encounters between Estella and Logroño has been recognized as deadly for the men and the horses that drink from it, and their fish is no less dangerous to eat. Should you anywhere in Spain or in Galicia eat either the fish vulgarly called *barbo*, or the one those of Poitou call *alose* and the Italians *clipia*, or even the eel or the tenca, you will no doubt die shortly thereafter or at least fall sick. And if somebody by chance ate them without falling sick, this is either because he was healthier than most, or because he had stayed in that country for a long time. All fish and the meat of beef and pork from all of Spain and Galicia cause sickness to foreigners.

Concerning the rivers whose waters are sweet and healthy to drink, these are the names by which they are ordinarily known: the Pisuerga, a stream that flows, to be sure, under the bridge of Itero; the Carrión that runs by Carrión; the Cea, at Sahagún; the Esla, at Mansilla; the Porma, under a certain large bridge between Mansilla and León; the Torio which flows by León underneath the encampment of the Jews; the Bernesga which flows by the same city, but on the other side, that is to say, towards Astorga; the Sil that waters Ponferrada in Valverde; the Cua that flows by Cacabelos; the Burbia that runs by the bridge of Villafranca; the Valcarce that flows in its own valley; the Miño that runs by Puertomarín. There is furthermore a certain river located at a distance of two miles from the city of Santiago, in a wooded place, and which is called Lavamentula, because there the French pilgrims that go to St. James, for the love of the Apostle, use to wash not merely their virile member but, having taken off their clothes, wash off the dirt from their entire body. The river Sar which flows between Monte del Gozo and the city of Santiago is considered healthy; similarly, the river Sarela which runs from the other side of the city towards the west is also reported as healthy.

If I have thus described these rivers, it was in order that the pilgrims that proceed to Santiago may strive to avoid unhealthy waters and may choose to drink those that are good for them and for their mounts.

Chapter 11: The Proper Welcoming of the Pilgrims of St. James

Pilgrims, whether poor or rich, who return from or proceed to Santiago, must be received charitably and respectfully by all. For he who welcomes them and provides them diligently with lodging will have as his guest not merely the Blessed James, but the Lord himself, who in His Gospels said: "He who welcomes you, welcomes me." Many are those who in the past brought upon themselves the wrath of God because they refused to receive the pilgrims of Saint James or the indigent.

In Nantua, which is a city between Genève and Lyon, a weaver refused to hand out some bread to a pilgrim who had asked for it; all of a sudden some linen of his dropped to the ground torn in its middle. In Villeneuve, a woman kept some bread under hot ashes. A needy pilgrim of Saint James asked her for alms by the love of God and the Blessed James. When she answered that she had no bread, the pilgrim exclaimed: "May the bread you have turn into stone!" And when the pilgrim left her house and was already at a considerable distance, this vicious woman turned to the ashes with the idea of retrieving her bread, but found only a round stone instead. With contrite heart she set out to look for the pilgrim, but could not find him anymore.

Two valiant Frenchmen, returning one day from Santiago destitute of all, kept asking for lodging, by the love of God and Saint James, all about the city of Poitiers from the house of Jean Gautier and as far as Saint-Porchaire--and they could find none. And having finally been put up by some poor man in the last house of that street next to the basilica of Saint-Porchaire, by the effects of divine vengeance, a violent fire burned to the ground that very night the entire street, starting from the house where they first asked for lodging and up to the one which had welcomed them. And these were about one thousand houses in all. But the one in which the servants of God had been put up remained, by divine grace, untouched.

That is the reason why it should be known that the pilgrims of Saint James, whether poor or rich, have the right to hospitality and to diligent respect.

from *The Pilgrim's Guide to Compostela*, edited and translated by William Melczer. New York: Italica Press. 1993.
By permission of Italica Press

Devout Bees

While the church condemned most kinds of folk magic, its teachings on miracles stimulated a belief in supernatural events of a religious nature. The story of the bees who constructed a church is one of many tales concerning the miraculous powers of the host, the bread that, according to church teaching, when elevated by the priest becomes the body of Christ.

For I have heard that a certain rustic, wishing to become wealthy and having many hives of bees, asked certain evil men how he could get rich and increase the number of his bees. He was told by someone that if he retained the sacred communion on Easter and placed it in some one of his hives, he would entice away all of his neighbor's bees, which leaving their own hives, would come to the place where the body of our Lord was and there would make honey. He did this.

Then all the bees came to the hive where the body of Christ was, and just as if they had felt compassion for the irreverence done to it, by their labor they began to construct a little church and to erect foundations, and bases, and columns, and an altar with like labor. And with the greatest reverence they placed the body of our Lord upon the altar. And within that little bee-hive they formed that little church with wonder and the most beautiful workmanship. The bees of the vicinity leaving their hives came to that one; and over that work they sang in their own manner certain wonderful melodies like hymns.

The rustic hearing this, wondered. But waiting until the fitting time for collecting the honey, he found nothing in his hives in which the bees had been accustomed to make honey. And finding himself impoverished through the means by which he had expected to be enriched, he went to that one where he had placed the host, where he saw the bees had come together. But when he approached, just as if they had wanted to vindicate the insult to our Saviour, the bees rushed upon the rustic and stung him so severely that he escaped with difficulty, and in great agony. Going to the priest he related all that he had done and what the bees had done.

The priest, by the advice of his bishop, collected his parishioners and made a procession to the place. Then the bees leaving the hive, rose in the air, making sweet melody. Raising the hive they found inside the noble structure of that little church, and the body of our Lord placed upon the altar. Then returning thanks they bore to their own church that little church of the bees constructed with such skill and elegance, and placed it on the altar.

By this deed those, who do not reverence, but offer insult instead to the sacred body of Christ or the sacred place where it is, ought to be put to great confusion.

from *Translation and Reprints from the Original Sources of European History*, Vol I. University of Pennsylvania Press, 1902.

Unit 21: Secular and Religious Authority

After the fall of the Roman Empire in the West, the Christian church was the only institution with an administrative hierarchy that stretched across the former Empire. Popes, bishops, and abbots became important feudal lords. As kings consolidated their authority, the strife between temporal rulers and church officials increased. The Investiture Controversy of the eleventh century pitted two strong leaders—Henry IV of Germany and Pope Gregory VII—against each other.

Dictatus Papae, 1075

These dictates of Pope Gregory VII are the most extravagant claims of the papacy to authority over secular rulers, as well as over all aspects of the church.

That the Roman church was founded by God alone.

That the Roman pontiff alone can with right be called universal.

That he alone can depose or reinstate bishops.

That, in a council, his legate, even if a lower grade, is above all bishops, and can pass sentence of deposition against them.

That the pope may depose the absent.

That, among other things, we ought not to remain in the same house with those excommunicated by him.

That for him alone is it lawful, according to the needs of the time, to make new laws, to assemble together new congregations, to make an abbey of a canonry; and, on the other hand, to divide a rich bishopric and unite the poor ones.

That he alone may use the imperial insignia.

That of the pope alone all princes shall kiss the feet.

That his name alone shall be spoken in the churches.

That this is the only name in the world.

That it may be permitted to him to depose emperors. That he may be permitted to transfer bishops if need be.

That he has power to ordain a clerk of any church he may wish.

That he who is ordained by him may preside over another church, but may not hold a subordinate position; and that such a one may not receive a higher grade from any bishop.

That no synod shall be called a general one without his order.

That no chapter and no book shall be considered canonical without his authority.

That a sentence passed by him may be retracted by no one; and that he himself, alone of all, may retract it.

That he himself may be judged by no one.

That no one shall dare to condemn one who appeals to the apostolic chair.

That to the latter should be referred the more important cases of every church.

That the Roman church has never erred; nor will it err to all eternity, the Scriptures bearing witness.

That the Roman pontiff, if he have been canonically ordained, is undoubtedly made a saint by the merits of St. Peter; St. Ennodius, bishop of Pavia, bearing witness, and many holy fathers agreeing with him. As is contained in the decrees of St. Symmachus the pope.

That he may depose and reinstate bishops without assembling a synod.

That he who is not at peace with the Roman church shall not be considered catholic.

That he may absolve subjects from their fealty to wicked men.

from E. F. Henderson, *Historical Documents of the Middle Ages*. London: George Bell & Sons, 1896.

Letter of Henry IV to Gregory VII, 1076

Henry's answer to the *Dictates* of Gregory was to demand that he step down from the papacy, an office which, Henry claims, he has gained unlawfully. He addresses Gregory as Hildebrand, the name he held before he became Pope.

Henry, king not through usurpation but through the holy ordination of God, to Hildebrand, at present not pope but false monk. You have deserved this because of your disturbances, since there is no grade in the church which you have omitted to make a partaker not of honor but of confusion, not of benediction but of malediction. For, to mention few and especial cases out of many, not only have you not feared to lay hands upon the rulers of the holy church, the anointed of the Lord--namely, the archbishops, bishops and priests--but you have trodden them under foot like slaves ignorant of what their master is doing. You have won favor from the common herd by crushing them; you have looked upon all of them as knowing nothing, upon yourself alone, moreover, as knowing all things. This knowledge, however, you have used not for edification but for destruction; so that with reason we believe that St. Gregory, whose name you have usurped for yourself, was prophesying concerning you when he said: "The pride of him who is in power increases the more, the greater the number of those subject to him; and he thinks that he himself can do more than all." And we, indeed, have endured all this, being eager to guard the honor of the apostolic see; you, however, have understood our humility to be fear, and have not, accordingly, shunned to rise up against the royal power conferred upon us by God, daring to threaten to divest us of it. As if we had received our kingdom from you! As if the kingdom and the empire were in your hands, and not in God's! And this although our Lord Jesus Christ did call us to the kingdom; did not, however, call you to the priesthood. For you have ascended by the following steps. By wiles, namely, which the profession of monk abhors, you have achieved money; by money, favor; by the sword, the throne of peace. And from the throne of peace you have disturbed peace, inasmuch as you have armed subjects against those in authority over them; inasmuch as you, who were not called, have taught that our bishops called of God are to be despised; inasmuch as you have usurped for laymen the ministry over their priests, allowing them to depose or condemn those whom they themselves had received as teachers from the hand of God through the laying on of hands of the bishops. On me also who, although unworthy to be among the anointed, have nevertheless been anointed to the kingdom, you have lain your hand; me who--as the tradition of the holy Fathers teaches, declaring that I am not to be deposed for any crime unless, which God forbid, I should have strayed from the faith--am subject to the judgment of God alone. For the wisdom of the holy fathers committed even Julian the apostate not to themselves, but to God alone, to be judged and to be deposed. For himself the true pope, Peter, also exclaims: "Fear God, honor the king." But you do not fear God; you dishonor in me his appointed one. Wherefore St. Paul, when he has not spared an angel of Heaven if he shall have preached otherwise, has not excepted you either; you who teach otherwise upon earth. For he says: "If any one, either I or an angel from Heaven, should preach a gospel other than that which has been preached to you, he shall be damned. You, therefore, damned by this curse and by the judgment of all our bishops and by our own, descend and relinquish the apostolic chair which you have usurped. Let another ascend the throne of St. Peter, who shall not practice violence under the cloak of religion, but shall teach the sound doctrine of St. Peter. I Henry, king by the grace of God, do say unto you, together with all our bishops: Descend, descend, to be damned throughout the ages.

modified from E. F. Henderson, *Historical Documents of the Middle Ages*. George Bell & Sons. London, 1896.

Excommunication and Deposition of Henry IV, 1076

Gregory retaliated by excommunicating Henry and declaring that Henry's vassals should no longer keep the oaths they have made to him. While technically an oath was made before God and therefore marginally within the jurisdiction of the Church, Gregory's declaration would have been ineffective had Henry's vassals not been looking for an excuse to defy him.

O St. Peter, chief of the apostles, incline to us, I beg, your holy ears, and hear me your servant whom you have nourished from infancy, and whom, until this day, you have freed from the hand of the wicked, who have hated and do hate me for my faithfulness to you. You, and my mistress the mother of God, and your brother St. Paul are witnesses for me among all the saints that your holy Roman church drew me to its helm against my will; that I had no thought of ascending your chair through force, and that I would rather have ended my life as a pilgrim than, by secular means, to have seized your throne for the sake of earthly glory. And therefore I believe it to be through your grace and not through my own deeds that it has pleased and does please you that the Christian people, who have been especially committed to you, should obey me. And especially to me, as your representative and by your favor, has the power been granted by God of binding and loosing in Heaven and on earth. On the strength of this belief therefore, for the honor and security of they church, in the name of Almighty God, Father, Son and Holy Ghost, I withdraw, through your power and authority, from Henry the king, son of Henry the emperor, who has risen against your church with unheard of insolence, the rule over the whole kingdom of the Germans and over Italy. And I absolve all Christians from the bonds of the oath which they have made or shall make to him; and I forbid any one to serve him as king. For it is fitting that he who strives to lessen the honor of your church should himself lose the honor which belongs to him. And since he has scorned to obey as a Christian, and has not returned to God whom he had deserted—holding intercourse with the excommunicated; practicing numerous iniquities; spurning my commands which, as you bear witness, I issued to him for his own salvation; separating himself from your church and striving to tear it apart—I bind him in your stead with the chain of the anathema. And, leaning on you, I so bind him that the people may know and have proof that you are Peter, and above your rock the Son of the living God has built His church, and the gates of Hell shall not prevail against it.

modified from E. F. Henderson, *Historical Documents of the Middle Ages*. George Bell & Sons. London, 1896.

France Placed Under the Interdict by Innocent III, 1200

Excommunication denied to the individual the right to participate in the life of the church and to receive the sacraments. The interdict, in effect, did the same to an entire territory. It was used in the hope that the people would pressure the ruler to comply with the Pope's demands. This interdict was placed against the realm of Philip II Augustus of France because of his refusal to give up Agnes of Meran and return to his wife, Ingeborg of Denmark, from whom he had separated in 1193.

Let all the churches be closed; let no one be admitted to them except to baptize infants; let them not be otherwise opened except for the purpose of lighting the lamps, or when the priest shall come for the Eucharist and holy water for the use of the sick. We permit mass to be cele-brated once a week on Friday early in the morning to consecrate the Host for the use of the sick, but only one clerk is to be admitted to assist the priest. Let the clergy preach on Sunday in the vestibules of the churches, and in place of the mass let them disseminate the word of God. Let them recite the canonical hours outside the churches, where the people do not hear them; if they recite an epistle or a gospel let them beware lest the laity hear them; and let them not permit the dead to be interred, or their bodies to be placed unburied in the cemeteries. let them, moreover, say to the laity that they sin and transgress grievously by burying bodies in the earth, even in unconsecrated ground, for in so doing they arrogate to themselves an office pertaining to others. Let them forbid their parishioners to enter churches that may be open in the king's territory, and let them not bless the wallets of pilgrims except outside the churches. Let them not celebrate the offices in Passion week, but refrain even till Easter day, and then let them celebrate in private, no one being admitted except the assisting priest, as above directed; let no one communicate even at Easter, except he be sick and in danger of death. During the same week, or on Palm Sunday, let them announce to their parishioners that they may assemble on Easter morning before the church and there have permission to eat flesh and consecrated bread. Women are expressly forbidden to be admitted into the churches for purification, but are to be warned to gather their neighbors together on the day of purification and pray outside the church, nor may the women who are to be purified enter even to raise their children to the sacred font for baptism until they are admitted by the priest after the expiration of the interdict. Let the priest confess all who desire it in the portico of the church; if the church have no portico we direct that in bad or rainy weather, and not otherwise, the nearest door of the church may be opened and confessions heard on its threshold (all being excluded except the one who is to confess) so that the priest and the penitent can be heard by those who are outside the church. If, however, the weather be fair, let the confession be heard in front of the closed doors. Let no vessels of holy water be placed outside of the church, nor shall the priests carry them anywhere, for all the sacraments of the church beyond these two which were reserved are absolutely prohibited. Extreme unction, which is a holy sacrament, may not be given.

from *Translation and Reprints from the Original Sources of European History*, Vol. IV. University of Pennsylvania Press, 1895.

CHAPTER 10: CITIES IN THE HIGH MIDDLE AGES

Unit 22: Life in a Medieval City

By 1300, there were more than 200 towns in France and 100 in England. Most had a population of 1,000 to 10,000, but a few were much larger. Paris probably had about 200,000 people at this time. Kingdoms were becoming states, governing through bureaucracies rather than by personal relationships. Many cities received charters, giving them the right to govern themselves. The traders and craftspersons regulated manufacture and trade.

Paris was not a chartered town. It was under the direct rule of the French king, governed through his provost. Parisian craft guilds were the first to have their regulations written, with details of how the rules were to be enforced. The provost said he was ordering this collection of rules so that buyers would not be disappointed by the poor quality of merchandise sometimes found.

Jean of Jandun, Description of Les Halles. c. 1323

The first buildings at Les Halles, the central market in Paris, were constructed in 1181 by King Philip Augustus. The buildings were surrounded by walls and a gate that locked, to protect the goods, which could then be left overnight. Covered stalls were erected between the buildings and the wall for those who could not find space inside. On Wednesdays, Fridays, and Saturdays the merchants left their workshops in the charge of wives or assistants and displayed their wares at Les Halles.

There, if you have the desire and the means, you can buy all kinds of ornaments which the most industrious workers, the most inventive spirits hasten to imagine to fulfill your desires. In the lower galleries are found cloths, each more beautiful than the other: superb pelisses, some made of animal skins, some of silk, others of delicate and strange materials, whose Latin names I don't know.[34]

On the upper level of the building, which forms an astonishingly long arcade, are all the objects which serve to adorn the different parts of the body: for the head, crowns, tresses, bonnets; ivory combs for the hair; mirrors for looking at oneself; belts for the waist; purses to suspend at the side, gloves for the hands, necklaces for the chest; others which I cannot list because of the insufficiency of Latin words, not for lack of having seen them. . . .

Among these stalls, the large number of decorations for the amusement (of guests) at weddings and great feasts make passersby smile with their eyes so that after they have walked half the length of one side, an impetuous desire pulls them toward the other; and after having traversed the whole length, an insatiable ardor for repeating this pleasure, not once or twice, but

---

[34] Jean is writing in Latin. By the fourteenth century, knowledge and use of Latin was limited to the educated elite, mostly clergy. The fact that no Latin words can be found for some of these items may indicate that they are relatively new and have names only in French or another vernacular language.

indefinitely, brings them back to the beginning and causes them to begin again, if they wish to increase their pleasure.

There is far too much that could be said about the animals, plants, fruits, and vegetables which, baked or roasted, nourish man; suffice it to say that a palace filled with hunger would never have trouble satisfying itself here. What seems even more marvelous is that, the more the population grows, the more is brought in, an exuberant abundance and an abundant exuberance of goods, without a proportional rise in prices. . . .

Regulations of the Paris Guilds

The mutual obligations of apprentice, journeyman, and master, the quality of merchandise, the hours of work, and the methods of sale were regulated by associations of master artisans and traders. These associations, or guilds, fulfilled other functions, as well, sometimes through a separate association called a confraternity. They provided pensions for widows and orphans and "sick pay" for members too ill to work. They took care of the funerals of members. They were also social clubs and had religious functions. Each guild had a patron saint whom they honored with a holiday, and often with weekly masses. The selections in this unit describe life in Paris in the thirteenth century. The guild of *crespiniers* admitted women to membership; the goldsmiths did not.

REGULATIONS OF THE GOLDSMITHS' GUILD, 1268.

I. (Whoever wants and knows how can be) a goldsmith in Paris, as long as he works according to the usages and customs of the metier[35], which are:

II. No goldsmith can work with gold at Paris if it is not (of the quality of) the *touche*[36] of Paris, or better, which *touche* surpasses all the gold that is worked in any (other) land.

III. No goldsmith can work with silver at Paris, if it is not (of the quality of) sterling or better.

IV. No goldsmith can have more than one foreign apprentice.[37] But of his own lineage or the lineage of his wife, whether distant or close, he can have as many as he likes.

V. No goldsmith can have an apprentice, either foreign or family, for less than ten years, unless the apprentice is so skilled that he knows how to earn 100 *sous* per year plus the cost of his food and drink.

VI. No goldsmith can work by night, unless the work is for the King, the Queen, their children, their brothers, or the bishop of Paris.

VII. No goldsmith owes tolls or other taxes on anything he buys or sells pertaining to the metier.

VIII. No goldsmith can work at his forge on the Day of the Apostle, unless it falls on Saturday, except in one workshop, which each will work in his turn on this holiday and on Sunday. And whatever he earns, whose workshop is open, he will put in the "box" of the

---

[35] "Metier" is sometimes used to mean "trade" or "craft"; sometimes it denotes the guild made up of people who follow a certain trade.

[36] "*Touche*" denotes the percentage of pure gold in the alloy, as "sterling" does for silver.

[37] A "foreign" apprentice is anyone from outside the family .

Confraternity of Goldsmiths, into which "box" are put the "pennies for God" which the goldsmith makes on things that he buys and sells, pertaining to the metier. And from all the money in this "box" is provided each year, on Easter Sunday, a dinner for the poor at the Hotel-Dieu of Paris.[38]

IX. The goldsmith is sworn to keep and uphold all the aforesaid regulations fully and in good faith. And if a foreign goldsmith comes to Paris, he will swear to uphold all these regulations.[39]

X. The goldsmiths at Paris are exempt from the guet, but they owe the other customary dues to the King.[40]

XI. And let it be known that the *preudhommes*[41] of the metier select two or three *preudhommes* to oversee the metier, which *preudhommes* swear that they will oversee the metier fully and in good faith according to the usages and customs described above. And when these *preudhommes* have finished their term of office, the community of goldsmiths cannot select them again to oversee the metier before three years, unless they choose to serve of their own free will.

XII. And if the three *preudhommes* find a man of the metier who works with inferior gold or inferior silver, and if he does not wish to cease this practice, the three *preudhommes* will take him before the provost of Paris, and the provost will punish him by banishing him for four years or six, whichever he deserves.

REGULATIONS OF THE *Crespiniers'* GUILD,[42] 1268.

I. Whoever wants to be a *crespinier* of linen or silk at Paris, that is a maker of bonnets for women, and pillowcases, and *paveillons* which one puts on the altars, that are made with a needle or on a loom, can be one freely, as long as he works according to the usages and customs of the metier, which are:

II. No *crespinier* of Paris can have more than one apprentice unless it is his child born of legal marriage, or the child of his wife, if his wife is a *crespiniere*. Which apprentice he cannot and must not take for less than seven years' service, but he can take more years plus money if he can get it.[43]

III. If a man is a *crespinier* and his wife is a *crespiniere*, and she customarily works at the metier, he can take and hold two apprentices in the manner described above.

IV. No male or female *crespinier* may or ought to take an apprentice except in front of the sworn overseers who guard the metier, or before at least two of them. And these sworn over-

---

[38] The Hotel-Dieu was a hospital for the poor.

[39] A "foreign" goldsmith was one who was not a resident of Paris.

[40] The *guet* was a patrol of nightwatchmen for which each guild, in turn, was required to provide either men or a payment to hire someone else.

[41] A *preudhomme* was a male businessman of good character. In a few guilds, the overseers are *preudfemmes*, or businesswomen of good character.

[42] As Article I states, the *crespiniers* made women's bonnets, pillowcases, and altar cloths.

[43] In many guilds, the length of apprenticeship was shorter if the apprentice or his or her parents paid a fee. From this it is evident that a part of the reason for long apprenticeships was to allow the master or mistress to benefit from the skilled labor an apprentice provided in the later years. In the *Livre des métiers*, the collection of guild regulations for Paris, the length of apprenticeship varied from four to 10 years, with an average of seven years.

seers ought to investigate and learn whether the person has enough, both of goods and of knowledge, so that he can provide for and teach the apprentice for the entire term agreed on.

V. No one may or ought to take an apprentice without paying 12 *deniers*[44] to the confraternity of the metier before the apprentice sets his hand to the work.

VII. No one who has taken an apprentice may or ought to take another until the seven years (of the first) are completed, unless the apprentice dies or foreswears the metier forever.

VIII. The master *crespinier* can have as many paid laborers as he wants, but he cannot hire them before they have finished the labor owed to their former master.

VIII. No *crespinier* may or ought to work or have work done at any time of year after the curfew has sounded at St. Merri, nor on any feast day proclaimed by the people of the town as a fair day. Nor (shall he work or have work done) on Saturdays outside Lent after the first note of vespers is sounded at Notre Dame, nor during Lent after compline is sounded in the same places.[45]

IX. No one may or ought to colport or have colported through the town of Paris a stack higher than one coif and a pillowcase together, except on Friday and Saturday.[46]

X. The aforesaid metier has eight men, whom the provost of Paris hires and fires at will, who have taken an oath on behalf of the King, that they will oversee the metier fully and in good faith, as much as is in their power, and that they will bring to the attention of the provost of Paris or his delegate all infractions of which they are aware, as soon as they reasonably can.

XI. Whoever does anything prohibited above will pay a fine to the King of five *sous*, each time he is caught, of which five *sous* the *preudhommes* who oversee the metier should have, from the hand of the provost of Paris, twelve deniers for their expenses.

XII. The *crespiniers* of Paris owe the *taille* and the *guet* and the other dues that the other bourgeois of Paris owe to the King.

XIII. The eight sworn men who oversee the metier on behalf of the King are exempt from the *guet* because of the nuisance and the work involved in overseeing the metier. Those who are older than sixty years of age and those whose wives are "lying in" after childbirth, as long as they are "lying in," do not owe the *guet*, but they are required to notify the one who oversees the *guet* on behalf of the King.

The Well-Furnished Kitchen. Alexander of Neckham. c. 1178.

The final two selections deal with food and its preparation. They are from the journal of a young English cleric, Alexander of Neckham, who traveled to Paris in about 1178 and described what he saw. In the first, Alexander describes the utensils necessary for a well-furnished kitchen; in the second, he describes the preparation of various dishes. You should keep in mind as you read that only a rather wealthy family would own such a variety of utensils and of food.

---

[44] A small coin.

[45] Medieval time was usually reckoned by the bells of the churches, which sounded to announce religious offices throughout the day. The day was divided into twenty-four hours ,but the hours were not of equal length. Vespers was rung at twilight and compline later, but before bedtime.

[46] A colporter carried goods in a basket on his or her shoulders, for sale to people on the streets.

In a kitchen there should be a small table on which cabbage may be minced, and also lentils, peas, shelled beans, beans in the pod, millet, onions, and other vegetables of the kind that can be cut up. There should be also pots, tripods, a mortar, a hatchet, a pestle, a stirring stick, a hook, a cauldron, a bronze vessel, a small pan, a baking pan, a meathook, a griddle, small pitchers, a trencher, a bowl, a platter, a pickling vat, and knives for cleaning fish. In a vivarium let fish be kept, in which they can be caught by net, fork, spear, or light hook, or with a basket. The chief cook should have a cupboard in the kitchen where he may store away aromatic spices, and bread flour sifted through a sieve--and used also for feeding small fish--may be hidden away there. Let there be also a cleaning place where the entrails and feathers of ducks and other domestic fowl can be removed and the birds cleaned. Likewise there should be a large spoon for removing foam and skimming. Also there should be hot water for scalding fowl.

Have a pepper mill, and a hand mill. Small fish for cooking should be put into a pickling mixture, that is, water mixed with salt. . . .To be sure, pickling is not for all fish, for these are of different kinds: mullets, soles, sea eels, lampreys, mackerel, turbot, sperlings, gudgeons, sea bream, young tunnies, cod, plaice, stargazers, anglers, herring, lobsters fried in half an egg, bougues, sea mullets, and oysters. There should be also a garde-robe pit through which the filth of the kitchen may be evacuated. In the pantry let there be shaggy towels, tablecloth, and an ordinary hand towel which shall hang from a pole to avoid mice. Knives should be kept in the pantry, an engraved saucedish, a saltcellar, a cheese container, a candelabra, a lantern, a candlestick, and baskets. In the cellar or storeroom should be casks, tuns, wineskins, cups, cup cases, spoons, ewers, basins, baskets, pure wine, cider, beer, unfermented wine, mixed wine, claret, nectar, mead . . . .piument, pear wine, red wine, wine from Auvergne, clove-spiced wine for gluttons whose thirst is unquenchable. . . .

from Urban Tigner Holmes, Jr. *Daily Living in the Twelfth Century. Based on the Observations of Alexander Neckam in London and Paris.* © University of Wisconsin Press, 1952. Reprinted by permission of University of Wisconsin Press.

Cooking Advice. Alexander of Neckham. c. 1178.

A roast of pork is prepared diligently on a grid, frequently basted, and laid on the grid just as the hot coals cease to smoke. Let condiment be avoided other than pure salt or a simple garlic sauce. It does not hurt to sprinkle a cut-up capon with pepper. A domestic fowl may be quite tender, having been turned on a long spit, but it needs a strong garlic sauce, diluted with wine or vinegar (that is, green juice of grapes or apples). Flavor a hen which has been cleaned and cut up into pieces, with cumin, if it is well boiled; but if it has been roasted, let it be treated with frequent drippings of fat, nor does it refuse garlic sauce; it will be most tasty with simple sauce. Let fish that have been cleaned be cooked in a mixture of wine and water; afterwards they should be taken with green "savory" which is made from sage, parsley, dittany, thyme, costus, garlic, and pepper; do not omit salt. One who takes this is especially exhilarated and restored by a raisin wine which is clear to the bottom of the cup, in its clarity similar to the tears of a penitent, and the color is that of an oxhorn. It descends like lightning upon one who takes it—most tasty as an almond nut, quick as a squirrel, frisky as a kid, strong in the manner of a house of Cistercians or gray monks, emitting a kind of spark; it is supplied with the subtlety of a syllogism of Petit Pont; delicate as a fine cotton, it exceeds crystal in its coolness.

from Urban Tigner Holmes, Jr. *Daily Living in the Twelfth Century. Based on the Observations of Alexander Neckam in London and Paris.* © University of Wisconsin Press, 1952. Reprinted by permission of University of Wisconsin Press.

CHAPTER 11: CRUSADES AND CULTURE

Unit 24: The Crusades

It is not a coincidence that the Crusades began while the Investiture Controversy[47] was still unsettled. An army of knights from all the kingdoms of Christendom, united under the banner of the Pope, would enhance the prestige of the papacy and, in addition, provide the force to back up claims of papal primacy. Innocent III would, in fact, call for a crusade against the German king and Holy Roman Emperor Frederick II in the early thirteenth century.

Several other factors led Urban II to call for European conquest of the Middle East. With invasions at an end, more Europeans were able to make the pilgrimage to Jerusalem, which was held by Muslims. While the Muslims generally welcomed the pilgrims and the trade they brought, pilgrims were occasionally robbed or beaten. Some saw crusaders simply as armed pilgrims. Urban II, who called Christian knights to the first crusade, had been active in the *reconquista* in Spain and saw the liberation of the Holy Places as an extension of that activity. Finally, knights no longer needed to protect their homelands from invasion sought new enemies, new ways of making their fortunes.

There are a number of eyewitness accounts of the crusades, found in letters and chronicles. Theologians discussed the theory of a "just war" and pontiffs made speeches and declarations. Songs lauded the brave knights who fought for their Lord.

from Song of Roland, c. 1100

In August of 778, as Charlemagne's army was returning from fighting in Spain, a rear guard was ambushed and killed by a party of Basques. Three hundred years later, in the best known of the *chansons de geste*, the small party of Basques has become an army of 100,000 Muslims and the French rear guard a crusading army of 20,000, spurred on by the Archbishop Turpin who exhorts them "Christendom needs you, so help us to preserve it." Roland's companion, Oliver, when he sees the size of the opposing army, begs Roland to sound his horn and call back the main army for aid. Roland scoffs that such a display of fear would stain his family's honor. Roland and his men embody the ideals sought in those who would wrest the Holy Places from other Muslims in another time.

Oliver's climbed a hill above the plain,
Whence he can look on all the land of Spain,
And see how vast the Saracen array;
All those bright helms with gold and jewels
    gay,
And all those shields, those coats of
    burnished mail;
And all those lances from which the
    pennons wave;

Even their squadrons defy all estimate,
He cannot count them, their numbers are so
    great;
Stout as he is, he's mightily dismayed.
He hastens down as swiftly as he may,
Comes to the French and tells them all his
    tale.

---

[47] See Chapter 9, Unit 21.

Quoth Oliver: "The Paynim[48] strength I've
    seen;
Never on earth has such a hosting been:
A hundred thousand in van ride under shield
Their helmets laced, their hauberks all
    agleam
Their spears upright, with heads of shining
    steel.
You'll have such battle as ne'er was fought
    on field.
My lords of France, God give you strength at
    need!
Save you stand fast, this field we cannot
    keep."
The French all say: "Foul shame it were to
    flee!
We're yours till death; no man of us will
    yield."

Quoth Oliver: "Huge are the Paynim
    hordes,
And of our French the numbers seem but
    small.
Companion Roland, I pray you sound your
    horn,
That Charles may hear and fetch back all his
    force."
Roland replies: "Madman were I and more,
And in fair France my fame would suffer
    scorn.
I'll smite great strokes with Durendal my
    sword,
I'll dye it red high as the hilt with gore.
This pass the Paynims reached on a luckless
    morn;
I swear to you death is their doom therefor."

"Companion Roland, your Olifant[49] now
    sound!
King Charles will hear and turn his armies
    round;
He'll succour us with all his kingly power."

---

[48] Muslim.

49 Roland's horn, made of ivory from an
elephant's tusk.

Roland replies: "May never God allow
That I should cast dishonour on my house
Or on fair France bring any ill renown!
Rather will I with Durendal strike out,
With this good sword, here on my baldrick
    bound;
From point to hilt you'll see the blood run
    down.
Woe worth the Paynims that e'er they made
    this rout!
I pledge my faith, we'll smite them dead on
    ground."

"Companion Roland, your Olifant now
    blow;
Charles in the passes will hear it as he goes,
Trust me, the French will all return right so."
"Now God forbid," Roland makes answer
    wroth,
"That living man should say he saw me go
Blowing of horns for any Paynim foe!
Ne'er shall my kindred be put to such
    reproach.
When I shall stand in this great clash of
    hosts
I'll strike a thousand and then sev'n hundred
    strokes,
Blood-red the steel of Durendal shall flow.
Stout are the French, they will do battle
    bold,
These men of Spain shall die and have no
    hope."

Quoth Oliver; "Herein I see no blame:
I have beheld the Saracens of Spain;
They cover all the mountains and the vales,
They spread across the hillsides and the
    plains;
Great is the might these foreigners display,
And ours appears a very small array."
"I thirst the more," quoth Roland, "for the
    fray.
God and His angels forbid it now, I pray,
That e'er by me fair France should be
    disfamed!

I'd rather die than thus be put to shame;
If the King loves us it's for our valour's
    sake."

Roland is fierce and Oliver is wise
And both for valour may bear away the
    prize,
Once horsed and armed the quarrel to
    decide,
For dread of death the field they'll never fly.
The counts are brave, their words are stern
    and high.
Now the false Paynims with wondrous fury
    ride.
Quoth Oliver: "Look, Roland, they're in
    sight,
Charles is far off, and these are very nigh;
You would not sound your Olifant for pride;
Had we the Emperor we should have been
    all right,
To Gate of Spain turn now and lift your
    eyes,
See for yourself the rear-guard's woeful
    plight.
Who fights this day will never more see
    fight."
Roland replies: "Speak no such foul despite!
Curst be the breast whose heart knows
    cowardise!
Here in our place we'll stand and here abide;
Buffets and blows be ours to take and
    strike!"

When Roland sees that battle there must be
Leopard nor lion ne'er grew so fierce as he.
He calls the French, bids Oliver give heed;
"Sir friend and comrade, such words you
    shall not speak!
When the King gave us the French to serve
    this need
These twenty thousand he chose to do the
    deed;
And well he knew not one would flinch or
    flee.

Men must endure much hardship for their
    liege,
And bear for him great cold and burning
    heat,
Suffer sharp wounds and let their bodies
    bleed.
Smite with your lance and I with my good
    steel,
My Durendal the Emperor gave to me;
And if I die, who gets it may agree
That he who bore it, a right good knight was
    he."

Then to their side comes the Archbishop
    Turpin,
Riding his horse and up the hillside spurring.
He calls the French and preaches them a
    sermon:
"Barons, my lords, Charles picked us for this
    purpose;
We must be ready to die in our King's
    service.
Christendom needs you, so help us to
    preserve it.
Battle you'll have, of that you may be
    certain,
Here come the Paynims--your own eyes
    have observed them.
Now beat your breasts and ask God for His
    mercy:
I will absolve you and set your souls in
    surety.
If you should die, blest martyrdom's your
    guerdon;
You'll sit on high in Paradise eternal."
The French alight and all kneel down in
    worship;
God's shrift and blessing the Archbishop
    conferreth,
And for their penance he bids them all strike
    firmly.

The French rise up and on their feet stand
    close;
All of their sins are shriven and made whole,

And the Archbishop God's blessing has
    bestowed.
Then on swift steeds they leap to saddlebow.
Armed with the arms prescribed by knightly
    code;
All are now ready into the field to go.
Count Roland said to Oliver right so;
"Sir my companion, too true the word you
    spoke,
That all of us by Ganelon were sold.[50]
He's ta'en his wage of wealth and goods and
    gold.
The Emperor's vengeance I think will not be
    slow!
Marsile the King has bargained for our
    bones:
He'll need the sword to fetch his purchase
    home."

Through Gate of Spain Roland goes riding
    past
On Veillantif, his swiftly-running barb;
Well it becomes him to go equipped in arms,
Bravely he goes, and tosses up his lance,
High in the sky he lifts the lancehead far,
A milk-white pennon is fixed above the
    shaft
Whose falling fringes whip his hands on the
    haft.
Nobly he bears him, with open face he
    laughs;
And his companion behind him follows
    hard;
The Frenchmen all acclaim him their strong
    guard.
On Saracens he throws a haughty glance
But meek and mild looks on the men of
    France,
To whom he speaks out of a courteous heart:
"Now, my lord barons, at walking pace--
    advance!
Looking for trouble these Paynims ride at
    large--

A fine rich booty we'll have ere this day's
    past;
Never French king beheld the like by half."
E'en as he speaks, their battles join and
    charge.

Quoth Oliver: "I have no more to say:
To sound your horn for help you would not
    deign,
So here you are, you've not got Charlemayn;
Little he knows, brave heart! he's not to
    blame.
Nor those with him, nowise in fault are they.
Ride forward then and do the best you may!
Barons my lords, hold firm amid the fray!
Now for God's sake be resolute, I pray,
To strike hard blows, to give them and to
    take.
King Carlon's[51] war-cry forget not to
    proclaim!"
A mighty shout the Frenchmen give
    straightway;
Whoso had heard the cry "Mountjoy" they
    raise
He would remember its valiance all his days.
They charge--Lord God, was ever sight so
    brave?
They spur their steeds to make the greater
    haste,
They fall afighting—there is no other way—
The Saracens join battle undismayed;
Paynims and Franks are fighting face to
    face.

Now Adelroth, (he was King Marsile's
    nephew),
Before the host comes first of all his fellows;
With evil words the French he thus
    addresses:
"Villainous Franks, with us you have to
    reckon!
You've been betrayed by him that should
    protect you,

---

50 Roland and his rear guard had been
betrayed by Roland's stepfather, Ganelon.

[51] Carlon is another form of Charlemagne.

Your king lacked with who in the passes left
you.
Fair France will lose her honour in this
venture;
From Carlon's body the right arm will be
severed."
When Roland hears him, God! but his rage
is reckless!
He spurs his horse, gives full rein to his
mettle,
His blow he launches with all his mightiest
effort;
The shield he shatters, and the hauberk he
rendeth,
He splits the breast and batters in the breast-
bone,
Through the man's back drives out the
backbone bended,

And soul and all forth on the spear-point
fetches;
Clean through he thrusts him, forth of the
saddle wrenching,
And flings him dead a lance-length from his
destrier;
Into two pieces he has broken his neckbone.
No less for that he speaks to him and tells
him:
"Out on thee, churl! no lack-wit is the
Emperor,
He is none such, nor loved he treason ever;
Right well he did who in the passes left us,
Neither shall France lose honour by this
venture.
First blood to us! Go to it, gallant
Frenchmen!
Right's on our side, and wrong is with these
wretches!"

translated by Dorothy Sayers. Penguin. 1957

Urban II's Call to the First Crusade, 1095

This version, by Robert the Monk, is one of several recorded recollections of the speech made at the
Council of Clermont in which Pope Urban II urged European nobles, especially the Franks, to go to Jerusalem and its neighboring territories and win them back from the Muslims, who had wrested them from
the Byzantine Empire shortly after Muhammed's death in the seventh century.

Oh, race of Franks, race from across the mountains, race chosen and beloved by God—as
shines forth in very many of your works—set apart from all nations by the situation of your
country, as well as by your catholic faith and the honor of the holy church! To you our discourse
is addressed and for you our exhortation is intended. We wish you to know what a grievous cause
has led us to your country, what peril threatening you and all the faithful has brought us.

From the confines of Jerusalem and the city of Constantinople a horrible tale has gone forth
and very frequently has been brought to our ears, namely, that a race from the kingdom of the
Persians, an accursed race, a race utterly alienated from God, a generation forsooth which has not
directed its heart and has not entrusted its spirit to God, has invaded the lands of those Christians
and has depopulated them by the sword, pillage and fire; it has led away a part of the captives
into its own country, and a part it has destroyed by cruel tortures; it has either entirely destroyed
the churches of God or appropriated them for the rites of its own religion. They destroy the altars,
after having defiled them with their uncleanness. They circumcise the Christians, and the blood
of the circumcision they either spread upon the altars or pour into the vases of the baptismal font.
When they wish to torture people by a base death, they perforate their navels, and dragging forth
the extremity of the intestines, bind it to a stake; then with flogging they lead the victim around
until the viscera having gushed forth the victim falls prostrate upon the ground. Others they bind
to a post and pierce with arrows. Others they compel to extend their necks and then, attacking

them with naked swords, attempt to cut through the neck with a single blow. What shall I say of the abominable rape of the women? To speak of it is worse than to be silent. The kingdom of the Greeks is now dismembered by them and deprived of territory so vast in extent that it can not be traversed in a march of two months. On whom therefore is the labor of avenging these wrongs and of recovering this territory incumbent, if not upon you? You, upon whom above other nations God has conferred remarkable glory in arms, great courage, bodily activity, and strength to humble the hairy scalp of those who resist you.

Let the deeds of your ancestors move you and incite your minds to manly achievements; the glory and greatness of king Charles the Great, and of his son Louis, and of your other kings, who have destroyed the kingdoms of the pagans, and have extended in these lands the territory of the holy church. Let the holy sepulchre of the Lord our Saviour, which is possessed by unclean nations, especially incite you, and the holy places which are now treated with ignominy and irreverently polluted with their filthiness. Oh, most valiant soldiers and descendants of invincible ancestors, be not degenerate, but recall the valor of your progenitors.

But if you are hindered by love of children, parents and wives, remember what the Lord says in the Gospel, "He that loveth father or mother more than me, is not worthy of me." "Every one that hath forsaken houses, or brethren, or sisters, or father, or mother, or wife, or children, or lands for my name's sake shall receive an hundred-fold and shall inherit everlasting life." Let none of your possessions detain you, no solicitude for your family affairs, since this land which you inhabit, shut in on all sides by the seas and surrounded by the mountain peaks, is too narrow for your large population; nor does it abound in wealth; and it furnishes scarcely food enough for its cultivators. Hence it is that you murder one another, that you wage war, and that frequently you perish by mutual wounds. Let therefore hatred depart from among you, let your quarrels end, let wars cease, and let all dissensions and controversies slumber. Enter upon the road to the Holy Sepulchre; wrest that land from the wicked race, and subject it to yourselves. That land which as the Scripture says "floweth with milk and honey," was given by God into the possession of the children of Israel.

Jerusalem is the navel of the world; the land is fruitful above others, like another paradise of delights. This the Redeemer of the human race has made illustrious by His advent, has beautified by residence, has consecrated by suffering, has redeemed by death, has glorified by burial. This royal city, therefore, situated at the centre of the world, is now held captive by His enemies, and is in subjection to those who do not know God, to the worship of the heathens. She seeks therefore and desires to be liberated, and does not cease to implore you to come to her aid. From you especially she asks succor, because, as we have already said, God has conferred upon you above all nations great glory in arms. Accordingly undertake this journey for the remission of your sins, with the assurance of the imperishable glory of the kingdom of heaven.

When Pope Urban had said these and very many similar things in his urbane discourse, he so influenced to one purpose the desires of all who were present, that they cried out, "It is the will of God! It is the will of God!" When the venerable Roman pontiff heard that, with eyes uplifted to heaven he gave thanks to God and, with his hand commanding silence, said:

Most beloved brethren, to-day is manifest in you what the Lord says in the Gospel, "Where two or three are gathered together in my name there am I in the midst of them." Unless the Lord God had been present in your spirits, all of you would not have uttered the same cry. For, although the cry issued from numerous mouths, yet the origin of the cry was one. Therefore I say to you that God, who implanted this in your breasts, has drawn it forth from you. Let this then be your war-cry in combats, because this word is given to you by God. When an armed attack is made upon the enemy, let this one cry be raised by all the soldiers of God: It is the will of God! It is the will of God!

And we do not command or advise that the old or feeble, or those unfit for bearing arms, undertake this journey; nor ought women to set out at all, without their husbands or brothers or legal guardians. For such are more of a hindrance than aid, more of a burden than advantage. Let the rich aid the needy; and according to their wealth, let them take with them experienced soldiers. The priests and clerks of any order are not to go without the consent of their bishop for this journey would profit them nothing if they went without permission of these. Also, it is not fitting that laymen should enter upon the pilgrimage without the blessing of their priests.

Whoever, therefore, shall determine upon this holy pilgrimage and shall make his vow to God to that effect and shall offer himself to Him as a living sacrifice, holy, acceptable unto God, shall wear the sign of the cross of the Lord on his forehead or on his breast. When, truly, having fulfilled his vow he wishes to return, let him place the cross on his back between his shoulders. Such, indeed, by the two-fold action will fulfill the precept of the Lord, as He commands in the Gospel, "He that taketh not his cross and followeth after me, is not worthy of me."

from *Translations and Reprints from the Original Sources of European History*, Vol I. Philadelphia, 1895.

Fulcher of Chartres: The Start of the First Crusade

In this account, Fulcher paints a dramatic and idealistic picture of knights taking leave of their families to depart for the land across the sea.

Such then was the immense assemblage which set out from the West. Gradually along the march and from day to day this army grew by the addition of other armies, coming from every direction and composed of innumerable people. Thus one saw massed together an infinite multitude, speaking different languages and come from divers countries. All did not, however, melt into a single army until we had reached the city of Nicaea. What shall I add? The isles of the sea and the kingdoms of the whole earth were moved by God, so that one might believe that he saw the fulfillment of the prophecy of David, who said in his Psalm: "All nations whom Thou hast made shall come and worship before Thee, O Lord; and shall glorify Thy name," and so that those who have reached the holy places may say justly: "We will worship where His feet have stood." Concerning this journey we read very many other predictions in the prophecies.

Oh, how great was the grief, how deep the sighs, what weeping, what lamentation among the friends when the husband left the wife so dear to him, his children also, and all his possessions of any kind; or his father, his mother, his brethren or his other kindred! And yet, in spite of these floods of tears which those who remained shed for their friends about to depart, and in their very presence, the latter did not suffer their courage to fail, and, out of love for the Lord, in no way hesitated to leave all that they would gain a hundred-fold in receiving the recompense which God has promised to those who follow Him.

Then the husband announced to his wife the exact time of his return, assuring her that if he lived he would return to his country and to her at the end of three years. He commended her to the Lord, gave her a kiss and promised to come back to her. But the latter, who feared that she would never see him again, overcome with grief, was unable to stand, fell almost lifeless to the ground and wept over her dear one, whom she was losing in life, as if he were already dead. He then, as if he had no pity—and was not moved by lamentations of his wife or children or friends—and yet he was secretly moved—departed with mind firmly set upon his purpose. The sadness was for those who remained, and the joy for those who departed. What more can we say? "This is the Lord's doings; and it is marvelous in our eyes."

from *Translations and Reprints from the Original Sources of European History*, Vol I. Philadelphia, 1895.

Privilege Granted to Crusaders by Pope Eugenius III, 1146

This is typical of the privileges and protections, both religious and practical, offered by popes and kings to those who took up the cross.

Moreover, by the authority vested by God in us, we who with paternal care provide for your safety and the needs of the church, have promised and granted to those who from a spirit of devotion have decided to enter upon and accomplish such a holy and necessary undertaking and task, that remission of sins which our predecessor Pope Urban instituted. We have also commanded that their wives and children, their property and possessions, shall be under the protection of the holy church, of ourselves, of the archbishops, bishops and other prelates of the church of God. Moreover, we ordain by our apostolic authority that until their return or death is fully proven, no law suit shall be instituted hereafter in regard to any property of which they were in peaceful possession when they took the cross.

Those who with pure hearts enter upon such a sacred journey and who are in debt shall pay no interest. And if they or others for them are bound by oath or promise to pay interest, we free them by our apostolic authority. And after they have sought aid of their relatives or lords of whom they hold their fiefs, and the latter are unable or unwilling to advance them money, we allow them freely to mortgage their lands and other possessions to churches, ecclesiastics or other Christians, and their lords shall have no redress.

Following the institution of our predecessor, and through the authority of omnipotent God and of St. Peter, prince of the Apostles--which is vested in us by God--we grant absolution and remission of sins, so that those who devoutly undertake and accomplish such a holy journey, or who die by the way, shall obtain absolution for all their sins which they confess with humble and contrite heart, and shall receive from the Remunerator of all the reward of eternal life.

Granted at Vetralle on the *Kalends* of December.

from *Translations and Reprints from the Original Sources of European History*, Vol I. Philadelphia, 1895.

Unit 25: Medieval Learning

Scholasticism is the name given to the method of the Schoolmen, those who taught in cathedral schools and early universities. Their focus was on giving rational form to their beliefs and on creating a systematic framework for understanding the world and man and their relationship to God. Unlike such church fathers as Jerome, they did not reject the philosophy of the preChristian Greeks, but attempted to find a common ground where Christianity and philosophy could meet.

Abelard: *Sic et Non*

Abelard is probably best known for his tragic romance with Heloise and the powerful enmity he engendered, which resulted in the condemnation of some of his teachings by the church. His book *Sic et Non* is, however, an outstanding example of the scholastic method. In the Prologue, he explains his method and the reasoning behind it.

PROLOGUE

I wish to collect various sayings of the Fathers which occur to my memory and which, because of the apparent contradiction in them, present a problem. They impel young readers to exert themselves most eagerly in the search for the truth, and render their minds more acute by means of the inquiry. This investigation is in fact the first key to wisdom, that is to say, assiduous of frequent inquiry, which is very strongly advocated by that most farsighted of all philosophers, Aristotle, when he says in exhorting the studious, "Perhaps it is difficult to express oneself with confidence on such matters, unless these have often been discussed. To entertain doubt concerning some of them is not without advantage." For it is through doubting that we arrive at inquiry, and through inquiry we perceive the truth, according to the Truth Himself.[52] "Seek," He says, "and you shall find, knock and it shall be opened unto you." And, in order to instruct us by His own example, He chose to be found at the age of twelve interrogating the doctors, sitting in their midst, showing us the appearance of a pupil asking questions, rather than that of a master who teaches, although there is in Him the complete and perfect wisdom of God.

Inasmuch as some words of the Scriptures have been quoted, it follows that the greater is the authority commanded by the Scriptures, the more these words induce one to search for the truth. Hence I have compiled in this volume sayings of the saints, observing the decree of Pope Gelasius concerning the authentic books, having included nothing from apocryphal books. . . .Here follow the propositions collected from these books which seem to contradict each other. Because of this contradiction this compilation of propositions is called *Sic et Non* (Yes and No).

I.	That faith is based on reason, and the opposite.
II.	That faith is of things not seen, and the opposite.
IV.	That one must believe in God only, and the opposite.
XXVII.	That Divine Providence is the cause of things happening, and the opposite.
XXVIII.	That nothing happens by chance, and the opposite.
XXXII.	That all things are possible to God, and the opposite.
XXXIII.	That God does not have a free will, and the opposite.
XXXVIII.	That God knows all things, and the opposite.
LIV.	That man's first sin did not begin through the persuasion of the devil, and the opposite.
LV.	That Eve only, and not Adam, was beguiled, and the opposite.
LVI.	That by sinning man lost free will, and the opposite.
CXVI.	That the sins of the fathers are visited upon the children, and the opposite.
CXXII.	That everybody should be allowed to marry, and the opposite.

---

[52] i.e., Jesus.

CLVI. THAT IT IS PERMITTED TO KILL MEN, AND THE OPPOSITE.

<u>Jerome on Isaiah, Book V</u>. He who cuts the throat of a man of blood, is not a man of blood.

<u>The Same, On the Epistle to the Galatians</u>: He who smites the wicked because they are wicked and whose reason for the murder is that he may slay the base, is a servant of the Lord.

<u>The Same, on Jeremiah</u>: For the punishment of homicides, impious persons and poisoners is not bloodshed, but serving the law.

<u>Cyprian, in the Ninth Kind of Abuse</u>: The King ought to restrain theft, punish deeds of adultery, cause the wicked to perish from off the face of the earth, refuse to allow parricides and perjurers to live.

<u>Augustine</u>: Although it is manslaughter to slaughter a man, a person may sometimes be slain without sin. For both a soldier in the case of a n enemy and a judge or his official in the case of a criminal, and the man from whose hand, perhaps without his will or knowledge, a weapon has flown, do not seem to me to sin, but merely to kill a man.

<u>Likewise</u>: The soldier is ordered by law to kill the enemy, and if he shall prove to have refrained from such slaughter, he pays the penalty at the hands of his commander. Shall we not go so far as to call these laws unjust or rather no laws at all? For that which was not just does not seem to me to be a law.

<u>The Same, on Exodus chapter xxvii</u>: The Israelites committed no theft in spoiling the Egyptians, but rendered a service to God at his bidding, just as when the servant of a judge kills a man whom the law has ordered to be killed; certainly if he does it of his own volition he is a homicide, even though he knows that the man whom he executes ought to be executed by the judge.

<u>The Same, on Leviticus chapter lxxv</u>: When a man is justly put to death, the law puts him to death, not you.

<u>The Same, Book I of the "City of God"</u>: You shall not kill, except in the case of those whose death God orders, or else when a law has been passed to suit the needs of the time and express command has been laid upon a person. But he does not kill who owes service to the person who gives him his orders, for he is as it were a mere sword for the person who employs his assistance.

<u>Likewise</u>: When a soldier, in obedience to the power under which he is legitimately placed, kills a man, by no law of the state is he accused of murder; nay if he has not done it, he is accused of desertion and insubordination. But if he had acted under his own initiative and of his own will, he would have incurred the charge of shedding human blood. And so he is punished if he does not do when ordered that for which he would receive punishment if he did it without orders.

<u>The Same, to Publicola</u>: Counsel concerning the slaying of men pleases me not, that none may be slain by them, unless perhaps a man is a soldier or in a public office, so that he does the deed not in his own behalf, but for others and for the state, accepting power legitimately conferred, if it is consonant with the task imposed on him.

Likewise: It has been said: let us not resist the evil man, let not the vengeance delight us which feeds the mind on others' ill, let us not neglect the reproofs of men.

The Same, to Marcella: If that earthly commonwealth of yours keeps to the teachings of Christ, even wars will not be waged without goodwill, for with pitying heart even wars if possible will be waged by the good, so that the lusts of desire may be subdued and those faults destroyed which ought under just rule to be either rooted out or chastised. For if Christian training condemned all wars, this should rather be the advice given in the gospel for their safety to the soldiers who ask for it, namely to throw aside their arms and retire altogether from the field. But this is the word spoken to them: Do violence to no man, neither accuse any falsely; and be content with your wages.

He warns them that the wages that belong to them should satisfy them, but he by no means forbids them to take the field.

The Same, to his comrade Boniface: "I will give you and yours a useful counsel: Take arms in your hands; let prayer strike the ears of the creator; because in battle the heavens are opened, God looks forth and awards the victory to the side he sees to be the righteous one."

The Same: The wars to be waged we undertake either at the command of God or under some lawful rule. Else John when the soldiers to be baptized came to him saying, "And what shall we do?" would make answer to them: "Cast aside your arms, leave the service; smite no man; ruin no man."

But because he knew that they did these things because they were in the service, that they were not slayers of men, but servants of the law; and not avengers of their own injuries, but guardians of the public safety, his answer to them was: "Do violence to no man," etc.

Isidore, Etymologiae, Book xviii, chapter iii: A righteous war is one waged according to orders, to recover property or drive back the enemy.

Pope Nicholas to the questions of the Bulgarians: If there is no urgent need, not only in Lent but at all times, men should abstain from battles. If however there is an unavoidable and urgent occasion, and it is not Lent, beyond all doubt preparations for wars should be sparingly made in one's own defence or in that of one's country or the laws of one's fathers: lest forsooth this word by said: A man if he has an attack to make, does not carefully take counsel beforehand for his own safety and that of others, nor does he guard against injury to holy religion.

Adapted from Arthur Norton, *Readings in the History of Education, Medieval Universities*. Harvard University Press. 1909.

from *The Summa Theologiae* of Thomas Aquinas, 1265: The Will of God

Aquinas is widely considered the greatest of the medieval philosophers. With the aid of new, more accurate translations of Aristotle directly from the Greek, he constructed a system of rational theology. He went beyond Abelard's simple listing of contradictory opinions, using reason to bring about a synthesis of the teachings of the Bible, the Church Fathers, and Aristotle.

SEVENTH ARTICLE. WHETHER THE WILL OF GOD IS MUTABLE?

Objection 1: It seems that the Will of God is mutable. For the Lord says: *It repenteth me that I have made man*. (Genesis 6:7). But whoever repents of what he has done, has a mutable will. Therefore God has a mutable Will.

Objection 2: Further, it is said to Jeremias in the person of the Lord: *I will speak against a nation and against a kingdom, to root out, and to pull down, and to destroy it; but if that nation shall repent of its evil, I also will repent of the evil that I have thought to do to them* (Jeremiah 18:7,8). Therefore God has a mutable Will.

Objection 3. Further, whatever God does, He does voluntarily. But God does not always do the same thing, for at one time He ordered the law to be observed, and at another time forbade it. Therefore He has a mutable Will.

Objection 4. Further, God does not will of necessity what He wills, as said before. Therefore He can both will and not will the same thing. But whatever can incline to either of two opposites, is mutable; as that which can exist and not exist is mutable substantially; and that which can exist in a place or not in that place, is mutable locally. Therefore God is mutable as regards His will.

On the contrary, It is said: *God is not as a man, that He should lie, nor as the son of man, that He should be changed* (Numbers 23:19).

I answer that, The Will of God is entirely immutable. On this point we must consider that to change the will is one thing; to will that a thing should be changed is another. It is possible to will a thing to be done now, and its contrary afterwards; and yet for the will to remain permanently the same. The will would be changed, if anyone should begin to will what before he had not willed; or cease to will what he had willed before. This cannot happen, unless we presuppose change either on the part of knowledge; or in the disposition of the substance of him who wills. Since the will regards good, a man may in two ways begin to will a thing. In one way when that thing begins to be good for him, which does not take place without a change in him. Thus when the cold weather begins, it becomes good to sit by the fire; though it was not so before. In another way when he knows for the first time that a thing is good for him, though he did not know it before. We take counsel for this reason, to know what is good for us. It has already been shown that both the Substance of God and His Knowledge are entirely immutable. Therefore His Will must be entirely immutable.

Reply to Objection 1: These words of the Lord are to be understood metaphorically, and after the fashion of our own nature. When we repent of having made a thing, we destroy what we have made; although we may even destroy a thing without change of will; as, when a man wills to make a thing, at the same time intending to destroy it later. Therefore God is said to have repented, as His deed seems to represent Him doing; when by the Deluge He destroyed from the face of the earth man whom He had made.

Reply to Objection 2: The Will of God, as it is the first and universal cause, does not exclude intermediate causes that have power to produce certain effects. Since all intermediate causes are inferior in power to the first cause, there are many things in the Divine Power and Knowledge and Will that are not included in the order of inferior causes. Thus in the case of the raising of Lazarus, one who looked only at inferior causes might have said that Lazarus would not rise again; but looking at the Divine First Cause might have said that he would rise again. And God wills both: that is, that in the order of the inferior cause a thing should happen; but that in the order of the higher cause it should not happen; or He may will conversely. We may say, then, that God sometimes declares that a thing shall happen according as it falls under the order of inferior causes, as of nature, or merit, which yet does not happen as not being in the designs of the Divine and higher cause. Thus He foretold to Ezechias: *Take order with thy house, for thou shalt die, and not live* (Isaiah 38:1). Yet this did not take place, since from eternity it was otherwise disposed in the Divine Knowledge and in the Divine Will, which is immutable. Hence Gregory says: *The sentence of God changes, but not His counsel*—that is to say, the counsel of His Will. When therefore He says, 'I also will repent,' His words must be understood metaphorically. For men seem to repent, when they do not fulfil what they have threatened.

Reply to Objection 3: It does not follow from this argument that God has a will that changes, but that He sometimes wills that things should change.

Reply to Objection 4. Although God's willing a thing is not by absolute necessity, yet it is necessary by supposition, on account of the immutability of the Divine Will, as has been said above.

Question 19. Translated by Fathers of the English Dominican Province. *Summa Theologica*, New York: Benziger Brothers, 1911.

Regulating the Professors at the University of Bologna

Some universities were governed by associations of masters, or professors, others by associations of students. At Bologna, the students fined professors who did not cover the prescribed material offered in their courses. Bologna was known for its courses in law, both canon (Church Law) and civil.

We have decreed also that all Doctors actually lecturing must read the glosses immediately after reading the chapter or the law, unless the continuity of the chapters or of the laws requires otherwise, taking the burden in this matter on their own consciences in accordance with the oath they have taken. Nor, with regard to those things that are not to be read, must they yield to the clamor of the scholars. Furthermore we decree that Doctors, lecturing ordinarily or extraordinarily, must come to the sections assigned de novo, according to the regulations below. And we decree, as to the close observance by them of the passages, that any Doctor, in his ordinary lecturing in Canon or Civil Law, must deposit, fifteen days before the Feast of Saint Michael, twenty-five Bologna pounds with one of the treasurers whom the rectors have appointed; which treasurer shall promise to give said money to the rectors, or the general beadle in their name, all at once or in separate amounts, as he shall be required by them or by him.

The form, moreover, to be observed by the Doctors as to the sections is this: Let the division of the book into sections be determined, and then let him be notified. And if any Doctor fails to reach any section on the specified date he shall be fined five pounds, and for a third and each succeeding violation of the rule, ten pounds. And if the twenty-five pounds are exhausted, he must deposit in said place a second twenty-five pounds; and the second deposit must be made within eight days from the time when the first was exhausted. . .

We decree also that no Doctor shall hereafter exceed one section in one lecture. And if the contrary be done by any one he shall be charged with perjury and punished to the extent of three pounds, to be taken from the money deposited for the purpose; and as often as the violation occurs, so often shall the penalty be inflicted, so long as the statute is in force; and the Rector also must exact it.

We add that at the end of a section the Doctors must announce to the scholars at what section they are to begin afterwards, and they shall be obliged to follow that section which they have begun, even to the end of the section. But if by chance, after due weight is given to the glosses or text, it seems useful to transfer a part of the lecture to another section, he shall be obliged in his preceding lecture to announce that to the scholars, so that those who wish may make provision before-hand; under penalty of five Bologna shillings for each occasion for the Doctor who does to the contrary.

We order this statute to be published in each school at the beginning of the term. . .

Since topics not read by the Doctors are completely neglected and consequently are not known to the scholars, we have decreed that no Doctor shall omit from his sections any chapter, decretal, law, or paragraph. If he does this he shall be obliged to read it within the following section. We have also decreed that no decretal or decree or law or difficult paragraph shall be reserved to be read at the end of the lecture if, through such reservation, promptness of exit at the sound of the appointed bell is likely to be prevented.

from *Readings in the History of Education: Mediaeval Universities*, edited by Arthur O. Norton. Harvard University press, 1909.

CHAPTER 12: THE FOURTEENTH-CENTURY CRISIS

Unit 26: The Hundred Years' War

The phrase "Hundred Years' War" covers the period from 1337 to 1453, a series of wars between the English and the French in which the English won most of the battles but ended by being ousted from French soil, except for a tiny toehold at Calais. For many English noblemen, the wars provided an opportunity to seek fame and fortune. For the French, it meant the devastation of much of the country. On both sides, the wars created legends, such as those of Edward, the Black Prince, John the Good, the French king who died in an English prison rather than break his word, and Joan of Arc, the Maid of Orléans, who was burned as a heretic and later made a saint.

From Froissart's *Chronicle*

Froissart was born the year the war began. He began his *Chronicle* at the age of twenty, and much of what he reports is what he himself witnessed, or what he learned from interviewing participants. He traveled widely, accepted at the courts of nobles on both sides, and he reports "Wherever I went I enquired of old knights and squires who had shared in deeds of arms, and could speak with authority concerning them, and also spoke with heralds in order to verify and corroborate all that was told me. In this way I gathered noble facts for my history . . ."

CAUSE OF THE WAR

History tells us that Philip, king of France, surnamed the Fair, had three sons, besides his beautiful daughter Isabella, married to the king of England. These three sons were very handsome. The eldest, Louis, king of Navarre, during the lifetime of his father, was called Louis Hutin; the second was named Philip the Great, or the Long; and the third, Charles. All these were kings of France, after their father Philip, by legitimate succession, one after the other, without having by marriage any male heirs. Yet on the death of the last king, Charles, the twelve peers and barons of France did not give the kingdom to Isabella, the sister, who was queen of England, because they said and maintained, and still insist, that the kingdom of France is so noble that it ought not to go to a woman; consequently neither to Isabella nor to her son, the king of England; for they held that the son of a woman cannot claim any right of succession where that woman has none herself. For these reasons the twelve peers and barons of France unanimously gave the kingdom of France to the lord Philip of Valois, nephew of King Philip, and thus put aside the queen of England (who was sister to Charles, the late king of France) and her son. Thus, as it seemed to many people, the succession went out of the right line, which has been the occasion of the most destructive wars and devastations of countries, as well in France as elsewhere, as you will learn hereafter; the real object of this history being to relate the great enterprises and deeds of arms achieved in these wars, for from the time of good Charlemagne, king of France, never were such feats performed.

ALLIANCE OF THE ENGLISH AND THE FLEMISH (1340)

When King Edward had departed from Flanders and arrived at Brabant he set out straight for Brussels, whither he was attended by the duke of Gueldres, the duke of Juliers, the marquis of Blanckenburg, the earl of Mons, the lord John of Hainault, the lord of Fauquemont, and all the barons of the Empire who were allied to him, as they wished to consider what was next to be done in this war which they had begun. For greater expedition, they ordered a conference to be held in the city of Brussels, and invited James van Arteveld[53] to attend it, who came thither in great array, and brought with him all the councils from the principal towns of Flanders.

At this parliament the king of England was advised by his allies of the Empire to solicit the Flemings to give him their aid and assistance in this war, to challenge the king of France, and to follow King Edward wherever he should lead them, and in return he would assist them in the recovery of Lisle, Douay, and Bethune.[54] The Flemings heard this proposal with pleasure; but they requested of the king that they might consider it among themselves and in a short time they would give their answer.

The king consented and soon after they made this reply: "Beloved sire, you formerly made us a similar request; and we are willing to do everything in reason for you without prejudice to our honor and faith. But we are pledged by promise on oath, under a penalty of two millions of florins, to the apostolical chamber,[55] not to act offensively against the king of France in any way, whoever he may be, without forfeiting this sum, and incurring the sentence of excommunication. But if you will do what we will tell you, you will find a remedy, which is, that you take the arms of France, quarter them with those of England, and call yourself king of France. We will acknowledge your title as good, and we will demand of you quittance for the above sum, which you will grant us as king of France. Thus we shall be absolved and at liberty to go with you wherever it please you."

The king summoned his council, for he was loath to take the title and arms of France, seeing that at present he had not conquered any part of that kingdom and that it was uncertain whether he ever should. On the other hand, he was unwilling to lose the aid and assistance of the Flemings, who could be of greater service to him than any others at that period. He consulted, therefore, with the lords of the Empire, the lord Robert d'Artois, and his most privy councilors, who, after having duly weighed the good and bad, advised him to make for answer to the Flemings, that if they would bind themselves under their seals, to an agreement to aid him in carrying on the war, he would willingly comply with their conditions, and would swear to assist them in the recovery of Lisle, Douay, and Bethune. To this they willingly consented. A day was fixed for them to meet at Ghent, where the king and the greater part of the lords of the Empire, and in general the councils from the different towns in Flanders, assembled. The above-mentioned proposals and answers were then repeated, sworn to, and sealed; and the king of England bore the arms of France, quartering them with those of England. He also took the title of king of France from that day forward.

From *A Source Book of Mediaeval History*, edited by Austin Ogg. New York, 1907

---

[53] Van Arteveldt was a brewer from Ghent, leader of the popular party, which opposed French influence in Flanders.

[54] Cities that had been taken from Flanders by the French.

[55] The papal court.

THE BATTLE OF CRÉCY

The battle of Crécy, fought in 1356, was the greatest of an early string of English victories. A badly outnumbered English force won the battle by taking a defensive position and withstanding sixteen attacks by the French. The English longbow and their reliance on foot soldiers rather than mounted, armored knights carried the day.

[Having reached a point near Crécy,] the king of England was well informed how the French king followed after him to fight. Then he said to his company: "Let us take here some plot of ground, for we will go no farther till we have seen our enemies. I have good cause here to await them, for I am on the very heritage of the queen, my mother, which land was given her at her marriage; I will challenge it of mine adversary, Philip of Valois." And because he had not the eighth part in number of men that the French king had, therefore he commanded his marshals to choose a plot of ground that would be to his advantage; and so they did, and there the king and his host went. . . .

That night the king made a supper to all his chief lords of his host, and made them good cheer; and when they had all departed to take their rest, then the king entered into his oratory and kneeled down before the altar, praying God devoutly that if he fought the next day he might achieve the expedition to his honor. Then about midnight he laid down to rest, and in the morning he rose early and heard mass, and the prince his son with him; and the most part of his company were confessed and received the communion; and after the mass was said, he commanded every man to be armed and to draw to the field, to the same place before appointed. Then the King caused a park to be made by the wood side behind his host, and there were set all the carts and carriages, and within the park were all their horses, for every man was afoot . . . .

Then [after arranging his army in three divisions,] the king leaped on a palfrey, with a white rod in his hand, one of his marshals on the one hand and the other on the other hand. He rode from rank to rank, asking every man to take heed that day to his right and honor. He spoke it so sweetly and with such good countenance and merry cheer that all those who were discomfited took courage in seeing and hearing him. And when he had thus visited all his divisions it was then nine of the day. Then he caused every man to eat and drink a little, and so they did at their leisure. And afterward they ordered again their divisions. Then every man lay down on the earth, his helmet and his bow by him, to be fresher when their enemies should come.

This Saturday the French king rose early and heard mass in Abbeville, in his lodging in the abbey of St. Peter, and he departed after the sun rising. [He dispatched four knights to view the English, who let them alone and permitted them to return to the king as they had come. The knights advised the king that the French should defer the attack until the morrow.] Then the king commanded that it should be so done. Then his two marshals rode, one before, another behind, saying to every banner, "Tarry and abide here in the name of God and St. Denis." They that were in front tarried, but they that were behind would not wait, but rode forth, and said how they would in no wise abide till they were as far forward as the foremost. And when they that were in front saw them come on behind, then they rode forward again, so that neither the king nor his marshals could rule them.

So they rode without order or good array till they came in sight of their enemies; and as soon as the foremost saw them, they recoiled in disorder; those behind marveled and were abashed, and thought that the foremost company had been fighting. Then they might have had leisure and room to have gone forward if they had wished, but some went forward while some stayed still.

The commons, of whom all the ways between Abbeville and Crécy were full, when they saw that they were near their enemies, took their swords and cried, "Down with them! Let us slay them all." There were no man, though he were present, that could imagine or show the truth of the disorder that was among the French party,—and yet they were a marvelous great number. What I write in this book I learned especially from the Englishmen, who beheld their dealing; and also certain knights of Sir John of Hainault's who was always near King Philip, showed me what they knew.

The Englishmen, who were in three divisions lying on the ground to rest them, as soon as they saw the Frenchmen approach, they rose upon their feet, fair and easily without any haste, and arranged their divisions. The first was the prince's division, and the archers there stood in manner of a harrow and the men-at-arms in the bottom of the division. The earl of Northampton and the earl of Arundel with the second division were on the wing in good order, ready to aid the prince's division, if they were needed.

The lords and knights of France did not come to the engagement together in good order, for some came before and some came after, in such disorder that one of them did trouble another. When the French king saw the Englishmen his blood changed and he said to his marshals, "Make the Genoese go on before and begin the battle in the name of God and St. Denis." There were of the Genoese crossbows about fifteen thousand, but they were so weary of going afoot that day six leagues armed with their crossbows that they said to their constables, "We are not well ordered to fight this day. We are not in a condition to do any great deed of arms; we have more need of rest." . . .

Also the same season there fell a great rain, and a flash of lightning with a terrible thunder, and before the rain there came flying over both armies a great number of crows for fear of the tempest coming. Then anon the air began to wax clear, and the sun to shine fair and bright, which was right in the Frenchmen's eyes and on the Englishmen's backs.

When the Genoese were assembled together and began to approach, they uttered a great cry to abash the Englishmen, but these stood still and stirred not for all that. Then the Genoese a second time made a fell cry and stepped forward a little, but the Englishmen did not retreat one foot. Thirdly they shouted again and went forth until they came within shot. Then they shot fiercely with their crossbows. Then the English archers stepped forth one pace and let fly their arrows so wholly and so thick that it seemed snow. When the Genoese felt the arrows piercing through heads, arms, and breasts, many of them cast down their crossbows and cut their strings and returned discomfited.[56]

When the French king saw them fly away he said, "Slay these rascals, for they shall hinder and trouble us without reason." Then you should have seen the men-at-arms dash in among them and they killed a great number of them; and ever still the Englishmen shot where they saw the thickest press. The sharp arrows ran into the men-at-arms and into their horses, and many fell, horses and men, among the Genoese, and when they were down they could not rise again; the

---

[56] The English longbow could be loaded and fired about ten times faster than the crossbow used by the French.

press was so thick that one overthrew another.[57] And also among the Englishmen there were certain rascals that went afoot with great knives, and they went in among the men-at-arms and slew and murdered many as they lay on the ground, both earls, barons, knights, and squires. The king of England was later displeased, for he had rather that they had been taken prisoners. . . .[58]

[The division led by the king's son, the Black Prince, being hard pressed,] they sent a messenger to the king, who was on a little windmill hill. Then the knight said to the king, "Sir, the earl of Warwick and the earl of Oxford, Sir Raynold Cobham, and others, such as are around the prince your son, are fiercely fought withal and are sorely handled; wherefore they ask that you and your division come and aid them; for if the Frenchmen increase, as they fear they will, your son and they will have much ado." Then the king said, "Is my son dead, or hurt, or on the earth felled?" "No, sir," quoth the knight, "but he is well matched, wherefore he has need of your aid." "Well," said the king, "return to him and to them that sent you here, and say to them that they should send no more to me for any adventure that falleth, as long as my son is alive; and also say to them that they allow him this day to win his spurs; for if God be pleased, I will that this expedition be his, and the honor thereof, and to them that are with him."

Adapted from *The Harvard Classics*, vol. 35. Edited Charles W. Eliot. New York: Collier, 1910.

from The Trial of Joan of Arc, 1431

Joan was a thirteen-year-old girl when, according to her testimony, she first heard voices. At the age of 17, the voices told her to go to Charles, the dauphin, and help him to aid the city of Orleans, which was besieged by the English, and then to see Charles crowned at Rheims, the traditional place for French coronations. She succeeded in both, but shortly after was captured by the Burgundians and turned over to the English. She was tried in a church court on charges of heresy and witchcraft. Questioning centered on whether the voices were from God or from the devil, and on her insistence on dressing in men's clothing. She was convicted and burned at the stake in 1431. In 1456 a new trial exonerated her of all charges. The following selection is excerpted from transcripts of the trial.

FIRST PUBLIC SESSION

The following day, which was Wednesday the twenty-first day of February, in the chapel royal of the castle of Rouen, in the presence of the bishop and of my lords and masters, my lord Gilles, Abbot of Fécamp, Jean Beaupère, Jean de Chatillon, Jacques le Tessier, Nicolas Midi, Gerard Feuillet, Guillaume Haiton, Thomas de Courcelles and Maître Richard Praty, were read the letters of the King of England wherein he commanded the ordinary judges of Rouen to hand over and deliver the Pucelle[59] to the bishop to be tried;[60] the letters of the Chapter of Rouen showing that they had given permission to the bishop to hold the trial within the territory of

---

[57] The English were defending a hillside. The French mounted knights were attacking. As those in front were felled by English arrows, they became mired in the mud. Those behind continued to press forward and were entangled in the mired carcasses.

[58] Medieval wars were not fought simply to gain political control. The taking of prisoners to hold for ransom was an important means of raising money.

[59] The word means girl or young woman, but was sometimes used to denote a virgin and sometimes, cynically, a prostitute.

[60] Being tried in the bishop's court meant that she was accused of crimes against canon, or church, law, rather than of civil crimes.

Rouen; and the citation to the Pucelle to appear before him, together with the account of him who had cited her.

These being read, Maître Jean Estivet, appointed promoter at the trial by the bishop, required the Pucelle to be brought and questioned in accordance with law. Which was granted by the bishop.

And since Jeanne had made a supplication that she might be allowed to hear Mass, the bishop said that he had consulted with several wise and notable persons, on whose advice he had come to the conclusion that, in view of the crimes of which she was accused, and of the fact that she wore man's dress, they ought to defer this request; and thus he declared it.

Very soon after, Jeanne was led in to the presence of the bishop and the assessors afore-mentioned.

She being present, the judge spoke to her and explained that she had been taken within the boundaries of his diocese. And since there was common report of a number of her deeds which were contrary to our faith, not only within the realm of France but in all the States in which they were known and published, and since she was accused of heresy, she had been handed over to him to be tried in a matter of faith.

After these words, the promoter showed how at his request she had been cited and convened to answer in a matter of faith, as appeared from the letters and acts which he then exhibited, begging that she should be adjured to speak the truth, and then questioned upon the accusations that he would deliver.

This was granted by the bishop and the court.

This request being granted, as has been said, the bishop caused Jeanne to come before him, and charitably admonished her.

And told her that she should tell the truth concerning the things which would be asked her, as much for the shortening of her trial as for the unburdening of her conscience, without subterfuge or craft; and that she should swear on the Holy Gospels to tell the truth concerning everything she should be asked.

Jeanne answered: I do not know on what you may wish to question me. Perhaps you may ask such things as I will not answer.

Whereupon the bishop said to her:

You will swear to tell the truth about whatever you are asked concerning the Catholic Faith, and all else that you may know.

To which Jeanne answered that concerning her father and mother, and concerning everything she had done since she took the road for France, she would willingly swear. But as for revelations sent her from God, never had she told or revealed them save to Charles, who she said was her king. And if they cut her head off, she would not reveal them; for she knew from her visions that she must keep them secret. But within eight days she would know if she ought to reveal them.

After these words the bishop admonished her, and asked her to take the oath to tell the truth concerning the faith.

Jeanne knelt down, her two hands on the book, that is to say a missal, and swore that she would tell the truth in all matters asked her concerning the Faith. But that, about the aforesaid revelations, she would not tell anyone.

The same day, after several questions had been put to her concerning the name of her father and mother, the place where she was born, and her age, Jeanne complained of the fetters which she had on her legs.

She was told by the bishop that several times she had endeavoured to escape from her prisons, wherefore, in order that she might be kept the more securely, he had ordered that she should be fettered.

To which Jeanne answered that it was true that on these previous occasions she would have much liked to escape from prison, as was lawful for every prisoner. She said further that if she had been able to escape, no one could have said that she had broken faith, for she had never given her parole[61] to anyone. On account of this answer, the bishop ordered John Rice, John Bernard, and William Talbot, to whom the guardianship of Jeanne was committed, that they should guard her strictly, and that they should not allow anyone to speak to her unless they had his express permission; and made the guards place their hands on the missal, upon which they took a solemn oath to do all that they had been ordered.

The same day, Jeanne, being questioned as to her name and surname,

Answered that, in the place where she was born, she was called Jeannette, and in France, Jeanne; of a surname she knew nothing.

Questioned as to the place of her birth,

She answered that she was born in a village called Domremy de Greux, and in Greux is the principal church.

Questioned as to the name of her father and mother,

She answered that her father was named Jacques Tart and her mother Ysabeau.

Questioned as to where she had been baptised,

She answered that it was in the church of Domremy.

Questioned as to who were her godfathers and godmothers,

She answered that they were a woman named Agnes and another called Jeanne; and a man called Jean Bavent was her godfather. She said also that she had heard her mother say that she had other godfathers and godmothers as well as these.

Questioned as to who was the priest who baptised her,

She answered that he was called Messire Jean Nynet, to the best of her belief.

Questioned as to whether the said Nynet was still alive,

She answered yes, to the best of her belief.

Questioned as to how old she was,

---

[61] Her word.

She answered that she was nineteen or thereabouts. She said also that her mother taught her the Pater Noster, Ave Maria and Credo; and that no one else save her mother taught her her faith.

Being required to repeat the Pater Noster and Ave Maria,

She answered that she would say it willingly, provided that my lord Bishop of Beauvais, who was present, would hear her confession.

And then the bishop said: I will give you one or two notable persons of this company to whom you will say your Pater Noster and Ave Maria,

To which she answered: I will not say them at all, if they do not hear me in confession.

SECOND SESSION

The year one thousand four hundred and thirty, the twenty-second day of February. . . .[62]

. . . Asked whether she made her confession every year,

She said yes, to her own curé. And if he were prevented, she confessed to another priest, with her curé's leave. And she also said that she had confessed two or three times to mendicant friars. And that she received the Body of Our Lord every year at Easter.

Asked whether she had not received the Body of Our Lord at other feasts than Easter,

She answered: Go to the next question. And she said that, from the age of thirteen, she received revelation from Our Lord by a voice which taught her how to behave. And the first time she was greatly afraid. And she said that the voice came that time at noon, on a summer's day, a fast day, when she was in her father's garden, and that the voice came on her right side, in the direction of the church. And she said that the voice was hardly ever without a light, which was always in the direction of the voice.

She said further that, after she had heard it three times, she knew that it was the voice of an angel.

She said also that this voice had always taken good care of her.

Questioned as to what teaching this voice gave her as to the salvation of her soul,

She answered that it taught her how to behave. And it said to her that she ought to go often to church. And later it said to her that it was necessary that she should go into France.

And it said to her two or three times a week that she must leave and go into France. And that her father knew nothing of her going.

And with this, it said to her that she must hurry and go and raise the siege of Orleans; and that she should go to Robert de Baudricourt, captain of Vaucouleurs; and that he would give her men to accompany her.

To which she answered that she was only a poor woman, who knew nothing of riding or of making war.

---

[62] In this time and place, the year began on March 25. Thus dates before March 25 were 1430, Old Style, but 1431 in the current style.

And after these words, she went to an uncle's house, where she stayed a week, after which her uncle brought her to Robert de Baudricourt, whom she recognized, although she had never seen him before.

And she said that she recognized him by her voices, which had told her that it was he.

She said further that de Baudricourt refused her twice. The third time he received her, and gave her people to conduct her to France, as the voice had told her.

[She said also that before she received her king's commands, the Duke of Lorraine asked for her to be sent to him. She went, and told him that she wished to be sent into France. He questioned her concerning his health, of which she told him she knew nothing. She said to him little about her journey, but asked him to lend her his son and some others to conduct her to France, and then she would pray God for his restoration to health. She went to him with a safe conduct, and returned to the town of Vaucouleurs.]

She said further that when she left Vaucouleurs, she took man's dress, and also a sword which de Baudricourt gave her, but no other armour. And she said she was accompanied by a knight and four other men; and that day they spent the night in the town of Saint Urbain, where she slept in the Abbey.

She said also that as for her route, she passed through Auxerre, where she heard Mass in the great church; and that she often had her voices with her.

Questioned as to who advised her to take male dress,

To this question I have found in one book that her voices had commanded her to take man's dress; and in the other I found that, although she was several times asked, she never made any other reply than "I charge nobody." And I found in this book that several times she answered variously.

She said further that Robert de Baudricourt made her escort swear that they would conduct her well and safely.

She also said that when they left, de Baudricourt said to her: Go, and let come what may.

She said that she was well assured that God greatly loved the Duke of Orleans, and that she had more revelations concerning him than any man in France, except her king.

She said further that it was absolutely essential for her to change her dress.

Questioned as to what letters she sent the English and what they contained,

She said that she sent letters to the English[63], who were before Orleans, wherein she wrote to them that they must leave. And she said that in these letters, as she had heard it said, they have altered two or three words; for example, Render to the Pucelle, where it should be Render to the king; and where there is Body for body, and Chieftain of war; this was not in the letters.

She said also that she went to her king without hindrance.

Further, she said that she found her king at Chinon, where she arrived about noon, and lodged at an inn, and after dinner went to the king who was in the castle.

---

[63] It is not clear whether Joan knew how to read and write, or whether she dictated the letters to others.

She said that she went right into the room where the king was; whom she recognized among many others by the advice of the voice.

She said that she told the king that she wished to make war on the English.

Questioned whether, when the voice pointed the king out to her, there was any light,

She answered: Go on to the next question.

Questioned if she saw an angel above the king,

She answered: Forgive me. Pass on to the next.

She said also that before the king set her to work, he had several apparitions and glorious revelations.

Questioned as to what revelations,

She answered: I shall not tell you yet; go to the king and he will tell you.

She said further that the voice promised her that very soon after she arrived the king would receive her.

She said also that those of her party well knew that the voice came from God; and that they saw and knew the voice; and that she knows this well.

She said that the king and several members of his Council heard and saw the voices who came to her; and amongst others, Charles, Duke of Bourbon. . . .

NINTH SESSION

Monday afternoon, March 12.

Questioned concerning her father's dreams,

She replied that when she was still with her father and mother, she was often told by her mother that her father had said that he dreamed his daughter Jeanne would go off with the soldiers; and that her mother and father took great care to keep her safely; that they were very strict with her; and that she was always obedient to them save in the incident at Toul, the action for marriage.[64]

She said further that she had heard her mother say that her father had said to her brothers; If I thought that such a thing could happen as I have dreamed, I should want you to drown her; and if you did not, I would drown her myself. And that she greatly feared that they would lose their minds when she left to go to Vaucouleurs.

Asked if his thoughts and dreams had come to her father after she had her visions,

She replied: Yes, more than two years after she first heard the voices.

Questioned as to whether it was at the request of Robert [de Baudricourt] that she took man's dress,

She replied that she had done so of her own wish, and not at the request of anyone in the world.

---

[64] Joan had been sued for breach of promise to marry.

Asked if the voice had told her to take man's dress,

She said: Everything good that I have done, I did by command of the voices.

And she said moreover that concerning this dress she would answer later on; at present she could not do so; but would answer tomorrow.

Questioned whether in taking male dress she thought that she had done wrong,

She answered no; and that even at this moment if she were with her own people and wearing this male dress, it seemed to her it would be for the great good of France to do as she used to do before she was taken prisoner.

Asked how she would have delivered the Duke of Orleans,[65]

She said that she would have taken enough English prisoners to ransom him; and if she had not taken enough for that, she would have crossed the sea and brought him from England by force.

Asked whether Saint Margaret and Saint Catherine had told her, absolutely and without condition, that she would take enough prisoners to ransom the Duke of Orleans who was in England, or that she would cross the sea to bring him from England by force, bringing him back within three years,

She answered yes. And she told her king to allow her to take prisoners.

She said also that if she had lasted three years without hindrance she would have delivered him.

She said moreover that it would have been a shorter time than three years, and longer than one; but she does not at the moment know [exactly how long.]

FOURTEENTH SESSION

On Thursday the XVth day of March in the year MCCCCXXX,

Jeanne was questioned on the aforesaid sworn testimony,

And firstly, as to what she had said concerning the manner in which she believed she could escape from the castle of Beaulieu, between two planks,

She answered that she was never a prisoner anywhere but she would escape gladly. And when she was in that castle she would have shut up her gaolers in the tower, had it not been that the porter saw her and caught her.

She said also that it seemed to her that it was not God's will that she should escape that time, and that she must see the King of the English, as her voices had told her, and as it is written above.

Asked whether she had leave from God or from her voices to escape from prison whenever she pleased,

She replied: I have often asked for it, but so far have not had it.

---

[65] The Duke was a prisoner in the Tower of London, awaiting ransom.

Asked whether she would go at once if she saw her opportunity,

She said that if she saw the door open she would go, for this would be Our Lord's permission. And she believes firmly that if she saw the door open and her guards and the rest of the English were unable to resist, she would understand that she had permission, and that Our lord would send her help. But without leave she would not go; unless she made an attempt so that she might know whether Our Lord would be pleased. And she quoted: Help yourself and God will help you. And she said this so that, if she escaped, no-one could say that she had gone without leave.

Questioned as to whether, since she asks to hear Mass, she does not think it more proper that she should wear a woman's dress. And therefore she was asked, which she would rather do: wear a woman's dress and hear Mass, or continue in her man's clothing and not hear Mass,

She answered: Promise me that I may hear Mass if I wear a woman's dress, and then I will answer you.

To which her questioner said: I promise you that you will hear Mass if you put on woman's dress.

She replied: And what do you say, if I have sworn and promised our King not to put off these clothes? Nevertheless I say, Make me a long dress, right down to the ground, without a train, and give it to me to go to Mass, and then when I come back I will put on the clothes I now have.

Asked if she would wear woman's dress at all to go and hear Mass,

She said: I will think this over, and then answer you. She further asked, for the honour of God and Our Lady, that she might hear Mass in this good town.

They then told her that she must take a woman's dress, unconditionally and absolutely,

And she replied: Bring me a dress like that of a citizen's daughter; that is a long houppelande, and I will wear it, and also a woman's hood, to go and hear Mass.

But she also begged, with the greatest urgency, that they should leave her the clothes she was wearing, and let her go and hear Mass without changing them.

Asked if she is willing to submit and refer all she has said and done to the judgment of the Church,

She replied: All my deeds are in God's hand, and I commit myself to Him. And I assure you that I would neither do nor say anything contrary to the Christian Faith; and if I had done or said anything, or there were anything in me that the churchmen could say was contrary to the Christian Faith established by Our Lord, I should not wish to uphold it, but would cast it from me.

Questioned as to whether she would submit to the ordinance of the Church,

She answered: I will not answer you anything further now; but on Saturday send me a clerk, if you do not wish to come yourself, and with God's help I will answer him, and it shall be set down in writing.

Asked if, when the voices come, she does them reverence absolutely, as to a saint,

She said yes. And if at any time she has not done so, she has afterwards begged their pardon. And she could not show them as great reverence as properly belongs to them. For she firmly believes that they are Saint Catherine and Saint Margaret.

And she said the same concerning Saint Michael.

Questioned as to whether, since candles were frequently offered to the saints in heaven, she has ever made oblation of lighted candles or such other things to the saints who visit her, either in church or elsewhere; or whether she has ever had Masses said,

She answered no, save in offering once a Mass, in the priest's hand, in honour of Saint Catherine; for she firmly believes her to be one of those who appeared to her; nor has she lit as many as she would have wished to Saint Catherine and Saint Margaret in Paradise, firmly believing as she does that it is they who come to her.

Questioned whether, when she puts candles before the statue of Saint Catherine, she believes that she is putting them in honour of her who appeared to her,

She replied: I do so in honour of God, Our Lady, and Saint Catherine who is in heaven. And I see no difference between Saint Catherine in heaven and her who appears to me.

Asked if she puts them in honour of her who appeared to her

She replied: Yes. For she sees no difference between her who appears to her and her who is in heaven.

Asked if she always did and accomplished what her voices commanded her,

She said that she obeyed the commands of Our Lord with all her power, which He told her by her voices, as far as she could understand, and they never command her to do anything save by Our Lord's good pleasure.

Asked whether in war she had ever done anything without the permission of her voices,

She answered: You have been answered. Read your book[66] carefully, and you will find it.

Translated W. S. Scott. London: The Folio Society, 1956

Unit 27: The Black Death

The Black Death, which killed somewhere between a quarter and half the population of Europe in 1347-48, inspired terror and fascination. It spawned a new genre of literature, the *Art of Dying*. Poets and novelists expressed the fear and awe felt by all. The devastation wrought by this plague is reported in chronicles, diaries, and letters. Scientists offered explanations and suggestions for warding it off. Religious leaders offered prayers and sermons.

from the Chronicle of Henry Knighton

Henry Knighton was an eyewitness to the devastation of the Black Death, though he was only a boy at the time.

---

[66] That is, the minutes of the previous sessions.

In this (1348) and the following year there was a general death of people throughout the world. It began first in India, then it passed to Tharsis, thence to the Saracens, Christians and Jews in the course of one year, from one Easter to the next . . .

In one day there died 812 people in Avignon according to the reckoning made to the pope. . . . 358 Dominicans died in Provence in Lent; in Montpellier only seven friars were left from 149. . . . At Marseilles only one Franciscan remained of 150. . . .

Then the grievous plague came to the seacoasts from Southampton, and came to Bristol, and it was there as if all the strength of the town had died, as if they had been hit with sudden death, for there were few who stayed in their beds more than three days, or two days or even one half a day. Then the death broke out everywhere the sun goes. And more than 380 died at Leicester in the small parish of St. Leonard. More than 400 died in the parish of the Holy Cross; 700 died in the parish of St. Margaret of Leicester. And so it was in greater number in each parish. Then the bishop of Lincoln sent throughout his diocese and gave general power to each and every priest, regular as well as secular, to hear confessions and absolve with full and complete episcopal authority, except only in the instance of debt. In which case, if he was able by himself while he lived he should pay it, or others surely would do this for him from his possessions after his death. Likewise the pope granted full remission of all sins to whoever was absolved while in peril of death,[67] and he granted this power to last from Easter to the next following. And everyone could select his confessor as it pleased him. In this year there was a great pestilence among the sheep everywhere in the kingdom; so that in one place more than 500 sheep died in one pasture, and they became so putrid that neither beasts nor birds would touch them. And because of the fear of death there were low prices for everything. . . For a man could have one horse which before was worth 40s for one half a mark. . . And sheep and cattle wandered through fields and among crops and there was no one who was concerned to drive and collect them, but an unknown number died in ditches and hedges throughout every region for lack of herders. For there was such a lack of servants and helpers that there was not one who knew what he ought to do. . .

The workers, nevertheless, were so elated and contrary that they did not heed the mandate of the king (prohibiting higher wages) but if anyone wanted to hire them, he had to give them as they desired; either lose their crops and fruit or grant the selfish and lofty wishes of the workers. .

.

After the aforesaid pestilence, many large and small buildings in all the cities, boroughs and villages collapsed and were leveled with the earth for lack of inhabitants; likewise many villages and hamlets were deserted. No house was left in them for everyone who had lived in them had died, and it was probable that many such villages were never to be inhabited again. . .

from the Rolls Series, ed. J. R. Lumby. 1895.

The three selections following are examples of the kinds of explanations offered to account for the devastating illness. Academics sought a scientific explanation. Many clerics thought it a punishment sent by God. Others blamed a human conspiracy, usually directed against the Jews.

---

[67] The fifteenth-century church taught that sins committed after baptism were forgiven after the sinner completed a threefold path: contrition of the heart, confession with the mouth, and satisfaction by good deeds or self-denial. If the sinner died before completing the penance imposed, a period of suffering in purgatory would be needed to atone for the sins. Since those who contracted the Black Death only lived three to eight days, there was no time for penance. This decree of the Pope thus freed them from the threatened pains of purgatory.

Report of the Paris Medical Faculty, 1348

We say that the distant and first cause of this pestilence was and is the configuration of the heavens. In 1345, at one hour after noon on 20 March, there was a major conjunction of three planets in Aquarius. This conjunction, along with other earlier conjunctions and eclipses, by causing a deadly corruption of the air around us, signifies mortality and famine—and also other things about which we will not speak here because they are not relevant. Aristotle testifies that this is the case in his book *Concerning the causes of the properties of the elements*, in which he says that mortality of races and the depopulation of kingdoms occur as the conjunction of Saturn and Jupiter, for great events then arise, their nature depending on the *trigon* in which the conjunction occurs. And this is found in ancient philosophers, and Albertus Magnus in his book, *Concerning the causes of the properties of the elements* (treatise 2, chapter 1) says that the conjunction of Mars and Jupiter causes a great pestilence in the air, especially when they come together in a hot, wet sign, as was the case in 1345. For Jupiter, being wet and hot, draws up evil vapours from the earth and Mars, because it is immoderately hot and dry, then ignites the vapours, and as a result there were lightnings, sparks, noxious vapours and fires throughout the air. . . .

Although major pestilential illnesses can be caused by the corruption of water or food, as happens at times of famine and infertility, yet we still regard illnesses proceeding from the corruption of the air as much more dangerous. This is because bad air is more noxious than food or drink in that it can penetrate quickly to the heart and lungs to do its damage. We believe that the present epidemic or plague has arisen from air corrupt in its substance, and not changed in its attributes. By which we wish it be understood that air, being pure and clear by nature, can only become putrid or corrupt by being mixed with something else, that is to say, with evil vapours. What happened was that the many vapours which had been corrupted at the time of the conjunction were drawn up from the earth and water, and were then mixed with the air and spread abroad by frequent gusts of wind in the wild southerly gales, and because of these alien vapours which they carried the winds corrupted the air in its substance, and are still doing so. And this corrupted air, when breathed in necessarily penetrates to the heart and corrupts the substance of the spirit there and rots the surrounding moisture, and the heat thus caused destroys the life force, and this is the immediate cause of the present epidemic.

And moreover these winds, which have become so common here, have carried among us (and may perhaps continue to do so in future) bad, rotten and poisonous vapours from elsewhere: from swamps, lakes and chasms, for instance, and also (which is even more dangerous) from the epidemic. Another possible cause of corruption, which needs to be borne in mind, is the escape of the rottenness trapped in the centre of the earth as a result of earthquakes—something which has indeed recently occurred. But the conjunctions could have been the universal and distant cause of all these harmful things, by which air and water have been corrupted. . . .

No wonder, therefore, that we fear that we are in for an epidemic. But it should be noted that in saying this we do not intend to exclude the possibility of illnesses arising from the character of the present year—for as the aphorism of Hippocrates has it: a year of many fogs and damps is a year of many illnesses. On the other hand, the susceptibility of the body of the patient is the most immediate cause in the breeding of illnesses, and therefore no cause is likely to have an effect unless the patient is susceptible to its effects. We must therefore emphasise that although, because everyone has to breathe, everyone will be at risk from the corrupted air, not everyone will be made ill by it but only those, who will no doubt be numerous, who have a susceptibility to it; and very few indeed of those who do succumb will escape.

The bodies most likely to take the stamp of this pestilence are those which are hot and moist, for they are the most susceptible to putrefaction. The following are also more at risk: bodies bunged up with evil humours, because the unconsumed waste matter is not being expelled as it should; those following a bad life style, with too much exercise, sex and bathing; the thin and weak, and persistent worriers; babies, women and young people; and corpulent people with a ruddy complexion. . . .

Translated by Rosemary Horrox, in *The Black Death*. Manchester University Press, 1994.

The Sins of the Times

See how England mourns, drenched in tears. The people, stained by sin, quake with grief. Plague is killing men and beasts Why? Because vices rule unchallenged here.

Alas! The whole world is now given over to spite. Where can a kind heart be found among the people? No one thinks on the crucified Christ, and therefore the people perish as a token of vengeance.

Peace and patience are thoroughly plundered; love and justice are not at home. Men cuddle up to errors and vices; children die for the sins of their father.

The sloth of the shepherds leaves the flocks straying. The trusting are tricked by the cunning of traders; fraud and avarice go hand in hand like sisters; the poor suffer through the depravity of the rich. . . .

The priests of God are unchaste; their deeds not matching their name. They should be teaching and administering the sacraments, but they behave in ways inappropriate to their order. . . .

Alas! Love and charity have grown cold in kingdoms. It is spite and harshness which blaze up in the people. Truth and faith are lukewarm in laymen and clerics alike. Nobility and renown are asleep in this realm.

Women are no longer bound by the restraints of their sex; the subtlety of merchants shifts into fraud; the guild of brothers turns the world topsy turvy. Man, if truth now reigns in you, rejoice.

from *Political Poems and Songs* I, edited by Thomas Wright. Rolls Series, 1839.

From the Chronicle of Herman Gigas, 1349

In 1347 there was such a great pestilence and mortality throughout almost the whole world that in the opinion of well-informed men scarcely a tenth of mankind survived. The victims did not linger long, but died on the second or third day. The plague raged so fiercely that many cities and towns were entirely emptied of people. In the cities of Bologna, Venice, Montpellier, Avignon, Marseilles and Toulouse alike, a thousand people died in one day, and it still rages in France, Normandy, England and Ireland. Some say that it was brought about by the corruption of the air; others that the Jews planned to wipe out all the Christians with poison and had poisoned wells and springs everywhere. And many Jews confessed as much under torture: that they had bred spiders and toads in pots and pans, and had obtained poison from overseas; and that not every Jew knew about this wickedness, only the more powerful ones, so that it would not be betrayed. As evidence of this heinous crime, men say that bags full of poison were found in many wells and springs, and as a result, in cities, towns and villages throughout Germany, and in fields and woods too, almost all the wells and springs have been blocked up or built over, so that no one can drink from them or use the water for cooking, and men have to use rain or river water instead. God, the lord of vengeance, has not suffered the malice of the Jews to go unpunished. Throughout Germany, in all but a few places, they were burnt. For fear of that punishment many accepted baptism and their lives were spared. This action was taken against the Jews in 1349, and it still continues unabated, for in a number of regions many people, noble and humble alike, have laid plans against them and their defenders which they will never abandon until the whole Jewish race has been destroyed.

Translated by Rosemary Horrox, in *The Black Death*. Manchester University Press. 1994.

Statute of Laborers, 1349

> The rapid decrease in population that resulted from the Black Death created a labor shortage. Many governments passed laws intended to keep wages and prices down. Some of these laws attempted to control wages and prices. Others shortened apprenticeship periods and lifted restrictions on the number of apprentices and journeymen a master might keep. Preachers exhorted people not to give alms to able-bodied beggars.

The King to the sheriff of Kent, greeting: Because a great part of the people, and especially of workmen and servants, have lately died in the pestilence, many seeing the necessity of masters and great scarcity of servants, will not serve unless they may receive excessive wages, and others preferring to beg in idleness rather than by labor to get their living; we, considering the grievous incommodities which of the lack especially of ploughmen and such laborers may hereafter come, have upon deliberation and treaty with the prelates and the nobles and learned men assisting us, with their unanimous counsil ordained:

That every man and woman of our realm of England, of whatever condition he may be, free or bond, able in body and within the age of sixty years, not living in merchandise, nor exercising any craft, nor having of his own whereof he may live, nor land of his own about whose tillage he may occupy himself, and not serving any other, if he be required to serve in suitable service, his estate considered, he shall be required to serve him who so shall require him; and take only the wages, livery, meed or salary which were accustomed to be given in the places where he oweth to serve, the twentieth year of our reign of England, or five or six other common years immediately before. Provided always, that the lords be preferred before others in their bondmen or their land tenants to be retained in their service; so that, nevertheless, the said lords shall retain no more than necessary for them. And if any such man or woman, being so required to serve, will not do this, and this being proved by two true men before the sheriff (or the bailiffs of our sovereign lord, the king, or the constables) of the town where this shall happen to be done, he shall anon be taken by them, or any of them, and committed to the next jail, there to remain under straight keeping till he find surety to serve in the form aforesaid.

If any reaper, mower, or other workman or servant, of whatever estate or condition that he be, retained in any man's service, do depart from the said service without reasonable cause or license before the term agreed, he shall have the penalty of imprisonment. And no one, under the same penalty, shall presume to receive or retain any such person in his service.

If the lords of the towns or manors presume in any point to come against this present ordinance, either themselves or their servants, then suit shall be made against them in the counties, wapentakes, tithings or such other courts for a penalty of thrice the sum paid or promised by them or their servants. And if any, before this present ordinance hath covenanted with anyone so to serve for more wages, he shall not be bound, by reason of the same covenant, to pay more than at another time was wont to be paid to such person; nor, under the same penalty, shall he presume to pay any more.

Saddlers, skinners, white-tawers, cordwainers, tailors, smiths, carpenters, masons, tilers, shipwrights, carters and all other artisans and workmen shall not take for their labor and workmanship above the same that was wont to be paid to such persons in the said twentieth year, and other common years immediately before, as before is said, in the place where they shall happen to work; and if any man take more, he shall be committed to the nearest jail in the manner as before is said.

Butchers, fishmongers, hostlers, brewers, bakers, poulters and all other sellers of all manner of victual shall be bound to sell the same victual for a reasonable price, having respect to the price that such victual be sold at in the adjoining places, so that the same sellers have moderate gains, and not excessive, reasonably to be required according to the distance of the place from whence the said victual be carried. . . .

Because many strong beggars as long as they may live by begging, do refuse to labor, giving themselves to idleness and vice, and sometime to theft and other abominations; none, under the said penalty of imprisonment shall under the color of pity or alms give anything to such who may possibly labor, or presume to favor them in their sloth, so that thereby they may be compelled to labor for their necessary living.

adapted from *Translations and Reprints from the Original Sources of European History.* Vol. 1. University of Pennsylvania Press, 1897.

Unit 28: The Great Schism

Shortly after Boniface VIII suffered humiliation at the hands of Philip IV of France[68], a Pope friendly to the French monarchy, Clement V, had himself crowned in Lyons and settled with his court in Avignon, where the papacy would remain for two generations. The Pope's primary claim to headship of the Church lay in his position as Bishop of Rome and thus successor to Saint Peter. To some Christians, a Pope not in residence in Rome was a scandal. While in Avignon, the papacy also underwent significant changes in finance and administration, mirroring the increasing centralization of secular states. The wealth and magnificence of the Avignonese court also drew criticism and demands that the court return to Rome.

In 1377, Pope Gregory XI did return the court to Rome. When he died a few months later, an Italian, Urban VI, was chosen as his successor in a hasty election. The French cardinals quickly withdrew from Rome and declared Urban's election invalid,

---

[68] See Chapter 9.

claiming that they had voted for him under duress. They elected Clement VII, who returned with the French contingent to Avignon. Now there were two popes.

A council was convened in Pisa in 1409 to resolve the situation and reunite the Church. The council deposed both the Roman and the Avignonese claimants and elected a new pope, Alexander V. Neither the Roman nor the Avignonese pontiff would step down. Now there were three.

The Council of Constance, convened in 1414, deposed the three popes and elected a new one. Because of the crisis and scandal inherent in the situation, the secular governments tended to support the decisions of this council, and the situation was resolved, but it was another decade before competing claims were laid to rest. Several decrees of the Council of Constance deal with the issue of a council's authority over the Pope.

Petrarch: The Babylonian Captivity of the Church

Petrarch likened the papal sojourn in Avignon to the captivity of the ancient Hebrew people by the Babylonians. In this essay, he compares the luxurious life of the Avignonese court to the poverty of Jesus' disciples.

I am now living in France, in the Babylon of the West. The sun, in its travels, sees nothing more hideous than this place on the shores of the wild Rhone, which suggests the hellish streams of Cocytus and Acheron. Here reign the successors of the poor fishermen of Galilee; they have strangely forgotten their origin. I am astounded, as I recall their predecessors, to see these men loaded with gold and clad in purple, boasting of the spoils of princes and nations; to see luxurious palaces and heights crowned with fortifications, instead of a boat turned downwards for shelter. We no longer find the simple nets which were once used to gain a frugal sustenance from the Lake of Galilee, with which, having labored all night and caught nothing, they took, at daybreak, a multitude of fishes, in the name of Jesus. One is stupefied nowadays to hear the lying tongues, and to see worthless parchments, turned by a leaden seal, into nets which are used, in Christ's name, but by the arts of Belial, to catch hordes of unwary Christians. These fish, too, are dressed and laid on the burning coals of anxiety before they fill the insatiable maw of their captors. Instead of holy solitude we find a criminal host and crowds of the most infamous satellites; instead of soberness, licentious banquets; instead of pious pilgrimages, preternatural and foul sloth; instead of the bare feet of the apostles, the snowy coursers of brigands fly past us, the horses decked in gold and fed on gold, soon to be shod with gold, if the Lord does not check this slavish luxury. In short, we seem to be among the kings of the Persians or Parthians, before whom we must fall down and worship, and who can not be approached except presents be offered. O, ye unkempt and emaciated old men, is it for this you labored? Is it for this that you have sown the field of the Lord and watered it with your holy blood? Let us leave the subject.

From *Translations and Reprints from the Original Sources of European History.*University of Pennsylvania Press, 1902.

Marsilius of Padua: *Defensor Pacis*, 1324

Drawing on the Politics of Aristotle, Marsilius constructed a political theory that locates political authority in the state, which is made up of the body of citizens. The prince, he says, rules by the consent of the citizens. The church is an establishment of the state and subject to its control. In the disputes between the Pope and secular rulers and between the Pope and a general council of the Church, Marsilius sides firmly with the anti-papal parties. The essay ends with a series of Conclusions. Five of the Conclusions were declared heretical by Pope John XXII in 1327.

Conclusion 1. The one divine canonical Scripture, the conclusions that necessarily follow from it, and the interpretation placed upon it by the common consent of Christians, are true, and belief in them is necessary to the salvation of those to whom they are made known.

2. The general council of Christians or its majority alone has the authority to define doubtful passages of the divine law, and to determine those that are to be regarded as articles of the Christian faith, belief in which is essential to salvation; and no partial council or single person of any position has the authority to decide these questions.

5. No mortal has the right to dispense with the commands or prohibitions of the new divine law; but the general council and the Christian "legislator" alone have the right to prohibit things which are permitted by the new law, under penalties in this world or the next, and no partial council or single person of any position has that right.

6. The whole body of citizens or its majority alone is the human "legislator."

7. Decretals and decrees of the bishop of Rome, or of any other bishops or body of bishops, have no power to coerce anyone by secular penalties or punishments, except by the authorization of the human "legislator."

8. The "legislator" alone or the one who rules by its authority has the power to dispense with human laws.

9. The elective principality or other office derives its authority from the election of the body having the right to elect, and not from the confirmation or approval of any other power.[69]

10. The election of any prince or other official, especially one who has the coercive power, is determined solely by the expressed will of the "legislator."

11. There can be only one supreme ruling power in a state or kingdom.

12. The number and the qualifications of persons who hold state offices and all civil matters are to be determined solely by the Christian ruler according to the law or approved custom [of the state.]

13. No prince, still more, no partial council or single person of any position, has full authority and control over other persons, laymen or clergy, without the authorization of the "legislator."

14. No bishop or priest has coercive authority or jurisdiction over any layman or clergyman, even if he is a heretic.

15. The prince who rules by the authority of the "legislator" has jurisdiction over the persons and possessions of every single mortal of every station, whether lay or clerical, and over every body of laymen or clergy.

---

[69] Since the eighth century, anointing of a new ruler by the Pope or another bishop had been an important part of the coronation ritual. It symbolized the belief that God recognized this claimant to the throne as the legitimate ruler. For some churchmen, it symbolized more: that the new ruler's authority came from God through the Church. Thus the Church had a claim to some sort of authority over the ruler.

16. No bishop or priest or body of bishops or priests has authority to excommunicate anyone or to interdict the performance of divine services, without the authorization of the "legislator."[70]

17. All bishops derive their authority in equal measure immediately from Christ, and it cannot be proved from the divine law that one bishop should be over or under another, in temporal or spiritual matters.[71]

18. The other bishops, singly or in a body, have the same right by divine authority to excommunicate or otherwise exercise authority over the bishop of Rome, having obtained the consent of the "legislator," as the bishop of Rome has to excommunicate or control them.

21. The "legislator" alone has the right to promote to ecclesiastical orders, and to judge of the qualifications of persons for these offices, by a coercive decision, and no priest or bishop has the right to promote anyone without its authority.

22. The prince who rules by the authority of the laws of Christians, has the right to determine the number of churches and temples, and the number of priests, deacons, and other clergy who shall serve in them.

23. "Separable" ecclesiastical offices may be conferred or taken away only by the authority of the "legislator"; the same is true of ecclesiastical benefices and other property devoted to pious purposes.[72]

27. The human "legislator" has the right to use ecclesiastical temporalities for the common public good and defence, after the needs of the priests and clergy, the expenses of divine worship, and the necessities of the poor have been satisfied.

28. All properties established for pious purposes or for works of mercy, such as those that are left by will for the making of a crusade, the redeeming of captives, or the support of the poor, and similar purposes, may be disposed of by the prince alone according to the decision of the "legislator" and the purpose of the testator or giver.

29. The Christian "legislator" alone has the right to forbid or permit the establishment of religious orders or houses.

30. The prince alone, acting in accordance with the laws of the "legislator," has the authority to condemn heretics, delinquents, and all others who should endure temporal punishment, to inflict bodily punishment upon them, and to exact fines from them.

32. The general council of all Christians alone has the authority to create a metropolitan bishop or church, and to reduce him or it from that position.

---

[70] See Chapter 9, Unit 21, for an example of the use of the interdict.

[71] By this statement, and those following, Marsilius would deny the Pope much of the authority the position had acquired over the centuries.

[72] Marsilius defines "separable" as those functions of the clergy that are not essentially spiritual in character. "Inseparable powers", he said, "are the power to bless the bread and wine, and turn them into the blessed body and blood of Christ, to administer the other sacraments of the church, and to bind and to loose men from their sins." Separable functions were the control of one priest over others and the administration of temporal possessions of the church. In this and the following statement, Marsilius would deny to ecclesiastical officials the right to amass wealth while exercising their "separable" functions.

33. The Christian "legislator" or the one who rules by its authority over Christian states, alone has the right to convoke either a general or local council of priests, bishops, and other Christians, by coercive power; and no man may be compelled by threats of temporal or spiritual punishment to obey the decrees of a council convoked in any other way.

39. The people as a community and as individuals, according to their several means, are required by divine law to support the bishops and other clergy authorized by the gospel, so that they may have food and clothing and the other necessaries of life; but the people are not required to pay tithes or other taxes beyond the amount necessary for such support.

41. The bishop of Rome and any other ecclesiastical or spiritual minister may be advanced to a "separable" ecclesiastical office only by the Christian "legislator" or the one who rules by its authority, or by the general council of Christians; and they may be suspended from or deprived of office by the same authority.

From *A Source Book for Medieval History*, edited by Oliver J. Thatcher and Edgar H. McNeal. New York: Charles Scribner's Sons, 1907.

Manifesto of the Revolting Cardinals, 1378

After the election of Urban VI in Rome, the French cardinals withdrew to Fondi, in the kingdom of Naples, deposed Urban, and elected a new pope, Clement VII. Urban was so disliked that the Italian cardinals assented to the election of Clement VII. Urban selected a new College of Cardinals supportive of him. Clement and his court returned to Avignon.

. . . After the apostolic seat was made vacant by the death of our lord, pope Gregory XI, who died in March, we assembled in conclave for the election of a pope, as is the law and custom, in the papal palace, in which Gregory had died. . . . Officials of the city with a great multitude of the people, for the most part armed and called together for this purpose by the ringing of bells, surrounded the palace in a threatening manner and even entered it and almost filled it. To the terror caused by their presence they added threats that unless we should at once elect a Roman or an Italian they would kill us. They gave us no time to deliberate but compelled us unwillingly, through violence and fear, to elect an Italian without delay. In order to escape the danger which threatened us from such a mob, we elected Bartholomew, archbishop of Bari, thinking that he would have enough conscience not to accept the election, since every one knew that it was made under such wicked threats. But he was unmindful of his own salvation and burning with ambition, and so, to the great scandal of the clergy and of the Christian people, and contrary to the laws of the church, he accepted this election which was offered him, although not all the cardinals were present at the election, and it was extorted from us by the threats and demands of the officials and people of the city. And although such an election is null and void, and the danger from the people still threatened us, he was enthroned and crowned, and called himself pope and apostolic. But according to the holy fathers and to the law of the church, he should be called apostate, anathema, Antichrist, and the mocker and destroyer of Christianity. . .

From *A Source Book for Medieval History,* edited by Oliver J. Thatcher and Edgar H. McNeal. New York: Charles Scribner's Sons, 1907.

Council of Constance: "Sacrosancta", 1415

In this decree, the Council declares its authority over all the Church, including the Pope.

In the name of the Holy and indivisible Trinity; of the Father, Son, and Holy Ghost. Amen.

This holy synod of Constance, forming a general council for the extirpation of the present schism and the union and reformation, in head and members, of the Church of God, legitimately assembled in the Holy Ghost, to the praise of Omnipotent God, in order that it may the more easily, safely, effectively and freely bring about the union and reformation of the church of God, hereby determines, decrees, ordains and declares what follows:—

It first declares that this same council, legitimately assembled in the Holy Ghost, forming a general council and representing the Catholic Church militant, has its power immediately from Christ, and every one, whatever his state or position, even if it be the Papal dignity itself, is bound to obey it in all those things which pertain to the faith and the healing of the said schism, and to the general reformation of the Church of God, in head and members.

It further declares that any one, whatever his condition, station or rank, even if it be the Papal, who shall contumaciously refuse to obey the mandates, decrees, ordinances or instructions which have been, or shall be issued by this holy council, or by any other general council, legitimately summoned, which concern, or in any way relate to the above mentioned objects, shall, unless he repudiate his conduct, be subject to condign penance and be suitably punished, having recourse, if necessary, to the other resources of the law. . .

From *Translations and Reprints from the Original Sources of European History* University of Pennsylvania Press, 1902.

Council of Constance: "Frequens," 1417

To ensure that its reforms would not be brushed aside, the Council formulated a plan by which a general council of the Church would be convened at regular intervals.

A good way to till the field of the Lord is to hold general councils frequently, because by them the briers, thorns, and thistles of heresies, errors, and schisms are rooted out, abuses reformed, and the way of the Lord made more fruitful. But if general councils are not held, all these evils spread and flourish. We therefore decree by this perpetual edict that general councils shall be held as follows: The first one shall be held five years after the close of this council, the second one seven years after the close of the first, and forever thereafter one shall be held every ten years. One month before the close of each council the pope, with the approval and consent of the council, shall fix the place for holding the next council. If the pope fails to name the place, the council must do so.

From *A Source Book for Medieval History*, edited by Oliver J. Thatcher and Edgar H. McNeal. New York: Charles Scribner's Sons, 1907.

CHAPTER 13: THE RENAISSANCE

Unit 29: Humanism

Humanism is the name given to that face of the Renaissance that concerned itself with education, textual criticism, the dignity of man, and an acceptance and legitimation of vernacular languages. Because humanism was primarily a literary phenomenon, an abundance of written sources are available. I make no claim that the following selections are the best, or the most representative, as such a choice would be impossible. I claim only that each of them highlights a significant aspect of humanism.

Petrarch: Letter to Posterity

In this essay, Petrarch reveals a self-awareness and sense of his own place in history that is typical of the Renaissance man.

Greeting. It is possible that some word of me may have come to you, though even this is doubtful, since an insignificant and obscure name will scarcely penetrate far in either time or space. If, however, you should have heard of me, you may desire to know what manner of man I was, or what was the outcome of my labors, especially those of which some description or, at any rate, the bare titles may have reached you.

To begin with myself, the utterances of men concerning me will differ widely, since in passing judgment almost everyone is influenced not so much by truth as by preference, and good and evil report alike know no bounds. I was, in truth, a poor mortal like yourself, neither very exalted in my origin nor, on the other hand, of the most humble birth, but belonging, as Augustus Caesar says of himself, to an ancient family. As to my disposition, I was not naturally perverse or wanting in modesty, however the contagion of evil associations may have corrupted me. My youth was gone before I realized it; I was carried away by the strength of manhood; but a riper age brought me to my senses and taught me by experiences the truth I had long before read in books, that youth and pleasure are vanity—nay, that the Author of all ages and times permits us miserable mortals, puffed up with emptiness, thus to wander about, until finally, coming to a tardy consciousness of our sins, we shall learn to know ourselves. In my prime I was blessed with a quick and active body, although not exceptionally strong; and while I do not lay claim to remarkable personal beauty, I was comely enough in my best days. I was possessed of a clear complexion, between light and dark, lively eyes, and for long years a deep vision, which however deserted me, contrary to my hopes, and forced me, to my great annoyance, to resort to glasses. Although I had previously enjoyed perfect health, old age brought with it the usual array of discomforts. . . .

I possessed a well-balanced rather than a keen intellect, one prone to all kinds of good and wholesome study, but especially inclined to moral philosophy and the art of poetry. The latter, indeed, I neglected as time went on, and took delight in sacred literature. Finding in that a hidden sweetness which I had once esteemed but lightly, I came to regard the works of the poets as only amenities. Among the many subjects which interested me, I dwelt especially upon antiquity, for our own age has always repelled me, so that had it not been for the love of those dear to me, I should have preferred to have been born in any other period than our own. In order to forget my own time, I have constantly striven to place myself in spirit in other ages, and consequently I delight in history; not that the conflicting statements did not offend me, but when in doubt I accepted what appeared to me most probably, or yielded to the authority of the writer.

My style, as many claimed, was clear and forcible; but to me it seemed weak and obscure. In ordinary conversation with friends, or with those about me, I never gave any thought to my language, and I have always wondered that Augustus Caesar should have taken such pains in this respect. When, however, the subject itself, or the place or listener seemed to demand it, I gave some attention to style, with what success I cannot pretend to say; let them judge in whose presence I spoke. If only I have lived well, it matters little to me how I talked. Mere elegance of language can produce at best but an empty renown.

translated by James Harvey Robinson in *Petrarch: The First Modern Scholar and Man of Letters*. New York: Putnam's, 1907.

Lorenzo Valla: On the Forgery of the Alleged Donation of Constantine, 1440

The Donation of Constantine had been used since the late eighth century as a basis for papal claims of sovereignty over much of central Italy, a territory known as the Papal States.[73] Valla, a humanist scholar, philosopher, and court secretary, used the techniques of textual criticism developed by the humanists to prove that the Donation was a forgery. Valla wrote this essay while he was secretary to King Alfonso of Aragon, who ruled Naples at the time. This position may explain the polemical tone of the piece.

II, 5. I understand that the ears of men have been waiting for a long time to hear with what crime I am about to charge the Roman Pontiffs. Surely it is a most serious crime, of either lackadaisical ignorance or enormous greed, which is a form of idolatry, or the vain will to power, which is always accompanied by cruelty. In fact, for several centuries now either the Popes have not understood that the donation of Constantine is a forgery and a fabrication, or they have invented it themselves, or else, as followers treading in the footsteps of their predecessors' deceit, they have defended it as being true, even while knowing it was false. Thus they have disgraced the dignity of the Pontificate and the memory of the early Popes, dishonored the Christian religion and caused general confusion with their massacres, destruction, and shameful actions. They say that theirs are the city of Rome, the Kingdom of Sicily and Naples, the whole of Italy, Gaul, Spain, the lands of the Germans and Britons, and finally, all of the West. And all these things, purportedly, are contained in the document describing the donation. Are these lands then all yours, oh Supreme Pontiff? Do you intend to recover all of them? Do you plan to strip all the kings and princes in the West of their cities or compel them to pay annual taxes to you? On the contrary, I deem it to be more just if the rulers are allowed to deprive you of all the dominion you hold, since, as I shall demonstrate, that donation, from which the Popes claim their rights derive, was unknown either to Pope Sylvester or to the Emperor Constantine.

6. However, before I come to the confutation of the text of the donation, the only defence they have, and one that is foolish as well as false, I must go back to an earlier period for the sake

---

[73] See Chapter 8.

of order. And, first of all, I maintain that neither Constantine nor Sylvester was able to carry out the transaction; the former had no motive to make the donation, had no right to make it, and no power to hand over his possessions to someone else; while the latter had no motive to accept the gift and had no right to do so. Secondly, even if this were not absolutely true and evident, as it is, the pope did not receive nor did the Emperor transmit possession of what is supposed to have been donated. It always remained in the power and dominion of the Caesars. Thirdly, Constantine gave nothing to Sylvester, but rather to the previous Pope, even before he received Baptism, and those gifts were modest ones on which the Pope could barely subsist. Fourthly, it is incorrect to say that the deed of the donation is to be found in the *Decretum*[74] or that it was taken from the *Life of Sylvester* since it is not included either in this or in any other historical work. Moreover, it contains certain elements that are contradictory, impossible, foolish, strange, and ridiculous . . . I shall add, in supernumerary argument, that even if at one time Sylvester had held title, yet, because either he himself or some successive pope was dispossessed, it can not, after such a long interval of time, be reclaimed either according to divine law or to human law. Finally, the Pope's possessions could not have been won through prescription, no matter how long he held them.

IX, 31. Since you can not prove your theory, I shall demonstrate, on the contrary, that Constantine ruled over the Empire until the last day of his life, as did all the other Caesars who followed him. Thus I shall silence you, who tell me it is a very difficult and laborious task to demonstrate this. Let all the Latin and Greek histories be consulted, let all the other authors who mention that period be cited; you will find discrepancies in none regarding this matter. Of the thousand testimonies available, one will suffice: Eutropius saw Constantine and wrote that, when he died, his three sons were made rulers over the whole world . . . . This historian would not have kept silent about the donation of the Western Empire had it taken place . . . .

32. At this point I wish to summon all of you recent Roman Pontiffs although you are dead and you, Eugenius, who are living. . . . Why do you boast loudly of the donation of Constantine and often present yourselves threateningly before certain kings and rulers as claimants of the Empire which has been usurped? Why do you force the Emperor and other rulers—the King of Naples and Sicily, for instance—to acknowledge submission at the time of their coronation? None of the early Popes of Rome did this . . . They always recognized that Rome and Italy along with the provinces belonged to the Emperors. Furthermore, golden coins exist, not to mention other monuments and temples in Rome, that bear not Greek but Latin inscriptions of Constantine, when he was already a Christian, and of almost all the successive emperors. I own many of these myself . . . . If ever you had ruled over Rome, an infinite number of coins would be found commemorating the Supreme Pontiffs, whereas none are to be found either of gold or silver and no one remembers having seen any. Yet, at that time, whoever ruled over the Roman Empire would have had to mint his own currency, probably with the image of the Saviour or of Saint Peter . . . .

XI, 44. As for the text of the document, it is still more absurd and unnatural that Constantinople [75] should be referred to as one of the patriarchal sees, when it was not yet either patriarchal or a see or a Christian city; it was not yet called Constantinople; it had not yet been

---

74The Decretum was a collection of nearly 3800 texts, compiled by the Benedictine monk Gratian about 1140, which became the basic text for the study of canon law.

75 Constantinople was the city in Asia Minor that Constantine created as a "second Rome" and which eventually replaced Rome as the capital of the Roman Empire.

founded or even planned. In fact, the privilege was supposedly granted three days after Constantine was converted to Christianity, when Byzantium still existed and not Constantinople. . . . Who fails to see, therefore, that he who drew up the privilege lived a long time after the age of Constantine? . . .

50. . . . Now, let us speak to this deceiver about his crude language. Through his babbling, he reveals his most impudent forgery himself. . . .Where he deals with the gifts, he says "a diadem . . . . made of pure gold and precious jewels". The ignoramus did not know that the diadem was made of cloth, probably silk. . . . He thinks it had to be made of gold, since nowadays kings usually wear a circle of gold set with jewels. But Constantine was not a king and he would never have dared to call himself a king or to adorn himself in regal fashion. He was Emperor of the Romans, not a king. . . .

XVIII, 58. . . .Is the barbarousness of his style not sufficient proof that such a piece of nonsense was forged not in Constantine's day but much later? . . .

XX, 65. . . . Therefore this text is not by Constantine but by some foolish petty cleric who does not know what to say or how to say it. Fat and full, he belches out ideas and words enveloped in fumes of intoxicating wine. But these sentences do not touch others; rather, they turn against the originator himself. . .

Translated by Olga Zorzi Pugliese, *The Profession of the Religious and the principal arguments from The Falsely-Believed and Forged Donation of Constantine*. Toronto: Victoria University Centre for Reformation and Renaissance Studies, 1985. Printed by permission.

Vespasiano: On the Founding of the Vatican Library

Owing to the jubilee of 1450 a great quantity of money came in by this means to the apostolic see, and with this the pope commenced building in many places, and sent for Greek and Latin books, wherever he was able to find them, without regard to price. He gathered together a large band of writers, the best that he could find, and kept them in constant employment. He also summoned a number of learned men, both for the purpose of composing new works and of translating such existing works as were not already translated, giving them most abundant provision for their needs meanwhile; and when the works were translated and brought to him, he gave them large sums of money, in order that they should do more willingly that which they undertook to do.

He made great provision for the needs of learned men. He gathered together great numbers of books upon every subject, both Greek and Latin, to the number of five thousand volumes. So at his death it was found by inventory that never since the time of Ptolemy had half that number of books of every kind been brought together. All books he caused to be copied, without regard to what it cost him, and there were few places where his Holiness had not copiers at work. When he could not procure a book for himself in any way, he had it copied.

After he had assembled at Rome, as I said above, many learned men at large salaries, he wrote to Florence to Messer Giannozzo Manetti, that he should come to Rome to translate and compose for him. And when Manetti left Florence and came to Rome, the pope, as was his custom, received him with honor, and assigned to him, in addition to his income as secretary, six hundred *ducats*, urging him to attempt the translation of the books of the Bible and of Aristotle, and to complete the book already commenced by him *Contra Judaeos et gentes*[76]; a wonderful work, if it had been completed, but he carried it only to the tenth book. Moreover he translated the New Testament, and the Psalter, . . .with five apologetical books in defense of this Psalter, showing that in the Holy Scriptures there is not one syllable that does not contain the greatest of mysteries.

It was Pope Nicholas' intention to found a library in St. Peter's, for the general use of the whole Roman curia, which would have been an admirable thing indeed, if he had been able to carry it out, but death prevented his bringing it to completion. He illumined the Holy Scriptures through innumerable books, which he caused to be translated; and in the same way with the works of the pagans, including certain works upon grammar, of use in learning Latin,—the *Orthography* of Messer Giovanni Tortelle, who was of his Holiness' household and worked upon the library, a worthy book and useful to grammarians; the *Iliad* of Homer; Strabo's *De situ orbis* he caused to be translated by Guerrino, and gave him five hundred *florins* for each part,—that is to say, Asia, Africa, and Europe; that was in all fifteen hundred *florins*. Herodotus and Thucydides he had translated by Lorenzo Valla, and rewarded him liberally for his trouble; Zenophon and Diodorus, by Messer Poggio; Polybius, by Nicolo Perotto, whom, when he handed it to him, he gave five hundred brand-new papal *ducats* in a purse, and said to him that it was not what he deserved, but that in time he would take care to satisfy him.

From *Readings in European History*, edited by J. H. Robinson. Boston: Ginn, 1906.

Laura Cereta: Letter to Bibulus Sempronius, 1488

Laura Cereta was widowed at the age of seventeen, after eighteen months of marriage to a businessman. Before and after her husband's death from the plague, she wrote a number of letters that reveal a fine humanist education. She was attacked by both men and women who claimed that a woman could not be learned and that her father must have written the letters for her. In this letter she uses her knowledge of antiquity to refute her critics.

My ears are wearied by your carping. You brashly and publicly not merely wonder but indeed lament that I am said to possess as fine a mind as nature ever bestowed upon the most learned man. You seem to think that so learned a woman has scarcely before been seen in the world. You are wrong on both counts, Sempronius, and have clearly strayed from the path of truth and disseminate falsehood. I agree that you should be grieved; indeed, you should be ashamed, for you have ceased to be a living man, but have become an animated stone; having rejected the studies which make men wise, you rot in torpid leisure. Not nature but your own soul has betrayed you, deserting virtue for the easy path of sin.

You pretend to admire me as a female prodigy, but there lurks sugared deceit in your adulation. You wait perpetually in ambush to entrap my lovely sex, and overcome by your hatred seek to trample me underfoot and dash me to the earth. It is a crafty ploy, but only a low and vulgar mind would think to halt Medusa with honey. You would better have crept up on a mole than on a wolf. For a mole with its dark vision can see nothing around it, while a wolf's eyes glow in the dark. For the wise person sees by force of mind, and anticipating what lies ahead, proceeds by the light of reason. For by foreknowledge the thinker scatters with knowing feet the evils which litter her path.

---

76 Against the Jews and Pagans

I would have been silent, believe me, if that savage old enmity of yours had attacked me alone. For the light of Phoebus cannot be befouled even in the mud. But I cannot tolerate your having attacked my entire sex. For this reason my thirsty soul seeks revenge, my sleeping pen is aroused to literary struggle, raging anger stirs mental passions long chained by silence. With just cause I am moved to demonstrate how great a reputation for learning and virtue women have won by their inborn excellence, manifested in every age as knowledge, the purveyor of honor. Certain, indeed, and legitimate is our possession of this inheritance, come to us from a long eternity of ages past.

To begin, we read how Sabba of Ethiopia, her heart imbued with divine power, solved the prophetic mysteries of the Egyptian Salomon. And the earliest writers said that Amalthea, gifted in foretelling the future, sang her prophecies around the banks of Lake Avernus, not far from Baiae. A sibyl worthy of the pagan gods, she sold books of oracles to Priscus Tarquinius. The Babylonian prophetess Eriphila, her divine mind penetrating the distant future, described the fall and burning of Troy, the fortunes of the Roman Empire, and the coming birth of Christ. Nicostrata also, the mother of Evander, learned both in prophecy and letters, possessed such great genius that with sixteen symbols she first taught the Latins the art of writing. The fame of Inachian Isis will also remain eternal who, an Argive goddess, taught her alphabet to the Egyptians. Zenobia of Egypt was so nobly learned, not only in Egyptian, but also in Greek and Latin, that she wrote histories of strange and exotic places. Manto of Thebes, daughter of Tiresias, although not learned, was skilled in the arts of divination from the remains of sacrificed animals or the behavior of fire and other such Chaldaean techniques. Examining the fire's flames, the bird's flight, the entrails and innards of animals, she spoke with spirits and foretold future events. What was the source of the great wisdom of the Tritonian Athena by which she taught so many arts to the Athenians, if not the secret writings, admired by all, of the philosopher Apollo? The Greek women Philiasia and Lasthenia, splendors of learning, excite me, who often tripped up, with tricky sophistries, Plato's clever disciples. Sappho of Lesbos sang to her stone-hearted lover doleful verses, echoes, I believe, of Orpheus' lyre or Apollo's lute. Later, Leontia's Greek and poetic tongue dared sharply to attack, with a lively and admired style, the eloquence of Theophrastus. I should not omit Proba, remarkable for her excellent command of both Greek and Latin and who, imitating Homer and Virgil, retold the stories from the Old Testament. The majesty of Rome exalted the Greek Semiamira, invited to lecture in the Senate on laws and kings. Pregnant with virtue, Rome also gave birth to Sempronia, who imposingly delivered before an assembly a fluent poem and swayed the minds of her hearers with her convincing oratory. Celebrated with equal and endless praise for her eloquence was Hortensia, daughter of Hortensius, an oratrix of such power that, weeping womanly and virtuous tears, she persuaded the Triumvirs not to retaliate against women. Let me add Cornificia, sister of the poet Cornificius, to whose love of letters so many skills were added that she was said to have been nourished by waters from the Castalian spring; she wrote epigrams always sweet with Heliconian flowers. I shall quickly pass by Tulliola, daughter of Cicero, Terentia, and Cornelia, all Roman women who attained the heights of knowledge. I shall also omit Nicolosa of Bologna, Isotta Nogarola and Cassandra Fedele of our own day. All of history is full of these examples. Thus your nasty words are refuted by these arguments, which compel you to concede that nature imparts equally to all the same freedom to learn.

Only the question of the rarity of outstanding women remains to be addressed. The explanation is clear; women have been able by nature to be exceptional, but have chosen lesser goals. For some women are concerned with parting their hair correctly, adorning themselves with lovely dresses, or decorating their fingers with pearls and other gems. Others delight in mouthing carefully composed phrases, indulging in dancing, or managing spoiled puppies. Still others wish to gaze at lavish banquet tables, to rest in sleep, or, standing at mirrors, to smear their lovely faces. But those in whom a deeper integrity yearns for virtue, restrain from the start their youthful souls, reflect on higher things, harden the body with sobriety and trials, and curb their tongues, open their ears, compose their thoughts in wakeful hours, their minds in contemplation, to letters bonded to righteousness. For knowledge is not given as a gift, but is gained with diligence. The free mind, not shirking effort, always soars zealously toward the good, and the desire to know grows ever more wide and deep. It is because of no special holiness, therefore, that we women are rewarded by God the Giver with the gift of exceptional talent. Nature has generously lavished its gifts upon all people, opening to all the doors of choice through which reason sends envoys to the will, from which they learn and convey its desires. The will must choose to exercise the gift of reason.

But where we women should be forceful we are too often devious; where we should be confident we are insecure. Even worse, we are content with our condition. But you, a foolish and angry dog, have gone to earth as though frightened by wolves. Victory does not come to those who take flight. Nor does he remain safe who makes peace with the enemy; rather, when pressed, he should arm himself all the more with weapons and courage. How nauseating to see strong men pursue a weakling at bay. Hold on! Does my name alone terrify you? As I am not a barbarian in intellect and do not fight like one, what fear drives you? You flee in vain, for traps craftily-laid rout you out of every hiding place. Do you think that by hiding, a deserter from the field of battle, you can remain undiscovered? A penitent, do you seek the only path of salvation in flight? If you do you should be ashamed.

I have been praised too much; showing your contempt for women, you pretend that I alone am admirable because of the good fortune of my intellect. But I, compared to other women who have won splendid renown, am but a little mousling. You disguise your envy in dissimulation, but cloak yourself in apologetic words in vain. The lie buried, the truth, dear to God, always emerges. You stumble half-blind with envy on a wrongful path that leads you from your manhood, from your duty, from God. Who, do you think, will be surprised, Bibulus[77], if the stricken heart of an angry girl, whom your mindless scorn has painfully wounded, will after this more violently assault your bitter words? Do you suppose, O most contemptible man on earth, that I think myself sprung like Athena from the head of Jove? I am a school girl, possessed of the sleeping embers of an ordinary mind. Indeed I am too hurt, and my mind, offended, too swayed by passions, sighs, tormenting itself, conscious of the obligation to defend my sex. For absolutely everything—that which is within us and that which is without—is made weak by association with my sex.

I, therefore, who have always prized virtue, having put my private concerns aside, will polish and weary my pen against chatterboxes swelled with false glory. Trained in the arts, I shall block the paths of ambush. And I shall endeavor, by avenging arms, to sweep away the abusive

---

77 The name means "drunkard" and is probably fictitious.

infamies of noisemakers with which some disreputable and impudent men furiously, violently, and nastily rave against a woman and a republic worthy of reverence. January 13

from *Her Immaculate Hand: Selected Works By and About the Women Humanists of Quattrocento Italy*. edited by Margaret L. King and Albert Rabil, Jr. Binghamton, New York: Medieval & Renaissance Texts & Studies. 1983

Unit 30: The Artist and the Viewer

Having shared with students examples of Romanesque art, followed by Gothic, when I arrive at the Renaissance, I display a slide and ask them "How is this different?" Almost unanimously, they say, "Well, finally, they learned how to paint (or sculpt)." Whether by indoctrination or instinct, they are only echoing what Renaissance artists said about themselves, and each other.

from Vasari's *Lives of the Painters, Sculptors and Architects*

Vasari, who lived from 1511 to 1574, was an artist and friend of artists. He believed that the art of his own time was the culmination of 300 years of increasing skill and constant progress toward perfection. He collected anecdotes and legends about many of the artists from Cimabue, who was born in 1240, to those of his own time. He divided his history into three parts, describing in detail what the artists of each phase contributed to the development of "modern" Italian, and especially Florentine, art. While not all of his details are correct, he describes with great enthusiasm an image of perfection in art that was shared by most of his contemporaries—a realistic likeness, the portrayal of emotion, and a passion for ideal beauty.

FROM THE INTRODUCTION TO PART II

Distinction in the arts may be attained in many ways. One man may work hard at it; another may study; another may imitate; a fourth may approach his problems with scientific inquiry; others, by several of these methods together, or even by all of them. I divide the time from the revival of the arts down to the present century into three parts, and in each of these there will be found a very obvious difference. In the first, the formative period, as we have seen, a beginning was made, and though obviously imperfect, the work has deserved a larger share of glory than if it were being judged by the strict rules of art. In the second period, richer invention was displayed, with more correct drawing, a better manner, and improved execution. The arts were freed from that rust of old age which still clung to them. Still, who can say that any artist of those times could do what we can do today? The third period has the credit of reaching such perfection that we must fear that art will sink rather than hope that it may still rise to a greater achievement.

. . . When Giotto improved the art of design, figures in marble and stone improved also. The forms became less rigid, the draperies flowed more freely, and expression began to appear in the heads. . . . We have seen the hard angular lines of Byzantine mosaic and painting first attacked by Cimabue and then entirely extinguished by Giotto. Then began what I would like to call the manner of Giotto, originated by him, imitated by his disciples, and finally honored by all. The hard lines by which every figure was bound, the senseless eyes, the feet planted upright on their extremities, the sharp, formless hands, and the absence of shadow, and every other monstrosity of those Byzantine painters were done away with. The heads began to express vivacity and spirit, the draperies began to have natural folds. Human passions were, in some sort, expressed in the faces. The early manner had been harsh and rugged; that of Giotto became softer and more harmonious. If in Giotto the figures did not have the limpidity and beauty of life, if his hands had not the articulation of nature, or his beards the flow of hair, remember that Giotto had never seen a better painter than himself. Giotto's followers improved manner, outline, expression, and color without originating a new direction.

FROM THE INTRODUCTION TO PART III

The perfection and bloom of art is a power, a boldness, a lightness, beauty, and grace. This we do not find in the second period, though we see diligent endeavor. Nor can this ultimate perfection be reached by studious effort. It was the sight of the antique, of the Laocoön, the Hercules, the mighty torso of the Belvedere, the Venus, the Cleopatra, the Apollo, that made success possible. Softness and power are visible; freedom from distortion, flexibility, and ease of nature are everywhere exhibited. These statues caused the banishment of the hard, dry sharpness of manner of Piero della Francesca, Andrea del Castagno, Giovanni Bellini, Ghirlandaio, Botticelli, Magnegna, Filippo Lippi, and Luca Signorelli.

These masters of the second period labored continually to produce the impossible in art, especially in foreshortening and in the rendering of ugly things, which are as difficult to do as they are unattractive. Francia of Bologna and Pietro Perugino began a new treatment. People rushed like madmen to see their works, so lifelike in their beauty. They believed that it would be impossible for future artists to do better. But then came Leonardo, who, besides the power and boldness of his drawing and the exactitude with which he copied the most minute particulars of nature exactly as they are, displays perfect rule, improved order, correct proportion, just design, and a most divine grace. Abounding in resource, and deeply versed in art, Leonardo may be said to have imparted to his figures not beauty only, but life and movement.

FROM "LEONARDO DA VINCI"

Leonardo was the quintessential renaissance man, with his wide-ranging intellectual interests.

Truly admirable, indeed, and divinely endowed was Leonardo da Vinci, the son of Ser Piero da Vinci. He might have been a scientist if he had not been so versatile. But the instability of his character caused him to take up and abandon many things. In arithmetic, for example, he made such rapid progress during the short time he studied it that he often confounded his teacher by his questions. He also began the study of music and resolved to learn to play the lute, and as he was by nature of exalted imagination, and full of the most graceful vivacity, he sang and accompanied himself most divinely, improvising at once both verses and music.

Though he divided his attention among pursuits so varied, Leonardo never abandoned his drawing, and also continued to model in relief, occupations which attracted him more than any others. His father, Ser Piero, observing this and taking into account the extraordinary character of his son's genius, took some of Leonardo's drawings to Andrea del Verrochio, his intimate friend. He begged Andrea to tell him whether the boy showed promise. Verrochio was amazed at these early efforts of Leonardo's and advised Ser Piero to see to it that his son become a painter. Leonardo was therefore sent to study in the shop of Andrea, whither he went most willingly. He studied not one branch of art only, but all. Admirably intelligent, and an excellent geometrician besides, Leonardo not only worked in sculpture—certain terra-cotta heads of smiling women and others of children done in early boyhood seem to be the work of a master—but, as an architect, designed ground plans and entire buildings; and, as an engineer, was the one who first suggested making a canal from Florence to Pisa by altering the river Arno. Leonardo also designed mills and water-driven machines. But, as he had resolved to make painting his profession, he spent most of his time drawing from life. He sometimes modeled clay figures on which he draped soft cloth dipped in plaster, and from these he made careful drawings on fine linen. He drew on paper also with so much care and so perfectly that no one has equaled him. Leonardo, imbued with power and grace, was endowed with so marvelous a facility, and his mind, his memory, and his hand were so efficient in the service of his intellect, that he confounded every antagonist.

Leonardo was frequently occupied in the preparation of plans to remove mountains or to pierce them with tunnels from plain to plain. By means of levers, cranes, and screws, he showed how to lift or move great weights. Designing dredging machines and inventing the means of drawing water from the greatest depths were among the speculations from which he never rested. Many drawings of these projects exist which are cherished by those who practice our arts. . . .

Leonardo afterward (after a series of paintings and sculptures, which Vasari describes in detail) gave his attention to human anatomy, in company with Messer Marcantonio della Torre, an eminent philosopher. Messer Marcantonio was then lecturing in Pavia and writing on anatomy, a subject which had, until that time, been lost in the darkness of ignorance. Leornado filled Marcantonio's book with drawings in red crayon outlined with the pen. These were drawn with the utmost care from bodies dissected by his own hand. He set forth the structure, arrangement, and disposition of the bones. Later he added the nerves in their due order, and then the muscles. He wrote an explanation, left-handed and backward, that can be read only with a mirror.

Translated by Mrs. Jonathan Foster. 1850.

Leonardo da Vinci on Painting

As Vasari says, Leonardo's notebooks were filled with detailed observations on the various problems he had encountered and his suggestions for dealing with them. He insists that the painter must observe and analyze what he would portray.

HOW IT IS NECESSARY FOR THE PAINTER TO KNOW THE INTERNAL STRUCTURE OF MAN

That painter who has knowledge of the chords, muscles and tendons will know well in moving a limb which chord is the cause of its motion, and which muscle in swelling is the cause of the contraction of this chord, and which chord, transformed into thinnest cartilage, surrounds and binds together the said muscle. By these means he will become a varied and comprehensive demonstrator of the various muscles according to their various effects in the figure, and he will not, as many do, tender diverse actions in such a way that the figures always display the same features in their arms, backs, breasts and legs. Such things are not to be counted as minor errors.

Remember, painter, in the movements you depict as being made by your figures to disclose only those muscles which are involved in the motion and action of your figure, and in each case make the most relevant muscle the most apparent, and that which is less relevant less evident, while that which is not involved at all remains slack and limp and is little displayed. And for this reason I urge you to learn the anatomy of the muscles, chords and bones, without attention to which you will accomplish little. If you are drawing from life, perhaps the person you have selected lacks fine muscles in that action which you wish him to adopt, but you do not always have access to good nudes, and nor is it always possible to portray them. It is better for you and more useful to be practised in such variety and to have committed it to memory. . . .

Muscular men have thick bones and are short and stocky, and have a dearth of fat, because the fleshiness of the muscles, through their growth, are pressed together, and there is no place for the fat that would otherwise be interposed between them. The muscles in such lean men, being in direct contact with each other, cannot widen, but increase in thickness and grow most in that part which is most distant from their ends, that is to say, towards the middle of their breadth and length . . . . Whereas fat men are themselves short and stocky, like the aforesaid muscular men, they have slight muscles, but their skin covers much fat sponginess and vacuity, that is to say, it is full of air, and therefore, these fat men sustain themselves better on water than can the muscular men, whose skin is full inside and who have a lesser quantity of air within it.

All the parts of each creature should be in keeping with its overall age, that is to say, that the limbs of the young, should not be contrived with pronounced muscles, chords or blood vessels, as is done by those who, wishing to display artistry and great draughtsmanship, ruin the whole effect through switching limbs, and the same thing is done by others who, lacking draughtsmanship, make old people with young limbs.

Youths have limbs with small muscles and blood vessels, and the surfaces of the body are delicate and rounded and of agreeable colour. In men the limbs will be sinewy and full of muscles. Old men will have rough and wrinkled surfaces, venous and with prominent sinews.

HOW AN ANGRY FIGURE IS TO BE MADE

Show an angry figure hold someone up by the hair—wrenching that person's head against the ground, with one knee upon the person's ribcage—and raising high the fist of his right arm. The angry figure will have his hair standing on end, his eyebrows lowered and drawn together, and teeth clenched, with the two lateral corners of his mouth arched downwards. His neck will bulge and overlap in creases at the front as he stoops over his enemy.

HOW A DESPAIRING MAN IS TO BE REPRESENTED

Give the despairing man a knife and let him have rent his garments with his hands. One of his hands will be tearing at his wound. Show him standing on his feet with his legs somewhat bent, and his body accordingly inclined towards the ground, with his hair torn and bedraggled.

HOW YOUNG CHILDREN SHOULD BE REPRESENTED

Little children must be represented with lively, wriggling actions when they are seated, and when they stand upright with timid and fearful actions.

HOW OLD MEN SHOULD BE REPRESENTED

Old men should be made with sluggish and slow movements, and their legs will be bent at the knees when they stand still, both when their feet are together and some distance apart, stooping with their heads tilted forwards and their arms not too extended.

HOW WOMEN SHOULD BE REPRESENTED

Women should be represented with demure actions, their legs tightly closed together, their arms held together, their heads lowered and inclined to one side.

HOW OLD WOMEN SHOULD BE REPRESENTED

Old women should be represented as shrewlike and eager, with irascible movements in the manner of the infernal furies, and their movements will be more apparent in their arms and heads than in their legs.

OF THE POSES OF WOMEN AND GIRLS

In women and girls there must be no actions where the legs are raised or too far apart, because that would indicate boldness and a general lack of shame, while legs closed together indicate the fear of disgrace.

Translated by Martin Kemp and Margaret Walker, in *Leonardo on Painting*. New Haven: ©Yale University Press, 1989. Reprinted by permission of Yale University Press.

Michelangelo: Sonnet

Looking at great art may fill one with joy and serenity, but Michelangelo made it clear in several poems that creating them had quite a different effect.

In this hard toil I've such a goiter grown,
Like cats that water drink in Lombardy.
(Or wheresoever else the place may be.)
That chin and belly meet perforce in one.
My beard doth point to heaven, my scalp its
    place
Upon my shoulder finds; my chest, you'll
    say,

A harpy's is, my paint-brush all the day
Doth drop a rich mosaic on my face.
My loins have entered my paunch within;
My nether end my balance doth supply,
My feet unseen move to and fro in vain.
In front to utmost length is stretched my skin
And wrinkled up in folds behind, while I
Am bent as bowmen bend a bow in Spain.

Translated by S. Elizabeth Hall, *Sonnets of Michelangelo*. London: Routledge & Kegan Paul, 1905

CHAPTER 14: THE REFORMATIONS

Unit 31: Martin Luther

The posting or publication of his "Ninety-Five Theses on the Power and Efficacy of Indulgences" by the young professor Martin Luther is generally considered the event that precipitated the Reformation. The writings of Luther alone fill many volumes. The works of his colleagues and opponents are myriad. When Luther posted his theses, the printing press had revolutionized the spread of information. The Ninety-five Theses would not have attracted so much attention had they not been printed and circulated. As the Reformation expanded, public debates were recorded and written treatises battled for the opinions of the learned. Posters and booklets, cartoons and doggerel ensured that the main arguments of both sides were known to the man, and woman, on the street.

Tetzel's Sermon on Indulgences

A papal fund drive to finance the construction of a new St. Peter's in Rome coincided with the ambition of Albert of Hohenzollern to become Archbishop of Mainz. Albert was too young to be a bishop, and he already held two bishoprics. To realize his ambition, he would need a papal dispensation exempting him from the rules regarding age and the holding of multiple offices. This would require money. An arrangement was made with the Fuggers banking family: they would finance the papal dispensation. To ensure repayment, they would oversee a massive sale of indulgences, from which half the money would go to pay off the loan; the other half would be sent to Rome for the building of St. Peter's. Johann Tetzel was one of the "commissioners" appointed to sell the indulgences.

You may obtain letters of safe conduct from the vicar of our Lord Jesus Christ, by means of which you are able to liberate your soul from the hands of the enemy, and convey it by means of contrition and confession, safe and secure from all pains of Purgatory, into the happy kingdom. For know, that in these letters are stamped and engraven all the merits of Christ's passion there laid bare. Consider, that for each and every mortal sin it is necessary to undergo seven years of penitence after confession and contrition, either in this life or in Purgatory.

How many mortal sins are committed in a day, how many in a week, how many in a month, how many in a year, how many in the whole extent of life! They are well-nigh numberless, and those that commit them must needs suffer endless punishment in the burning pains of Purgatory.

But with these confessional letters you will be able at any time in life to obtain full indulgence for all penalties imposed upon you, in all cases except the four reserved to the Apostolic See. Thence throughout your whole life, whenever you wish to make confession, you may receive the same remission, except in cases reserved to the Pope, and afterwards, at the hour of death, a full indulgence as to all penalties and sins, and your share of all spiritual blessings that exist in the church militant and all its members.

Do you not know that when it is necessary for anyone to go to Rome, or undertake any other dangerous journey, he takes his money to a broker and gives a certain per cent--five or six or ten—in order that at Rome or elsewhere he may receive again his funds intact, by means of the letters of this same broker? Are you not willing, then, for the fourth part of a florin, to obtain these letters, by virtue of which you may bring, not your money, but your divine and immortal soul, safe and sound into the land of Paradise?

From *Translations and Reprints from the Original Sources of European History.* Vol. 2. University of Pennsylvania Press. 1897.

Luther's Ninety-Five Theses, 1517

In response to the preaching of Tetzel, Luther posted, on the door of the Castle Church in Wittenberg (or so tradition says), an invitation to debate the nature and efficacy of indulgences.

In the desire and with the purpose of elucidating the truth, a disputation will be held on the underwritten propositions at Wittenberg, under the presidency of the Reverend Father Martin Luther, Monk of the Order of St. Augustine, Master of Arts and of Sacred Theology, and ordinary Reader of the same in that place. He therefore asks those who cannot be present and discuss the subject with us orally, to do so by letter in their absence. In the name of our Lord Jesus Christ. Amen.

5. The Pope has neither the will nor the power to remit any penalties, except those which he has imposed by his own authority, or by that of the canons.

6. The Pope has no power to remit any guilt, except by declaring and warranting it to have been remitted by God; or at most by remitting cases reserved for himself; in which cases, if his power were despised, guilt would certainly remain.

8. The penitential canons are imposed only on the living, and no burden ought to be imposed on the dying, according to them.

10. Those priests act unlearnedly and wrongly, who, in the case of the dying, reserve the canonical penances for purgatory.

13. The dying pay all penalties by death, and are already dead to the canon laws, and are by right relieved from them.

20. Therefore the Pope, when he speaks of the plenary remission of all penalties, does not mean really of all, but only of those imposed by himself.

21. Thus those preachers of indulgences are in error who say that, by the indulgences of

the Pope, a man is loosed and saved from all punishment.

22. For in fact he remits to souls in purgatory no penalty which they would have had to pay in this life according to the canons.

23. If any entire remission of all penalties can be granted to any one, it is certain that it is granted to none but the most perfect, that is to very few.

24. Hence, the greater part of the people must needs be deceived by this indiscriminate and high-sounding promise of release from penalties.

25. Such power as the Pope has over purgatory in general, such has every bishop in his own diocese, and every curate in his own parish, in particular.

29. Who knows whether all the souls in purgatory desire to be redeemed from it, according to the story told of Saints Severinus and Paschal.

32. Those who believe that, through letters of pardon, they are made sure of their own salvation, will be eternally damned along with their teachers.

33. We must especially beware of those who say that these pardons from the Pope

are that inestimable gift of God by which man is reconciled to God.

36. Every Christian who feels true compunction has of right plenary remission of punishment and guilt even without letters of pardon.

37. Every true Christian, whether living or dead, has a share in all the benefits of Christ and of the Church, given him by God, even without letters of pardon.[78]

42. Christians should be taught that it is not the wish of the Pope that the buying of pardons is to be in any way compared to works of mercy.

43. Christians should be taught that he who gives to a poor man, or lends to a needy man, does better than if he bought pardons.

44. Because by a work of charity, charity increases, and the man becomes better; while by means of pardons, he does not become better, but only freer from punishment.

45. Christians should be taught that he who sees any one in need, and, passing him by, gives money for pardons, is not purchasing for himself the indulgences of the Pope, but the anger of God.

50. Christians should be taught that, if the Pope were acquainted with the executions of the Preachers of pardons, he would prefer that the Basilica of St. Peter should be burnt to ashes, than that it should be built up with the skin, flesh, and bones of his sheep.

65. Hence the treasures of the Gospel are nets, wherewith of old they fished for the men of riches.

66. The treasures of indulgences are nets, wherewith they now fish for the riches of men.

81. This license in the preaching of pardons makes it no easy thing, even for learned men, to protect the reverence due to the Pope against the calumnies, or, at all events, the keen questionings of the laity.

82. As for instance: Why does not the Pope empty purgatory for the sake of most holy charity and of the supreme necessity of souls—this being the most just of all reasons—if he redeems an infinite number of souls for the sake of that most fatal thing, money, to be spent on building a basilica—this being a very slight reason?

86. Again; why does not the Pope, whose riches are at this day more ample than those of the wealthiest of the wealthy, build the one Basilica of St. Peter with his own money, rather than with that of poor believers?

From *Translations and Reprints from the Original Sources of European History.* Vol. 2. University of Pennsylvania Press, 1897.

---

[78] The doctrine of indulgences was based on the idea that a "Treasury of Merit" exists, made up of the good deeds of Jesus and the saints and not needed for their own salvation. These merits were deemed available to the Pope, to be granted as he wished to atone for the sins of others.

The Freedom of a Christian, 1520

After being threatened with excommunication, Luther sent this treatise to Pope Leo X with an open letter "as a token of peace and good hope."

To make the way smoother for the unlearned—for only them do I serve—I shall set down the following two propositions concerning the freedom and the bondage of the spirit:

A Christian is a perfectly free lord of all, subject to none.
A Christian is a perfectly dutiful servant of all, subject to all.

These two theses seem to contradict each other. If, however, they should be found to fit together they would serve our purpose beautifully. Both are Paul's own statements, who says in I Corinthians 9, "For though I am free from all men, I have made myself a slave to all," and in Romans 13, "Owe no one anything, except to love one another." Love by its very nature is ready to serve and be subject to him who is loved. So Christ, although he was Lord of all, was "born of woman, born under the law" and therefore was at the same time a free man and a servant, "In the form of God" and "of a servant"

Let us start, however, with something more remote from our subject, but more obvious. Man has a twofold nature, a spiritual and a bodily one. According to the spiritual nature, which men refer to as the soul, he is called a spiritual, inner, or new man. According to the bodily nature, which men refer to as flesh, he is called a carnal, outward, or old man, of whom the Apostle writes in II Corinthians 4, "Though our outer nature is wasting away, our inner nature is being renewed every day." Because of this diversity of nature the Scriptures assert contradictory things concerning the same man, since these two men in the same man contradict each other, "for the desires of the flesh are against the Spirit, and the desires of the Spirit are against the flesh," according to Galatians 5.

First, let us consider the inner man to see how a righteous, free, and pious Christian, that is, a spiritual, new, and inner man, becomes what he is. It is evident that no external thing has any influence in producing Christian righteousness or freedom, or in producing unrighteousness or servitude. A simple argument will furnish the proof of this statement. What can it profit the soul if the body is well, free, and active, and eats, drinks, and does as it pleases? For in these respects even the most godless slaves of vice may prosper. On the other hand, how will poor health or imprisonment or hunger or thirst or any other external misfortune harm the soul? Even the most godly men, and those who are free because of clear consciences, are afflicted with these things. None of these things touch either the freedom or the servitude of the soul. It does not help the soul if the body is adorned with the sacred robes of priests or dwells in sacred places or is occupied with sacred duties or prays, fasts, abstains from certain kinds of food, or does any work that can be done by the body and in the body. The righteousness and the freedom of the soul require something far different since the things which have been mentioned could be done by any wicked person. Such works produce nothing but hypocrites. On the other hand, it will not harm the soul if the body is clothed in secular dress, dwells in unconsecrated places, eats and drinks as others do, does not pray aloud, and neglects to do all the above-mentioned things which hypocrites can do.

Furthermore, to put aside all kinds of works, even contemplation, meditation, and all that the soul can do, does not help. One thing, and only one thing, is necessary for Christian life, righteousness, and freedom. That one thing is the most holy Word of God, the gospel of Christ, as Christ says, John 11, "I am the resurrection and the life; he who believes in me, though he die, yet shall he live"; and John 8, "So if the Son makes you free, you will be free indeed"; and Matthew 4, "Man shall not live by bread alone, but by every word that proceeds from the mouth of God." Let us then consider it certain and firmly established that the soul can do without anything except the Word of God and that where the Word of God is missing there is no help at all for the soul. If it has the Word of God it is rich and lacks nothing since it is the Word of life, truth, light, peace, righteousness, salvation, joy, liberty, wisdom, power, grace, glory, and of every incalculable blessing. This is why the prophet in the entire Psalm and in many other places yearns and sighs for the Word of God and uses so many names to describe it.

On the other hand, there is no more terrible disaster with which the wrath of God can afflict men than a famine of the hearing of his Word, as he says in Amos. Likewise there is no greater mercy than when he sends forth his Word, as we read in Psalm 107: "He sent forth his word, and healed them, and delivered them from destruction." Nor was Christ sent into the world for any other ministry except that of the Word. Moreover, the entire spiritual estate—all the apostles, bishops, and priests—has been called and instituted only for the ministry of the Word.

You may ask, "What then is the Word of God, and how shall it be used, since there are so many words of God?" I answer: The Apostle explains this in Romans 1. The Word is the gospel of God concerning his Son, who was made flesh, suffered, rose from the dead, and was glorified through the Spirit who sanctifies. To preach Christ means to feed the soul, make it righteous, set it free, and save it, provided it believes the preaching. Faith alone is the saving and efficacious use of the Word of God, according to Romans 10: "If you confess with your lips that Jesus is Lord and believe in your heart that God raised him from the dead, you will be saved." Furthermore, "Christ is the end of the law, that every one who has faith may be justified". Again, in Romans 1, "He who through faith is righteous shall live." The Word of God cannot be received and cherished by any works whatever but only by faith. Therefore it is clear that, as the soul needs only the Word of God for its life and righteousness, so it is justified by faith alone and not any works; for if it could be justified by anything else, it would not need the Word, and consequently it would not need faith.

Unit 32: The Radical Reformation

The reforms sparked by Luther drew support from a wide variety of people for a wide variety of reasons. Some supported him for political or economic reasons. Others shared his enthusiasm for a new, evangelical approach to faith, but insisted that his reforms did not go far enough. Those who insisted on more extensive and radical reforms are usually labeled "radical reformers" or "the left wing of the Reformation."

Twelve Articles of the Swabian Peasants

Revolts of peasants and of city-dwellers were not new, but in the 1520's some groups used the language of the reformers, drawing on Luther's concept of "the freedom of a Christian," to articulate their discontent.

1. First, it is our humble petition and desire, as also our will and resolution, that in the future we should have power and authority so that each community should choose and appoint a pastor, and that we should have the right to depose him should he conduct himself improperly. The pastor thus chosen should teach us the Gospel pure and simple, without any addition, doctrine or ordinance of man. For to teach us continually the true faith will lead us to pray God that through His grace this faith may increase within us and become a part of us. For if His grace work not within us we remain flesh and blood, which availeth nothing; since the Scripture clearly teaches that only through true faith can we come to God. Only through His Mercy can we become holy. Hence such a guide and pastor is necessary and in this fashion grounded upon the Scriptures.

2. According as the just tithe is established by the Old Testament and fulfilled in the New, we are ready and willing to pay the fair tithe of grain. The word of God plainly provides that in giving according to right to God and distributing to His people, the services of a pastor are required. We will that for the future our church provost, whomsoever the community may appoint, shall gather and receive this tithe. From this he shall give to the pastor, elected by the whole community, a decent and sufficient maintenance for him and his as shall seem right to the whole community. What remains over shall be given to the poor of the place, as the circumstances and the general opinion demand. . . . The small tithes, whether ecclesiastical or lay, we will not pay at all, for the Lord God created cattle for the free use of man. We will not, therefore, pay farther an unseemly tithe which is of man's invention.

3. It has been the custom hitherto for men to hold us as their own property, which is pitiable enough, considering that Christ has delivered and redeemed us all, without exception, by the shedding of His precious blood, the lowly as well as the great. Accordingly, it is consistent with Scripture that we should be free and wish to be so. Not that we would wish to be absolutely free and under no authority. God does not teach us that we should lead a disorderly life in the lusts of the flesh, but that we should love the Lord our God and our neighbor. . . . We are thus ready to yield obedience according to God's law to our elected and regular authorities in all proper things becoming to a Christian. We, therefore, take it for granted that you will release us from serfdom as true Christians, unless it should be shown us from the Gospel that we are serfs.

4. In the fourth place it has been the custom heretofore, that no poor man should be allowed to touch venison or wild fowl or fish in flowing water, which seems to us quite unseemly and unbrotherly as well as selfish and not agreeable to the word of God. In some places the authorities preserve the game to our great annoyance and loss, recklessly permitting the unreasoning animals to destroy to no purpose our crops which God suffers to grow for the use of man and yet we must remain quiet. This is neither godly nor neighborly. For when God created man he gave him dominion over all the animals, over the birds of the air and over the fish in the water. Accordingly it is our desire, if a man holds possession of waters, that he should prove from satisfactory documents that his right has been unwittingly acquired by purchase. We do not wish to take it from him by force, but his rights should be exercised in a Christian and brotherly fashion. But whosoever cannot produce such evidence should surrender his claim with good grace.

5. In the fifth place we are aggrieved in the matter of wood-cutting, for the noble folk have appropriated all the woods to themselves alone. If a poor man requires wood he must pay double for it. It is our opinion in regard to a wood which has fallen into the hands of a lord, whether spiritual or temporal, that unless it was duly purchased it should revert again to the community. It

should, moreover, be free to every member of the community to help himself to such fire wood as he needs in his home. . . .

6.   Our sixth complaint is in regard to the excessive services demanded of us which are increased from day to day. We ask that this matter be properly looked into so that we shall not continue to be oppressed in this way, but that some gracious consideration be given us, since our forefathers were required only to serve according to the word of God.

7.   Seventh, we will not hereafter allow ourselves to be farther oppressed by our lords, but will let them demand only what is just and proper according to the word of the agreement between the lord and the peasant. The lord should no longer try to force more services or other dues from the peasant without payment, but permit the peasant to enjoy his holding in peace and quiet. The peasant should, however, help the lord when it is necessary, and at proper times when it will not be disadvantageous to the peasant and for a suitable payment.

8.   In the eighth place, we are greatly burdened by holdings which cannot support the rent exacted from them. The peasants suffer loss in this way and are ruined, and we ask that the lords may appoint persons of honor to inspect these holdings, and fix a rent in accordance with justice, so that the peasant shall not work for nothing, since the laborer is worthy of his hire.

9.   In the ninth place, we are burdened with a great evil in the constant making of new laws. We are not judged according to the offence, but sometimes with great ill will, and sometimes much too leniently. In our opinion we should be judged according to the old written law so that the case shall be decided according to its merits, and not with partiality.

10.   In the tenth place, we are aggrieved by the appropriation by individuals of meadows and fields which at one time belonged to a community. These we will take again into our own hands. . . .

11.   In the eleventh place we will entirely abolish the due called *Todfall* [79] and will no longer endure it, nor allow widows and orphans to be thus shamefully robbed against God's will, and in violation of justice and right, as has been done in many places, and by those who should shield and protect them. . . .

Conclusion: In the twelfth place it is our conclusion and final resolution, that if any one or more of the articles here set forth should not be in agreement with the word of God, as we think they are, such article we will willingly recede from when it is proved really to be against the word of God by a clear explanation of the scripture. Or if articles should now be conceded to us that are hereafter discovered to be unjust, from that hour they shall be dead and null and without force. . . .

From *Translations and Reprints from the Original Sources of European History*. Vol. 2. University of Pennsylvania Press. 1897.

Thomas Müntzer: Letter to Count Ernst of Mansfeld, May 1525

Martin Luther and Philip Melanchthon referred to Thomas Müntzer as the "arch-devil of Allstedt," because he insisted that the Reformation must go much further and have more radical consequences than

---

[79] Payment due on the death of a tenant

those supported by Luther. At the Battle of Frankenhausen in 1525, he supported the peasants in their uprising. He was captured, tortured, and eventually executed.

An open letter for the conversion of Brother Ernst at Heldrungen.

May the whole power of God, the mighty fear of him, and the constant basis of his just will be with you, brother Ernst. I, Thomas Müntzer, formerly minister at Allstedt, warn you—as a superfluous encouragement—that, for the sake of the name of the living God, you should give up your tyrannical raging and no longer call down the wrath of God over you. You have begun to torture Christians. You have upbraided the holy Christian faith as a roguery. You have dared to wipe out Christians. Say, you miserable, needy bag of maggots, who made you a prince of people whom God has won with his precious blood? You must and shall prove whether you are a Christian. You shall and must give an accounting of your faith, as I Peter 3 commanded. In a fair trial, you shall have a good, secure chance to bring your faith to light. A whole community, meeting in a circle, has promised you this. And you must also apologize for your evident tyranny. And you should also declare who it is that has made you so bloodthirsty that you want to be a heathen evil doer, one who in the name of being a Christian seeks to harm all Christians. If you reject this challenge and do not settle the matter that has been put to you, then I will cry aloud to the whole world that all the brothers should confidently risk their blood against you, as they did formerly against the Turks. You shall be persecuted and annihilated. For each one who has bought an indulgence from you will become much more zealous (in this anger) than those who formerly bought them from the pope. We know of no other way to reach you. You are shameless; God has hardened you like King Pharaoh and like the kings that God wanted to wipe out, Joshua 5 and 11. May it always be complained about to God that the world did not perceive your coarse, bullish, raging tyranny earlier. Since you have caused such manifest and irreparable damage, what else can happen except that God himself take pity on you? In brief, through God's mighty power, you have been delivered up for destruction. If you do not want to humble yourself before the little people, then an eternal shame before all Christendom will fall on your neck, and you will become a martyr for the devil.

So that you also know that we have a strict order about it, I say: The eternal living God has ordered us to push you from your throne with the power that has been given us. For you are of no use to Christendom. To the friends of God you are a harmful scourge. God has spoken of you and your kind, Ezekiel 34 and 39, Daniel 7, Micah 3. Obadiah the prophet says that your lair must be torn apart and smashed to pieces.

We want to have your answer by the end of the day, or, in the name of the God of hosts, we will afflict you. You may depend on this. We will unhesitatingly do what God has ordered us. You do your best as well. I will be there.

Written at Frankenhausen the Friday after Jubilate (May 12) in the year of our Lord 1525.

Thomas Müntzer with the sword of Gideon.

Translated by Michael G. Baylor, in *Revelation and Revolution: Basic Writings of Thomas Müntzer*. Bethlehem: Lehigh University Press. 1993. Reprinted with permission of Cambridge University Press.

Menno Simons: from the Epistle to Martin Micron, 1556

In this letter Menno takes a stand against capital punishment, in stark contrast to the teachings of Luther and most other reformers.

. . . Seven. It is also manifest that you encourage and strengthen the rulers in their impenitent lives not a little by your writing; rulers who are usually quite obdurate, proud, ambitious, puffed up, self-conceited, pompous, selfish, earthly, carnal, and often bloodthirsty. And that you may gain their favor and praise the more therewith I, miserable man, must be your blind and imprisoned Samson as a spectacle and derision, although I never in my life spoke an insulting word against the rulers or against their office and service.

I have from the beginning of my ministry fraternally warned them in my writings in faithful, unadulterated truth from my soul against the destruction of their souls, admonishing them to a godly, penitent, Christian life, pointing them with the Scriptures to the perfect Spirit, Word, commandment, prohibition, ordinance, and example of Christ. And when you proposed your pharisaical, Herod-like question concerning the magistracy, I said nothing more to you than that it would hardly become a true Christian ruler to shed blood. For this reason, If the transgressor should truly repent before his God and be reborn of Him, he would then also be a chosen saint and child of God, a fellow partaker of grace, a spiritual member of the Lord's body, sprinkled with His precious blood and anointed with His Holy Ghost, a living grain of the Bread of Christ and an heir to eternal life; and for such an one to be hanged on the gallows, put on the wheel, placed on the stake, or in any manner be hurt in body or goods by another Christian, who is of one heart, spirit, and soul with him, would look somewhat strange and unbecoming in the light of the compassionate, merciful, kind nature, disposition, spirit, and example of Christ, the meek Lamb--which example He has commanded all His chosen children to follow.

Again, if he remain impenitent, and his life be taken, one would unmercifully rob him of the time of repentance of which, in case his life were spared, he might yet avail himself. It would be unmerciful to tyrannically offer his poor soul which was purchased with such precious treasure to the devil of hell, under the unbearable judgment, punishment, and wrath of God, so that he would forever have to suffer and bear the tortures of the unquenchable burning, the consuming fire, eternal pain, woe, and death. Never observing that the Son of man says: Learn of me, I have given you an example, Follow me, I am not come to destroy souls, but to save them.

Behold, this was the foundation of my guileless words which I at that time spoke to you in sincerity of heart, according to the style and spirit of the Gospel of Christ. These words you daub with this hateful color before all men saying that I make many pious rulers homicides, that I protect and encourage the hoodlums in their wickedness. I will leave it to your judgment what kind of spirit prompted you thus enviously to write about my plain words. O Micron, you misbehaved too grossly! For what else do you do by your writing but upbraid and blaspheme Christ Himself, whose example I follow in this matter, for pointing unto repentance the adulterous woman who was already adjudged by the law of Moses and letting her go uncondemned. Paul also did not punish the Corinthian further (according to the Mosaic and human law he was deserving of death) than with separation whereby he won him unto God, something which with your putting to death he could not have done. Dear Micron, reflect and see if I do not teach correctly.

I do not doubt in the least but that all reasonable men who shall read my writings, if they have any Scriptural knowledge at all, will say that I have not spoken unreasonably but truly and Christianly, although I have to hear such an ugly greeting from you.

Profane history shows that the Lacedaemonians, who were heathen, did not practice capital punishment, but they imprisoned their offenders and put them to work. It happened that when some of them showed natural piety, ability, counsel, deeds, honor, and self-restraint, they raised them to high office. They were not driven by the bloodthirsty spirit of murder as are some of the preachers and writers who dare boast of the crucified Christ . . .

Reprinted by permission of Heral Press, Scottdale Pennsylvania 15683, from *The Complete Writings of Menno Simons*. Translated by Leonard Verduin, edited by John Christian Wenger. 1956.

Balthazar Hubmaier: On the Sword, 1527

Hubmaier wrote this treatise to make clear his position in a dispute within the Anabaptist community over whether Christians should participate in government and, more specifically, whether they might use force in doing so. In each "passage," he analyzes a Scriptural argument that has been used by his opponents. There are fifteen passages in all. In the second passage he condemns the use of violence by the commoners during the Peasants' War. He claims in the dedication that he has never advocated sedition, but he was burned at the stake in 1528 for alleged activities against the rule of the Habsburgs.

THE FIRST PASSAGE

Christ said to Pilate, "My kingdom is not of this world. If it were of this world, without a doubt my servants would fight for me, so that I would not be delivered to the Jews," John 18.

Concerning this passage some brothers say, "If the kingdom of the Christians is not of this world, a Christian may not wield the sword." To this I answer: if such people would really open their eyes, they would have to say something very different, namely that our kingdom should not be of this world. But unfortunately—may we complain about it to God—it is of this world, as we confess in the "Our Father," where we pray, "Father, thy kingdom come" (Matthew 6). For we are in the kingdom of the world, which is a kingdom of sin, death, and hell (Luke 11). But, father, help us out of this kingdom. We are immersed in it over our ears and here on earth we can never be independent of it. It clings to us until death. Lord, release us from this evil and help us to come home to your kingdom.

Such brothers now see the truth and must admit that out kingdom is of this world, which should grieve our hearts. But Christ alone could truly say, "My kingdom is not of this world," since he was conceived and born without sin, an innocent lamb, in whom there is no deception and who is without sin or stain. And he alone could also truly say, "The prince of this world, the devil, has come but found no evil in me" (John 14). We here on earth could never truthfully say this. For as often as the prince comes—the devil—he finds in us evil lusts, evil desires, and evil inclinations. For this reason St. Paul, while filled with the holy spirit, also calls himself unholy (Romans 7). Thus, the most pious and godly Christians must also confess that they are unsaved until their death. May God help us to make something of our lives.

THE SECOND PASSAGE

Jesus says to Peter, "Put up your sword, for he who takes up the sword shall die by the sword. Do you think that I could not request my father to send me more than twelve legions of angels? But how then could Scripture be fulfilled? It must take place so," Matthew 26.

Pay sharp attention here, pious Christian, to the words of Christ, and then you will already have an answer to the accusation of the brothers. First Christ says, "Put up your sword." It is not proper for you to wield it. You are not in power. You have not been commanded to use it. You have been neither called upon nor elected to use it. For he who takes up the sword shall die by the sword. They perish by the sword who use it without being elected, who are disorderly, and who use it without rules and in the service of their own arbitrariness. And no one should take up the sword unless he has been elected and thus required to do so. For then he himself does not take up the sword, but it is brought to him and given to him. Then he can say, "I have not taken up the sword, I would rather be without it, for I myself am most deserving of punishment. But since I have been called to use it, I bid God to grant me grace and to lend me wisdom so that I may wield it and govern according to his word and will." So Solomon prayed, and God gave him great wisdom to wield the sword in the right way (I kings 3).

In addition, in this passage you hear that Christ says to Peter, "Put your sword in its sheath." He does not say, "Get rid of it and throw it away." For Christ rebuked him because he drew it, not because he had a sword at his side. Otherwise, if it were wrong to carry it, he would have rebuked him long before. In addition, the following part of the text says that he who takes up the sword shall die by the sword. That is, he has fallen to the judgment of the sword, even if he is not always executed by the sword for just reasons. Notice here how Christ confirms the sword, with which one should punish those who pursue their own arbitrary power and crime. And those who have been elected for it should do this punishing, whoever they may be. Thus it is evident that the more pious rulers are, the better and more justly will they wield the sword according to the will of God, to protect the innocent and to induce fear in evildoers. God has appointed and ordained them for this reason (Romans 13).

Thirdly, there is what Christ said to his disciples when they wanted to prevent him from going to Jerusalem. For the Jews wanted to stone him at once. Christ said, "There are not twelve hours in the day" (John 11). As if he wanted to say, "They will not kill me until the twelfth hour comes—that is, the hour that god has ordained for my death," which Christ also calls "the hour of darkness"(Luke 22). But when this same twelfth hour had come, Christ himself said to his disciples on the Mount of Olives, "Arise and let us go down. The hour is here in which I shall be given over to death, so that the Scriptures are fulfilled" (Matthew 26). Note this! Peter hears that the hour has come which had been determined and ordained by God, yet he wanted to prevent it, and he drew his sword on his own authority. That was the greatest error. Therefore Christ said, "No protection or defense is of use any longer. The hour decided by God is here, and even if twelve legions of angels were here, they would not be able to help me against the will of God, my heavenly father. So put away your sword. It is useless. I told you before that the hour has come. Scripture shall and must be fulfilled."

Here every Christian learns that a person should not cease protecting and guarding all pious and innocent people, as long as he is not certain that the hour of their death has arrived. But when the hour comes, whether you know it or not, no protection or defense is then able to help.

Therefore the authorities are bound, on the salvation of their souls, to protect and defend all innocent and peaceful people until a definite voice comes from God clearly saying, "You should no longer protect this person." Abraham heard such a voice, telling him that he should kill his son, contrary to the commandment, "Thou shalt not kill" (Genesis 22, Exodus 20). Thus, the authorities are responsible for protecting and liberating all oppressed and coerced people, widows and orphans—whether familiar to them or strangers—without regard to the person, according to the will and earnest commandment of God. Isaiah 1, Jeremiah 21 and 22, Romans 13, and in many other places. They must do this until they are called by God to do something different, for which they must wait a long time. For this reason God has hung the sword at their side and ordered them to be his handmaidens (Romans 13). . . .

From *Revelation and Revolution: Basic Writings of Thomas Müntzer*, edited and translated by Michael G. Baylor. Lehigh University Press, 1993.

Expulsion of the Jews from Regensburg, 1519

Jews had been expelled from England, France, and Spain before the Reformation, as canon law was relaxed to allow Christians to lend money at interest. In Germany, the rhetoric of reformers and their challenge to the church hierarchy encouraged resentment and rebellion against others seen as oppressors. The following anonymous popular rhyme includes the most prevalent accusations against Jews: wealth, perceived as gained at the expense of Christians, the killing of Christ, and ritual murder of Christian children. Protected by Emperor Maximilian, Jews were expelled from Regensburg after his death in 1519. Their property was confiscated, the synagogue and cemetery destroyed, and a chapel dedicated to the Virgin Mary erected on property they had occupied.

By murder and usury, the Jews
Had done our city grave abuse.
Stirred by laments from young and old,
By pleas from all the land, I'm told,
The council acted. Otherwise,
Had council members shut their eyes
And left the Jews in impunity
They would have wrecked our community.
May our brave councillors be blessed
For having rid us of this pest.
God's purpose was behind their action,
For our Lord feels satisfaction
Whenever Jews are driven from
A famous city in Christendom.
God heeds the cries of honest folk
Oppressed beneath the Jewish yoke.
No craftsman's income is too small
For Jews to demand it all.
He needs a suit, a pair of shoes?
Off he goes trudging to the Jews;
There he finds pewter, silver plate,
Velvet and linen stuffs, brocade,
The things that he himself not owns

Jews hold as pledges for their loans,
Or buy from highwayman and thief
To make their pile from Christian grief.
Stolen or found, cheap stuff or rare,
Look at the Jew's; you'll find it there.
He's got the cash to lend on it,
No questions asked, depend on it.
A piece worth fifty *gulden* when
Bought new, the Jew gets it for ten,
Holds on to it two weeks or three,
Then claims it as his property,
Converts his house into a store
With pants and coats stuffed roof to floor;
A cobbler can't sell a pair of shoes,
Townfolk buy only from the Jews. . . .

Jewish malignity was foretold
by the prophet Isaiah in days of old;
And if further evidence you desire,
Ask Doctor Balthasar Hubmair
To tell you why it is that we
Treat the Jews with such hostility.
He'll waste no time convincing you

(By quoting God's own Gospel, too)
That there's no punishment too painful
For a tribe so openly disdainful
Not only of Christ, their adversary,
But of his mother, the Virgin Mary.
For a Christian there's no sin so great
As to merit a Jew's love, not his hate.
Unceasingly the Jewish swine
Scheme how to violate, malign,
Dishonor the pure Virgin maid,
Our Christian solace, hope, and aid,
Whose son died on the cross that we
Might live in bliss eternally.
No city therefore can fare well
Until it's sent its Jews to hell.

Now listen and pay careful heed
To a horrendous, bestial deed
Of Christian bloodshed without pity
By murderous Jews in our city.
It happened in Emperor Frederick's reign;
Six children they killed with dreadful pain,
Into a dungeon then they threw them
To hide the bodies, bleeding and gruesome.
But soon their crime was indicated,
All of the Jews incarcerated,
And the burghers resolved, for the Virgin's
    sake,
To burn the damned Jews at the stake.
But--though to tell it is a disgrace--
The Jews found help in an exalted place.
Our council spent what money it could
To keep the Jews from winning their suit,
But with the emperor to defend
Their case, the Jews won in the end.
This caused complaints and lamentations;
Citizens sent deputations
To ask why Jewish dogs who spilled
Pure Christian blood should not be killed.
As for the Jews, they caught the drift
Of things, made many a handsome gift
Where money counts; their silver and gold

Regained for them their old foothold.
The burghers would have burned the Jews,
But the emperor saw fit to refuse.
The might and glory of his crown
Served to keep Jews in our town.
Our councillors resented this intervention,
Which frustrated their good intention
Of just revenge on the blaspheming Jew
For the innocent children whom they slew.
The gold sent abroad also caused them grief;
It could have been used for poor relief.
Three years they wasted in vain appeal,
But the emperor adhered to his deal.
Nothing the councillors could say
Would change his mind; the Jews must stay.

For forty years we pressed our case
Against the murderous Jewish race.
Of money paid out, the total score
Was a hundred and thirty-five thousand
    gulden or more;
The city registers record it.
Our citizens could scarcely afford it,
While the Jews, who had much more to
    spend,
Bribed the emperor's courtiers to pretend
To Maximilian, double-tongued,
That the Jews of Regensburg had been
    wronged.
Money makes lies like truth appear,
And the facts were kept from the emperor's
    ear.
Thus matters stood, justice defied,
Until the day Maximilian died,
And God eliminated a few
Of our Jew-loving burghers, too,
Which left the Jews without a friend
Their horrid actions to defend.
That's all I'll say about them here,
Their stubborn blindness cost them dear.
We're free at last of their oppressions;
May God forgive them their transgressions.

Translated by Gerald Strauss, in *Manifestations of Discontent in Germany on the Eve of the Reformation.*
Bloomington: Indiana University Press. 1971

Unit 33: The Catholic Reformation

The Catholic Reformation is sometimes called the Counter-Reformation, but it was not solely a response to the threat posed by those who would come to be called Protestants. The Fifth Lateran Council, held from 1512 to 1517, had already addressed some of the worst clerical abuses. A new mysticism, led by St. John of the Cross and others, led some to a new spirituality. In 1540, the Pope recognized a new order, the Society of Jesus, or Jesuits, led by Ignatius of Loyola. Unlike traditional monastic orders, the Jesuits were dedicated to preaching and missions—the propagation of the faith. On the negative side, the Inquisition was revitalized and directed against the new heresies. In 1559, Pope Paul IV issued the first *Index Librorum Prohibitorum*, the Index of Prohibited Books, to stop the spread of the Reformation by means of printed materials. The most direct response to the Protestant movement was the Council of Trent, which dealt directly with many of the issues raised by Luther and others who followed his lead.

Decrees of the Council of Trent

The Council of Trent, which met intermittently during the years 1545-1563, dealt with many of the issues raised by reformers, both those who remained loyal to the Church at Rome and those who did not. Humanists such as Erasmus wanted a new Latin translation of the Bible, more accurate than the Vulgate, which was the standard translation of the Middle Ages. Luther and others translated the Bible into the vernacular languages so that people who did not know Latin could read and interpret the Scripture for themselves. The question of whether or not the bread and wine of the mass actually becomes the body and blood of Christ was central to the whole issue of the need for a separate order of priests. The issue of indulgences was, of course, the subject of Luther's 95 Theses, the publication of which is traditionally regarded as the beginning of the Reformation.

DECREE CONCERNING THE EDITION AND THE USE OF THE SACRED BOOKS

Moreover, the same sacred and holy Synod,—considering that no small utility may accrue to the Church of God, if it be made known which out of all the Latin editions, now in circulation, of the sacred books, is to be held as authentic,—ordains and declares, that the said old and vulgate edition, which, by the lengthened usage of so many ages, has been approved of in the Church, be, in public lectures, disputations, sermons and expositions, held as authentic; and that no one is to dare, or presume to reject it under any pretext whatever.

Furthermore, in order to restrain petulant spirits. It decrees, that no one, relying on his own skill, shall,—in matters of faith, and of morals pertaining to the edification of Christian doctrine,—wrestling he sacred Scripture to his own senses, presume to interpret the said sacred Scripture contrary to that sense which holy mother Church,—whose it is to judge of the true sense and interpretation of the holy Scriptures,—hath held and doth hold; or even contrary to the unanimous consent of the Fathers; even though such interpretations were never (intended) to be at any time published. Contraveners shall be made known by their Ordinaries, and be punished with penalties by law established.

ON THE MOST HOLY SACRAMENT OF THE EUCHARIST

Canon I. If any one denieth, that, in the sacrament of the most holy Eucharist, are contained truly, really and substantially, the body and blood together with the soul and divinity of our Lord

Jesus Christ, and consequently the whole Christ; but saith that He is only therein as in a sign, or in figure, or virtue; let him be anathema.

Canon II. If any one saith, that, in the sacred and holy sacrament of the Eucharist, the substance of the bread and wine remains conjointly with the body and blood of our Lord Jesus Christ, and denieth that wonderful and singular conversion of the whole substance of the bread into the Body, and of the whole substance of the wine into the Blood—the species only of the bread and wine remaining—which conversion indeed the Catholic Church most aptly calls Transsubstantiation; let him be anathema.

Canon VIII. If any one saith, that Christ, given in the Eucharist, is eaten spiritually only, and not also sacramentally and really; let him be anathema.

DECREE CONCERNING INDULGENCES

Whereas the power of conferring Indulgences was granted by Christ to the Church; and she has, even in the most ancient times, used the said power, delivered unto her of God; the sacred holy Synod teaches, and enjoins, that the use of Indulgences, for the Christian people most salutary, and approved of by the authority of sacred Councils, is to be retained in the Church; and It condemns with anathema those who either assert, that they are useless; or who deny that there is in the Church the power of granting them. In granting them, however, It desires that, in accordance with the ancient and approved custom in the Church, moderation be observed; lest, by excessive facility, ecclesiastical discipline be enervated. And being desirous that the abuses which have crept therein, and by occasion of which this honourable name of Indulgences is blasphemed by heretics, be amended and corrected, It ordains generally by this decree, that all evil gains for the obtaining thereof,--whence a most prolific cause of the abuses amongst the Christian people has been derived,--be wholly abolished. But as regards the other abuses which have proceeded from superstition, ignorance, irreverence, or from whatever other source, since by reason of the manifold corruptions in the places and provinces where the said abuses are committed, they cannot conveniently be specially prohibited; It commands all bishops, diligently to collect, each in his own church, all abuses of this nature, and to report them in the first provincial Synod; that, after having been reviewed by the opinions of the other bishops also, they may forthwith be referred to the Sovereign Roman Pontiff, by whose authority and prudence that which may be expedient for the universal Church will be ordained; that thus the gift of holy Indulgences may be dispensed to all the faithful, piously, holily, and incorruptly. . .

from *The Canons and Decrees of the Sacred and Oecumenical Council of Trent*, translated by J. Waterworth. London, 1848.

Ignatius of Loyola: Letters

The first letter reveals the importance of foreign missions to the Jesuit program. The second outlines the tactics Loyola considered most likely to bring about the desired results: respect for the natives, a mild approach to correcting abuses, widespread education, and the use of the vernacular language. Ethiopia had been Christianized in the fourth century by Monophysite missionaries, considered heretics by the Roman Church. The conquest of North Africa and the Middle East by Muslims in the seventh century had cut off the Ethiopian Christians from other Christians and they developed independently. The Jesuits were sent to bring them into conformity with the Roman church.

To Bertram Loyola, 1540

May our Lord be always our help and support.

Owing to the extreme pressure I am under in suddenly having to send some of our men to the Indies, some to Ireland, and others to different parts of Italy, I will not have the time to write at length as I should wish. Master Francis Xavier of Navarre, son of the lord of Xavier, one of our Society, is the bearer of this letter. At the request of the king of Portugal and at the command of the pope he with two others are going overseas in the interests of the same king. Master Francis will give you full details and will speak to you about everything in my name as though I myself were present.

The ambassador of the king of Portugal, in whose company Francis is traveling, is, you must know, one of our dearest friends, one to whom we are very deeply in debt, and who in the service of our Lord can do us many favors with the king and with all with whom he deals. I beg you therefore, for the service of God our Lord, to show him every courtesy and treat him with all the honor you can.

Araoz, if he is there with you, should consider this letter as written to him. As regards Master Francis, I would have you take his word for everything that concerns me as though I myself had uttered it. Remember me very especially to the lady of the household and all the family.

To Father John Nuñez Barreto, new Patriarch of Ethiopia, c. 1555

Some suggestions which may help to bring the kingdoms of Prester John[80] into union with the Catholic faith and Church.

Since, humanly speaking, the principal factor in this undertaking will be found primarily in Prester John, king of Ethiopia, and secondarily in the people, a few suggestions will be offered which may be of help in winning over Prester John. They will be followed by others which may help in dealing with the people and Prester John conjointly.

For the king

Besides the bulls which the pope addresses to him, the letters which are written him from here will afford some help in winning over the heart of Prester John. They recall to mind the submission which his father David sent to the Holy See, and contain certain recommendations of those who are sent and accredited to him. They also make other friendly advances. But the principal and final help, after that of God our Lord, for winning the heart of Prester John must come from the king. Not merely letters from his highness, but, if he will agree to it, a special ambassador will be required, who on the part of the king will call on Prester john and present the patriarch, the coadjutor bishops, and the other priests, and explain the order that will be followed, so that it will be no longer necessary to take patriarchs from Moorish lands or from schismatic Christians. The more solemnly this presentation is made on the part of his highness, the more authority it seems the patriarch will have for God's service.

It might be good to see whether his highness thinks that some presents should be sent, especially of things that are held in esteem in Ethiopia; and in offering them he could indicate

---

[80] Prester John was a legendary Christian king of India, whose identity had somehow been attached to the king of Ethiopia.

that a true union of friendship will exist among Christian princes when they all hold the one religion. When this is recognized, he could send him every kind of official he desired, and God will give him the grace to overcome the Moors, so far as this will be for God's greater service.

Some letters from the king to individuals will also be of help, especially to those who are closer to Prester John and with whom he consults and whom he holds in esteem, notably the Portuguese. Other letters, if the king agrees, could be brought unaddressed, the proper addresses being supplied in Ethiopia. But whether by letter or otherwise an effort should be made to make such men friendly.

The viceroy of India likewise could do much to add to the authority of the patriarch with Prester John, by letter or a personal representative, if the king does not send one.

The patriarch and those with him should try to be on familiar terms with Prester John and gain his good will by every honorable means. Should he be receptive and the opportunity present itself, give him to understand that there is no hope of salvation outside the Roman Catholic Church, and whatever she determines about faith or morals must be believed if one is to be saved. If you succeed in convincing Prester John of this general truth, you have already gained many particular points which depend on this fundamental truth and which can little by little be deduced from it.

If you can win over men of influence who have great weight with Prester John, or, on the other hand, if you can get him to make the Exercises[81] and give him a taste for prayer and meditation and spiritual things, this will be the most efficacious means of all to get them to think less of and even to abandon the extreme views which they entertain concerning material things.

Remember that they have a prophecy to the effect that in these times a king from this part of the West (apparently they have no other in mind than the king of Portugal) is destined to destroy the Moors. This is an additional reason for a closer friendship with him, and this in turn will be recommended by a closer uniformity. For if there is no opposition in the matter of religion, there will be a closer union of love between them.

You should also remember that up to this Prester John holds both ecclesiastical and civil jurisdiction. Consider whether it would be good to let him know that kings and great princes of the Catholic Church usually have the right of presentation to important positions, but that the actual conferring of the dignity is done by the supreme pontiff and by bishops, archbishops, and patriarchs in their respective spheres of authority. Conforming himself in this matter with the Roman Church and her princes could be of much help to him.

For the people and king conjointly

Take along with you the amplest faculties and see that you are able to explain them. The exterior appearance of the bulls or briefs should be as beautiful to the eye as possible. It will be all the better if they are translated into Abyssian.

To the best of your ability you should have ready the proofs for the dogmas against which they err, with the definition of the Apostolic see or the councils when there is any. For if they can be brought to admit this one truth, that the Holy See cannot err when it speaks *ex cathedra* on

---

[81] Loyola is perhaps best known for his "Spiritual Exercises," a four-week program of study and meditation designed to fuse a mystical spirituality with a practical dedication to God and the Church.

matters of faith and morals, it will be easy to convince them of the others. You should be well prepared, therefore, to prove this thesis and you should approach this matter in a way that is accommodated to those people, or the understanding of anyone.

Concerning the abuses which exist, first try to bring over Prester John and a few individuals of wider influence, and then, without making a fuss over it once these are disposed of, see what can be done about calling a meeting of those in the kingdom who are held in high esteem for their learning. Without taking away from them anything in which they are particularly interested or which they especially value, try to get them to accept the truths of Catholicism and all that must be held in the Church, and encourage them to try to help the people to come to some agreement with the Roman Catholic Church.

After having removed the more substantial abuses—those which are in conflict with a sincere belief, such as the obligatory observance of the Old Law[82]—it would be better to begin, with the support of Prester John, to remove or lessen other abuses if it can be done. If this cannot be done, try at least to make it as plain as possible that there can be no obligation to observe such practices and that, even though they are tolerated, it would be better not to observe them. In this way they will lapse, especially if some of the leading men can be induced to give the example.

The austerities which they practice in their feats and other corporal penances might be gently moderated, it seems, and brought within a measure of discretion. This could be done in four ways. The first would be to quote the testimony of Holy Scripture, to praise spiritual exercises over those that are corporal, since these latter are but of little avail. But you should not withdraw your approval from external exercises, which are necessary up to a certain point. Thus if they lose that esteem for things which they now hold in honor, these things will fall of their own weight, since they are rather repugnant to the flesh anyway. The second is rather to praise and prefer a golden mean to its extremes. The third means is taken from reason, which will convince them that it is against charity and the common good so to weaken themselves for good works by their fasting that their enemies invade their lands and put them to the sword, with so many offenses against God our Lord. This is an argument which will readily appeal to Prester John, and others too who have more than ordinary intelligence. The fourth means is that of example, which could be given by some of those whom they regard as holy, once you convince them that they should so act for God's greater service. It is quit likely that they will do so. Observe too that God calls some individuals to a life of penance and austerity; and when He does, praise what they do in this matter. But in general a measure of discretion is necessary if such austerities are to be praised.

Perhaps some exterior feast would be a great help in getting rid of certain abuses. I am thinking of Corpus Christi processions and others which are in use in the Catholic Church. These would replace their baptisms, and so forth. Our own people, who are not so coarse, are helped by these feasts.

Be very careful that public services such as Mass and Vespers are conducted in a way that will be edifying to the people. The recitation should be slow and distinct, since they do the opposite, and think that our way is more perfect. If the king approves having a choir with organ, this might be a help in the beginning. But let them be in charge of some externs, as it is foreign to our Institute.

---

[82] The Ethiopian church emphasized adherence to Old Testament teachings.

Vestments of priest, deacon, and subdeacon, altar ornaments, chalices, altar stones, and equipment for making hosts ought to be of the best. Try to get them into the habit of making hosts for the Blessed Sacrament as they are made here. In bringing them to Communion let them know that confession should precede, and that Communion is not distributed any day one comes to the church. In the case of the sick who cannot come to the church, see that the Blessed Sacrament is brought to their homes.

It would be good to instruct them in the ceremonies of baptism. It must be conferred but once and not many times, accustomed as they are to baptize every year

As they have never made use of confirmation, it ought to be administered to all the people after they have been prepared for the sacrament. You should also introduce the practice of extreme unction, as they know nothing about it there.

At first you could hear the confessions of those who can understand you. For the others, it would be good for you to bend your efforts to learn the Abyssinian language. The confessors they have among them could be instructed in the proper procedure by means of interpreters. They should be told of reserved cases, which are restricted to bishops and patriarchs; and very severe penalties should be meted out to confessors who reveal matter of confession, something which they say is done there. Lastly, see that the abuses regarding these sacraments are diligently corrected.

With regard to holy orders, some reform is necessary with respect to age, integrity, competence, and other aspects in the candidate for orders, as far as circumstances which prevail there permit.

As to matrimony, and generally speaking the same must be said of all the sacraments, give heed to the form which must be observed. Ceremonies can be introduced gradually, in the measure in which they contribute to greater edification. These exterior rites should not be few in number, considering that the people are much given to ceremonies.

It would be a great help for the complete conversion of those lands, both at the beginning and throughout the rest of the time, to open a large number of elementary schools there, and secondary schools and colleges, for the education of young men, and even of others who may need it, in Latin and in Christian faith and morals. This would be the salvation of that nation. For when these youngsters grow up, they would be attached to what they have learned in the beginning and to that in which they seem to excel their elders. Before long the errors and abuses of the aged would lapse and be forgotten. If it appears hard to the people of that kingdom, habituated as they are to their old ways, to see their children properly trained, think about the advisability of Prester John's sending abroad a large number of those who have talent. A college could be opened in Goa and, if circumstances called for it, another in Coimbra, another in Rome, another in Cyprus, on the opposite side of the sea. Then, armed with sound Catholic teaching, they could return to their lands and help their fellow countrymen. If they came to love the practices of the Latin Church, they would be all the more firmly grounded in her ways.

The patriarch could, by himself or through an interpreter or someone else, begin to give discourses and exhortations to the people within the limits of their capacity. The bishops and others could do likewise. Teaching the catechism in many different places by good teachers would also be of great importance.

Those among the native population who excel in talent and exercise some influence by reason of their good lives should be won over by making much of them. They could be given some ecclesiastical revenues and dignities, but only under the probability that they would turn out to be faithful ministers. You could even have some of these preach.

Some Portuguese who are acquainted with the Abyssinian language would be good as interpreters, should any of Ours preach, and for conferences, after the manner of the Abyssinian preachers. Some could even be brought from Goa or other parts of India; and if there were children's catechism classes in India, they could serve as a beginning for a children's school in the kingdom of Prester John. This would seem to be very much to the point.

Take thought of beginning in the course of time some universities or liberal-arts courses.

Consider the abuses or disorders which can be corrected gently and in a way that will give the people of the country a chance to see that a reform was necessary, and that it begins with them. This will furnish you with authority for the reform of other abuses.

Since Ours have to lessen the esteem for corporal penance which the Abyssinians have, in the use of which they go to extremes, set before them charity in word and example. To this end it would be good to establish hospitals where pilgrims and the sick, curable and incurable, could be gathered, to give and cause others to give public and private alms to the poor, to arrange for the marriage of young girls, and to establish confraternities for the redemption of captives and the care of exposed children of both sexes. They would thus see that there are better works than their fast. It seems that Prester John, who is generous with his alms, should if possible have a finger in all these pious works.

In works of spiritual mercy also the people of the country should behold in you a tender solicitude for souls. This would be shown in teaching them virtue and their letters, all of which should be done gratis and for the love of Christ. These works should be praised in sermons and conversations and supported with texts from Holy Scripture and the example and sayings of the saints, as we indicated above.

Although you are ever intent on bringing them to conformity with the Catholic Church, do everything gently, without any violence to souls long accustomed to another way of life. Try to win their love and their respect for your authority, preserving their esteem of learning and virtue, without harm to your humility, so that they will be helped in proportion as they esteem those by whom they are to be helped. . . .

From Letters of St. Ignatius of Loyola, translated by William J. Young. Chicago: Loyola University Press, 1959.

CHAPTER 15: DISCOVERY AND CRISIS

Unit: 34: European Exploration

Bernal Diaz spoke for most of his fellow explorers when he wrote that he went to the Indies "to serve God and His Majesty, to give light to those who were in darkness, and to grow rich, as all men desire to do." Much of the documentation of early voyages of discovery is concerned with the dual motives of religious zeal and the hunger for wealth.

From the Diary of Columbus' First Voyage to America, 1492-93

This is the first voyage and the courses and way that the Admiral Don Christóbal Colón took when he discovered the Indies, summarized except for the prologue that he composed for the king and queen, which is given in full and begins this way:[83]

In the Name of Our Lord Jesus Christ

Whereas, Most Christian and Very Noble and Very Excellent and Very Powerful Princes, King and Queen of the Spains and of the Islands of the Sea, our Lords: This present year of 1492, after Your Highnesses had brought to an end the war with the Moors who ruled in Europe and had concluded the war in the very great city of Granada, where this present year on the second day of the month of January I saw the Royal Standards of Your Highnesses placed by force of arms on the towers of the Alhambra, which is the fortress of the said city; and I saw the Moorish King come out to the gates of the city and kiss the Royal Hands of Your Highnesses and of the Prince my Lord; and later in that same month, because of the report that I had given to Your Highnesses about the lands of India and about a prince who is called "Grand Khan," which means in our Spanish language "King of Kings"; how, many times, he and his predecessors had sent to Rome to ask for men learned in our Holy Faith in order that they might instruct him in it and how the Holy Father had never provided them; and thus so many peoples were lost, falling into idolatry and accepting false and harmful religions; and Your Highnesses, as Catholic Christians and Princes, lovers and promoters of the Holy Christian Faith, and enemies of the false doctrine of Mahomet and of all idolatries and heresies, you thought of sending me, Christóbal Colón, to the said regions of India to see the said princes and the peoples and the lands, and the characteristics of the lands and of everything, and to see how their conversion to our Holy Faith might be undertaken. And you commanded that I should not go to the East by land, by which way it is customary to go, but by the route to the West, by which route we do not know for certain that anyone previously has passed.

So, after having expelled all the Jews from all of your Kingdoms and Dominions, in the same month of January Your Highnesses commanded me to go, with a suitable fleet, to the said regions of India. And for that you granted me great favors and ennobled me so that from then on I might call myself "Don" and would be Grand Admiral of the Ocean Sea and Viceroy and perpetual Governor of all the islands and lands that I might discover and gain and [that] from now on might be discovered and gained in the Ocean Sea; and likewise my eldest son would succeed me and his son him, from generation to generation forever.

---

[83] The diary was abstracted by Fray Bartolomé de las Casas. This is his introduction.

And I left the city of Granada on the twelfth day of May in the same year of 1492 on Saturday, and I came to the town of Palos, which is a seaport, where I fitted out three vessels very well suited for such exploits; and I left the said port, very well provided with supplies and with many seamen, on the third day of August of the said year, on a Friday, half an hour before sunrise; and I took the route to Your Highnesses' Canary Islands, which are in the said Ocean Sea, in order from there to take my course and sail so far that I would reach the Indies and give Your Highnesses' message to those princes and thus carry out that which you had commanded me to do.

And for this purpose I thought of writing on this whole voyage, very diligently, all that I would do and see and experience, as will be seen further along. Also, my Lord Princes, besides writing down each night whatever I experience during the day and each day what I sail during the night, I intend to make a new sailing chart. In it I will locate all of the sea and the lands of the Ocean Sea in their proper places under their compass bearings and, moreover, compose a book and similarly record all of the same in a drawing, by latitude from the equinoctial line and by longitude from the west; and above all it is very important that I forget sleep and pay much attention to navigation in order thus to carry out these purposes, which will be great labor.

FRIDAY, AUGUST 3

We departed Friday the third day of August of the year 1492 from the bar of Saltés at the eighth hour. We went south with a strong sea breeze 60 miles, which is 15 leagues, until sunset; afterward to the southwest and south by west, which was the route for the Canaries. . . .

SUNDAY, SEPTEMBER 9

He made 15 leagues that day and he decided to report less than those actually traveled so in case the voyage were long the men would not be frightened and lose courage. In the night they made 120 miles at ten miles per hour, which is 30 leagues. The sailors steered badly, straying to the west by north and even to the half division [west-northwest], because of which the Admiral rebuked them many times.

WEDNESDAY, OCTOBER 10

He steered west-southwest; they traveled ten miles per hour and at times 12 and for a time seven and between day and night made 59 leagues; he told the men only 44 leagues. Here the men could no longer stand it; they complained of the long voyage. But the Admiral encouraged them as best he could, giving them good hope of the benefits that they would be able to secure. And he added that it was useless to complain since he had come to find the Indies and thus had to continue the voyage until he found them, with the help of Our Lord.

> After thirty-three days of sailing, Columbus landed at an island the natives called Guanahani, which he named San Salvador.

THURSDAY, OCTOBER 11

He steered west-southwest. They took much water aboard, more than they had taken in the whole voyage. They saw petrels and a green bulrush near the ship. The men of the caravel Pinta saw a cane and a stick, and took on board another small stick that appeared to have been worked with iron, and a piece of cane, and other vegetation originating on land, and a small plank. The men of the caravel Niña also saw other signs of land and a small stick loaded with barnacles. With these signs everyone breathed more easily , , ,

What follows are the very words of the Admiral in his book about his first voyage to, and discovery of, these Indies. I, he says, in order that they would be friendly to us—because I recognized that they were people who would be better freed [from error] and converted to our Holy Faith by love than by force—so some of them I gave red caps, and glass beads which they put on their chests, and many other things of small value, in which they took so much pleasure and became so much our friends that it was a marvel. Later they came swimming to the ships' launches where we were and brought us parrots and cotton thread in balls and javelins and many other things, and they traded them to us for other things which we gave them, such as small glass beads and bells. In sum, they took everything and gave of what they had very willingly. But it seemed to me that they were a people very poor in everything. All of them go around as naked as their mothers bore them; and the women also, although I did not see more than one quite young girl.

And all those that I saw were young people, for none did I see of more than 30 years of age. They are very well formed, with handsome bodies and good faces. Their hair [is] coarse—almost like the tail of a horse—and short. They wear their hair down over their eyebrows except for a little in the back which they wear long and never cut. Some of them paint themselves with black, and they are of the color of the Canarians, neither black nor white; and some of them paint themselves with white, and some of them with red, and some of them with whatever they find. And some of them paint their faces, and some of them the whole body, and some of them only the eyes, and some of them only the nose. They do not carry arms nor are they acquainted with them, because I showed them swords and they took them by the edge and through ignorance cut themselves. They have no iron. Their javelins are shafts without iron and some of them have at the end a fish tooth and others of other things. All of them alike are of good-sized stature and carry themselves well. I saw some who had marks of wounds on their bodies and I made signs to them asking what they were; and they showed me how people from other islands nearby came there and tried to take them, and how they defended themselves; and I believed and believe that they come here from *tierra firme* to take them captive. They should be good and intelligent servants, for I see that they say very quickly everything that is said to them; and I believe that they would become Christians very easily, for it seemed to me that they had no religion. Our Lord pleasing, at the time of my departure I will take six of them from here to Your Highnesses in order that they may learn to speak. No animal of any kind did I see on this island except parrots. All are the Admiral's words.

Saturday, October 13

As soon as it dawned, many of these people came to the beach—all young as I have said, and all of good stature—very handsome people, with hair not curly but straight and coarse, like horsehair; and all of them very wide in the forehead and head, more so than any other race that I have seen so far. And their eyes are very handsome and not small; and none of them are black, but of the color of the Canary Islanders. Nor should anything else be expected since this island is on an east-west line with the island of Hierro in the Canaries. All alike have very straight legs and no belly but are very well formed. They came to the ship with dugouts that are made from the trunk of one tree, like a long boat, and all of one piece, and worked marvelously in the fashion of the land, and so big that in some of them 40 and 45 men came. And others smaller, down to some in which came one man alone. They row with a paddle like that of a baker and go marvelously. And if it capsizes on them they then throw themselves in the water, and they right and empty it with calabashes that they carry. They brought balls of spun cotton and parrots and javelins and other little things that it would be tiresome to write down, and they gave everything for anything that was given to them. I was attentive and labored to find out if there was any gold; and I saw that some of them wore a little piece hung in a hole that they have in their noses. And by signs I was able to understand that, going to the south or rounding the island to the south, there was there a king who had large vessels of it and had very much gold. I strove to get them to go there and later saw that they had no intention of going. I decided to wait until the afternoon of the morrow and then depart for the southwest, for, as many of them showed me, they said there was land to the south and to the southwest and to the northwest and that these people from the northwest came to fight them many times. And so I will go to the southwest to seek gold and precious stones. . . .

Translated by Oliver Dunn and James E. Kelley, Jr. *The Diario of Christopher Columbus's First Voyage to America 1492-1493.* ©University of Oklahoma Press, 1989. Reprinted by permission.

Michele Soriano: The Gold of the Indies, 1559

Michele Soriano explains that sometimes the two goals—spreading Christianity and acquiring wealth—are contradictory.

From New Spain are obtained gold and silver, cochineal (little insects like flies), from which crimson dye is made, leather, cotton, sugar and other things; but from Pero nothing is obtained except minerals. The fifth part of all that is produced goes to the king, but since the gold and silver is brought to Spain and he has a tenth part of that which goes to the mint and is refined and coined, he eventually gets one-fourth of the whole sum, which fourth does not exceed in all four or five hundred thousand ducats, although it is reckoned not alone at millions, but at millions of pounds. Nor is it likely that it will long remain at this figure, because great quantities of gold and silver are no longer found upon the surface of the earth, as they have been in past years; and to penetrate into the bowels of the earth requires greater effort, skill and outlay, and the Spaniards are not willing to do the work themselves, and the natives cannot be forced to do so, because the Emperor has freed them from all obligation of service as soon as they accept the Christian religion. Wherefore it is necessary to acquire negro slaves, who are brought from the coasts of Africa, both within and without the Straits, and these are selling dearer every day, because on account of their natural lack of strength and the change of climate, added to the lack of discretion upon the part of their masters in making them work too hard and giving them too little to eat, they fall sick and the greater part of them die.

from *Translations and Reprints from the Original Sources of European History.* vol. 3. University of Pennsylvania Press, 1896.

Unit 35: Disorderly Women and Witchcraft

In the sixteenth and seventeenth centuries, between 60,000 and 100,000 people, most of them women, were executed for alleged witchcraft. Carlo Ginsburg, in his book *The Night Walkers*, has demonstrated how a benign folk belief could be transformed, by the questions and accusations of officials, into a belief in worship of the devil, accompanied by supernatural acts of malice toward the enemies of the alleged witch. Throughout Europe, folk healers used herbs and incantations to treat illness. In the popular view, a person who could cure illness might also cause it. A particularly malevolent person with such powers might even cause death or failure of crops. Prosecutions for such acts focused on the act itself. A different view of witchcraft developed among theologians who claimed that a human could not do these evils without the aid of the devil. Accusations switched from a focus on actions performed to the condition of being a witch—of having made a pact with the devil. The stereotypical witch was an independent adult woman, often a widow, who did not conform to male ideas of proper female behavior. She was assertive and not under the authority of a male relative.

Innocent VIII: The Witch-Bull of 1484

In the fifteenth and sixteenth centuries, the Inquisition was used to seek out and prosecute witches.

Desiring with supreme ardor, as pastoral solicitude requires, that the catholic faith in our days everywhere grow and flourish as much as possible, and that all heretical pravity be put far from the territories of the faithful, we freely declare and anew decree this by which our pious desire may be fulfilled, and, all errors being rooted out by our toil as with the hoe of a wise laborer, zeal and devotion to this faith may take deeper hold on the hearts of the faithful themselves.

It has recently come to our ears, not without great pain to us, that in some parts of upper Germany, as well as in the provinces, cities, territories, regions, and dioceses of Mainz, Köln, Trier, Salzburg, and Bremen, many persons of both sexes, heedless of their own salvation and forsaking the catholic faith, give themselves over to devils male and female, and by their incantations, charms, and conjurings, and by other abominable superstitions and sortileges, offences, crimes, and misdeeds, ruin and cause to perish the offspring of women, the foal of animals, the products of the earth, the grapes of vines, and the fruits of trees, as well as men and women, cattle and flocks and herds and animals of every kind, vineyards also and orchards, meadows, pastures, harvests, grains and other fruits of the earth; that they afflict and torture with dire pains and anguish, both internal and external, these men, women, cattle, flocks, herds, and animals, and hinder men from begetting and women from conceiving, and prevent all consummation of marriage; that, moreover, they deny with sacrilegious lips the faith they received in holy baptism; and that, at the instigation of the enemy of mankind, they do not fear to commit and perpetrate many other abominable offences and crimes, at the risk of their own souls, to the insult of the divine majesty and to the pernicious example and scandal of multitudes. And, although our beloved sons Henricus Institoris and Jacobus Sprenger, of the order of Friars Preachers, professors of theology, have been and still are deputed by our apostolic letters as inquisitors of heretical pravity, the former in the aforesaid parts of upper Germany, including the provinces, cities, territories, dioceses, and other places as above, and the latter throughout certain parts of the course of the Rhine; nevertheless certain of the clergy and of the laity of those parts, seeking to be wise above what is fitting, because in the said letter of deputation the aforesaid provinces, cities, dioceses, territories, and other places and the persons and offences in question were not individually and specifically named, do not blush obstinately to assert that these are not at all included in the said parts and that therefore it is illicit for the aforesaid inquisitors to exercise their office of inquisition in the provinces, cities, dioceses, territories, and other places aforesaid, and that they ought not to be permitted to proceed to the punishment, imprisonment, and correction of the aforesaid persons for the offences and crimes above named. Wherefore in the provinces, cities, dioceses, territories, and places aforesaid such offences and crimes, not without evident damage to their souls and risk of eternal salvation, go unpunished.

We, therefore, desiring, as is our duty, to remove all impediments by which in any way the said inquisitors are hindered in the exercise of their office, and to prevent the taint of heretical pravity and of other like evils from spreading their infection to the ruin of others who are innocent, the zeal of religion especially impelling us, in order that the provinces, cities, dioceses, territories, and places aforesaid in the said parts of upper Germany may not be deprived of the office of inquisition which is their due, do hereby decree, by virtue of our apostolic authority, that it shall be permitted to the said inquisitors in these regions to exercise their office of inquisition and to proceed to the correction, imprisonment, and punishment of the aforesaid persons for their said offences and crimes, in all respects and altogether precisely as if the provinces, cities, territories, places, persons, and offences aforesaid were expressly named in the said letter. and, for the greater sureness, extending the said letter and deputation to the provinces, cities, dioceses, territories, places, persons, and crimes aforesaid, we grant to the said inquisitors that they or either of them, joining with them our beloved son Johannes Gremper, cleric of the dioceses of Constance, master of arts, their present notary, or any other notary public who by them or by either of them shall have been temporarily delegated in the provinces, cities, dioceses, territories, and places aforesaid, may exercise against all persons, of whatsoever condition and rank, the said office of inquisition, correcting, imprisoning, punishing, and chastising, according to their deserts, those persons whom they shall find guilty as aforesaid.

And they shall also have full and entire liberty to propound and preach to the faithful the word of God, as often as it shall seem to them fitting and proper, in each and all of the parish churches in the said provinces, and to do all things necessary and suitable under the aforesaid circumstances, and likewise freely and fully to carry them out. . . .

from *Translations and Reprints from the Original Sources of European History*. vol. 3. University of Pennsylvania Press, 1896.

Heinrich Krämer and Jacob Sprenger: *Malleus Maleficarum*, 1486

The "Hammer of Witches" was a handbook compiled by the two inquisitors named in the previous selection (Institoris is the Latinized version of Krämer's name). It is an extensive collection of beliefs about witches, with a code of procedure for detecting and punishing them.

DIRECTIONS FOR THE TORTURE OF A WITCH

The method of beginning an examination by torture is as follows: First, the jailers prepare the implements of torture, then they strip the prisoner (if it be a woman, she has already been stripped by other women, upright and of good report.) This stripping is lest some means of witch-craft may have been sewn into the clothing--such as often, taught by the Devil, they prepare from the bodies of unbaptized infants, (murdered) that they may forfeit salvation. And when the implements of torture have been prepared, the judge, both in person and through other good men zealous in the faith, tries to persuade the prisoner to confess the truth freely; but, if he will not confess, he bids attendants make the prisoner fast to the *strappado*[84] or some other implement of torture. The attendants obey forthwith, yet with feigned agitation. Then, at the prayer of some of those present, the prisoner is loosed again and is taken aside and once more persuaded to confess, being led to believe that he will in that case not be put to death.

Here it may be asked whether the judge, in the case of a prisoner much defamed, convicted both by witnesses and by proofs, nothing being lacking but his own confession, can properly lead him to hope that his life will be spared—when, even if he confess his crime, he will be punished with death.

It must be answered that opinions vary. Some hold that even a witch of very ill repute, against whom the evidence justifies violent suspicion, and who, as a ringleader of the witches, is accounted very dangerous, may be assured her life, and condemned instead to perpetual imprisonment on bread and water, in case she will give sure and convincing testimony against other witches; yet this penalty of perpetual imprisonment must not be announced to her, but only that her life will be spared, and that she will be punished in some other fashion, perhaps by exile. And doubtless such notorious witches, especially those who prepare witch-potions or who by magical methods cure those bewitched, would be peculiarly suited to be thus preserved, in order to aid the bewitched or to accuse other witches, were it not that their accusations cannot be trusted, since the Devil is a liar, unless confirmed by proofs and witnesses.

Others hold, as to this point, that for a time the promise made to the witch sentenced to imprisonment is to be kept, but that after a time she should be burned.

A third view is, that the judge may safely promise witches to spare their lives, if only he will later excuse himself from pronouncing the sentence and will let another do this in his place. . . .

But if, neither by threats nor by promises such as these, the witch can be induced to speak the truth, then the jailers must carry out the sentence, and torture the prisoner according to the accepted methods, with more or less of severity as the delinquent's crime may demand. And, while he is being tortured, he must be questioned on the articles of accusation, and this frequently and persistently, beginning with the lighter charges—for he will more readily confess the lighter than the heavier. And, while this is being done, the notary must write down everything in his record of the trial—how the prisoner is tortured, on what points he is questioned, and how he answers.

And note that, if he confesses under the torture, he must afterward be conducted to another place, that he may confirm it and certify that it was not due alone to the force of the torture.

But, if the prisoner will not confess the truth satisfactorily, other sorts of tortures must be placed before him, with the statement that, unless he will confess the truth, he must endure these also. But, if not even thus he can be brought into terror and to the truth, then the next day or the next but one is to be set for a continuation of the tortures—not a repetition,[85] for they must not be repeated unless new evidences be produced.

---

[84] The *strappado* was a rope passed through a pulley in the ceiling. The wrists of the accused were tied together behind his or her back, and attached to the rope. The accused was raised off the ground by means of the rope, allowed to fall, and then jerked up again.

[85] The law prohibited repeated torture. Inquisitors got around this by claiming that a series of tortures were simply one long session, with periods of respite.

The judge must then address to the prisoners the following sentence: We, the judge, etc., do assign to you, _____, such and such a day for the continuation of the tortures, that from your own mouth the truth may be heard, and that the whole may be recorded by the notary.

And during the interval, before the day assigned, the judge, in person or through approved men, must in the manner above described try to persuade the prisoner to confess, promising her (if there is ought to be gained by this promise) that her life shall be spared.

The judge shall see to it, moreover, that throughout this interval guards are constantly with the prisoner, so that she may not be left alone; because she will be visited by the Devil and tempted into suicide.

from *Translations and Reprints from the Original Sources of European History*. vol. 3. University of Pennsylvania Press. 1896.

Johannes Junius: How a Confession was Obtained, 1628

The Lord Mayor of Bamberg explained his confession of witchcraft in a letter secretly sent to his daughter. Junius was convicted and burned at the stake.

Many hundred thousand good-nights, dearly beloved daughter Veronica. Innocent have I come into prison, innocent have I been tortured, innocent must I die. For whoever comes into the witch prison must become a witch or be tortured until he invents something out of his head and—God pity him—bethinks him of something. I will tell you how it has gone with me. When I was the first time put to the torture, Dr. Braun, Dr. Kötzendörffer, and two strange doctors were there. Then Dr. Braun asks me, "Kinsman, how come you here?" I answer, "Through falsehood, through misfortune." "Hear, you," he says, "you are a witch; will you confess it voluntarily? If not, we'll bring in witnesses and the executioner for you." I said "I am no witch, I have a pure conscience in the matter; if there are a thousand witnesses, I am not anxious, but I'll gladly hear the witnesses." Now the chancellor's son was set before me . . .and afterward Hoppfen Elss. She had seen me dance on Haupts-moor. . . . I announced: "I have never renounced God, and will never do it—God graciously keep me from it. I'll rather bear whatever I must." And then came also—God in highest heaven have mercy—the executioner, and put the thumbscrews on me, both hands bound together, so that the blood ran out at the nails and everywhere, so that for four weeks I could not use my hands, as you can see from the writing. . . .Thereafter they first stripped me, bound my hands behind me, and drew me up in the torture. Then I thought heaven and earth were at an end; eight times did they draw me up and let me fall again, so that I suffered terrible agony. . . .[86]

. . . When at last the executioner led me back into the prison, he said to me: "Sir, I beg you, for God's sake, confess something, whether it be true or not. Invent something, for you cannot endure the torture which you will be put to; and, even if you bear it all, yet you will not escape, not even if you were an earl, but one torture will follow after another until you say you are a witch. . . .

And so I begged, since I was in wretched plight, to be given one day for thought and a priest. The priest was refused me, but the time for thought was given. Now, my dear child, see in what

---

[86] This was the torture of the *strappado*. See footnote in previous selection.

hazard I stood and still stand. I must say that I am a witch, though I am not,—must now renounce God, though I have never done it before. Day and night I was deeply troubled, but at last there came to me a new idea. I would not be anxious, but, since I had been given no priest with whom I could take counsel, I would myself think of something and say it. . . . and afterwards I would confess it to the priest, and let those answer for it who compel me to do it. . .

Then I had to tell what crimes I had committed. I said nothing. . . "Draw the rascal up!" So I said that I was to kill my children, but I had killed a horse instead. It did not help. I had also taken a sacred wafer, and had desecrated it. When I had said this, they left me in peace. . . .

Now, dear child, here you have all my confession, for which I must die. And they are sheer lies and made-up things, so help me God. For all this I was forced to say through fear of the torture which was threatened beyond what I had already endured. . . .

Dear child, keep this letter secret so that people do not find it, else I shall be tortured most piteously and the jailers will be beheaded. . . . Dear child, pay this man a dollar. . . .

Good night, for your father Johannes Junius will never see you more. July 24, 1628

From *Translations and Reprints of the Sources of European History*, vol. 3. University of Pennsylvania Press, 1907.

CHAPTER 16: ABSOLUTE AND LIMITED MONARCHIES

Unit 36: The Growth of Absolutism

"L'Etat, c'est moi." For Louis XIV of France, the nation and the king were indistinguishable. The Wars of Religion, the decline of feudalism, and rising secularism led the rulers of France, Russia, and Prussia in the seventeenth century to tighten control over as many aspects of government as they could. This theory of government was called absolutism.

The Edict of Nantes, 1598

The Reformation in France had led to three civil wars and, on St. Bartholomew's Day of 1572, to an indiscriminate massacre of most of the leading Huguenots[87] in Paris, and thousands in the rest of the country. After the assassination of Henry III in 1589, a Huguenot leader, Henry of Navarre, was named as his successor, provided that he would convert to Catholicism. He converted and, in 1598, as Henry IV, he issued the Edict of Nantes, granting the Huguenots political and religious freedom.

Henry, by the grace of God king of France and of Navarre, to all to whom these presents come, greeting:

Among the infinite benefits which it has pleased God to heap upon us, the most signal and precious is his granting us the strength and ability to withstand the fearful disorders and troubles which prevailed on our advent in this kingdom. The realm was so torn by innumerable factions and sects that the most legitimate of all the parties was fewest in numbers. God has given us strength to stand out against this storm; we have finally surmounted the waves and made our port of safety,—peace for our state. . . .

We have, by this perpetual and irrevocable edict, established and proclaimed and do establish and proclaim:

1. First, that the recollection of everything done by one party or the other between March, 1585, and our accession to the crown, and during all the preceding period of troubles, remain obliterated and forgotten, as if no such things had ever happened.

3. We ordain that the Catholic Apostolic and Roman religion shall be restored and reestablished in all places and localities of this our kingdom and countries subject to our sway, where the exercise of the same has been interrupted, in order that it may be peaceably and freely exercised, without any trouble or hindrance; forbidding very expressly all persons, of whatsoever estate, quality, or condition, from troubling, molesting, or disturbing ecclesiastics in the celebration of divine service, in the enjoyment or collection of tithes, fruits, or revenues of their benefices, and all other rights and dues belonging to them; and that all those who during the troubles have taken possession of churches, houses, goods or revenues, belonging to the said

---

[87] French Protestants

ecclesiastics, shall surrender to them entire possession and peaceable enjoyment of such rights, liberties, and sureties as they had before they were deprived of them.

6. And in order to leave no occasion for troubles or differences between our subjects, we have permitted, and herewith permit, those of the said religion called Reformed to live and abide in all the cities and places of this our kingdom and countries of our sway, without being annoyed, molested, or compelled to do anything in the matter of religion contrary to their consciences, . . .upon condition that they comport themselves in other respects according to that which is contained in this our present edict.

8. It is permitted to all lords, gentlemen, and other persons making profession of the said religion called Reformed, holding the right of high justice, to exercise the said religion in their houses.

9. We also permit those of the said religion to make and continue the exercise of the same in all villages and places of our dominion where it was established by them and publicly enjoyed several and divers times in the year 1597, up to the end of the month of August, notwithstanding all decrees and judgments to the contrary.

13. We very expressly forbid to all those of the said religion its exercise, either in respect to ministry, regulation, discipline, or the public instruction of children, or otherwise, in this our kingdom and lands of our dominion, otherwise than in the places permitted and granted by the present edict.

14. It is forbidden as well to perform any function of the said religion in our court or retinue, or in our lands and territories beyond the mountains, or in our city of Paris, or within five leagues of the said city.

18. We also forbid all our subjects, of whatever quality and condition, from carrying off by force or persuasion, against the will of their parents, the children of the said religion, in order to cause them to be baptized or confirmed in the Catholic Apostolic and Roman Church; and the same is forbidden to those of the said religion called Reformed, upon penalty of being punished with especial severity.

21. Books concerning the said religion called Reformed may not be printed and publicly sold, except in cities and places where the public exercise of the said religion is permitted.

22. We ordain that there shall be no difference or distinction made in respect to the said religion, in receiving pupils to be instructed in universities, colleges, and schools; nor in receiving the sick and poor into hospitals, retreats, and public charities. . . .

From *Readings in European History*, edited by J. H. Robinson. Boston: Ginn, 1906.

The Demolition of Feudal Castles, 1626

The French "Wars of Religion" were not fought only over religious differences. They were also a part of the struggle of many of the high nobles of the kingdom against the increasing centralization of authority. In 1626 Louis XIII ordered the destruction of all fortresses in the interior of France, from which these nobles had often defied royal power.

Whereas formerly the assemblies of the estates of this realm and those of notable persons chosen to give advice to ourselves, and to the late king, our very honorable lord and father, on important affairs of this realm, and likewise the assembly of the estates of the province of Brittany held by us in the year 1614, have repeatedly requested and very humbly supplicated our said lord and father and ourselves to cause the demolition of many strongholds in divers places of this realm, which, being neither on hostile frontiers nor in important passes or places, only serve to augment our expenses by the maintenance of useless garrisons, and also serve as retreats for divers persons who on the least provocation disturb the provinces where they are located; . . .

For these reasons, we announce, declare, ordain, and will that all the strongholds, either towns or castles, which are in the interior of our realm or provinces of the same, not situated in places of importance either for frontier defense or other considerations of weight, shall be razed and demolished; even ancient walls shall be destroyed so far as it shall be deemed necessary for the well-being and repose of our subjects and the security of this state, so that our said subjects henceforth need not fear that the said places will cause them any inconvenience, and so that we shall be freed from the expense of supporting garrisons in them.

From *Readings in European History*, edited by J. H. Robinson. Boston: Ginn, 1906.

Bossuet: from *Politics Drawn from the Very Words of Holy Scripture*

The medieval king had a quasi-sacred character, but his power and authority were limited. He ruled; he did not govern. His rule was based on personal relationships. As government was centralized, a new theory was needed to validate the kind of absolute authority for which Louis XIV strove. Jaques Bossuet was an outspoken proponent of the "divine right" of kings.

We have already seen that all power is of God. The ruler, adds St. Paul, "is the minister of God to thee for good. But if thou do that which is evil, be afraid; for he beareth not the sword in vain: for he is the minister of God, a revenger to execute wrath upon him that doeth evil."[88] Rulers then act as the ministers of God and as his lieutenants on earth. It is through them that God exercises his empire. Think ye "to withstand the kingdom of the Lord in the hand of the sons of David"?[89] Consequently, as we have seen, the royal throne is not the throne of a man, but the throne of God himself. The Lord "hath chosen Solomon my son to sit upon the throne of the kingdom of the Lord over Israel."[90] And again, "Solomon sat on the throne of the Lord."[91]

Moreover, that no one may assume that the Israelites were peculiar in having kings over them who were established by God, note what is said in Ecclesiasticus: "God has given to every people its ruler, and Israel is manifestly reserved to him."[92] He therefore governs all peoples and gives them their kings, although he governed Israel in a more intimate and obvious manner.

It appears from all this that the person of the king is sacred, and that to attack him in any way is sacrilege. God has the kings anointed by his prophets with the holy unction in like manner as he has bishops and altars anointed. But even without the external application in thus being anointed, they are by their very office the representatives of the divine majesty deputed by Providence for the execution of his purposes. Accordingly God calls Cyrus his anointed. "Thus saith the Lord to his anointed, to Cyrus, whose right hand I have holden, to subdue nations before

---

[88] See Romans 13: 1-7.
[89] II Chronicles 13:8.
[90] I Chronicles 28:5.
[91] I Chronicles 29:23.
[92] Ecclesiasticus 17:14,15.

him."[93] . . . Kings should be guarded as holy things, and whosoever neglects to protect them is worthy of death. . . .

There is something religious in the respect accorded to a prince. The service of God and the respect for kings are bound together. St. Peter unites these two duties when he says, "Fear God. Honour the king."[94] . . .

The royal power is absolute. With the aim of making this truth hateful and insufferable, many writers have tried to confound absolute government with arbitrary government. But no two things could be more unlike, as we shall show when we come to speak of justice.

The prince need render account of his acts to no one. "I counsel thee to keep the king's commandment, and that in regard of the oath of God. Be not hasty to go out of his sight; stand not on an evil thing for he doeth whatsoever pleaseth him. Where the word of a king is, there is power; and who may say unto him, What doest thou? Whoso keepeth the commandment shall feel no evil thng."[95] Without this absolute authority the king could neither do good nor repress evil. It is necessary that his power be such that no one can hope to escape him, and, finally, the only protection of individuals against the public authority should be their innocence. This conforms with the teaching of St. Paul: "Wilt thou then be afraid of power? Do that which is good."[96]

I do not call majesty that pomp which surrounds kings or that exterior magnificence which dazzles the vulgar. That is but the reflection of majesty and not majesty itself. Majesty is the image of the grandeur of God in the prince.

God is infinite, God is all. The prince, as prince, is not regarded as a private person; he is a public personage, all the state is in him; the will of all the people is included in his. As all perfection and all strength are united in God, so all the power of individuals is united in the person of the prince. What grandeur that a single man should embody so much!

The power of God makes itself felt in a moment from one extremity of the earth to another. Royal power works at the same time throughout all the realm. It holds all the realm in position, as God holds the earth. Should God withdraw his hand, the earth would fall to pieces; should the king's authority cease in the realm, all would be in confusion. . . .

Finally, let us put together the things so great and so august which we have said about royal authority. Behold an immense people united in a single person; behold this holy power, paternal and absolute; behold the secret cause which governs the whole body of the state, contained in a single head: you see the image of God in the king, and you have the idea of royal majesty. God is holiness itself, goodness itself, and power itself. In these things lies the majesty of God. In the image of these things lies the majesty of the prince. . . .

From *Readings in European History*, edited by J. H. Robinson. Boston: Ginn, 1906.

---

[93] Isaiah 14:1.

[94] I Peter 2:17.

[95] Ecclesiasticus 8:2-5

[96] Romans 13:3.

Louis XIV: Letter to the Officials of Marseilles, 1664

Under Colbert, France practiced an economic policy known as mercantilism, in which the state plays a significant role in protecting, regulating, and stimulating the economy. In this letter to the officials of Marseilles, France's principal port on the Mediterranean, Louis describes many of the elements of seventeenth-century French mercantilism.

Considering how advantageous it would be to this realm to reestablish its foreign and domestic commerce, . . . we have resolved to establish a council particularly devoted to commerce, to be held every fortnight in our presence, in which all the interests of merchants and the means conducive to the revival of commerce shall be considered and determined upon, as well as all that which concerns manufactures.

We also inform you that we are setting apart, in the expenses of our state, a million *livres* each year for the encouragement of manufactures and the increase of navigation, to say nothing of the considerable sums which we cause to be raised to supply the companies of the East and West Indies;

That we are working constantly to abolish all the tolls which are collected on the navigable rivers;

That there has already been expended more than a million *livres* for the repair of the public highways, to which we shall also devote our constant attention;

That we will assist by money from our royal treasury all those who wish to reestablish old manufactures or to undertake new ones;

That we are giving orders to all our ambassadors or residents at the courts of the princes, our allies, to make, in our name, all proper efforts to cause justice to be rendered in all cases involving our merchants, and to assure for them entire commercial freedom;

That we will comfortably lodge at our court each and every merchant who has business there during all the time that he shall be obliged to remain there, having given orders to the grand marshal of our palace to indicate a proper place for that purpose, which shall be called the House of Commerce; . . .

That all the merchants and traders by sea who purchase vessels, or who build new ones, for traffic or commerce shall receive from us subsidies for each ton of merchandise which they export or import on the said voyages.

We desire, in this present letter, not only to inform you concerning all these things, but to require you, as soon as you have received it, to cause to be assembled all the merchants and traders of your town of Marseilles, and explain to them very particularly our intentions in all matters mentioned above, in order that, being informed of the favorable treatment which we desire to give them, they may be the more desirous of applying themselves to commerce. Let them understand that for everything that concerns the welfare and advantage of the same they are to address themselves to Sieur Colbert. . . .

From *Readings in European History*, edited by J. H. Robinson. Boston: Ginn, 1906.

from the *Memoires* of the Duke of St. Simon

The rich descriptions of the Duke provide intimate details of Louis's life and his style of government.

The king's great qualities shone more brilliantly by reason of an exterior so unique and incomparable as to lend infinite distinction to his slightest actions; the very figure of a hero, so impregnated with a natural but most imposing majesty that it appeared even in his most insignificant gestures and movements, without arrogance but with simple gravity; proportions such as a sculptor would choose to model; a perfect countenance and the grandest air and mien ever vouchsafed to man; all these advantages enhanced by a natural grace which enveloped all his actions with a singular charm which has never perhaps been equaled. He was as dignified and majestic in his dressing gown as when dressed in robes of state, or on horseback at the head of his troops.

He excelled in all sorts of exercise and liked to have every facility for it. No fatigue nor stress of weather made any impression on that heroic figure and bearing; drenched with rain or snow, pierced with cold, bathed in sweat or covered with dust, he was always the same. I have often observed with admiration that except in the most extreme and exceptional weather nothing prevented his spending considerable time out of doors every day.

A voice whose tones corresponded with the rest of his person; the ability to speak well and to listen with quick comprehension; much reserve of manner adjusted with exactness to the quality of different persons; a courtesy always grave, always dignified, always distinguished, and suited to the age, rank, and sex of each individual, and, for the ladies, always an air of natural gallantry. So much for his exterior, which has never been equaled nor even approached.

In whatever did not concern what he believed to be his rightful authority and prerogative, he showed a natural kindness of heart and a sense of justice which made one regret the education, the flatteries, the artifice which resulted in preventing him from being his real self except on the rare occasions when he gave way to some natural impulse and showed that,—prerogative aside, which choked and stifled everything,—he loved truth, justice, order, reason,—that he loved even to let himself be vanquished.

Nothing could be regulated with greater exactitude than were his days and hours. In spite of all his variety of places, affairs, and amusements, with an almanac and a watch one might tell, three hundred leagues away, exactly what he was doing. . . . Except at Marly, any man could have an opportunity to speak to him five or six times during the day; he listened, and almost always replied, "I will see," in order not to accord or decide anything lightly. Never a reply or a speech that would give pain; patient to the last degree in business and in matters of personal service; completely master of his face, manner, and bearing; never giving way to impatience or anger. If he administered reproof, it was rarely, in few words, and never hastily. He did not lose control of himself ten times in his whole life, and then only with inferior persons, and not more than four or five times seriously.

Louis XIV's vanity was without limit or restraint; it colored everything and convinced him that no one even approached him in military talents, in plans and enterprises, in government. Hence those pictures and inscriptions in the gallery at Versailles which disgust every foreigner; those opera prologues that he himself tried to sing; that flood of prose and verse in his praise for which his appetite was insatiable; those dedications of statues copied from pagan sculpture, and the insipid and sickening compliments that were continually offered to him in person and which he swallowed with unfailing relish; hence his distaste for all merit, intelligence, education, and, most of all, for all independence of character and sentiment in others; his mistakes of judgment in matters of importance; his familiarity and favor reserved entirely for those to whom he felt himself superior in acquirements and ability; and, above everything else, a jealousy of his own authority which determined and took precedence of every other sort of justice, reason, and consideration whatever.

From Readings in European History, edited by J. H. Robinson. Boston: Ginn, 1906.

Louis XIV took great pains to be well informed of all that passed everywhere; in the public places, in the private homes, in society and familiar intercourse. His spies and tell-tales were infinite. He had them of all species; many who were ignorant that their information reached him; others who knew it; others who wrote to him direct, sending their letters through channels he indicated; and all these letters were seen by him alone, and always before everything else; others who sometimes spoke to him secretly in his cabinet, entering by the back stairs. These unknown means ruined an infinite number of people of all classes, who never could discover the cause; often ruined them very unjustly; for the King, once prejudiced, never altered his opinion, or so rarely, that nothing was more rare. He had, too, another fault, very dangerous for others and often for himself, since it deprived him of good subjects. He had an excellent memory; in this way, that if he saw a man who, twenty years before, perhaps, had in some manner offended him, he did not forget the man, though he might forget the offence. This was enough, however, to exclude the person from all favour. The representations of a minister, of a general, of his confessor even, could not move the King. He would not yield.

The most cruel means by which the King was informed of what was passing—for many years before anybody knew it—was that of opening letters. The promptitude and dexterity with which they were opened passes understanding. He saw extracts from all the letters in which there were passages that the chiefs of the post-office, and then the minister who governed it, thought ought to go before him; entire letters, too, were sent to him, when their contents seemed to justify the sending. Thus the chiefs of the post, nay, the principal clerks were in a position to suppose what they pleased and against whom they pleased. A word of contempt against the King or the government, a joke, a detached phrase, was enough. It is incredible how many people, justly or unjustly, were more or less ruined, always without resource, without trial, and without knowing why. The secret was impenetrable; for nothing ever cost the King less than profound silence and dissimulation. . . .

From The Memoires of the Duke of Saint-Simon, edited by Bayle St. John. New York: James Pott, 1901.

Revocation of the Edict of Nantes, 1685

The Catholic faith was probably more compatible than the Reformed with an absolutist state. Louis XIV revoked the Edict of Nantes. About 250,000 Protestants fled, most of them to England, Prussia, Holland, or America.

Louis, by the grace of God king of France and Navarre, to all present and to come, greeting:

King Henry the Great, our grandfather of glorious memory, being desirous that the peace which he had procured for his subjects after the grievous losses they had sustained in the course of domestic and foreign wars, should not be troubled on account of the religion called Reformed, as had happened in the reigns of the kings, his predecessors, by his edict, granted at Nantes in the month of April, 1598, regulated the procedure to be adopted with regard to those of the said religion, and the places in which they might meet for public worship, established extraordinary judges to administer justice to them, and, in fine, provided in particular articles for whatever could be thought necessary for maintaining the tranquillity of his kingdom and for diminishing mutual aversion between the members of the two religions, so as to put himself in a better position to labor, as he had resolved to do, for the reunion to the Church of those who had so lightly withdrawn from it.

As the intention of the king, our grandfather, was frustrated by his sudden death, and as the execution of the said edict was interrupted during the minority of the late king, our most honored lord and father of glorious memory, by new encroachments on the part of the adherents of the said religion known as Reformed, which gave occasion for their being deprived of divers advantages accorded to them by the said edict; nevertheless the king, our late lord and father, in the exercise of his usual clemency, granted them yet another edict at Nîmes, in July, 1629, by means of which, tranquillity being established anew, the said late king, animated by the same spirit and the same zeal for religion as the king, our said grandfather, had resolved to take advantage of this repose to attempt to put his said pious design into execution. But foreign wars having supervened soon after, so that the kingdom was seldom tranquil from 1635 to the truce concluded in 1684 with the powers of Europe, nothing more could be done for the advantage of religion beyond diminishing the number of places for the public exercise of the religion known as Reformed, interdicting such places as were found established to the prejudice of the dispositions made by the edicts, and suppressing of the bi-partisan courts, these having been appointed provisionally only.

God having at last permitted that our people should enjoy perfect peace, we, no longer absorbed in protecting them from our enemies, are able to profit by this truce (which we have ourselves facilitated), and devote our whole attention to the means of accomplishing the designs of our said grandfather and father, which we have consistently kept before us since our succession to the crown.

And now we perceive, with thankful acknowledgment of God's aid, that our endeavors have attained their proposed end, inasmuch as the better and the greater part of our subjects of the religion known as Reformed have embraced the Catholic faith. And since by this fact the execution of the Edict of Nantes and of all that has ever been ordained in favor of the said religion known as Reformed has been rendered nugatory, we have determined that we can do nothing better, in order wholly to obliterate the memory of the troubles, the confusion, and the evils which the progress of this false religion has caused in this kingdom, and which furnished occasion for the said edict and for so many previous and subsequent edicts and declarations, than entirely to revoke the said Edict of Nantes, with the special articles granted as a sequel to it, as well as all that has since been done in favor of the said religion.

1. Be it known that for these causes and others us hereunto moving, and of our certain knowledge, full power, and royal authority, we have, by this present perpetual and irrevocable edict, suppressed and revoked, and do suppress and revoke, the edict of our said grandfather, given at Nantes in April, 1598, in its whole extent, together with the particular articles agreed upon in the month of May following, and the letters patent issued upon the same date; and also

the edict given at Nîmes in July, 1629; we declare them null and void, together with all concessions, of whatever nature they may be, made by them as well as by other edicts, declarations, and orders, in favor of the said persons of the religion known as Reformed, the which shall remain in like manner as if they had never been granted; and in consequence we desire, and it is our pleasure, that all the temples of those of the said religion known as Reformed situate in our kingdom, countries, territories, and the lordships under our crown, shall be demolished without delay.

2. We forbid our subjects of the religion known as Reformed to meet anymore for the exercise of the said religion in any place or private house, under any pretext whatever, . . .

3. We likewise forbid all noblemen, of what condition soever, to hold such religious exercises in their houses or fiefs, under penalty to be inflicted upon all our said subjects who shall engage in the said exercises, of imprisonment and confiscation.

4. We enjoin all ministers of the said religion known as Reformed, who do not choose to become converts and to embrace the Catholic, apostolic, and Roman religion, to leave our kingdom and the territories subject to us within a fortnight of the publication of our present edict, without leave to reside therein beyond that period, or, during the said fortnight, to engage in any preaching, exhortation, or any other function, on pain of being sent to the galleys. . . .

7. We forbid private schools for the instruction of children of the religion known as Reformed, and in general all things whatever which can be regarded as a concession of any kind in favor of the said religion.

8. As for children who may be born of persons of the religion known as Reformed, we desire that from henceforth they be baptized by the parish priests. We enjoin parents to send them to the churches for that purpose, under penalty of five hundred *livres* fine, to be increased as circumstances may demand; and thereafter the children shall be brought up in the Catholic, apostolic, and Roman religion, which we expressly enjoin the local magistrates to see done.

10. We repeat our most express prohibition to all our subjects of the said religion known as Reformed, together with their wives and children, against leaving our kingdom, lands, and territories subject to us, or transporting their goods and effects therefrom under penalty, as respects the men, of being sent to the galleys, and as respects the women, of imprisonment and confiscation.

12. As for the rest, liberty is granted to the said persons of the religion known as Reformed, pending the time when it shall please God to enlighten them as well as others, to remain in the cities and places of our kingdom, lands, and territories subject to us, and there to continue their commerce, and to enjoy their possessions, without being subjected to molestation or hindrance on account of the said religion known as Reformed, on condition of not engaging in the exercise of the said religion, or of meeting under pretext of prayers or religious services, of whatever nature these may be, under the penalties above mentioned of imprisonment and confiscation. This do we give in charge to our trusty and well-beloved counselors, etc.

Given at Fontainebleau in the month of October, in the year of grace 1685, and of our reign the forty-third.

From *Readings in European History*, edited by J. H. Robinson. Boston: Ginn, 1906.

<u>Isabel Charras: Renewed Persecution, 1707</u>

Among the Huguenots who fled France because of the renewed persecution after the revocation of the Edict of Nantes were a group who experienced visions. One of them here describes the deaths she witnessed while still in France.

Isabel Charras of Les Roches, half a League from St. Greve, in the Vellay, declared the 19th of February 1706 (March 5, 1707, New Style):

I left France in the Year 1696. From the beginning of 1689, for seven years complete, until my leaving that country, I saw in the Velay abundance of people of every age and sex, that fell into violent agitations of body, in an extraordinary manner; during which they uttered large discourses, very pious, and strongly hortatory of repentance. They had also predictions of the ruin of mystical Babylon, with assurances that the Church would speedily be delivered out of affliction. They were forewarned and directed in a multitude of things, relating either to their own particular conduct, or to the religious assemblies (held almost daily in secret) for their safety. They always spoke good French in the inspiration, though they never could at other times; and during their discourses then, they spoke in the manner as if the Divine Spirit has spoken in them, saying "I tell thee," "I declare to thee," "my child," etc.

As 'tis many years ago, that I have left that country, I will not fix the times of several remarkable particulars here recited, though the certainty of them be no ways the less for it, for I relate nothing, but what I heard and saw, and what I well remember.

One John Heraut of our neighbourhood, and four or five of his children, had all of them the gift of inspiration, the two youngest were, one of five and a half, and the other seven years old, when they first had it. I have seen these many a time, in their ecstasies. Another of our neighbours, named Marliant, had two sons and three daughters in the same state. One of his daughters being big, and within a month of her time, went with the rest of her brothers and sisters, and a boy of her own about seven, to an assembly for worship. In that assembly, she with her child, a brother and sister, were massacred. The brother that escaped was wounded, but recovered. The youngest sister was left for dead among the slaughtered bodies, but had no harm. One of the two sisters butchered was brought home to her father's yet alive, but she died of her wounds a few days after. I was not at that assembly, but saw the sad spectacles of the slain and wounded. What was most remarkable on that occurrence is that the father, the surviving brother and sister, a nephew, and the whole family assured me that those martyrs were forewarned of their death by the inspiration. They acquainted their father as much, in taking leave of him, and asking him blessing, the same evening, when they went out of doors, to go to that assembly, which was by night. When the father beheld these lamentable objects, he did not abandon himself and sink under grief, but on the contrary only said, with a pious resignation "The Lord gave, and the Lord has taken away. Blessed by the name of the Lord."

From *A Cry from the Desart*, edited by François-Maximilien Misson, translated by John Lacy. London: B. Bragg, 1707.

Unit 37: Constitutional Government

After the death of Queen Elizabeth in 1603, James VI of Scotland became King James I of England. He, too, believed in the divine right of monarchs to rule without restriction, answerable only to God. But the Parliament of England had become accustomed to sharing authority with its kings, and England followed its own route to a new form of government—a monarchy subject to law and to the approval of representatives of the people.

The Petition of Right, 1628

The Scottish kings, James I and Charles I, were unable or unwilling to adapt to the expectations of Parliament. In 1628, Parliament delivered to Charles a list of grievances.

To The King's Most Excellent Majesty:

Humbly show unto our Sovereign Lord the King, the Lords Spiritual and Temporal, and Commons in Parliament assembled, that whereas it is declared and enacted by a statute made in the time of the reign of King Edward the First,[97] commonly called *Statutum de Tallagio non concedendo,* that no tallage or aid shall be laid or levied by the King or his heirs in this realm, without the goodwill and assent of the Archbishops, Bishops, Earls, Barons, Knights, Burgesses, and other the freemen of the commonalty of this realm: and by authority of Parliament held in the five and twentieth year of the reign of King Edward the Third[98], it is declared and enacted, that from thenceforth no person shall be compelled to make any loans to the King against his will, because such loans were against reason and the franchise of the land; and by other laws of this realm it is provided, that none should be charged by any charge or imposition, called a Benevolence, or by such like charge, by which the statutes before-mentioned, and other the good laws and statutes of this realm, your subjects have inherited this freedom, that they should not be compelled to contribute any tax, tallage, aid, or other like charge, not set by common consent in Parliament:

Yet nevertheless, of late divers commissions directed to sundry Commissioners in several counties with instructions have issued, by means whereof your people have been in divers places assembled, and required to lend certain sums of money unto your Majesty, and many of them upon their refusal so to do have had an oath administered unto them, not warrantable by the laws or statutes of this realm, and have been constrained to become bound to make appearnace and give attendance before your Privy Council, and in other places, and others of them have been therefore imprisoned, confined, and in sundry other ways molested and disquieted. . . .

And where also by the statute called, "The Great Charter of the Liberties of England,"[99] it is declared and enacted, that no freeman may be taken or imprisoned or be disseised of his freeholds or liberties, or his free customs, or be outlawed or exiled, or in any manner destroyed, but by the lawful judgment of his peers, or by the law of the land. . . .

And whereas of late great companies of soldiers and mariners have been dispersed into divers counties of the realm, and the inhabitants against their wills have been compelled to receive them into their houses, and there to suffer them to stay, against the laws and customs of this realm, and to the great grievance and vexation of the people. . . .

They do therefore humbly pray your Most Excellent Majesty, that no man hereafter be compelled to make or yield any gift, loan, benevolence, tax, or such like charge, without common

---

[97] 1272-1307

[98] 1352

[99] 1215

consent by Act of Parliament; and that none be called to make answer, or take such oath, or to give attendance, or be confined, or otherwise molested or disquieted concerning the same, or for refusal thereof; and that no freeman, in any such manner as is beforementioned, be imprisoned or detained; and that your majesty will be pleased to remove the said soldiers and mariners, and that your people may not be so burdened in time to come; . . .

All which they most humbly pray of your Most Excellent Majesty, as their rights and liberties according to the laws and statutes of this realm.

From *The Constitutional Documents of Constitutional History*, edited by G. Adams and H. Stephens. New York: Macmillan, 1916.

A Pamphlet on the Civil War

After a serious attempt by Parliament in 1629 to limit royal prerogatives, Charles refused to summon the Parliament for eleven years. Finally, when he was forced to call them together to raise money to put down a rebellion in Scotland, the confrontation resumed and resulted in Civil War.

The war went on with horrid rage in many places at one time; and the fire, when once kindled, cast forth, through every corner of the land, not only sparks but devouring flames; insomuch that the kingdom of England was divided into more seats of war than counties; nor has she more fields than skirmishes, nor cities than sieges; and almost all the palaces of lords, and other great houses, were turned everywhere into garrisons of war. They fought at once by sea and land; and through all England (who could but lament the miseries of his country!) sad spectacles were seen of plundering and firing villages; and the fields, otherwise waste and desolate, were rich only and terribly glorious in camps and armies.

From *Readings in European History*, edited by J. H. Robinson. Boston, Ginn, 1906.

Charles I: At His Execution, 1649

At the end of the Civil War, Oliver Cromwell purged Parliament of those who favored restoration of the monarchy. A rump Parliament deposed Charles I and created a High Court, which tried and convicted him for treason. At the scaffold, he continued to insist on the sovereignty of the monarch.

[As for the people,] truly I desire their liberty and freedom as much as anybody whomsoever; but I must tell you that their liberty and freedom consist in having of government, those laws by which their life and their goods may be most their own. It is not for having share in government, sirs; that is nothing pertaining to them; a subject and a sovereign are clear different things. And therefore until they do that, I mean that you do put the people in that liberty, as I say, certainly they will never enjoy themselves. Sirs, it was for this that now I am come here. If I would have given way to an arbitrary way, for to have all laws changed according to the power of the sword, I needed not to have come here; and therefore I tell you (and I pray God it be not laid to your charge) that I am the martyr of the people. . . .

From *Readings in European History*, edited by J. H. Robinson. Boston, Ginn, 1906.

Declaration of the Commonwealth, 1649

Be it declared and enacted by this present Parliament, and by the authority of the same, that the people of England, and of all the dominions and territories thereunto belonging, are and shall be, and are hereby constituted, made established, and confirmed, to be a Commonwealth and Free State, and shall from henceforth be governed as a Commonwealth and Free State by the supreme authority of this nation, the representatives of the people in Parliament, and by such as they shall appoint and constitute as officers and ministers under them for the good of the people, and that without any king or House of Lords.

From *The Constitutional Documents of the Puritan Revolution*, edited by S. R. Gardiner. 1899,

Burnet: The Act Against Dissenters, 1670

After the military rule of Oliver Cromwell, a limited monarchy was restored in 1660. Religious issues continued to plague the country. Parliament, in 1664, declared all religious meetings, except those in accordance with the rules of the Church of England, to be illegal. Eighteen years later, the "Glorious Revolution" would bring to the throne William of Orange and his wife Mary, to rule by grace of Parliament, not "by the grace of God."

When [after the great London fire of 1666] the city was pretty well rebuilt, they began to take care of the churches, which had lain in ashes some years; and in that time conventicles abounded in all parts of the city. It was thought hard to hinder men from worshiping God any way as they could, when there were no churches, nor ministers to look after them. But now they began to raise churches of boards, till the public allowance should be raised towards the building of churches. These they called tabernacles, and they fitted them up with pews and galleries as churches. So now an act was proposed reviving the former act against conventicles. . . . This act was executed in the city very severely in Starling's mayoralty, and put things in such disorder that many of the trading men of the city began to talk of removing with their stock over to Holland; but the king ordered a stop be put to further severities.

Many of the sects either discontinued their meetings or held them very secretly, with small numbers, and not in the hours of public worship; yet informers were encouraged and were everywhere at work. The behavior of the Quakers was more particular, and had something in it that looked bold. They met at the same place and at the same hour as before; and when they were seized, none of them would go out of the way: they went all together to prison; they stayed there till they were dismissed, for they would not petition to be set at liberty, nor would they pay the fines set on them, nor so much as the jail fees, calling these wages of unrighteousness. And as son as they were let out they went to their meeting-houses again; and when they found these were shut up by order, they held their meetings on the street, before the doors of those houses. They said that they would not disown or be ashamed of their meeting together to worship God; but in imitation of Daniel, they would do it the more publicly because they were forbidden doing it. Some called this obstinacy, while others called it firmness. But by it they carried their point, for the government grew weary of dealing with so much perverseness and so began with letting them alone.

From *Readings in European History*, edited by J. H. Robinson. Boston: Ginn, 1906

CHAPTER 17: THE SCIENTIFIC REVOLUTION

Unit 38: Astronomy and Mathematics

The word "revolution" suggests rapid change, but the change in scientific thinking from a primarily theoretical, deductive system to one based on observation and experimentation was spread over at least two centuries. Thomas Kuhn has said that a new scientific paradigm does not really become firmly entrenched until the old generation, keepers of the old paradigm, dies off.

Copernicus first published his heliocentric theory in 1534. When Galileo defended it ninety-eight years later, he was condemned by the Inquisition and ordered not to teach it. Several generations had to die before the new ideas would be generally accepted.

From William Harvey: *Circulation of the Blood,* 1628

Harvey's description of the circulation of the blood and the work of the heart as a pump opened the way for a new understanding of physiology. In this selection, his reliance on observation and experimentation is clear.

Chapter II: What Manner of Motion the Heart Has in the Dissection of living Creatures

First then in the hearts of all creatures, being dissected while they are yet alive, opening the breast, and cutting up the capsule which immediately surrounds the heart, you may observe that the heart moves sometimes, sometimes rests: and that there is a time when it moves, and when it moves not.

This is more evident in the hearts of colder creatures as the toads, serpents, frogs, housesnails, shrimps, crayfish, and all manner of little fishes. For it shows itself more manifestly in the hearts of hotter bodies, as of dogs, swine, if you observe attentively till the heart begin to die, and move faintly, and life is as it were departing from it. Then you may clearly and plainly see that the motions of it are more slow, and seldom, and the restings of it longer: and you may observe and distinguish more easily, what manner of motion it is, and which ways it is made, in the resting of it, as likewise in death, the heart is yielding, flagging, weak, and lies as it were dropping.

At the motion, and while it is moving, three things are chiefly to be observed.

That the heart is erected and that it raises itself upwards into a point, insomuch that it beats the breast at that time, so that the pulsation is felt outwardly.

That there is a contraction of it every way, especially of the sides of it, so that it appears lesser, longer and contracted. The heart of an eel, taken out and laid upon a trencher, or upon one's hand, evidences this: It appears likewise in the hearts of little fishes, and of those colder animals whose hearts are sharp at top and long.

That the heart being grasped in one's hand while it is in motion, feels harder. This hardness arises from tension, like as if one take hold of the tendons on one's arm by the elbow while they are moving the fingers, one shall feel them bent and more resisting.

It is moreover to be observed in fish and colder animals which have blood, as serpents, frogs, at that time when the heart moves it becomes whitish; when it leaves motion it appears full of sanguine colour. From hence it seemed to me, that the motion of the heart was a kind of tension in every part of it according to the drawing and constriction of the fibers every way, because it appeared that in all its motions, it was erected, received vigour, grew lesser, and harder, and that the motion of it was like that of the muscles, where the contraction is made according to the drawing of the nervous parts and fibers, for the muscles while thy are in motion, and in action, are envigorated, and stretched, of soft become hard, they are uplifted, and thickened, so likewise the heart.

From which observations with good reason we may gather that the heart at that time while it is in motion, suffers constriction and is thickened in its outside, and so straightened in its ventricle, thrusting forth the blood contained within it: which from the fourth observation is evident, because that in the tension it become white, having thrust out the blood contained within it and presently after in its relaxation, and rest, a purple and crimson colour returns to the heart. But of this no man needs to make any further scruple, since upon the inflicting of a wound into the heart, in the very tension, you shall see the blood within contained to leap out.

So then these things happen at one and the same time, the tension of the heart, the erection of the point, the beating (which is felt outwardly) by reason of its hitting against the breast, the thickening of the sides of it, and the forcible protrusion of the blood by constriction of the ventricles.

Hence the contrary of the commonly received opinion appears which is, that the heart at that time when it beats against the breast, and the pulsation is outwardly felt, it is believed that the ventricles of the heart are dilated, and replete with blood, though you shall understand that it is otherwise and that when the heart is contracted it is emptied. For that motion which is commonly thought the Diastole of the heart, is really the Systole, and so the proper motion of the heart is not a Diastole but a Systole, for the heart receives no vigour in the Diastole, but in the Systole, for then it is extended, moves and receives vigour.

Neither is that to be allowed, though it is confirmed by a comparison alleged by the Divine Vesalius,100 of a wreath of osiers, meaning of many twigs, joined together in fashion of a pyramid: that the heart does not only move by the straight fibers, and so while the top is brought near to the bottom, the sides of it are dilated round about, and do acquire the form of a little gourd, and so take in blood (for according to all the drawing of the fibers which it has, the heart is stiffened and gathered together). But that the outside and substance of it are rather thickened and dilated, and that while the fibers are stretched from the top of the corner to the bottom, the sides of the heart do not incline to an orbicular figure, but rather contrary, as every fiber circular lies placed, does in its contraction incline to straightness and as all the fibers of the muscles while they are contracted and shortened of their length so towards the sides they are extended, and are thickened after the same fashion as the bodies of the muscles.

---

100 Andreas Vesalius, *On the Fabric of the Human Body*, 1543; considered by some the foundation of modern anatomy.

To this add, that not only in the motion of the heart by erection and thickening of the sides of it, it so falls out, that the ventricles are straightened, but moreover all the sides inwardly are girt together as it were with a noose, for expelling the blood with greater force, by reason that those fibers or little tendons, amongst which there are none but straight ones, (for those in the outside are circular) called by Aristotle, nerves, are various in the ventricles of the heart of greater creatures, while they are contracted together with a most admirable frame.

Neither is it true which is commonly believed, that the heart by any motion or distention of its own draws blood into the ventricles, but while it is moved and bended, the blood is thrust forth, and when it is relaxed and falls, the blood is received in manner as follows. . .

Adapted from an anonymous English translation, 1653.

From Galileo: *Dialogue on the Two Chief Systems of the World, 1632*

Galileo's defense of Copernicus heliocentric theory takes the form of a dialogue.

The Probability of the Earth's Motion

Salviati: Let our contemplation begin therefore with this consideration, that whatever motion may be ascribed to the Earth, it is necessary that it be to us, (as inhabitants upon it, and consequently partakers of the same) totally imperceptible, as if it did not exist, so long as we have regard only to terrestrial things; yet it is on the contrary, as necessary that the same motion seem common to all other bodies and visible objects that, being separated from the Earth, do not participate in its motion. So that the true method to find whether any kind of motion may be ascribed to the Earth, and that found, to know what it is, is to consider and observe if, in bodies separated from the Earth, one may discover any appearance of motion, which equally suits to all the rest. For a motion that is only seen, e.g. in the Moon, and that has nothing to do with Venus or Jupiter, or any other Stars, cannot any way belong to the Earth, or to any other save the Moon alone. Now there is a most general and grand motion above all others and it is that by which the Sun, the Moon, the other Planets, and the Fixed Stars, and in a word, the whole Universe, except for the Earth, appears in our thinking to move from the East towards the West, in the space of twenty-four hours. And this, as in this first appearance, has no obstacle to hinder it, that it may not belong to the Earth alone, as well as to all the world besides, the Earth excepted; for the same aspects will appear in the one portion, as in the other. Hence it is that Aristotle and Ptolemy, having hit upon this consideration, in going about to prove the Earth to be immoveable, argue only against the diurnal motion; except that Aristotle hints in obscure terms against another motion ascribed to it by an Ancient, of which we shall speak in its place. . .

Sagrado: I find my fancy disturbed with certain conjectures so confusedly sprung from your later discourses; that, if I am to apply myself with attention to what follows, I must of necessity attempt whether I can better methodize them, and gather thence their true construction, if haply any can be made of them; and peradventure, the proceeding by questions may help me the more easily to express myself. Therefore, I demand first of Simplicius, whether he believes that different motions may naturally agree to one and the same moveable body, or is it necessary that it have only one natural and proper motion.

Simplicius: For one moveable thing, there can naturally be only one motion, and no more; the rest all happen accidentally and by participation; like he who walks on the deck of a ship. His proper motion is that of his walk, his motion by participation that which carries him to his port, where he would never have arrived by walking, if the ship with its motion had not brought him there.

Sagrado: Tell me secondly. That motion, which is communicated to any moveable thing by participation, while it moves by itself with another motion different from the participated, is it necessary that it reside in a certain subject, or can it subsist in nature alone?

Simplicius: Aristotle gives an answer to all these questions, and says that, just as there is only one motion of any moveable thing, so there is only one moveable thing for any motion. Consequently, without the inherence in its subject, no motion can either subsist or be imagined.

Sagrado: Please tell me, in the third place, whether you believe that the Moon and other Planets and celestial bodies have their proper motions, and what they are.

Simplicius: They have so, and they are those according to which they run though the Zodiac—the Moon in a month, the Sun in a year, Mars in two, the Starry Sphere in so many thousand. And these are their proper, or natural, motions.

Sagrado: But that motion by which I see the Fixed Stars and the Planets move together from East to West, and return to the East again in twenty-four hours, what is its relationship to them?

Simplicius: It is their motion by participation.

Sagrado: This, then, does not reside in them. Since it does not reside in them, and since it cannot subsist without some subject in which it resides, there must be some other sphere whose natural and proper motion it is.

Simplicius: For this purpose Astronomers and Philosophers have found another high sphere, above all the rest, without Stars, to which the diurnal motion belongs. This they call the Primum Mobile, which carries along with it all the lesser spheres, contributing and imparting its motion to them.

Sagrado: But when, without introducing other spheres unknown and hugely vast, without other motions or communicated raptures, leaving to each sphere its sole and simple motion, without intermixing contrary motions, but making all turn one way, as it is necessary that they do, all depending on a single principle, all things proceed in an orderly fashion and correspond with perfect harmony, why do we reject this Phenomenon and agree to those prodigious and laborious conditions?

Simplicius: The difficulty lies in finding this natural and expeditious way.

Sagrado: In my judgement this is found. Make the Earth the *Primum Mobile*; that is, make it turn round its own axis in twenty-four hours, and towards the same point with all the other spheres. Without imparting this motion to any other Planet or Star, all shall have their risings and settings and, in a word, all their other appearances.

Simplicius: The problem is to be able to make the Earth move without a thousand inconveniences.

Salvati: All the inconveniences shall be removed as fast as you propound them; and the things spoken thus far are only the primary and more general inducements which lead us to believe that the diurnal conversion may not altogether with all probability be applied to the Earth rather than to all the rest of the universe; which inducements I impose on you not as inviolable axioms, but as hints, which carry with them some likelihood. And I know well that a single experiment or conclusive demonstration showing the contrary will suffice to batter to the ground these and a thousand other probably arguments; therefore it is not fit to stay here, but proceed forward and hear what Simplicius answers, and what greater probabilities or stronger arguments he may allege for the opposing view.

Simplicius: I will first say something in general upon all these considerations together, and then I will descend to some particular. It seems that you found all you say upon the greater simplicity and facility of producing the same effects, while you argue that, to explain the cause of them, the motion of the earth alone serves as well as the motion of all the rest of the world, not including the Earth. And the operation of the latter, you claim, is much easier than of the former. To which I reply that I agree with you, so long as I think of my own finite and feeble power. But considering the strength of the Mover, which is infinite, it is no less easy to move the universe than the Earth, or even than a straw. And if his power is infinite, why should he not rather exercise more of it than less? Therefore, I hold that your argument in general is not convincing.

Salvati: If I had at any time said that the universe stood still for lack of power in the Mover, I should have erred and your reproof would have been merited. I grant you that, for an infinite power, it is as easy to move a hundred thousand as one. But what I said concerns not the Mover, but only the moveable things; and within them not just their resistance, which no doubt is lesser in the Earth than in the universe, but their many other particulars. As to your next point, that it is better to exercise a greater than a lesser part of an infinite power, I answer that, when speaking of the infinite, no part is greater than another, since both are infinite. Nor can it be said that a hundred thousand is a larger portion of the infinite number than is two, even though a hundred thousand is fifty times greater than two. If for the moving of the universe a finite power is required, though very great in comparison to that which suffices to move the earth; yet that great power is no greater a portion of the infinite power, nor is the remaining unused part less infinite. So, to apply a little more, or a little less, power to achieve a particular effect is meaningless. Besides, the goal of such an operation is not the diurnal motion alone; there are several other motions in the world that we know of, and there may be many others unknown to us. Therefore, if we respect the moveable things, and grant as out of the question that it is a shorter and easier way to move the Earth than the universe; moreover, considering the many other abbreviations and facilites that can only be obtained in this way, an infallible maxim of Aristotle, which he teaches us—"It is vain to assign many causes when few will do"—renders it more probable that the diurnal motion belongs to the Earth alone, than to the whole universe except the Earth.

Adapted from *Dialogue on the Two Chief Systems of the World*, translated by Thomas Salusbury. London, 1661.

René Descartes: *Discourse on Method*, 1637

Descartes explains how he tried nearly every kind of traditional learning before he came to his celebrated decision to believe only what he could know without a doubt to be true.

Part 1: From my childhood, I have been familiar with letters; and as I was given to believe that by their help a clear and certain knowledge of all that is useful in life might be acquired, I was ardently desirous of instruction. But as soon as I had finished the entire course of study, at the close of which it is customary to be admitted into the order of the learned, I completely changed my opinion. For I found myself involved in so many doubts and errors, that I was convinced I had advanced no farther in all my attempts at learning, than the discovery at every turn of my own ignorance. And yet I was studying in one of the most celebrated Schools in Europe, in which I thought there must be learned men, if such were anywhere to be found. I had been taught all that others learned there; and not contented with sciences actually taught us, I had, in addition, read all the books that had fallen into my hands, treating of such branches as are esteemed the most curious and rare. I knew the judgment which others had formed of me; and I did not find that I was considered inferior to my fellows, although there were among them some who were already marked out to fill the places of our instructors. And, in fine, our age appears, to me, as flourishing, and as fertile in powerful minds as any preceding one. I was thus led to take the liberty of judging of all other men by myself, and of concluding that there was no science in existence that was of such a nature as I had previously been given to believe.

I still continued, however, to hold in esteem the studies of the Schools. I was aware that the Languages taught in them are necessary to the understanding of the writings of the ancients; that the grace of Fable stirs the mind; that the memorable deeds of History elevate it; and, if read with discretion, aid in forming the judgment; that the perusal of all excellent books is, as it were, to interview with the noblest men of past ages, who have written them, and even a studied interview, in which are discovered to us only their choicest thoughts; that Eloquence has incomparable force and beauty; that Poesy has its ravishing graces and delights; that in the Mathematics there are many refined discoveries eminently suited to gratify the inquisitive, as well as further all the arts and lessen the labour of man; that numerous highly useful precepts and exhortations to virtue are contained in treatises on Morals; that Theology points out the path to heaven; that Philosophy affords the means of discoursing with an appearance of truth on all matters, and commands the admiration of the more simple; that Jurisprudence, Medicine, and the other Sciences, secure for their cultivators honours and riches; and in fine, that it is useful to bestow some attention upon all, even upon those abounding the most in superstition and error, that we may be in a position to determine their real value, and guard against being deceived.

But I believed that I had already given sufficient time to Languages, and likewise to the reading of the writings of the ancients, to their Histories and Fables. For to hold converse with those of other ages and to travel, are almost the same thing. It is useful to know something of the manners of different nations, that we may be enabled to form a more correct judgment regarding our own, and be prevented from thinking that everything contrary to our customs is ridiculous and irrational,—a conclusion usually come to by those whose experience has been limited to their own country. On the other hand, when too much time is occupied in travelling, we become strangers to our native country; and the over curious in the customs of the past are generally ignorant of those of the present. Besides, fictitious narratives lead us to imagine the possibility of many events that are impossible; and even the most faithful histories, if they do not wholly mis-represent matters, or exaggerate their importance to render the account of them more worthy of perusal, omit, at least, almost always the meanest and least striking of the attendant circum-stances; hence it happens that the remainder does not represent the truth, and that such as regulate their conduct by examples drawn from this source, are apt to fall into the extravagances of the knight-errants of Romance, and to entertain projects that exceed their powers.

I esteemed Eloquence highly, and was in raptures with Poesy; but I thought that both were gifts of nature rather than fruits of study. Those in whom the faculty of Reason is predominant, and who most skillfully dispose their thoughts with a view to render them clear and intelligible, are always the best able to persuade others of the truth of what they lay down, though they should speak only in the language of Lower Brittany, and be wholly ignorant of the rules of Rhetoric; and those whose minds are stored with the most agreeable fancies and who can give expression to them with the greatest embellishment and harmony, are still the best poets, though unacquainted with the Art of Poetry.

I was especially delighted with the Mathematics, on account of the certitude and evidence of their reasonings; but I had not as yet a precise knowledge of their true use; and thinking that they but contributed to the advancement of the mechanical arts, I was astonished that foundations, so strong and solid, should have had no loftier superstructure reared on them. On the other hand, I compared the disquisitions of the ancient Moralists to very towering and magnificent palaces with no better foundation than sand and mud; they laud the virtues very highly, and exhibit them as estimable far above anything on earth; but they give us no adequate criterion of virtue, and frequently that which they designate with so fine a name is but apathy, or pride, or despair, or parricide.

I revered our Theology, and aspired as much as any one to reach heaven; but being given assuredly to understand that the way is not less open to the most ignorant than to the most learned, and that the revealed truths which lead to heaven are above our comprehension, I did not presume to subject them to the impotency of my Reason; and I thought that in order competently to undertake their examination, there was need of some special help from heaven, and of being more than man.

Of philosophy I will say nothing, except that when I saw that it had been cultivated for many ages by the most distinguished men, and that yet there is not a single matter within its sphere which is not still in dispute, and nothing, therefore, which is above doubt, I did not presume to anticipate that my success would be greater in it that that of others; and further, when I considered the number of conflicting opinions touching a single matter that may be upheld by learned men, while there can be but one true, I reckoned as well-nigh false all that was only probable.

As to the other Sciences, inasmuch as these borrow their principles from Philosophy, I judged that no solid superstructures could be reared on foundations so infirm; . . .

For these reasons, as soon as my age permitted me to pass from under the control of my instructors, I entirely abandoned the study of letters, and resolved no longer to seek any other science than the knowledge of myself, or of the great book of the world. I spent the remainder of my youth in travelling, in visiting courts and armies, in holding intercourse with men of different dispositions and ranks, in collecting varied experience, in proving myself in the different situations into which fortune threw me, and, above all, in making such reflection on the matter of my experience as to secure my improvement. . . . In addition, I had always a most earnest desire to know how to distinguish the true from the false, in order that I might be able clearly to discriminate the right path in life, and proceed in it with confidence.

It is true, that, while busied only in considering the manners of other men, I found here, too, scarce any ground for settled conviction, and remarked hardly less contradiction among them than in the opinions of the philosophers. So that the greatest advantage I derived from the study consisted in this, that, observing many things which, however extravagant and ridiculous to our apprehension, are yet by common consent received and approved by other great nations, I learned to entertain too decided a belief in regard to nothing of the truth of which I had been persuaded merely by example and custom; and thus I gradually extricated myself from many errors powerful enough to darken our Natural Intelligence, and incapacitate us in great measure from listening to Reason. But after I had been occupied several years in thus studying the book of the world, and in essaying to gather some experience, I at length resolved to make myself an object of study, and to employ all the powers of my mind in choosing the paths I ought to follow; and undertaking which was accompanied with greater success than it would have been had I never quitted my country or my books.

Part 2: . . .Among the branches of Philosophy, I had, at an earlier period, given some attention to Logic, and among those of the Mathematics to Geometrical Analysis and Algebra,— three Arts or Sciences which ought, as I conceived, to contribute something to my design. But, on examination, I found that, as for Logic, its syllogisms and the majority of its other precepts are of avail rather in the communication of what we already know, or even as the Art of Lully, in speaking without judgment of things of which we are ignorant, than in the investigation of the unknown; and although this Science contains indeed a number of correct and very excellent precepts, there are nevertheless, so many others, and these either injurious or superfluous, mingled with the former, that it is almost quite as difficult to effect a severance of the true from the false as it is to extract a Diana or a Minerva from a rough block of marble. Then as to the Analysis of the ancients and the Algebra of the moderns, besides that they embrace only matters highly abstract, and to appearance, of no use, the former is so exclusively restricted to the consideration of figures, that it can exercise the Understanding only on condition of greatly fatiguing the Imagination; and, in the latter, there is so complete a subjection to certain rules and formulas, that there results an art full of confusion and obscurity calculated to embarrass, instead of a science fitted to cultivate the mind. By these considerations I was induced to seek some other Method which would comprise the advantages of the three and be exempt from their defects. And as a multitude of laws often only hampers justice, so that a state is best governed when, with few laws, these are rigidly administered; in like manner, instead of the great number of precepts of which Logic is composed, I believed that the four following would prove perfectly sufficient for me, provided I took the firm and unwavering resolution never in a single instance to fail in observing them.

The first was never to accept anything for true which I did not clearly know to be such; that is to say, carefully to avoid precipitancy and prejudice, and to comprise nothing more in my judgment than what was presented to my mind so clearly and distinctly as to exclude all ground of doubt.

The second, to divide each of the difficulties under examination into as many parts as possible, and as might be necessary for its adequate solution.

The third, to conduct my thoughts in such order that, by commencing with objects the simplest and easiest to know, I might ascend by little and little, and, as it were, step by step, to the knowledge of the more complex; assigning in thought a certain order even to those objects which in their own nature do not stand in a relation of antecedence and sequence.

And the last, in every case to make enumerations so complete, and reviews so general, that I might be assured that nothing was omitted.

The long chains of simple and easy reasonings by means of which geometers are accustomed to reach the conclusions of their most difficult demonstrations, had led me to imagine that all things, to the knowledge of which man is competent, are mutually connected in the same way, and that there is nothing so far removed from us as to be beyond our reach, or so hidden that we cannot discover it, provided only we abstain from accepting the false for the true, and always preserve in our thoughts the order necessary for the deduction of one truth from another. . . .

Part 4: I am in doubt as to the propriety of making my first meditations in the place above mentioned a matter of discourse; for these are so metaphysical, and so uncommon, as not, perhaps, to be acceptable to every one. And yet, that it may be determined whether the foundations that I have laid are sufficiently secure, I find myself in a measure constrained to advert to them. I had long before remarked that, in practice, it is sometimes necessary to adopt, as if above doubt, opinions which we discern to be highly uncertain, as has been already said; but as I then desired to give my attention solely to the search after truth, I thought that a procedure exactly the opposite was called for, and that I ought to reject as absolutely false all opinions in regard to which I could suppose the least ground for doubt, in order to ascertain whether after that there remained aught in my belief that was wholly indubitable. Accordingly, seeing that our senses sometimes deceive us, I was willing to suppose that there existed nothing really such as they presented to us; and because some men err in reasoning, and fall into paralogisms, even on the simplest matters of Geometry, I, convinced that I was as open to error as any other, rejected as false all the reasonings I had hitherto taken for demonstrations; and finally, when I considered that the very same thoughts which we experience when awake may also be experienced when we are asleep, while there is at that time not one of them true, I supposed that all the objects that had ever entered into my mind when awake, had in them no more truth than the illusions of my dreams. But immediately upon this I observed that, whilst I thus wished to think that all was false, it was absolutely necessary that I, who thus thought, should be somewhat; and as I observed that this truth, I think, hence, I am, was so certain and of such evidence, that no ground of doubt, however extravagant, could be alleged by the Sceptics capable of shaking it, I concluded that I might, without scruple, accept it as the first principle of the Philosophy of which I was in search. . . .

In *The Harvard Classics*, vol. 34. New York: P. F. Collier & Son, 1910

Isaac Newton: The Laws of Motion, 1687

Newton's system of physical laws was the bedrock of the physical sciences until Einstein in 1905 posited another universe, one that runs by other rules. Still, in practical terms, in science on the scale of man, we still live in a Newtonian universe.

Law 1: Every body perseveres in its state of rest, or of uniform motion in a straight line, unless it is compelled to change that state by forces impressed thereon.

Projectiles persevere in their motions, so far as they are not retarded by the resistance of the air, or impelled downwards by the force of gravity. A top, whose parts by their cohesion are perpetually drawn aside from rectilinear motions, does not cease its rotation, otherwise that as it is retarded by the air. The greater bodies of the planets and comets, meeting with less resistance in more free spaces, preserve their motions both progressive and circular for a much longer time.

Law 2: The alteration of motion is every proportional to the motive force impressed; and is made in the direction of the straight line in which that force is impressed.

If any force generates a motion, a double force will generate double the motion, a triple force triple the motion, whether that force be impressed altogether and at once, or gradually and successively. And this motion (being always directed the same way with the generating force), if the body moved before, is added to or subtracted from the former motion, according as they directly conspire with or are directly contrary to each other or obliquely joined, when they are oblique, so as to produce a new motion compounded from the determination of both.

Law 3: To every action there is always opposed an equal reaction: or the mutual actions of two bodies upon each other are always equal, and directed to contrary parts.

Whatever draws or presses another is as much drawn or pressed by that other. If you press a stone with your finger, the finger is also pressed by the stone. If a horse draws a stone tied to a rope, the horse (if I may so say) will be equally drawn back towards the stone; for the distended rope, by the same endeavour to relax or unbend itself, will draw the horse as much towards the stone as it does the stone towards the horse, and will obstruct the progress of the one as much as it advances that of the other. If a body impinge upon another, and by its force change the motion of the other, that body also (because of the equality of the mutual pressure) will undergo an equal change, in its own motion, towards the contrary part. The changes made by these actions are equal, not in the velocities, but in the motions of bodies; that is to say, if the bodies are not hindered by any other impediments. For, because the motions are equally changed, the changes of the velocities made towards contrary parts are reciprocally proportional to the bodies. This law takes place also in attractions, as will be proved in the next *scholium*. . .

From *Principia Mathematica*, translated by Andrew Motte. London, 1729.